Border Tensions:
Dance and Discourse

Proceedings of the
Fifth Study of Dance Conference

University of Surrey

20–23 April 1995

Conference Chair and Proceedings Compiler:
Professor Janet Adshead-Lansdale

Conference Organiser and Proceedings Co-compiler:
Chris Jones

Published by: Department of Dance Studies, University of Surrey

Distributed by:
National Resource Centre for Dance
University of Surrey
Guildford, Surrey GU2 5XH
United Kingdom

This collection of papers has been compiled from camera-ready copy supplied by individual speakers and performers at the *Border Tensions: Dance and Discourse* conference. Papers have been reproduced as supplied; they have not be edited or proofread.

Reprinted 1997

ISBN: 0-946483-23-X

PREFACE AND ACKNOWLEDGEMENTS

Border Tensions: Dance and Discourse was the fifth Study of Dance Conference held by the Department of Dance Studies, University of Surrey. It addressed the changing character of discourse in and about dance and brought together dancers, choreographers, researchers, and academics to explore the inter-relationship of the many voices in dance research. Tensions and negotiations between critical, cultural, and historical practices—and between dance, visual art, and theatre practices—were demonstrated and debated.

It is a fitting, although sad, acknowledgement that this conference began shortly after the announcement of Peter Brinson's death (April 7th 1995). As Director of the Gulbenkian Foundation, he was critically important in negotiating the establishment of the first Dance Department in a UK university, here at the University of Surrey, in 1981. His continued interest in the work of both the Department and the National Resource Centre for Dance was recognised when the Duke of Kent conferred upon him an honorary doctorate of the University in July 1994. I hope you will see Peter Brinson's vision realised in this record of the conference. His commitment to dance research never wavered.

This is also an opportunity to record June Layson's inspired leadership of Dance Studies as its first Professor in the UK and Head of the Department at the University of Surrey from 1981-91. The gathering of such a substantial, international community of dance scholars is a fine tribute to her scholarship, her open-mindedness in the face of changes in the discipline, her leadership, drive and commitment.

I would like to thank the Conference Committee, which consisted of the Department of Dance Studies Research Committee, augmented by external advisors, Liz Aggiss, Sandra Carter and Ann Nugent, which met to review submissions and to plan the programme. Lesley Tutty, the Dance Department Administrator, acted with foresight, experience and energy in making the internal links between Departments in the University work so well. I am deeply grateful to Chris Jones, Conference Organiser, who has worked with imagination, flair and thoroughness in a manner far beyond the call of duty.

For their support of the conference, I wish to thank the South East Arts Board and the British Academy. For their involvement in other ways, acknowledgements are due to Campusdance, Dance Books, the National Resource Centre for Dance, and Routledge Book Publishers.

Professor Janet Adshead-Lansdale
Head of the Department of Dance Studies

June 1995

CONTENTS

Other Presentations

Appendices

DISCOURSE IN DANCE: ITS CHANGING CHARACTER

Janet Adshead-Lansdale
University of Surrey

Dance and Discourse and the University of Surrey

This conference was prompted by the awareness, shared worldwide, that the discipline of dance studies has expanded—exploded even—in many directions. Insularity does not serve the interests of the subject; indeed the question of what this subject is, and whether such things exist any more, is part of the debate. The possibilities for research that might loosely bear the title 'dance research' are now commensurately and terrifyingly vast, or excitingly varied, depending upon one's point of view and degree of confidence!

The Society for Dance History Scholars conference next month in Canada (May 1995), coincidentally titled *Border Crossings,* testifies to the topicality of the issue. Our two conferences were announced simultaneously in the Spring of 1994 without prior communication between the Committees. In the interim, the number of other conferences dealing specifically with disciplinary tensions, both across the arts and between other subjects, has been remarkable.

Equally, conferences which focus on the body (not dance) and its metaphoric position—the body in relation to almost anything, it seems, but particularly to feminist, philosophical and poststructuralist thought—have become commonplace. This de-stabilised 'body' questions issues of gender, language and meaning. We could be forgiven for feeling that our specific interests have been thoroughly hi-jacked. New MA courses are springing up like mushrooms to accommodate these ideas, in departments of literature, cultural studies, visual arts, performance studies, philosophy and sociology.

What we might be able to do in dance, uniquely, apart from stake our claim to an important research area and perhaps begin to make a contribution that is recognised outside dance, is to be particularly sensitive to these more metaphoric uses of the body as distinct from those which take account of real dancing bodies. The literary reference to a metaphoric body is part of a tradition which has a long history from angels dancing on pin-heads onwards. The actualities and physicalities of dancing are largely ignored, whether these references are dancing bodies in everyday life, to the use of dance in forms of popular culture, television and video or in the shifting complexities of an extensive and multiplying number of stylised dance forms.

In dance research, both metaphoric and physical potentialities can be explored, and the tensions delineated, as we hope this stimulating series of papers will demonstrate. The papers range freely between modes of being and thinking, between metaphor and physicality. *Written on the Body* is not just the title of Jeanette Winterson's novel, but a strategy for choreographic discourse, too. The female body as a site of oppression, culturally inscribed, presents great difficulties for the feminist choreographer.

A brief historical note of a different kind generates a touch of irony, which I appreciate and perhaps one which the other half dozen or so people who are here today and were present at the first Study of Dance Conference at Leeds University will appreciate. On that occasion, only 14 years ago, we were exploring for the first time the possibilities of a soundly based conceptual framework for Dance. There was no Society for Dance Research in the UK; few degree courses in dance; virtually no post-graduate development except at the University of Leeds, which had run dance courses since 1971, to be followed later by the Laban Centre. Our concerns in 1981 were much more with a traditional, epistemological model and with the distinctiveness of dance in a philosophical tradition where it was marked only by its absence. It always strikes me that we have been more Derridean than Derrida.

We were concerned with carving out our own field of study in the higher education sector; with establishing our independence from music, theatre, and physical education. In the course of these fourteen years, the irony is, the world seems to have turned upside down. Is it independence that we still desire?

At the 1981 conference, the first in this series, a model for the analysis of dances that some of you may recognise was given its first public airing[1] and we celebrated June Layson's pioneering work in setting up dance courses at Leeds University,[2] her imminent move here to the University of Surrey, and my own PhD, the first in Dance, at Leeds University.[3]

By the time of the second conference in 1983 on British Theatre Dance in the Twentieth Century we had MA and research students but no undergraduates at the University of Surrey. We welcomed 130 colleagues to sessions ranging across ballet, modern dance and new or postmodern dance. We had commissioned reconstructions of Richard Alston's early work and Fergus Early's *Trois Gymnopédies* and, among other highlights, invited the Royal Ballet to give demonstrations of *Manon*. Reconstruction of dances in the Natural Movement tradition, with Anita Heyworth, and of Revived Greek Dance, with Bice Bellairs, began a tradition of recovering British dance history.

Recognition of cultural diversity and the particular focus of the University of Surrey undergraduate Dance Degree programme titled *Dance and Society* (now *Dance and Culture*), prompted the 1984 conference, *Dance—A Multi-cultural Perspective*. It was one of the earliest attempts to bring research in this field to a wider audience and to enhance for our own students a perspective in which cultural ethnocentrism would be unthinkable.

At the fourth conference in 1987 we focussed on one of the trickiest problems of dance research, education and training; the question of how far new choreography might be discussed, critically reviewed, and taught. We asked how far the heritage of dance is interesting in a choreographic context, that is, how far existing and new dance works can be attributed to conventions, stylistic codes, and their rootedness in a dance culture. We were sensitive to both our classical and expressionistic dance heritage and to the making of new work. How far the notion of individual romantic genius would be tenable in a postmodern era was thought worthy of considerable debate. *Choreography: Principles and Practice* was a conference which 200 people enjoyed and which had far-reaching consequences.[4]

Now, in 1995, we have the fifth in the series, continuing the theme of critical debate on some of the many and various ways our discipline might be structured. Looking back over this period, the influence of our former Head of Department and Europe's first full Professor of Dance Studies, is unmistakable. June Layson's retirement, in 1991, marked the end of 10 arduous years spent establishing the first university Department of Dance in this country in the face of much scepticism and financial difficulty.

Distinctions between colleges, polytechnics and universities are no longer of much significance in the British system, but at the time, the Gulbenkian Foundation's initiative, and Peter Brinson's vision, in particular, enabled dance to grow in an alien field but one which was vital for its scholarly well-being.

June Layson brought this to fruition and it is my pleasant task, somewhat tardily, to acknowledge her work. The difficulties that we faced, inevitable in introducing a new subject in a time of recession, were also opportunities to put into practice the poststructuralist dictum of writing one's own history. Instead of telling someone else's stories, we could write a script from new, or should it be, from our own prejudices?

It was opportunity to re-invent the discipline, to devise courses from a blank sheet, to appoint the most qualified staff for this adventure and to choose our own sources and resources. It was no easy task: there was no money, there was no curriculum, no staff, no buildings, no books. But just as everyone who has engaged in a SWOT analysis knows, one's weaknesses can become one's strengths, threats can become opportunities and vice versa. I am reminded of Fergus Early's delightful exposure of the problem of characterisation and definition, in *New Dance* magazine, when he said in celebration of 10 years of this activity in the UK:

> New dance is not baggy trousers, rolling about, chinese shoes, contact improvisation.... New dance does not exclude baggy trousers, rolling about, chinese shoes, contact improvisation.
> Early 1987 p.10[5]

Consciousness of the problematics of constructing narratives and disciplines becomes particularly poignant therefore given this starting point, and we have remained self-conscious about the task ever since. I mean this in this sense of being alert to the tendency for such structures to become monolithic. If _we_ valued the freedom to create our own narrative, at a certain moment in time, so we must now be flexible in response to change whether in the practice of dance, in its allegiances with other media or in its theoretical musings.

Dancing and Writing Modernism

Turning to this conference, one of the monolithic concepts that the committee identified as worthy of debate is 'Modernism', which has come in for some criticism in recent years and is exposed in many of these papers for its tendency to produce inadequate generalisations.

Our reflection on the twentieth century seems to be reaching obsessional proportions as we near the millennium and it is evident that there were a multiplicity of strands which were perhaps never adequately covered by a single term, like modernism, particularly one which failed to recognise the differences between American and European culture. The benefits of hindsight!

Rosemary Butcher's work demonstrates vividly how crude these binarisms of form and content, abstraction and expression, can be. The intensification and condensation of meaning in her work evokes, with subtlety, aspects of life, our histories and moods, in the sensuous surface of movement and invites ascription of meaning from many sources. Formalist disinterestedness, as polarised somehow against meaning, gives way to a quest to understand the interaction of movement with other signifiers, recognising the position of the choreographer but also of the reader, of the present moment but also of the history of twentieth century dance and culture.

Iris Garland's paper on Tórtola València, the Spanish dance modernist working between 1908 and 1933, shows how the archeological and oriental, mystical and magical connotations of the Spanish and Latin American notions of modernism gave València's work a character which was quite distinct from the more abstract forms of Northern Europe and the USA.

In a similar vein but from a very different cultural context Sally Bowden offers a re-reading of some early Diaghilev ballets establishing their allegiance to medieval mystery and miracle plays. The limitations of turning only to ancient Greece as source and canon in Western European Dance forms is highlighted. Modernism in its autonomous, formalist sense is vulnerable, for the significance of medievalism lies in its ability to present theatre as an integral part of life, drawing spectator and actor closer in the allegorical treatment of commonly understood roles. In fact she also identifies conspicuous symbolist and neo-romantic references in *Petroushka*.

Ramsay Burt's is also a revisionist account, this time of the more subtle differences between modernism and minimalism in work of the Judson Dance Theatre. He challenges now-canonical views by arguing that Rainer and Paxton's radical minimalism may have been misconstrued as high modernism. By undermining the conventions through which performers relate to their audiences he suggests that minimalists disrupt the traditional audience-performer relationship and reveal their affinity with *post*modernism.

The Modernist assumption of progress, which in turn supports a story-telling, linear account of dance history has come under threat from new historicism. In the writings of dance history in the 1980s and early 1990s change is becoming apparent, closely tied to the very influential rise of feminist criticism. Not just in history but also in anthropology these trends are evident.

Using quite different subject matter, the *Tsámikos* dance of Greece, Maria Koutsouba analyses the changes that occur where women perform roles formerly associated with men, and explores the possibility that social changes in the role of the sexes are thus reflected.

Reflections on Dance and Narrative

At the forefront of critical reflection of this kind, which takes account of both new history and feminism, is Ann Daly, whose paper on Isadora Duncan takes a model of cultural reproduction from Bourdieu. She uses it to show how Duncan's choices along a number of axes might be seen to cohere to create a new, respectable form of high art, spiritual and intellectual in character, with woman elevated to Goddess. Explanatory models of this kind have powerful potential in re-writing the narrative of dance history.

In choreography this same concern with narrative, but now fragmented, is evident in the work of such choreographers as Susan Marshall and Bill T Jones. The return of expression, the reference to everyday life and autobiography provide subject matter for these and many choreographers of the present time. Philosophical reflections by Sherrie Barr and Philip Lewin on the proto-narrative unit, focus on a theme, a gesture, which suggests narrative possibility without specifying the exact nature of the narrative. This link between literal gesture and dance movement is perhaps found most obviously in semiotic theory where cultural signification can be made explicit.

The questioning of narrative—which new historicism demands—combined with a sensitivity to the position of women—which feminism provides—is used by Sandra Carter in analysis of the music hall ballets of the late Victorian and early Edwardian era. Although the control by men of these ballets has, in the past, prevented women's voices from being heard, Carter recovers attitudes and perceptions which constructed the image of the dancer's body. The paradox of chastity and impurity and negotiations between them are crucial to an understanding of the period, yet are largely ignored in other (male) accounts.

As with Iris Garland's discussion of Tórtola València, here the appearance of a so-called high art, ballet, in the context of popular entertainment, i.e. the music hall, has led, equally inexorably it seems, to disdain from dance historians. Closely related in theme is Caroline Kershaw's analysis of sites of tension generated by cultural clashes of regionality, class and gender in clog dancing, which was also prevalent in the music halls before the turn of the century. Written out of history in much the same way as ballet, but for different reasons, its lower-class image and association with betting and public houses was thought unsuited to the programmes of The Empire.

The most effective male protagonist of traditional or folk dance was Cecil Sharp who can be held largely responsible for the nature of the discourse which saw its revival this century. His ambivalence in categorising dance forms, which Kershaw highlights in relation to clog dance, is also a feature of Linda Tomko's study of English traditional dance which traverses geographic boundaries by scrutinizing its transmission to the United States in the 1900 to 1910 period.

What the two papers by Caroline Kershaw and Linda Tomko open up, methodologically, is that sources, documents, facts, are never neutral, that descriptions and accounts of the dance, however 'objective' their stance, reveal more than they conceal and give us a rich source for reconsideration of accepted accounts.

Politics, Boundaries, Art and Culture

Also from the USA, the specific characteristics of a cultural and geographical site is explored by M.A. Greenstein who posits a continuing historic role for Los Angeles in breaking with tradition, where rebellion is as natural as its earthquakes: 'revolt and innovate' the slogans for a town where life imitates art. In an analysis of Frank Guevera's performance work, his gay, Latino identity and his dance aesthetic are juxtaposed with the realities of suppression in American life.

The view from marginalised positions can bring into relief the role of dance in mainstream societies; this is the subject of Stacey Prickett's paper on Joe Goode, the San Francisco gay performance artist. His integration of dance with text, narrative, props and sets is put to the service of celebrating and subverting gender constructs through an eclectic mix of movement styles. Here boundaries are blurred and differences transcended within cultural pluralism.

Almost universally in our own time, the hierarchical tensions between high and popular art are still reflected in a canon of dance scholarship which focusses on theatre dance. Theresa Buckland's work on dance in pop music video challenges this absence of concern with popular forms of culture.

Oral and non-oral traditions, popular and high art, tradition and modernity, male and female, are among the binarisms which also intersect in any analysis of the problematics of writing the history of other forms of dance. These polarities, compounded by issues of colour and race, are explored by Mo Dodson in a discussion of the complex position of jazz dance and the relationships between its vernacular or social forms and its stage forms.

Interest in the plurality of cultures and their interactions has become a dominant theme of our time and we pursue this with two further papers. One, illustrated with danced examples, is from the choreographer Shobana Jeyasingh who argues in both words and in dance that the idea of two separate cultures that we conventionally consider to be 'east' and 'west' is irrelevant. She is not, she says (publicity material 1995), 'a cultural cook mixing Indian dance with western flavourings' or an 'artistic magpie', but a citizen of a 'global community'. In this community Asian women in Britain make postmodern dances which deny this East/West distinction and focus on the development of a new language. Her recent work, *Raid* (1995), pushes to extremes the idea that the languages of all cultures are open for all to use.

Jane Turner, on Balinese dance, offers the argument that intercultural work may remove the indigenous voice and become a form of colonial appropriation. The political implications of a global culture are pursued in her analysis of how Balinese dance is conceived and perceived in the West. The boundaries are down, but who is in control of the passes, she asks.

Comparisons between apparently remote dance forms are the subject of Georgiana Gore's exploration of the legitimacy of placing British rave in relation to southern Nigerian possession cult dance events. Rhythm, representation and ritual provide the focus for an analysis of these manifestations of rites of passage in which secrecy, journeying and transformation of consciousness, it is argued, are central. Disciplines from structuralism to postmodernism are employed.

It might not seem to be an obvious connection but the clue to the link with Romantic ballet is of methodology. Imagination and reality, spirituality and materiality, process and product, provide a contrasting set of polarities which bring the Romantic Ballet and Romanticism into complex relationship. Valerie Rimmer opens up the subtext of their intertwined existence to challenge the accepted wisdom of the ballerina's dominance and supremacy in this period.

The Crossing of Art Boundaries

Other accepted wisdoms which are now under threat can be seen in the performance by Liz Aggiss who has not always had the recognition that she deserves as a pivotal figure in dance in the UK. The reasons: that her work does not fit conventional funding or critical categories, and that it requires multi-skilled people, who can dance with great expressionist power, speak and, on occasion, sing.

The Fetching Bride (1995), described as an erotic black satire in the company's publicity material, brings a lyric opera singer and Liz Aggiss, herself, as dancer, into relationship with Billy Cowie's romantically dark music. Here she subverts her own well-established image of being an expressionist choreographer, whereas in *Hi Jinx,* commissioned especially for this conference, is a vibrant reflection of it. Knowledge of the expressionist dance and arts culture cannot be avoided. Spoof or tender recognition of its greatness? Ironic commentary or an attack on dance training practices?

In related sessions Ian Spink's workshops and his discussion with Richard Cave demonstrate the working practices of a particularly significant playwright and choreographer. His collaborations with Caryl Churchill have produced problematic and contentious works which question the relative power of words, movement, sound, image and their independence and interaction in performance.

The possibilities of integration, assimilation and juxtaposition of dance with other elements provides the focus for a group of three papers on the relationships of music and dance. Here the influence of structuralist and poststructuralist theory can be seen alongside theory from aesthetics and music/dance style analysis.

The relationship between dance and music analysis, in theory, practice and method, is a problematic which all three explore. While Stephanie Jordan deals with counterpoint, visualisation and narrative implications in examples from Ashton, Balanchine and Tudor; Rachel Richardson focuses upon gesture and its relationship to music, in Tudor's work. The question of the level at which relationships may be observed to function is also Sophia Preston's concern in analysing Siobhan Davies's *Bridge the Distance* danced to Britten's third string quartet.

In these three papers it is the detail of the inner workings of the music and the dance that begins to provide evidence of extraordinarily complex and subtle negotiations in the construction of both structure and meaning; an antidote to the sweeping generalisations common in many texts on the subject of their relationship.

We have not, yet, lost this particularity of dance research, of close reading of the dance text, which, rightly in my view, distinguishes dance analysis from other subjects of analysis. I maintain the view I first espoused 20 years ago when I completed an MA

Dissertation on Music and Dance relationships (1975) that dance cannot simply be a pale reflection, or even a dramatic extension of *something else*. It is a *dance*, not music, that we are interested in, *dance* not theatre, much as it may overlap, interact, share and engage with other ideas and media.

I feel like an unreconstructed, old-fashioned epistemologist but the frustration of seeing texts on postmodernism which have art examples but ignore dance and feminist analyses of art practices which ignore dance reinforces my prejudices. Are our interests best served by this constant amalgamation of media into performance?

Despite reservations about critical perspectives drawn from other fields it would be false to view Lea Anderson's *Perfect Moment* in any other terms given her use of postmodern strategies of fragmentation, incoherent signifiers, and open-ended meanings. Sherril Dodds illustrates the vital contribution of film and textuality theories in explanation of her work.

Alternative Bodies of Knowledge

Roger Copeland's paper, *Abstraction and Hysteria: The Place of the Body in American Non-literary Theatre,* links interactions between media with investigations into the body. The borders between dance and theatre are crossed to pursue the question of what might be meant by 'physical presence'. Examples from 1960s groups in North America, e.g. The Living Theatre, and later from Robert Wilson's work illustrate the problems inherent in understanding the eruption of physical activity within works distanced by technology.

But an older, early twentieth century tradition brings theory and practice, movement and text together: that of the Alexander technique. This principle will be followed through in Michael Huxley, Jayne Stevens, and Martin Leach's three-part spoken and danced illustration of the interfaces between dance, physiology, theatre, and history in application of the Alexander technique to the training of dancers.

The rise of interest in discourses of and on the body, common in poststructuralist and postmodernist literature links several papers. Helen Thomas questions the value of taking on these 'bodies' of literature, natural bodies, passive bodies, abject bodies, or celebratory bodies, addicted bodies even, where derivations from other fields of work which sometimes only see dance in metaphoric terms have long constrained the development of theoretical constructs for dance.

Anna Aalten's paper on femininity in performance provides something of a theoretical counterpoint to Carol Brown's performance. Aalten bases her ethnographic survey of dancers' gendered selves on Judith Butler's theorising of gender as a performative act. Carol Brown, in performing the work which successfully completed her PhD,[6] examines perspectives from Irigaray, Foucault and Butler as they illuminate feminist choreographic practice in constructing gendered identities.

In parallel, Jools Gilson-Ellis' analysis of Laurie Anderson and Rose English's use of text illustrates the force of Kristeva's arguments for rejection and disruption as strategies for re-negotiating the feminine. Brown and Gilson-Ellis separately question both gender and genre.

Johannes Birringer explores *The Obscene/Off-screen Body* in practical terms through his multi-media presentation, bringing several of these themes together. The problematics of visual communication across cultural borders and conventions of permissibility are explored in the ambivalent experience of the sexual self.

Equally imaginatively, Valerie Briginshaw brings together aspects of postmodern theory with feminism, notably concepts of mapping, of cultural diversity and of concern for the environment, to explore the gendered basis of travel metaphors.

Technologies and Choreologies

If metaphor is a problem in traditional accounts of dance, virtual reality poses extreme difficulties. Travel is a metaphor Susan Kozel uses in tracing a dancer's path through virtual reality, mimesis and a segment of recent feminist thought. The tendency of virtual reality to negate the physical body entirely, is countered through the concept of mimesis, seen in the moving, physical body. This is brought together with Braidotti's feminist writing on nomadic subjects.

The potential of modern technology for doing something rather different from questioning the physicality of bodies is demonstrated by the development of multimedia video discs. The usefulness of video discs for dance teaching is explored in Jacqueline Smith-Autard's presentation on technologies applied to Siobhan Davies's *White Bird Featherless.*

Technology underpins the Aerobics video, which gives Patricia Winter a starting point to illustrate the convergence of separately existing bodies of theory in explanation of this meeting of culture and corporeality. The body as a site of tension and ambiguity is thus exposed.

Likewise, corporeality, but in the context of bodily intelligence, links Aalten's paper with Andrée Grau's discussion of the character of bodily construction in terms of its biological as well as its social construction, arguing that intellectual divisions between what is social and what is biological are themselves a social construction. The possibilities of seeing recent research on intelligence in this light are explored in relation to diverse cultures.

Conclusion

The adoption of models from cultural, feminist and poststructuralist theory has brought new perspectives to the appraisal of dance and to the existing literature as written by earlier scholars. A massive revision is under way. Wanting to retain a physically-present dancing and watching body and dance text does not inevitably lead to a return to definitive meaning but the exposure of the many intertextual levels at which it is possible to operate and an awareness of the diverse, subtle and complex matters of interpretation.

The splintering of disciplinary structures and of dance forms is responsive to, and reflected in, the wider context in which dance exists. Linda Jasper's paper addresses these issues in the Community Dance movement; a case in point where concern over definitional identities, and the desire to draw on some common principles in this proliferating activity, has become a major issue.

Susan Foster, appropriately in my view, draws the conference to a close, not because I expect her to have the last word, or to summarise the previous days' experiences in conventional conference tradition to point to 'the way forward'. That would be both naive and inappropriate for this conference and its themes. But her commentary, in both words and movement, opens up rather than closes down the issues so that we might continue to think about them.

Notes

1. Published in Adshead, J. (ed) *Dance analysis: theory and practice* London: Dance Books 1988.

2. From the early 1970s MA courses in dance were available within the Physical Education Department's postgraduate courses. The first PhD student in dance registered in 1975.

3. *Dance as a discipline* Leeds University, 1980

4. Not least that the conference report, *Choreography: Principles and Practice* still sells in reasonable numbers (obtainable through the NRCD, University of Surrey).

5. Issue no. 40, April-June 1987 pp.10-12.

6. University of Surrey, 1995.

FEMININITY AS PERFORMANCE/PERFORMING FEMININITY: CONSTRUCTING THE BODY OF THE BALLERINA

Anna Aalten
Department of Cultural Anthropology
University of Amsterdam, The Netherlands

In my view 1992 was a landmark in the field of dance studies. In that year, we saw the publication of Christy Adair's *Women and Dance: Sylphs and Sirens* in Britain and Gabriele Klein's *Frauen, Körper, Tanz. Ein Zivilisationsgeschichte des Tanzes*, two books on dance that were written from an explicit feminist perspective. Looking back now, I think these books were a turning point in the hitherto feminist disdain of the world of dance and it's performers. At last, dance and dancers were considered an interesting field for feminist research. Of course in the late eighties we had read Judith Lynne Hanna's book on *Dance, Sex and Gender* (1988) and Ann Daly's inspiring articles about the *Balanchine Woman* (1987) and on *Classical Ballet as a Discourse on Difference* (1987/-88). However, in contrast to these authors, Klein and Adair provided us with feminist frameworks that would make it possible to rewrite dance history. In that sense both studies can be called 'ground breaking'.

Adair's book calls attention to the elitist, sexist ánd racist tendencies in the world of Western professional dance, while Klein shows us how the human body in the course of European dance history has been subject to oppressive and liberating movements. Both Adair and Klein take the subordination of women as their starting-point. Women are conceptualized as victims of patriarchal relationships in the world of dance and their representation on stage usually as oppressive. At the same time, both authors try to show that women have played a very important part in the development of dance and that their role must be described and acknowledged.

Although I have read these books with pleasure and I respect the authors' endeavours tremendously, I find the women-as-victims model a serious stumbling-block when trying to understand the complexity of gender relations in dance. To give an example, Adair first presents the innovative power of Martha Graham as proof of women's importance in the history of dance, but in a next chapter she criticizes the oppressiveness nature of the Graham-technique (1992: 132). I cannot help but thinking that here Adair wants to have her cake and eat it too.

Femininity as Performance/Performing Femininity

Last year I started research on 'Femininity and the Body of the Ballerina in Western Theatrical Dance'. I am an anthropologist with a strong commitment to feminist studies and a lifelong fascination for dance and dance practices. During my life, I have watched numerous dance performances and I have practiced many different dance styles, ranging from classical ballet to Argentinian tango and African dance. In my research project I am interested in the construction of the female body in ballet; it was Gabriele Klein's detailed account of the increasing control of the human body in Western society that first called my attention to this aspect of dance. To Christy Adair's work I owe my interest in the relationship between social inequalities and the world of dance. I have chosen dance as my research area, because of its potential to reflect culture, at the same time (re)producing it. I totally agree with Ted Polhemus, when he states 'that dance is the liqueur which is distilled of the stuff of culture' (1993: 9). In my research, I consider classical and neo-classical ballet a form of ethnic dance. In doing so, I am aware that I go against some conventions in theatre studies, but if challenged I think I can make a case for such a choice (see Kealiinohomoku 1983).

As I said earlier, I take as my point of departure the body and femininity, joining with Klein and Adair in their exploration of these research themes. However, contrary to both of them I have chosen an actor-oriented approach. It is my conviction that when theories portray human beings narrowly as either constructed by linguistic means or as the vehicles through which discourses gain expression, they neglect the dialectical ability of human beings to engage language, and their potential to confront, negotiate and maneuver in their worlds. Therefore, I want to use my research to give voice to the dancers themselves. I combine the anthropological tradition of focussing on the human subject as the creator of his or her world with feminist and dance studies' attention to the representation of femininity. In my research I study the construction of the body of the ballerina in relation to representations of femininity.

In search of theoretical tools, I have come upon the works of the feminist philosopher Judith Butler who provided me with the concepts I needed to cross the borders of dance studies and anthropology. In an attempt to develop a theory of gender identity inspired by Simone de Beauvoir's famous formulation "one is not born, but rather becomes a woman", Judith Butler proposes to see gender as "the corporeal locus of cultural meanings both received and innovated" (1987: 128). But when we define the body as a locus of meanings, which aspects of this body are hence natural or free of cultural imprint? Or, to quote Butler: "Indeed, how are we to find the body that preexists its cultural interpretation? If gender is the corporealization of choice, and the acculturation of the corporeal, then what is left of nature, and what had become of sex? If gender is determined in the dialectic between culture and choice, then what role does "sex" serve, and ought we to conclude that the very distinction between sex and gender is anachronistic?" (ibid: 129). To answer these questions Butler looks again at De Beauvoir's work in combination with the ideas of Wittig, Foucault and phenomenologists such as Merleau-Ponty.

On the face of it De Beauvoir's famous statement seems to adopt a Cartesian mind/body dualism, presenting the view of a disembodied agent taking on a gender. However, when examining it more closely it becomes clear that in saying that one becomes a woman, De Beauvoir "... does not imply that this "becoming" traverses a path from disembodied freedom to cultural embodment. Indeed, one is one's body from the start, and only thereafter becomes one's gender. The movement from sex to gender is internal to embodied life, a sculpting of the original body into a cultural form" (ibid: 131). Instead of reproducing the Cartesian view of a body that must be transcended, De Beauvoir introduces the notion of the body as a situation. There are at least two ways of interpreting this notion. The first is to see the body as a material reality: as something which is there and can be held. Yet also as a material reality a body is never just there; it always has a meaning, because it has already been defined in a social and cultural context. The second way of interpreting the notion of the body as a situation is to regard having a specific body as an obligation to take up these social and cultural definitions and to come to terms with them. The acceptance of the notion of the body as a situation poses a serious problem for the distinction between sex and gender, because "(i)f we accept the body as a cultural situation, then the notion of a natural body and, indeed, a natural "sex" seem increasingly suspect. The limits to gender, the range of possibilities for a lived interpretation of a sexually differentiated anatomy, seem less restricted by anatomy than by the weight of the cultural institutions that have conventionally interpreted anatomy. Indeed, it becomes unclear when we take Beauvoir's formulation to its unstated consequences, whether this linkage is itself cultural convention. If gender is a way of existing one's body, and one's body is a situation, a field of cultural possibilities both received and reinterpreted, then both gender and sex seem to be thoroughly cultural affairs" (ibid: 134). I can only fully agree with Butler here.

But if both sex and gender are cultural affairs, what then is the relation between a female body as a material reality and different representations of femininity? If we do not believe that the meaning of femininity can be derived from some physiological fact, if we do not regard the relation between sex and gender as a causal one, how do we view it then? Butler criticizes the idea that femininity and masculinity are to be seen as the cultural *expression* of a material fact, namely the female or male body, - an idea that is so common in Western cultures. Instead of a notion of gender as expressive she proposes to see gender as a *performative* act (Butler 1990: 279). She develops this notion of gender as a performative act using the phenomenological theory of acts as the ways in which social subjects constitute reality. Butler's notion of gender as a performative act can be seen as an elaboration of her earlier thoughts on the body as a situation. Gender, says Butler, is in no way a stable identity or a locus of agency from which various acts proceed, but it is an identity tenuously constituted in time. Gender must be considered as an identity instituted through a stylized repetition of acts (ibid: 270).

What is the importance of the body in this constituting process? How can we study the body in relation to meanings of femininity without falling into the trap of causality? In Butler's view, the body and gender are closely connected, but not as a biological facticity and as the cultural interpretation of that facticity. The body and gender are connected, because (to use Butler's own words) "gender is instituted through the stylization of the body and, hence, must be understood as the mundane way in which bodily gestures, movements, and enactments of various kinds constitute the illusion of an abiding gendered self" (ibid: 270. She goes on to say: "Consider gender, for instance, as *a corporeal style*, an 'act,' as it were, which is both intentional and performative, where 'performative' itself carries the double-meaning of 'dramatic' and 'non-referential'" (ibid: 272-273). The idea of gender as a performative act offers the possibility of looking at the ways in which individuals live their bodies, thereby constituting gender. In the process of constituting the body, be it female or male, offers infinite possibilities.

But human subjects do not act within a social or cultural vacuum; they constitute their genders within the confines of already existing historical directives. Or, to quote Butler once again: "As an intentionally organized materiality, the body is always an embodying *of* possibilities both conditioned and circumscribed by historical convention. In other words, the body *is* a manner of doing, dramatizing, and *reproducing* a historical situation" (ibid: 272). Here, I think, Butler offers us the foundations of a research agenda that gives attention to the body in relation to the construction of femininity, and frees itself from the "Cartesian ghost" that separates the mind from the body. In her proposal to see gender as a performative act which constitutes reality, Butler breaks away from the popular and academic notion which draws a distinction between the reality of sex and the appearance of gender. Instead, we consider gender reality to be created through a continuation of performances in which the body is stylized to fit existing gender directives and/or to produce new ones.

In the notion of the body as "not merely matter but a continual and incessant *materializing* of possibilities" (ibid: 272) lies the possibility to study femininity as performance and to look at the construction of the body of the female dancer. The tension between the body of the ballerina as object and the embodied feminine subject of the dancer will, thus, be the focus of my analysis. The material I collect consists of biographies and autobiographies of dancers. I visit performances of Dutch dance companies to look for representations of femininity. I study the trainings methods used by Dutch ballet academies and specifically look at the ways in which teachers and dancers treat the bodies of these dancers-to-be. And, last but not least, I interview Dutch professional ballet dancers about their ideas and experiences of femininity and the body in their own dancing practices.

This research is still in process. The methods I have chosen have only begun to indicate the direction to take to answer my research questions. Therefore, the next part of today's paper should be regarded as an elaboration of the main research question, and not as its answer.

Constructing the Body of the Ballerina

This is not the place to go into a detailed history of Western ballet; most of you are familiar with it. I will confine myself to a short sketch of the body images in present-day classical and neo-classical ballet. Western academic dance, better known as 'classical ballet', has its roots in the French court dances of the 15th and 16th century. Until the beginning of the nineteenth century, ballet is a male affair - male dancers are the stars - but this situation changes drastically during the days of the Romantic movement. The nineteenth-century Romantic conceptualisation of femininity is filled with ambivalence. In their rejection of Reason and rationality the Romantics honour women for their presupposed relation to Nature. Women are seen as creatures who are closer to their feelings than men; therefore they come to symbolize emotionality, one of the ideals that the Romantics strove for. On the other hand, there is the Romantic preoccupation with the dichotomy of the flesh and the spirit. In this dichotomy the body is seen in opposition to the soul, the physical in opposition to the spiritual. In this oppositional construct, body and soul are not seen as equals. The soul or the spirit is perceived as being superior.

Because of their presumed connection with the natural world, women are associated with the lowliness of the body. Thus, when ballerina's were worshipped not only as dancers, but as symbols of femininity, the public's admiration concerns a specific kind of femininity. The femininity these dancers perform is the staging of a female body as the representation of a celestial creature, an incorporeal nymph, a disembodied woman who has become a spirit. As Roger Copeland once wrote: "Hence the odd paradox that dance - the only art form whose raw material is the human body - began to idealise the image of the disembodied woman." (1990: 27; see also Klein 1992; Sayers 1993). Neo-classical ballet, exemplified by the work of George Balanchine, who has also had an enormous influence on European ballet, presents strikingly similar images of femininity. Balanchine's ballerinas are like contemporary nymphs: innocent, cool and with a natural purity.

Lightness is the keyword in ballet. "Light as weightlessness, light as luminosity: in English the same word serves both meanings" (Jowitt 1988: 39). Dancers are seen as artists who succesfully challenge the law of gravity. This is not only the consequence of taste and fashion, but can also be attributed to the ballet technique itself. The basic movement of ballet, the increased turn-out, makes it possible to raise the legs very high, and to change directions very rapidly and fluidly. High jumps, spectacular pirouettes and innovating *lifts* (whereby the male dancer lifts the female dancer and carries her across the stage) are part of standard technique. And, of course, there is the perfection of pointe work for women that makes it clear that the basic movement in ballet is upwards, constantly striving to disregard gravity and reach for the immortality of a heavenly creature (Kirstein 1983).

How can we relate the cultural meanings of femininity in ballet to the stylization of the body of the ballerina? How is the body of a female dancer used to perform these femininities that are required? What does the performative act of a nymph mean for the construction of the body of the performer? The major ballet academies in the Netherlands train their female students to dance the principal roles of the Romantic repertoire; every year they try to bring forth several young Giselles and young Sleeping Beauties. Their training is aimed at learning the right technique. Because the basic principle of the classical technique goes against the natural movements of the human body (human feet do not stand out in a 180 degree corner), the training process is long and arduous. A good turn-out is basic in ballet and since the eighteenth century dancers have gone to extremes to accomplish it. Adair describes how, in the days of Romanticism, a common practice used for beginning dancers was to put them in a box with braces that could be adjusted via a series of grooves; more advanced dancers had their maids or colleagues stand on their hips (1992: 87; Jowitt 1988: 43)). Nowadays a good turn-out is attained through extensive training starting at the earlist age possible. But even with extensive training the result may be unsatisfactory. One of the dancers I interviewed was sent from school because she had an insufficient turn-out. She is now training to be a modern dancer.

But the common thought is that talent and training can overcome possible physical shortcomings; young bodies are very flexible. Some of the dancers I interviewed talked about their bodies as being "easy". Others suffered enormously during their training years. I heard several stories of dancers whose recollections of their bodies, especially during the training years, were predominantly of the aches and pains they experienced. One dancer told me she had been in constant pain during the first four years of her training at the academy, but she "had got used to it". Another dancer told me about her stiff back that made it difficult to make a good arabesque; once she over-stretched and was seriously injured for weeks, but her back has been flexible ever since.

And what about dancing on pointe shoes; how does this affect the construction of the ballerina's body? Human toes are not made to walk on and the feet of female dancers are legendary because of their ugliness. Still, pointe shoes are used, not only in the choreographies of the nineteenth century repertoire, but also in neo-classical ballet and even in post-modern choreographies by William Forsythe and others. Good pointe work demands years of training and constant practice, and even then it is never easy; blisters and bleeding feet are part and parcel of a ballerina's life. But it does have its merits; a dancer moves faster and turns easier on pointe and, as one dancer told me "it is the closest a human being can ever come to flying".

Apart from a good turn-out, female dancers who aspire a career in ballet must possess certain body proportions. To impersonate the incorporeal nymph a dancer has to have long legs, a slim body and no hips. In present-day ballet a body with roundings at the hips, buttocks and breasts, is definitely not considered being well proportioned (Vincent 1979). For how could a dancer represent the celestial creature that is asked for on stage when her body 'betrays' her, revealing that she is an embodied woman? The striking thing is that dancers and their teachers firmly believe they can achieve the image of a disembodied woman if they work on it. The aesthetic ideal of the present-day ballet world is therefore the subject of a lot of feminist criticism (Adair 1992; Gordon 1983; Novack 1993) and the cause of much tension in the dancers' lives (Bentley 1983; Brady 1982; Kirkland and Lawrence 1986).

In my conversations with female dancers who are members of major Dutch companies they repeatedly expressed the enormous pressure they feel to be thin. Female dancers are constantly told to watch their weight by teachers, ballet masters, choreographers and directors. Some dancers experience a permanent struggle against food and the autobiographies of some present-day dancers can be read as the account of this struggle (Bentley 1983; Kirkland and Lawrence 1986). The preoccupation with their weight starts at the schools where young girls on the verge of puberty are scrutinized for the first physical signs of femininity. Most girls start training seriously at the age of eleven or twelve, before their body has taken shape and they are still skinny, but in the following years their bodies start blossoming into something they and their teachers dread. Both at school and in the company, any signs of feminine curves are met with disapproval. Too much breast and hips can be the reason that a young woman is asked to leave the school. One or two pounds of 'fat' (and I put 'fat' in quotation marks, because dancers can hardly be considered fat) can be the reason for not getting a role.

In their attempts to conform to the ideal body, many female dancers have eating disorders. Even the dancers who never had any problems staying slim, told me they experienced problems with their weight during a certain period in their lives. The fact that they were surrounded by girls who were told to lose weight, made them feel insecure about their own bodies. They started to diet with the others. This usually resulted in minor eating disorders which most of the women eventually overcame. On the other hand, the physical and aesthetic demands do not lead *all* dancers to experience eating disorders. Some of them are built slim; others perceive the need for a constant bodily control not as a threat, but as a challenge. Let us listen to Toni Bentley, former dancer with the New York City Ballet for an example of this: "We don't eat food, we eat music. We need artistic sustenance only. Emotional, inspiring sustenance. All our physical energy is the overflow of our spiritual feelings. We live on faith, belief, love, inspirations, vitamins and Tab. (...) I don't think that there is any dancer who does not harbor this dream of the future: to eat three meals a day - French toast with butter and syrup, ice cream soda and three-course diners with wine - and not to have to grab a yoghurt or coleslaw in a half-hour break for dinner. On the other hand, our minds and hearts are focused on other, far more important things - a flat tummy, warming up, makeup, and the endless toe-sewing. Food is unnecessary" (1983: 18-19).

To conclude

Looking back at the questions I posed and the material I presented I see several elements of tensions I would like to work on in the future. First, there is the strange paradox that ballet, the art form that centers on the human body, requires female performers to be disembodied. Maybe this is caused by the contempt for the body that is characteristic of

Western cultures, as Christy Adair has suggested. The second tension lies in the role of the ballerina who performs this disembodied femininity. In most of the literature, ballerinas are presented as the victims of a patriarchal system that degrades women, forcing them to mistreat their bodies constantly. But where does the happy dancers I talked to, the women who loved dancing and enjoyed their work fit into this picture of the mute and mutilated ballerina? And finally, I see a tension between the pleasure I experience when watching a ballet performance and my knowledge of the often degrading practices that it conceals. Am I admiring the craftmanship of a remarkable group of women or am I simply reiterating the dominant codes of this Western culture? I leave that as a question, and I hope this presentation has provided some food for thought concerning the performance of femininity in dance.

References

Adair, Christy
1992   *Women and Dance. Sylphs and Sirens*. London: Macmillan Press
Bentley, Toni
1983   *Winter Season: A Dancer's Journal*. New York: Random House
Brady, Joan
1982   *The Unmaking of a Dancer. An Unconventional Life*. Washington: Washinton Square Press
Butler, Judith
1987   'Variations on Sex and Gender. Beauvoir, Wittig and Foucault', in: Seyla Benhabib and Drucilla Cornell (eds), *Feminism as Critique. Essays on the Politics of Gender in Late-Capitalist Societies*, pp. 128-143. Cambridge: Polity Press
Butler, Judith
1990   'Performative Acts and Gender Constitution', in: Sue-Ellen Case (ed), *Performing Feminisms. Feminist Critical Theory and Theatre*, pp. 270-283. Baltimore: John Hopkins University Press
Copeland, Roger
1990   'Duncan, Graham, Rainer and Sexual Politics', *Dance Theatre Journal* vol. 8 no. 3: 60-10 en 27-30
Daly, Ann
1987/88   'Classical Ballet: A Discourse of Difference', *Women & Performance. A Journal of Feminist Theory* vol. 3 no. 2: 57-67
Daly, Ann
1987   'The Balanchine Woman. Of Hummingsbirds and Channel Swimmers', *The Drama Review* 1: 8-21
Gordon, Suzanne
1983   *Off Balance. The Real World of Ballet*. New York: Pantheon Books
Hanna, Judith Lynne,
1988   *Dance, sex and gender; signs of identity, dominance, defiance, and desire*. Chicago: University of Chicago Press
Jowitt, Deborah
1988   *Time and the Dancing Image*. New York: William Morrow and Co.

Kealiinohomoku, Joann
1983   'An Anthropologist Looks at Ballet as a Form of Ethnic Dance', in: R. Copeland and M. Cohen (eds), *What is Dance? Readings in Theory and Criticism*, pp. 533-550. Oxford: Oxford University Press

Kirkland, Gelsey and Greg Lawrence
1986   *Dancing on my grave: an autobiography*. New York: Doubleday

Kirstein, Lincoln
1983   'Classic Ballet: Aria of the Aerial', in: R. Copeland and M. Cohen (eds), *What is Dance? Readings in Theory and Criticism*, pp. 238-244. Oxford: Oxford University Press

Klein, Gabriel
1992   *Frauen Körper Tanz. Eine Zivilisationsgeschichte des Tanzes*. Berlin: Quadriga

Novack, Cynthia J.
1993   'Ballet, Gender and Cultural Power', in: Helen Thomas (ed), *Dance, Gender and Culture*, pp. 34-49. London: Macmillan Press

Polhemus, Ted
1993   'Dance, Gender and Culture', in: Helen Thomas (ed), *Dance, Gender and Culture*, pp. 3-16. London: Macmillan Press

Sayers, Lesley-Anne
1993   ''She might pirouette on a daisy and it would not bend' Images of Femininity and Dance Appreciation', in: Helen Thomas (ed), *Dance, Gender and Culture*, pp. 164-184. London: Macmillan Press

Vincent, L.M.
1979   *Competing with the Sylph: Dancers and the Pursuit of the Ideal Body Form*. New York: Andrews & McMeel Inc.

Straddling Borders: The Proto-Narrative Unit
by
Sherrie Barr, University of Oregon & Philip Lewin, Clarkson University

[Representative video clips were included in our original presentation]

The decade of the 1980s witnessed a return to expression within the dance world. Content, meaning, and emotion have come back into vogue. The re-occurring cycles within dance history again became evident as the choreographers of the 80s took their turn rebelling against what had become institutionalized as the analytical dance of the 70s. Choreographic inquiries which only a short time before had been rejected as "establishment" were re-examined, often receiving positive responses. However, as scholars such as Noëll Carroll suggest, with each revolution of the cycle there is a subtle new twist.[1] Each re-occurrence occurs within a unique socio-cultural-political climate.

In the late 70s and 80s features such as virtuosity, pop music, and gender bending re-appeared in the dance world at a moment when the larger culture became preoccupied with issues of narcissism, the emerging cultural hegemony of the electronic media, and the political empowerment of women and gays. In the 80s, and continuing into the 90s, the notion of expression is being re-considered and re-defined as theatricality, drama and narrative re -appear in dance and performance[2]; at the same moment, the larger culture has largely abandoned its flirtation with the dubious license of the postmodern, and in a post-theory phase, has begun tentative exploration of a new communitarian ethos grounded in commitments to local but potentially fragmented attachments. At one extreme, these are attachments to personal relationships conceived as apolitical ideals, islands of meaning in the seas of cultural chaos; at the other extreme, these are attachments to the various groups composing a muticultural identity politics.

The dances of Susan Marshall and Bill T. Jones exemplify these two extremes, Marshall in the sense of "the personal and apolitical," Jones in what might be thought of as "the personal as political." Each achieve their ends by utilizing, though in very different ways, what we call "the proto-narrative unit."

The re-surfacing of narrative arises naturally within the procession of dance cycles. Narrative is a response to both the expressiveness within dance of the modern dance era, and to the influences of crafting and vocabulary from contemporary choreographers' immediate avant-garde past. Working within narrative offers possibilites for choreographing in a middle domain, a domain that is less explicit than the storylines and heroic characters that inspired previous generations of modern choreographers while being more recognizably embedded within human experience than the abstract and emotionally-neutral vocabularies of early postmodern dance.

Second generation Judson choreographers rightfully claim the modern dance pioneers of the 40s and 50s as part of their heritage. They also inherit, as Marcia Siegel states, "the objectivity, nonlinearity, nonrepresentation of 60s, formalism and physicality of 70s, and eclecticism and parody of 80s."[3] Postmodern choreographers who pursue narrative as a means to explore the human condition need not do so literally, in the manner of Martha Graham's psychological drama *Night Journey* (1947) or in the ironic, pedestrian-esque style of David Gordon's work *Chair, Alternatives 1 through 5* (1978). Rather, choreographers such as Johanna Boyce, Bill T. Jones, Susan Marshall, and Jim Self approach narrative in a postmodern way, playfully and eclectically, without seeking the closure of a formal storyline.[4] The choreographers attracted by narrative are mining the terrain of the proto-narrative unit. The proto -narrative can be thought of as a semiotic unit of experience containing elements that lend themselves to being configured within narratives[5]; it is not a complete narrative in itself. We use the term proto-narrative unit to refer to elements such as themes, schemas, gestures, and postures that, like Mona Lisa's smile, suggest narrative posssibilites without specifying what these narratives might be. Such proto-narratives employ recognizable components of everyday life whose meanings remain ambiguous yet suggestive and open to interpretation.

As semiotic, the proto-narrative unit must be understood as having both semantic and behavioral components. Its signifier is the behavioral act, such as a waving hand. Its signified is the meaning attributed to the physical motion, as in a greeting. But any successful communication rests upon what Charles Peirce called the "interpretant," the condition that an audience already understands how a signifier can carry the meaning it does. Does a handwave <u>mean</u> a greeting rather than a cry for help, or is it simply a hand waving?

The work we are considering represents a departure from the stern aesthetic of formalism. It draws upon narrative as a frame for meaning. Story provides context; the meaning of a handwave is clear once we know that its setting is a crowded restaurant rather than a storm-tossed sea. But is it a greeting? Maybe it's a call for the waiter to bring the check, perhaps a gestural accompaniment to a private conversation, an invitation for a newcomer to join our table, a signal for the surprise birthday cake to appear. The handwave is meaningful, but its meaning is only partially determined by the narrative context.

In this paper, we focus in particular on how Bill T. Jones and Susan Marshall make meaning in their dances. Both choreographers draw upon the ambience of postmodernism in their work, utilizing the expanded movement vocabulary that results from cross-breeding between idioms such as contact improvisation, classical ballet, and the many forms of modern and folk dance, and the breaking of traditional boundaries between theatre and dance. Their choreography is produced through an interdisciplinary and collaborative process to which composers, set designers and dancers contribute. They mix and mingle elements of pop culture with elements of high culture. Both also doublecode in their dances, simultaneously referencing, revering, and commenting upon their predecessors.

But what makes Marshall's and Jones's work distinctive in our eyes is their fascination, in much of their work, with the everyday stuff of human life. Exploiting the ambiguities of ordinary experience becomes a means to achieve structural cohesion within their dances. For instance, the way physical contact between partners signifies varies with the genders of the dancers. The same caress between two men reads differently than it does between a man and a woman. Or does it? Such commonplace material provides fertile ground for choreographic possibilities focussing on expression, theatricality, pastiche, and proto-narrative. Yet Susan Marshall and Bill T. Jones use the proto-narrative unit in very different ways. Marshall makes the choreographic one with the semantic; one reads meaning into her movement directly, while the larger narrative frame remains implicit. Jones, in contrast, often provides an explicit narrative frame in the title of his work, and then fills the work with movement that is more purely formal and less obvious in meaning. As Marshall provides the interpretant through meaningful gesture, Jones does so through the narrative frame. Both provide minimal and open structures that support interpretive efforts by an audience.

Susan Marshall prefers to suggest a situation rather than present a storyline. Marshall builds many of her dances on the ambiguites of emotion. As spectators we see dancers as people in the physicality of moving; they do not represent a movement pattern or the structure of the music. They are people experiencing the everyday as the everyperson. One might ask whether they are people wearing costumes or whether their clothes are what came out of the closet that morning. In an interview with Richard Woodward concerning the premiere of *Spectators at an Event* (1994), Marshall quietly states "I don't relate to violent crime. No one in my circle of loved ones has ever been touched by that. Unfortunately, I do know something about illness."[6] This statement is revealing of Marshall's work in general as she typically begins with her own personal experience, but then distills it to reveal an emotional essence.[7]

Marshall's proto-narrative is both private and universal. The duet *Arms* (1984) is considered one of her signature works. It exemplifies why one can not separate Marshall's choreographic intent from her vocabulary or her movement structure. Two people standing side by side, never to move from that one spot, display their involvement, their on-again, off-again relationship. One feels intimacy and support, juxtaposed with resistance to being overpowered or dominated by the partner. They are not so much a couple as two individuals negotiating their coupling. There is need for the other in the same moment that need is shrugged off in favor of a precarious independence. Throughout, there is a longing and reaching for something transcendent, for something more than just the small comfort of another warm body. Yet the same unisex clothing, the repetitive and jarring music, the sense of enclosue within a proletarian environment undercuts transcendence. Watching *Arms* may evoke similar moments of struggle within one's own relationships. Feelings recalled are bittersweet, running the gamut from tenderness to aggression.

Gesturing arms and the duet form often serve as signifying units for Marshall's proto-narrative structure. Her movement material intricately links character and situation. In a 1994 interview, Marshall stated "I use a great deal of movement that's innately understood, whether someone looks away or looks toward, all the embraces, a separation. And I like working with those materials. They carry so much meaning. Then you have embedded in the work a whole vocabulary of movement that's very direct and that informs the more abstract material."[8] In the duet *Kiss* (1987), Marshall reveals information about characters and situation by placing the dancers in aerial harnesses and thus heightening physical risks. The swinging from the harnesses, the near misses of collision, and the fleeting embraces caught mid-air become the signifying unit of experience for passionate longing.

In *Contenders* (1990) Marshall once again blends and blurs the boundaries of character, mood, and emotion while providing a narratively evocative context. There is no doubt that the soundtrack comes from an athletic arena. The starting guns and the roar of the crowd help us keep track of the different events. In a film version made for public television, *Contenders* was taped in a gymnasium, which underscored the narrative theme of dancer-athlete. The film affords us the opportunity to become even more intimate with Marshall's proto-narrative unit through the close-ups and angles of the camera shots as well as the specificity of the set. And yet even in this exactness, there is room for interpretation.

In seeing the film, we as individuals may be personally inspired to keep going, to win, to strive for that which is most important to us. Or we may find ourselves questioning the costs of winning, the difficulty of enduring, the harm our willing can do to others. We may become conscious of how much even the most ardent individual effort relies upon the care and support of others, the gentle caress, the push to strive harder, and the intimacies of competition. Or we may find only fatigue and exhaustion, the grind of unrewarded and unending effort, of ceaseless training that wears down joy, the weariness that arises when there is no victory but only contending.

If Marshall's proto-narrative unit centers around human relationships, that of Bill T. Jones's is situated in social commentary. Jones's interest in narrative and story-telling are well documented.[9] During a pre-concert talk this past January in Eugene, Oregon, Jones commented that "...everything in my repertory of late has a story..."[10] Jones layers his storytelling, mixing and mingling visual imagery, spoken text and highly skilled movement with themes and images derived from his life experiences. This layering and mingling of Jones's personal associations, with a cross-bred movement vocabulary taken from modern dance, contact improvisation, and the everyday, makes his dances both autobiographical and impersonal. Dance critic Elizabeth Zimmer argues that Jones's true genre is multidisciplinary dance theatre. She claims that he is "more interested in authenticity than in originality, negotiating between impersonal ideals of avant-gardism and his more populist, personal passions."[11]

Authentic is a word often found when reading about Jones. It is a word he often uses in statements that he makes about his works. In a 1990 interview for *Ballet Review*, he says that if a work "is infused from the beginning with something that is authentic, if its roots are in some real experience, if it is true to the people performing... it should alter consciousness." [12] In a 1994 interview in *Discourse*, Jones emphatically states "I always speak from the personal."[13] He does not hide the fact that his works are made by a black American homosexual. But paradoxically, by celebrating who he is without apology, he makes works that transcend personal history. As he says about *Still/Here*, a work inspired by his personal confrontation with the ravages of AIDS, "My intention has been to create a work, not as a rumination on death and decline, but on the resourcefulness and courage necessary to perform the act of living."[14]

Jones's proto-narrative unit arises from the interweaving of the autobiographical and the expressive within a narrative frame that orients the spectator. As movement, it often appears as stillnesses that punctuate surrounding movement, quiet gestures juxtaposed with virtuosic locomotion that sweeps the stage. In an interview concerning *Still/Here* Jones commented how his work has always been very gestural. "I might show you five or six phrases that have meant something to me, phrases and shapes that talk about history, maybe my sexuality, my autobiography, my philosophy."[15]

The blurring of public and intimate selves, the overlapping of individual and universal spheres can be illustrated in Jones's solo *Last Night on Earth* (1992). He couples stillnesses with gestures that point to his mouth, chest, and groin. These pointing gestures reappear in varied forms throughout the solo. He mimics, signs, and emphatically gestures along with the lyrics. Yet Jones deconstructs the text as he deconstructs the movement. Is he caught up in the dance, or mocking it? Does he celebrate his homosexuality or merely vamp it? Is Jones trying to show us his different selves? This is material fraught with ambiguity. The critic Anne Tobias, for instance, feels the dynamic and at times dangerous drama of the work and acknowledges its autobiographical nature. But she wants to know why Jones is so angry. She writes, "Details of the dance, along with biographical information, would suggest issues inherent in

Jones's being a gay black man in a relentlessly straight white world. But choreographically speaking, this is never quite clear."16 This type of criticism is occasionally heard in reference to Jones's work. Perhaps he himself is so emphatic about the proto-narrativity of his work that a traditional storyline is expected. Or perhaps for some dances, the story telling is in the choreographic process more than in the performance, so that the dance is more expressive than mimetically narrative.

Jones acknowledges how the rebels of the 60s cleared a space by saying no. As he says, they proved that a duet could exist between a person and a teapot and therefore he no longer has to fight that battle.17 But Jones's work is not merely reactive, not simply personal in an exclusively idiosyncratic sense. Jones warmly claims his link to the early modern dance choreographers. "I owe a great deal to the psychological theatrical works of Martha Graham, José Limón, and also to Alvin Ailey in a special way. We are both in pursuit of all the resonances available in black Americana."18

In addition to elements of personal history and the influences of earlier choreographers, another element within Jones's works arises from his fascination with film. "I wanted to make a kind of art form inspired by the cinema I had been introduced to, the non-narrative cinema of the sixties."19 With Jones's 1990 full-length dance-theatre work, *Last Supper at Uncle Tom's Cabin/The Promised Land*, one can see cinematic associations and his fusion of dance and theatre. This full-length work has its roots in the story of Uncle Tom's Cabin as well as drawing upon the tales and anecdotes his mother shared with him. Jones considers the work a poem - sometimes formal structures are used, at other times the meaning is direct.20 But because of the frame provided by its biblical and emancipatory themes, even the most formally expressive movement becomes suggestive of possible meaning. Within the last section of the *Last Supper*, where at least forty local people join the company on stage at each performance, Jones uses the commonality of the body to invite us to experience the tragedy and hope embodied by the work. The performers shed their clothes, as individual performers did earlier in the piece. Earlier this disrobing signified humiliation before the dominating master, spectator, voyeur. At the end it signifies the resurrection of human dignity, a prelapsarian beauty. "The crowded stage full of naked bodies, with many races, ages, and sexual preferences duly represented, signal humankind's potential for returning to a before-the-Fall innocence and equality."21

During a 1993 television interview Jones stated that he is "looking for the gesture...that changes... the gesture... that changes."22 In many ways this belief drove the collection of movement material in the survival workshops upon which his latest full-length work, *Still/Here*, is based. Before the work premiered in France, Jones was asked about how this material emerged from the workshops he conducted (whose participants consisted of persons diagnosed with life threatening illness). He answered that the movement came "from untrained performers, movement coming from a very emotional place because I ask them to capsulize or crystallize their essential situation, dilemma, in a gesture." He continued by acknowledging how he manipulated the material for more dramatic content.[23] Anna Kisselgoff, in her review of the New York premiere wrote that Jones "succeeds as deeply as he does most of the time because he has realized the paradox of giving immediacy to emotion by distancing himself from it." She also commented on his highly formal structures which are "focused on the heightened distillation of gesture that is Mr. Jones's dance signature."[24]

The choreography of Susan Marshall and Bill T. Jones each offer responses to our historical moment, a moment in which persons are caught straddling the traditional and the modern in a world that is, at least in the developed democracies, increasingly postmodern. In the way of the traditional, we seek connection with others. We want more than the contingent association of being in the same place at the same time; we want community. Yet the commitments to community conflict with the universalist aspirations of modernity, its stress on individual autonomy and political equality, on the impartial state over affiliations with family and blood ties. The results of this conflict in the 20th century have been devastating, playing themselveselves out in the rise of fascism and the cultivation of ethnic hatred, in the stigmatizing of outgroups and the scapegoating of otherness. If we no longer celebrate postmodern play, still we are wary of too quickly embracing the (too) easy comfort of instant community.

Bill T. Jones celebrates the authentic in the context of larger historical and social narratives, but he does so within the diminished promise of the modern. Survival itself may be the only universal value left to the modern sensibility. And if Susan Marshall can find her sphere of creation in the close personal relationship, she hardly can be said to trust the promise of community. Even within this smallest and most intimate of spaces, her work suggests that what we share is the difficulty of relationship, and the struggle to achieve fulfillment. Even in community, we may not find transcendence.

The proto-narrative is not narrative. It suggests a story, but barely and tentatively, almost reluctantly. In a time when theory seems exhausted; when we seek to trust but are wary of who and what to trust, its hesitant gesture repeats our ambivalence.

Notes

1Noel Carroll, "Theatre, Dance and Theory: A Philosophical Narrative," *Dance Chronicle* 15, no. 3 (1992): 317-321.

2Ibid. Also see Sally Banes, "Dancing on the Edge," "Happily Ever After? The Postmodern Fairytale and the New Dance," in *Writing Dancing* (Hanover, NH: Univ. Press of New England, 1994): 252-258; 280-290; Deborah Jowitt, "Expression and Expressionism in American Modern Dance," in *Dance History*, 2nd. ed., J. Adshead-Lansdale and J. Layson, Eds. (NY: Routledge, 1994), 169-181.

3Marcia Siegel, "What has Become of Postmodern Dance," Ann Daly, Ed., *The Drama Review* 36, no. 1 (Spring 1992): 50.

4Sally Banes and Noel Carroll, "Dance and Spectacles in the United States in the Eighties and Nineties," in *Writing Dancing*, 333-340.

5Paul Ricoeur, *Time and Narrative*, Three volumes (Chicago, IL: University of Chicago Press, 1984, 1985, 1988).

6Richard Woodward, "Weegee's Grisley Images Gaze on These Dancers," *The New York Times* , 6 November 1994, Arts & Leisure, 23.

7"Dance Magazine Makes Its 1995 Awards," *Dance Magazine* (April 1995): 40.

8Anne Tobias, "Susan Marshall: A Place Beyond," *Dance Ink* 5, no. 2 (Summer 1994): 17.

9*New York Times Magazine* article states that Jones "...repeatedly works his biography into dance narratives." Elizabeth Kaye, "Bill T. Jones," 6 March 1994, 32.

10Bill T. Jones, Public Lecture, January 10, 1995, Hult Center of the Performing Arts, Eugene, Oregon.

11Henry Louis Gates, "The Body Politics," *The New Yorker*, 28 November 1994, 124.

12Maya Wallach, "A Conversation with Bill T. Jones," *Ballet Review* 18, no. 4 (Winter 1990-1991): 73.

13Nicole J. Cunningham and Thomas Piontek, "Still/Here: An Interview with Bill T. Jones," *Discourse* 16, no. 3 (Spring 1994): 82.

14Bill T. Jones, Program notes for *Still/Here* performance in Portland, Oregon, January 13-15, 1995.

15Nicole J. Cunningham and Thomas Piontek, 80.

16Anne Tobias, "Reality and Fantasy," *Dance View* 10, no. 3 (Spring 1993): 38.

17Bill T. Jones, *Retracing Steps: American Dance Since Postmodernism* (Michael Blackwood Production, 1988), videorecording.

18Bill T. Jones, *Bill T. Jones: Dancing to the Promised Land* (V.I.E.W. Video, 1994), videorecording.

19Henry Louis Gates, 117-8.

20See note 18.

21Anne Tobias, "Bill T. Jones/Arnie Zane & Co., BAM Opera House, November 7-10, 1990," *Dance Magazine* (February 1991): 121.

22Bill T. Jones, excerpt from "CBS Sunday Morning America," Fall 1993, television program.

23Nicole J. Cunningham and Thomas Piontek, 78-79.

24Anna Kisselgoff, "Anger Meets Elegy in Bill T. Jones's Lyrical Look at Survivors," *The New York Times*, 2 December 1994, B1.

Selected References

Banes, Sally. *Democracy's Body.* Ann Arbor: MI: UMI Press, 1980.

Banes, Sally. *Terpsichore in Sneakers.* Boston, MA: Houghton Mifflin, 1980.

Banes, Sally. *Writing Dancing in the Age of Postmodernism.* Hanover, NH: University Press of New England, 1994.

Boyce, Johanna, Daly, Ann, Jones, Bill T. Jones, and Martin, Carol. "A Roundtable Discussion," *The Drama Review* 32, no. 4 (Winter 1988): 82 -101.

"CBS Sunday Morning America," television segment on Bill T. Jones, Fall 1993.

Carroll, Noel. "Theatre, Dance, and Theory: A Philosophical Narrative," *Dance Chronicle* 15, no. 3 (1992): 317-334.

Cunningham, Nicole and Piontek, Thomas. "Still/Here: An Interview with Bill T. Jones," *Discourse* 16, no. 3 (Spring 1994): 78-85.

Daly, Ann, Ed. "What has Become of Postmodern Dance," *The Drama Review* 36, no. 1 (Spring 1992): 48-69.

"Dance Magazine Makes Its 1995 Awards," *Dance Magazine* (April 1995): 40.

Gates, Henry Louis. "The Body Politics," *The New Yorker*, 28 November 1994, 112-124.

Jones, Bill T. Program Notes for Still/Here, Bill T. Jones/Arnie Zane Dance Co., 1994.

Jones, Bill T. *Bill T. Jones: Dancing to the Promised Land.* V.I.E.W. Video Productions, 1994.

Jones, Bill T. Public Lecture, Hult Center for the Performing Arts, Eugene, OR, January 10, 1995.

Jowitt, Deborah. "Expression and Expressionism in American Modern Dance," in *Dance History*, 2nd ed., J. Adshead and J. Layson, Ed., NY: Routledge, 1994.

Kaye, Elizabeth. "Bill T. Jones," *New York Times Magazine*, 6 March 1994, 30-33.

Kisselgoff, Anna. "Anger Meets Elegy in Bill T. Jones's Lyrical Look at Survivors," *The New York Times*, 2 December 1994, B1, 11.

Manning, Susan. "Modernist Dogma and Post-modern Rhetoric," *The Drama Review* 32, no. 4 (Winter 1988): 32-39.

Retracing Steps: American Dance Since Postmodernism. Michael Blackwood Video Production, 1988.

Ricoeur, Paul. *Time and Narrative*. Three volumes. Chicago, IL: University of Chicago Press, 1984, 1985, 1988.

Tobias, Anne. "Bill T. Jones/Arnie Zane & Co., BAM Opera House, November 7-10, 1990," *Dance Magazine* (February 1991): 120-121.

Tobias, Anne. "Reality and Fantasy," *Dance View* 10. no. 3 (Spring 1993): 38.

Tobias, Anne. "Susan Marshall: A Place Beyond," *Dance Ink* 5, no. 2 (Summer 1994): 17.

Wallach, Maya. "A Conversation with Bill T. Jones," *Ballet Review* 18, no. 4 (Winter 1990-91): 73-75.

Woodward, Richard. "Weegee's Grisley Images Gaze on These Dancers," *The New York Times*, 6 November 1994, Arts & Leisure, 23.

MIRACLES OR MYSTERIES? READING BALLETS OF EARLY MODERNISM: DIAGHILEV AND MEDIEVALISM

Sally Bowden

To link Diaghilev, as impressario of the Ballets Russes, with medievalism is to juxtapose twentieth century modernism with antiquity. Is this apparent tension consistent with the sounds and images that fused Borodin's music with the bleak steppe lands of ancient Russia in 1909 or even Stravinsky's insistent rhythms with pagan ritual in 1913? Do the Polovtsian dances from *Prince Igor* and *Le Sacre du printemps* reconcile the anomaly? These ballets reiterated such theatre pieces as *Tsar Fyodor Ivanovich* that Stanislavsky directed at the Moscow Art Theatre in 1898 and Diaghilev's own presentation of Mussorgsky's opera *Boris Godunov* in Paris in 1908. As ethnographical stage reconstructions, the ballets were undoubtedly impressive. However, as experiments in mere living history, can the pieces be recognised as stemming from early twentieth century theatre modernism that in Russia challenged the established bourgeois theatre based on the realistic representation of life? The title of this paper is *Miracles or Mysteries*, since it is through these sacred dramatic forms of the Middle Ages that a reconciliation between Diaghilev's ballet modernism and medievalism, as a movement in Russian avant-garde theatre, might be accomplished.

In Russia, the first decade of the twentieth century inspired a new, or anti-representational drama, that rejected theatre realism with its proscenium framing and fourth wall conventions, authenticity of setting, costume and manners. The new drama was directed towards the exposure of the illusionary nature of theatrical art in the belief that theatre, as art, probed 'universal mysteries and the reassertion of eternal verities through new configurations of image and idea' (Segel, 1970, p 56). The exponents of this new drama found inspiration in the forms of ancient theatre: the conventions of Greek theatre of the fifth century BC, antique oriental theatre and European drama from the Middle Ages to the Renaissance. Medieval theatre was rediscovered, but in the absence of a recognised native Russian medieval theatre exemplary mystery and miracle plays were drawn from Western European historical tradition, notably the French mystères (mysteries). New versions were written as neo-romantic variants, such as Kuzmin's *The history of the knight of d'Allesio* (1905). This particular mystery is of note since *Schéhérazade*, as it was staged by the Ballets Russes (1910), bore certain similarities to the plot of Kuzmin's play.

Contemporary enthusiasm for the mysteries came from Symbolist circles in which Diaghilev's *World of Art* group and journal featured with prominence. The Symbolist movement in Russia was inspired by French symbolism which was contemporary with impressionism in painting and music, with the philosophy of the unconscious mind, mysticism and symbolism as expressed by the poets Rimbaud, Verlaine and Mallarmé. It was Mallarmé's verse that was the initial inspiration for the ballet *L'Après-midi d'un faune* that Nijinsky choreographed in 1912. The atmospheric quality of Verlaine's verse, which was often of a melancholic nature, but characterised by a general trend towards simplicity, was reflected in the dramas of the Belgian playwright,

Maeterlinck. Such plays as his trilogy of neo-mysteries, *The sightless, The intruder* and *The interior,* written between 1890 and 1894, were influential in the development of Russian theatre at the turn of the century and promoted the dramatisation of man's spiritual fears and longings.

The mystical qualities of the medieval dramas were derived from the chanted speech and processional movement that formed part of the regular liturgy or Christian Church service of the day, as in the earliest form that celebrated the resurrection at Easter time (*Resurrexi,* tenth century Limoges manuscript). It was the anti-representational nature of these allegorical pieces and their symbolic significance that recommended the ancient plays to the exponents of the new drama.

In order to locate Diaghilev's modernism with in the context of Russian neo-medievalism for this paper, two ballets have been selected that separately can be seen to mirror this trend of the new drama. The paper is a discussion of the relationship of *Petrouchka* (1911) to the 1907-08 season of medieval mysteries, miracles and farces as staged in St. Petersburg at The Ancient Theatre and that of *L'Après-midi d'un faune* (1912) to Meyerhold's direction of Maeterlinck's neo-medieval plays in Moscow (1905) and St. Petersburg (1906).

The Ancient Theatre and *Petrouchka*

Amongst the experiments in new drama, the most startling and significant achievement in establishing an ancient art as living theatre was the venture undertaken by Evreinov and Baron Driezen which was known as The Ancient Theatre. The theatre directorate published proposals for The Ancient Theatre in *Theatre and Art* of 3 June, 1907, that included provisions for 'archaeological and historical truthfulness of staging and communication of the spirit and character of the epoch under consideration' (Golub, 1984, p 109). This aim in itself was not original since there was a general impulse in Russian arts at that time to recreate antiquity. In the visual arts and architecture, besides the theatre, an obsessive reclamation of the past prevailed. The paintings of Riabushkin and Surikov, besides the collections of Mamontov and Tenisheva, bear witness to the intense interest in the antique that pervaded artistic circles. However, the further proposition that The Ancient Theatre would recreate on stage the characteristics of the actor-audience relationship, brought the venture in line with the avant-garde staging of the new drama.

The plan of the directorate of The Ancient Theatre was to accompany each performance of the medieval dramas with the responses of an on stage audience made up of actors, who were to characterise the spectators appropriate to each performance. The on stage spectators represented, at the same time, both observers and participants in the action of the play. The play-within-the-play was an intentional reminder to the theatre audience that it was participating in a theatrical performance, rather than assuming the passive role associated with the audience observing realistic drama. The introduction of the metatheatrical device of the play-within-the-play challenged the illusion of medieval theatre that was otherwise authentically reconstructed.

Diaghilev's *World of Art* group participated in The Ancient Theatre. For the 1907-08 season visual artists were occupied as theatrical designers. Benois, Bilibin, Dobuzhinsky, Lanseray and Roerich took part. Benois served as artistic and historical consultant, whilst Fokine, who choreographed *Petrouchka*, composed the dances for the pastoral *Robin and Marion* by Adam de la Halle.

An extract from the stage directions of *The fair on the day of St. Denis*, a fifteenth century street theatre piece, indicates a proposed manner of staging a play-within-a-play at The Ancient Theatre. It was Benois who created the designs for setting and costume for *Petrouchka*. The director, Evreinov, visualised the fair in a town square surrounded by multi-coloured, little shops. In the distance was a church. In the foreground was a brothel with its tempting notices and near by drunken citizens were enjoying themselves. The sounds of musical instruments could be heard mingled with the stamping of feet, laughter and the confused chatter of coarse, drunken conversation. A lively round dance was taking place. All this hubbub was dominated by the voice of a puppet master who was entertaining an animated crowd of spectators.

If the staging of Petrouchka is considered in the light of the stage directions for *The fair on the day of St. Denis*, the resemblance between the two is one that surpasses the mere notion that both were characterised by a stage-within-a-stage. Certain features are duplicated in the two pieces, notably the town square, the fair, multi-coloured shops, a brothel, a distant church and a puppet show. A drunken crowd of revellers, folk dance, sounds of musical instruments (impressions of the instruments of street musicians were included in Stravinsky's score for *Petrouchka*), stamping feet, laughter and a mood of happy animation, dominated by the characters of the puppeteers, feature in both productions.

The narrative and intention of *Petrouchka*, like that of the medieval plays in which the role of the spectator was intrinsic, are only explicable when the responses of the on stage spectators are integrated with the dramatic action. In the case of *Petrouchka*, the spectators are Russians of mid-nineteenth century St. Petersburg participating in the entertainments at the *Maslenitsa* fair. Although alternative productions of the new drama that utilised a stage-within-a-stage technique would have been part of Benois' experience as a theatre critic prior to the genesis of *Petrouchka*, in particular Blok's satirical harlequinade, *The fairground booth* (1906), it was at The Ancient Theatre that theatre realism with an on stage audience were harmoniously effective. However, the *Petrouchka* of 1911 owes more to the example of neo-medievalism than the techniques of avant-garde staging as exemplified at The Ancient Theatre. Within the make up of the ballet lie references to the allegory and ritual of the early liturgical dramas and mysteries. Consider *Petrouchka* as a neo-mystery!

The liturgical dramas of the Middle Ages were constructed to contain subject matter that was appropriate to the calendar feasts of the Christian church – Easter, Christmas and Epiphany. At that same time, the ancient folk festivals of the agrarian year, that marked the passing of the seasons with the sun's passage through the heavens, had not been supplanted completely by the Church feasts and became identified with them. The folk games and dances, mummers and carnival processions associated in the pagan mind with the seasonal deities were accommodated within the structure of the

Church year. Thus the pagan origins of the festivals were invested with Christian significance. For example, the death of winter and the rebirth of spring that was celebrated annually with carnival was later to be mirrored in the Christian celebration of the death and resurrection of Jesus Christ at Easter. This event was ritualised in the tenth century liturgical dramas of Good Friday and the Resurrection.

The fairground carnival in *Petrouchka* celebrates *Maslenitsa*, and marks Shrovetide or the last three days before Lent that preceeds Easter in the Christian Church. The intention of the seasonal rite was to bid farewell to winter and charm the sun's return in spring. The annual Shrove procession, that was still evident in Russia in the nineteenth century, was headed by a dressed effigy of the deity made of wood or straw. The climax of the celebration was the physical annihilation of this puppet figure, or god of darkness. In *Petrouchka*, the superstitions and customs of Shrovetide that permeate the fairground scenes are concluded with the substitution of winter for spring, when a straw dummy, symbolic of the former and personified by the Petrouchka puppet, is destroyed in an act of productive magic, albeit at the hands of the foolish Moor. Yet, Petrouchka is apparently restored to life as the ballet concludes. Is it the immortal soul of the puppet that is glimpsed in the half light gesticulating above the puppet theatre? The ballet is a dance drama of the fairground and an allegory for death and rebirth.

The fairground crowd is confronted with a double image of the Shrovetide festival. The illusion of revelry is underpinned by connotations of ritual that translate the humour of the scene into a mood of impending sacrifice and death. The congregations that witnessed the liturgical dramas in the Middle Ages were similarly presented with a duality within the celebration of Christ's resurrection in the *Ludus Paschalis*. The Easter drama was an ornate, seasonal ritual, undertaken by clerics. It was 'artificial, mystical and lyrical' (Wickham, 1987, p 33). Yet, the *Ludus Paschalis* was a dramatic representation of an event in Christian history that coincided with the pagan festival to reawaken the earth after its seeming death in winter. In *Petrouchka*, the puppet proves his immortality in the style of the traditional guignol, who inevitably was victorious over all his foes, even the Devil. At the same time Petrouchka's death and reappearance justifies the pagan belief that from death is derived life and the assurance that the sun would rise again to warm the earth and renew its fertility.

Meyerhold's 'motionless theatre' and *L'Après-midi d'un faune*

A further theatrical context for modernist mystery plays relevant to Diaghilev's neo-medievalism was that of the studio theatre of the Art Theatre, Moscow, during 1905, and that of the theatre of Vera Komissarzhevskaya the following year. Both were under the direction of Meyerhold. *L'Après-midi d'un faune* may be regarded as a reflection of Meyerhold's experimental staging of 1905 and 1906, when his visualisation of 'motionless theatre' and stylisation of stage grouping in the form of bas relief was realised. Of the work he undertook to stage Maeterlinck's neo-medieval tale, *The death of Tintagiles*, at the studio theatre, Meyerhold (1908) wrote that it inspired

> a method of placing figures on stage in bas-reliefs and frescoes and a means of expressing interior monologue with the help of the music of plastic motion, and

provided the possibility of trying out in practice the force of mystical accentuation.

Rudnitsky, 1981, p 58.

This was the beginning of 'motionless theatre' that Rudnitsky, the theatre critic and historian, claimed (1981) had determined in many respects the temper of all Russian symbolist theatre.

'Motionless theatre' was theatre of slow, considered motion. The plastic form of acting represented the hidden spirit of the play. Sometimes at moments of particular significance, characters would suddenly freeze as living statues, or bas-reliefs. The movement was not intended as a realistic image of human motion. *The death of Tintagiles* was performed on an unusually narrow stage to accentuate the impression of the bas-relief. Meyerhold brought forward the backcloth to create a shallow platform after the manner of the Japanese Kabuki stage.

It was at the theatre of Vera Komissarzhevskaya that Meyerhold continued his experiments in the staging of Symbolist plays in 1906. The production of Maeterlinck's neo-miracle play *Sister Beatrice* is relevant to this discussion. Meyerhold directed his crowd to move in unison, whilst the gestures of a chorus of nuns, who remained at Beatrice's side virtually throughout the play, he synchronised. Photographs of the production illustrate Meyerhold's grouping of these characters so as to create a plastic accompaniment of supporting gestures to the heroine's poses. It was probable that Meyerhold sought inspiration for his grouping in reproductions of paintings, ancient church artefacts and decorative schemes. With identical gestures, with slow restrained movements the nuns followed one another precisely, moving the whole time in profile so as to maintain the appearance of a bas-relief or frieze.

L'Après-midi d'un faune may be described as an animated Greek frieze. The ballet was danced in profile. A chorus of nymphs and the faun performed angular and parallel movements. This frieze of living figures, with bodies turned to the audience whilst heads and limbs were averted, suggested a two-dimensional surface. The effect of flatness was accentuated by lighting and the restriction of the stage space to a narrow ribbon by the forward positioning of Bakst's painted backcloth.

Numerous myths have grown up concerning the genesis of *L'Après-midi d'un faune*. Although Nijinska (1982), in her memoirs, has attributed its entire conception to her brother, Haskell, in his biography of Diaghilev, assigned the original ideas for the ballet to Diaghilev and Bakst. According to Haskell (1935) Diaghilev and Bakst resolved to marry Debussy's music with Mallarmé's verse. Moreover, it was with their judgement that the two-dimensional design that gave the piece so distinctive a stage appearance was incorporated. In 1906 Bakst had been involved in the organisation of Vera Komissarzhevskaya's new theatre, and painted the front curtain for Meyerhold's season of plays. Bakst undoubtedly was familiar with Meyerhold's experiments. The static images and rhythmical movement, restricted to a narrow stage space, of Meyerhold's Symbolist theatre is mirrored in *L'Après-midi d'un faune*. The depersonalised acting of the nuns in *Sister Beatrice* is reflected in the angular movements of the nymphs that emphasised the abstraction of Mallarmé's verse. Their synchronised gestures and stylised choric dance transferred 'motionless theatre' from the drama stage to the ballet theatre.

In conclusion, it can be said that Diaghilev's medievalism was consistent with early modernism, as exemplified in the new Russian drama of the first decade of the twentieth century. The experiments undertaken at The Ancient Theatre and by the director Meyerhold determined new methods of staging that influenced Russian Symbolist theatre and apparently infiltrated some early ballets of the Ballets Russes, so that *Petrouchka* and *L'Après-midi d'un faune* may be read as neo-mysteries or neo-miracles. A plastic convention of acting, based on the form of bas-relief and harmonious with the symbolic nature of the drama was introduced by Meyerhold and was reflected in the staging of *L'Après-midi d'un faune*. Whilst the sub-text of *Petrouchka* bears a resemblance to the ancient ritual celebration of Easter, there is an additional link between the ballet and contemporary stagings of neo-mysteries with which to end this discussion, or continue it at some future time. Do Fokine's choreographic plastiques that he devised for the duality of the Petrouchka role and the extrovert nature of the Moor reflect Meyerhold's experiments in 'motionless theatre' that expressed the interior monologues of his characters?

Bibliography

Golub, S. *Evreinov The theatre of paradox and transformation*. Ann Arbor: UMI Research Press, 1984.

Haskell, A. *Diaghileff: his artistic and private life*. In collaboration with Nouvel, W. London: Gollancz, 1935.

Nijinska, B. *Bronislava Nijinska Early Memoirs*. Nijinska, I. and Rawlinson, J. (eds and trans) London: Faber and Faber, 1982.

Rudnitsky, K. *Meyerhold the director*. Petrov, G. (trans) Ann Arbor: Ardis, 1981.

Segel, H. *Twentieth century Russian drama: from Gorky to the present*. New York: Columbia University Press, 1970.

Wickham, G. *The medieval theatre*. Cambridge: Cambridge University Press, 1987.

METAPHORS OF TRAVEL AND MAPPING IN POSTMODERN DANCE AND DISCOURSE
or an attempt to chart a course between feminism and postmodernism.

Valerie A. Briginshaw, Chichester Institute of Higher Education

This paper explores the extent to which some recent dance films and
videos, which focus on travel, are gendered in a specific sense
because of this subject-matter and its treatment.(1) The interest
in travel as subject-matter for dance parallels the use of travel
metaphors in some recent postmodern theory. Consequently by looking
at the way in which such work is gendered this paper also
contributes to current debates concerning the often vexed
relationships between feminism and postmodernism.

After briefly outlining some uses of travel and mapping metaphors
in postmodern discourse and showing how travel is gendered, six
dance films are considered where the choreography and filming of
bodies in space is shown to support or subvert this claim. In
conclusion some reasons for this current interest in travel
metaphors are suggested and some examples of reappropriation of the
metaphors for feminism are given.

Metaphors of travel and mapping in postmodern discourse

New experiences of space and time are claimed to be characteristic
of the present postmodern era(Bird et al., 1993). A central concept
in Harvey's *The Condition of Postmodernity*(1989) is that of 'time-
space compression' which he partly derives from Heidegger(1971)
whom he quotes as stating 'all distances in time and space are
shrinking'. These new experiences are manifest in 'an increase
in...cultural flows' and 'transnational encounters'(Featherstone in
Bird et al., 1993). The world, through new technologies, is in many
senses a much smaller, more accessible place than it used to be.
Travelling of all kinds, of information as well as people, through
time as well as space is escalating. Whereas the motorcar, the
train and the aeroplane could be seen to be signs of modernity,
postmodernity is rather characterised by a range of electronic,
computerised, telecommunication, video and virtual reality
developments.(2)

These developments have revealed tensions between 'the global' and
'the local', between 'space' and 'place'. Attempts to express,
understand or resolve these tensions are evident in a nostalgic
fascination with local cultures and the vernacular or the 'other'
in some postmodern culture. 'Travel' as a metaphor gives access to
the 'other' and postmodernism has brought an awareness of
'otherness' through, as Elizabeth Grosz has put it, 'the
replacement of geographical space with the screen interface'(Grosz
in Colomina, 1992 p.251). Metaphors of travel and mapping position
the 'other' as either 'natural' or constructed and in doing so they
either hide or reveal key constituents of the construction, such as
gender.

Whilst on the one hand the links between different cultures, times and places perhaps stress integration or a kind of globalisation, in another sense recognition of the range of cultural groups and 'others' that exist, emphasises notions of fragmentation or localisation, which are also manifest in concepts of a 'fragmented subject'. This is described by some as a 'nomadic subjectivity': 'individuality functions as and is articulated out of, a nomadic wandering through everchanging positions and apparatuses'(Grossberg quoted in Probyn, 1990 p.184).(3) The metaphor of the tourist is sometimes also used. Tourists and nomads are seen as 'unthreatening, merely passing through;' (ibid.,p.184). Travel allows the possibility of being 'simultaneously everywhere' (Chambers, 1987 p.1).

It is because postmodern discourse needs to address such fluidity not only of subjects and identities, but also of concepts of 'meaning' and 'truth', that it has employed metaphors of travel. In a recent text, tellingly titled *Cartographies - poststructuralism and the mapping of bodies and spaces* (Diprose & Ferrell eds., 1991), it is suggested that 'the philosopher of the future will be a "wanderer", a transient who abjures attachments to existing institutions and ideas,... the desert in which he or she wanders is..., a mobile space characterised by the variable directions and the multiple dimensions in which movement is possible'(Patton, 1991 p.53). Culture can be rethought in terms of travel to accommodate the shifting 'truths', encounters, horizons and landscapes of postmodernity so that culture as a 'rooted body that grows lives and dies is questioned' and replaced by 'constructed and disputed *historicities*, sites of displacement, interference, and interaction'(Clifford,1992 p.101). Recognition that the terrain is varied and complex results in an extension of these travel metaphors to include the notion of worldviews becoming 'maps', 'topographies' or grids with 'coordinates' as reference points. The notion of 'cognitive mapping' as a postmodern way of 'seeing the world' has been championed by Jameson(1988) and the term 'conceptual map'(Connor,1989) has also been used. Another recent text is entitled *Mapping the Futures*(Bird et al. 1993) and a recent series of texts all entitled *Mapping* something, for instance, *Mapping Ideology, Mapping the Nation* is another example. Given that everything, from identities to ideas to cultures characterised as postmodern, is essentially fluid, forever shifting and changing, on the move, it is perhaps not surprising that travel metaphors of various kinds have become current in postmodern discourse.

Travel and gender

The ways in which travel is gendered often remain hidden. Some of the theorists who use travel metaphors, particularly Jameson(1991) and Harvey(1989), almost entirely ignore gender in their analyses (Massey,1993, Morris, 1993). Arguing that travel metaphors in cultural criticism are gendered, Janet Wolff(1993) claims that 'just as the practices and ideologies of *actual* travel operate to exclude or pathologise women, so the use of that vocabulary as

metaphor necessarily produces androcentric tendencies in
theory'(p.224).

Having examined vocabularies of travel in postmodern theory,
postcolonial criticism and poststructuralism, Wolff(1993) looks at
women and travel and concludes that 'histories of travel make it
clear that women have never had the same access to the road as
men'(p.229). She quotes Cynthia Enloe as stating 'being feminine
has been defined as sticking close to home. Masculinity by contrast
has been the passport for travel'(p.229). Wolff points out that
women do travel and have a place in travel, but often that place is
marginalised and degraded, as in tourism where women are often
hotel maids or active in sex-tourism. Those women who have
travelled in the past have often been masculinised and seen as
eccentric for taking up a 'male pursuit'. Wolff cites the hostile
criticism of the film *Thelma and Louise* as partly to do with the
unacceptable notion of women starring in a road movie, normally the
domain of men. Thelma and Louise also become masculinised as the
film progresses as they move from the 'supposedly female space of
the home to the supposedly male space of the great outdoors' and
take to the road which acts as a sign for 'a certain mythicised
freedom'(Tasker, p.136.). It is claimed that '"Good travel"
(heroic, educational, scientific, adventurous, ennobling) is
something men(should) do. Women are impeded from serious
travel'(Clifford,1992 p.105) and Dea Birkett(1990), reviewing books
on women travellers in the last two centuries, comments, 'it is
far...more demanding for a woman to wander now than ever
before'(p.41).

Space, power and gender

It is not just travel itself but also concepts associated with
travel, such as space, that are gendered. This is relevant when the
chosen dance films are analysed. It is important to recognise that
space is not transparent and innocent, rather it is socially
constructed and imbued with power of different kinds. There is a
politics of space and of movement through space or travel. Travel
is closely associated with power and knowledge in different
ways.(1) For example, the forced migration of people in the face of
lack of resources or employment and the regulation associated with
refugee camps and immigration demonstrate the powerlessness of some
kinds of travel. Doreen Massey(1993) employs the term 'power-
geometry' to describe the differential power associated with
movement flows and travel. She compares those who are doing the
moving and communicating and importantly are in control of these
processes - the 'jet-setters' - and those who, although moving a
lot, are not in charge in the same way - the refugees, migrant
workers, third world peasants,etc. As she states: 'mobility and
control over mobility both reflect and reinforce power'(p.62). This
power differential is based to a certain extent on power structures
and institutions that operate elsewhere, such as patriarchy.
Gillian Rose(1993) claims that space is often seen as 'transparent'
and it can be known only through a certain masculinity and that
'like the masculine subjectivity on which it relies, transparent

space hides what it depends on for its meaning: an other'(p.71),
which Rose sees as 'place'. Characteristics of this 'transparent'
space are its infinitude, its unboundedness and the freedom it
provides. Rose(1993) cites one geographer(Gould) describing the
freedom to run, leap, stretch and reach out without bounds in this
'transparent' space. She comments 'these claims of power over
space...suggest to me that [the] space is that of hegemonic
masculinity. Only white heterosexual men usually enjoy such a
feeling of spatial freedom. Women know that spaces are not
necessarily without constraint; sexual attacks warn them that their
bodies are not meant to be in public spaces'(pp.75-76).

Postmodern dance and travel

In postmodern dance travel is not being used as a metaphor in the
same sense as it is in postmodern discourse. The dances actually
focus on and create images of, or associated with, 'real' travel,
but in the sense that any dance or art work is re-presenting ideas
about the 'real world', I would argue that these representations of
travel can sometimes act as metaphors.

There are several examples of recent dances which demonstrate a
fascination with local cultures and the 'other' and hence suggest
or re-present travel in this way. Wim Vandekeybus's *On a Mountain
Barking*(1993/4), which includes film footage of life in a Moroccan
village, Gallotta's *Mammame*(1985-7) about refugees and his later *Un
Chant Presque Etient*(1989), drawing on *Mammame*, come to mind. There
is also Mark Morris's *O Rangasayee*(1984), which appropriates Indian
classical dance, his *Hard Nut*(1991) with its dances from other
cultures and Preljocaj's *Noces*(1989), which looks at his Albanian
cultural traditions through the lens of the Ballets Russes' earlier
modernist appropriation of similar traditions. It can be countered
that appropriations from other cultures have been evident in dances
and other art forms prior to postmodernism. Petipa and Ivanov's
various national dances in ballets such as *Swan Lake*(1895) and *The
Nutcracker*(1892) are well-known examples, but a key difference is
that these were not produced in the context of an awareness of
'otherness' that has come about with postmodernism.

Six dance films which have travel as their focus have been selected
for consideration. Their details are provided in Fig. 1. The first
point of commonality to note is that they are importantly all
films/videos. This allows for a range of locations that suggest
travel of various kinds such as quays, ports, stations, hotels,
shorelines, beaches, railtracks and roads(see Fig.2). Crucially the
relationships created by choreographing and filming the body in
performance in these particular locations, are key sources of
meaning in these works. The body and its environment construct or
produce each other(Grosz, 1992). These juxtapositions conjure up
notions of travel, journeys, uprooted peoples, spaces, places,
maps. It goes without saying that all pieces, being dances, involve
movement, but importantly, all involve a considerable amount of
pedestrian movement of the most direct or obvious kind for going
places; walking and running.

The kinds of travel covered by these texts can be seen to fall into three loose, sometimes overlapping, categories; those of exploration, migration and tourism(see Fig.2). There are various clues in the works that point to or suggest these categories; first, the titles or notes quoted on video covers. *Ellis Island* refers to a reception centre that was used for immigrants to the USA from the end of the last century throughout the first part of this century. There are hints of travel in some of the other titles: *Carnets de Traversée, Quais Ouest(Carnets* from now on) can be loosely translated as Crossing(or passage) Notebooks(notes or jottings), West Quays, *La Deroute*, the Route and *Cross-Channel*. Cover notes for the video of *Carnets* and *La Deroute* state: 'Two dance performances on the theme of migration' and those for *Land-Jäger* state: 'An imaginary journey. Three characters are stranded on the coast of the Baltic Sea, in a country which is unknown to them.' It is relatively straightforward to categorise *Ellis Island*, *Carnets* and *La Deroute* as dances about migration and *Cross-Channel* since, as well as the title, it includes hotel, beach, camping site and bar settings and cycling, swimming and sunbathing activities, as a dance focussing on holidaymaking or tourism. The others are less straightforward. *Land-Jäger* I have decided to classify as a kind of exploration piece, since activities such as striding through high undergrowth, sitting or sleeping around a campfire in front of what looks like a kind of primitive shelter built out of wood, are included. There is also no evidence of any 'civilisation' in the landscape. *A Mossa* is more of a metaphor for travel than any of the other pieces, in that it is not about travel, migration or journeys as such, but it suggests such, in that it is set on Corsica, an 'exotic', faraway location, and, as the video cover note states, 'it combines the traditions of Corsica with contemporary dance.'

Some examples of gendering in the dance films

The kind of gendering of space and travel that is evident in some postmodern discourse is also apparent in some of these dance films.

(Video clips from *Land-Jäger* and *La Deroute*)

The wide open spaces filmed in *Land-Jäger* and *La Deroute* in particular, especially when seen with figures running and leaping across them, are being presented, I would suggest, as 'transparent' and hence from a masculine perspective. There is also a sense in four of the films, *Carnets, Land-Jäger, La Deroute* and *A Mossa*, that the space is innocent and 'transparent' because it is not clearly identifiable as a specific place. A generalised, almost abstract, sense of space, rather than a specific place is being evoked.

Massey(1993) suggests that what is needed to expose the 'transparency' at work is 'a progressive sense of place', 'an understanding of "its character", which can only be constructed by linking that place to places beyond....it would be about the relationship between place and space...a global sense of the

local'(p.68). I would suggest that that is what is presented in
Ellis Island and *Cross Channel*. The understanding of the character
of Ellis Island as a specific place is suggested by what goes on
and by how people are identified with places beyond Ellis Island,
where they have come from. In very different ways the characters in
Cross Channel are also identified with places beyond the channel
crossing and the French coast by markers on their journey; London's
Victoria Station and a pub in the English countryside, for example.
Importantly also gender is not at all 'transparent', it
characterises the places passed through on the journey. In a
similar way particular ethnic identities characterise *Ellis Island*.

In accounting for the masculinist nature of much geography
Rose(1993) describes the geographer's gaze as 'penetrating' with a
'strong claim to knowledge' which she claims depends on the
'transparency' of space which appears to be unmediated and 'utterly
knowable'(p.70). Theories of the 'look' or the 'gaze' and the ways
in which looking is gendered are prevalant in feminist scholarship
from John Berger's(1973) statement that 'men look' whilst 'women
appear' and connote 'to-be-looked-at-ness', to Laura Mulvey's(1975)
theory of the male gaze at work in Hollywood cinema, to Luce
Irigaray's(1978) statement that 'investment in the look is not
privileged in women as in men. More than the other senses, the eye
objectifies and masters'(p.50). The associations of
objectification, mastery, control, possession, manipulation,
exploitation and voyeurism with this kind of masculine penetrative
looking can be seen to relate to those travellers who were also
explorers and conquerors in colonial times as well as to tourists
today. The use of telephoto lenses in game parks comes particularly
to mind. In the sense that tourism is 'a form of entertainment
dependent on exploitation'(Chaney, 1994, p.79), a notion of 'the
tourist gaze' has been suggested(Urry, 1990) and the tourist has
been described as a voyeur(Chaney, 1994.p.173). The geographer's
gendered gaze can be synthesized with Mulvey's masculine gaze since
both objectify and rationalise from a masculine perspective; the
geographer's gaze objectifies the land and the masculine gaze
objectifies woman.

The synthesis of these two gazes is demonstrated in the dance films
being considered in the way space is filmed as 'transparent' and in
the way the women in some of the pieces are also presented as
'transparent', when clearly they are gendered by certain filmic and
choreographic devices. As Mulvey claims both the camera and the
other(male) performers position the viewer to see the female
performer(s) through the masculine gaze, or through masculine eyes.

(Video clip from *Carnets*)

The men in *Carnets* are seen actively moving through space; climbing
steps, walking along the quay side, jumping on the quay wall. The
women are often seen looking, but nearly always stationary, often
in close-up, focussing on their faces, well-lit, with hair blowing
in the wind. When the women move it is often in a sensitive,
interior kind of way. In *La Deroute* there are similar close-up

shots of women's faces but there is also a long solo dance of a
woman in water which arrests the narrative in just the way Mulvey
describes for female stars in mainstream Hollywood narrative films.
Both the woman and the land, in the sense of mud and water, are
seen as 'transparent' and objectified by the gaze. *Cross-Channel*
also presents women as passive and to-be-looked-at; sunbathing,
leaning over the side of the ship, sitting in a train, etc. and men
as active; cycling, swimming, directing traffic onto the boat,
cleaning windows,etc. But I would argue that through various
structural devices such as editing and repetition, the passivity of
the women and the activity of the men in *Cross-Channel* is
emphasised, foregrounded and played with and thus exposed and
critiqued through ridicule. In no way is gender 'transparent' in
the same sense as it is in *Carnets* and *La Deroute*.

The choreography in *Cross-Channel* also emphasises gender
differences.

(Video clip from *Cross-Channel*)

For example, the women are given mainly whole body, fluid
movements, as in a hotel corridor when they emerge from doorways
spin across the hallway and disappear into the rooms opposite.
Whereas the choreography for the men consists mainly of rigid,
movements of isolated body parts, for example when they are
swatting flies on the clifftops or when paddling on the beach. The
choreography particularly when combined with the costumes results
in the women tending to look suave, sophisticated and in control
and the men often looking clumsy, awkward and silly. The women
appear as competent 'natural' travellers, whereas the men look
uncomfortable in this role, reversing, and hence questioning, the
dominant viewpoint.

Mapping can be seen as a kind of extension of the gaze. It is
another kind of visualisation depending crucially on perspective
and a point of view. As Harvey(1989) has stated, 'it turned out to
be far from ideologically neutral'(p.228). Like space, maps and
mapping are invested with power. Western mapping skills developed
during the Renaissance when perspective was being developed in art,
the same aesthetic principles of geometrical harmony were required.
In terms of values there are obvious links with classical ballet,
which is similarly not ideologically neutral, and, as I and others
have shown elsewhere, is gendered in a particular way.(4) Mapping
is to do with ordering, with territorial organisation, with
boundaries, with surveillance, possession and control. Current
events in Bosnia are a telling reminder of this. In some of the
dance films being considered mapping metaphors could be said to be
present.

(Video clip of *Carnets*)

I am thinking about moments when the land is viewed from a distance
or from above and people are scattered about it. They often walk or
run in straight lines across the space. The choreography creates

grids. Again the view of space and people appears 'transparent',
the audience is placed in the position of surveyor. In *Ellis Island*
however this perspective is subverted by the choreography and the
filming. When there is a slight movement in an otherwise completely
still group tableau, the audience is surprised, taken unawares, it
is no longer in the position of surveyor with a controlling gaze.
Similarly when the camera roves around the space in *Ellis Island*
the audience is disorientated, it loses its sense of space, the
performers are in control, they are continually illuding the
camera. Whereas in *Carnets* and *La Deroute* there is a sense in which
everything in the frame of the camera is composed or mapped,
putting the audience in the position of the masculine geographer
who has knowledge, power and control.

There is a sense in which postmodern tensions between the global
and the local or space and place could be said to be suggested in
these dance films by particular relations that are constructed
between the performers and the land and seascapes presented.
Distance shots of land or sea and sky also show horizons which have
a particular metaphorical, also often romantic or mythic resonance,
in terms of travel, journeys and distance, especially when figures
are placed looking towards them as they are in *Carnets* and *Cross-
Channel*, for example. Such scenes conjure up images from familiar
Romantic paintings such as *'The Monk by the Sea'* by
Friedrich,(slide) where the size of the figure,(small, almost
minute) in relation to the size of the land or seascape(vast), is
powerfully evocative of a certain kind of liminality. This is a
romantic, masculine view of the world where nature is seen as
'other'. This view is reinforced in *Carnets* but subverted in *Cross-
Channel* because instead of a single, lone figure gazing
romantically towards the horizon, in *Cross-Channel* there is a line
of figures gazing out to sea at the sunset. They are equally
spaced, self-reflexively underlining the fact that this is an image
that is constructed and that carries certain meanings. It is not
'natural'.

Conjunctions of land and sea are also often evident and particular
meanings are suggested when people are filmed against such. There
are plenty of examples of shots of people walking along shorelines,
beaches and quays and also sometimes 'playing with' these points of
conjunction by crossing the dividing line in different ways as in
Carnets when the men jump on the quay wall.

(Video clip from *Cross-Channel*)

In *Cross-Channel* the male performers are seen walking into the sea,
but their movements are off-balance and wobbly, sharply contrasting
with the deft skill of the men in *Carnets* and importantly also in
Cross-Channel they contrast with intercut shots of women lying on
loungers sunbathing on the beach, again where land meets sea.
Whereas the men look cold, wet and out of control, especially when
the film speeds up their antics in 'keystone cop' fashion and when
bathing with rubber rings at the water's edge they are 'beached' by
the waves, the women look warm, sensual and very much in control as

44

they run their polished fingernails through the sand and raise their legs in the air in unison, enjoying soaking up the sun. The precisely spaced lines of men and women on the shoreline again underline the constructed nature of this performance.

Some reasons for the current interest in travel metaphors

Sarah Kent(1984) claims that postmodern painting is 'a form of mourning for lost power, lost belief and lost confidence, in which actual significance is replaced by overblown self-importance,....It is a masculine artform - a witness to the crumbling of certainty' (p.61). In a similar sense I am suggesting that the use of travel metaphors in postmodern discourse also represents mourning, but for different kinds of lost masculine, colonial power. Some theorists have proposed that postmodernism is 'a response by intellectuals to their own discomfiture, their sense of dislodgement from previous authority'(Massey, 1991 p.33). Practices of de-centering and destabilising that postmodernism champions clearly pose threats to established, centered power bases which are traditionally masculine. A mode of thinking which sets up a centre and a periphery in opposition to one another, apart from being modernist, is also imperialist and colonialist(Docherty, 1993). As Steven Connor(1989) suggests the use of 'metaphorical-topographical terms of space and territory' which include 'centre and margin, inside and outside, position and boundary....can conjure up an oddly antique-seeming map of the world and global political relations, when struggles for power and conquest could be represented in much more reassuringly visible terms.' He continues: 'in their mimicking of this...vanished territorialization of power relationships, these metaphors also seem to embody a nostalgia for what has been lost with that sort of map of the world.'(p.227)

(Video clip of *A Mossa*)

This sense of nostalgia for a lost world can be seen in *A Mossa* in particular where traditional culture is privileged. By its juxtaposition with the natural environment and at times with the female performers and its aesthetic treatment in the filming, the perspective or viewpoint, I would argue, can be seen to be masculine.

Postmodernism has heralded a series of crises, and one of the most central is the fragmentation, destabilisation and decentering of the subject, which can be seen as a sense of loss. Partly in response to this crisis, metaphors of travel and mapping are employed to re-position or orientate fragmented, displaced subjects. Jameson in particular has suggested that the 'means to orientate oneself spatially' in the postmodern world are missing(ibid. p.227) and he proposes his concept of mapping to address this problem.

Mapping, however, through its global visualisation, positions and controls the 'other' which includes the feminine. This can be compared with the traditional treatment of landscape in painting as 'inanimate'(Oulton quoted in Lee, 1987 p.23) derived from the male artist's search for 'beauty' and perfection, and seen in terms of his ability to transform and subjugate 'nature', where 'nature' is traditionally constructed as feminine and 'other'. The 'transparent' ways in which the landscape and nature are filmed and constructed in the dance films *Land-Jäger, La Deroute, Carnets* and *A Mossa* can be seen as gendered in the context of these ideas. For example, there are hints of the subjugation of nature in *Land-Jäger* with the 'boy scout/Iron John/new man' activities of the male performers. There are also several long shots of a triangular structure in *Land-Jäger*; its geometry could suggest rationality which could be associated with the masculinity of the men in those suits which dissociate them from the femininity of the landscape. Nature's association with the feminine is also evidenced in *La Deroute* with the 'water solo' where woman and nature become one. A yearning for a lost colonialism as well as notions of exploration are also conjured up in *Land-Jäger*, by the use of accompaniment of African traditional music which creates an eerie, faraway, exotic, almost jungle-like atmosphere.

Travel can be seen as a response to the postmodern crisis of identity when viewed as a metaphor for a search for self or a quest. It has been claimed that tourists 'embody a quest for authenticity'(Urry,1990 p.8). However, as Wolff(1993) points out this is another example of how the metaphor is gendered in that 'men have...an exaggerated investment in a concept of a "self"'(p.231). The exploration kind of travel represented in *Land-Jäger* has strong associations with this kind of search for 'self'. The notion of quest also brings to mind Romantic ballet narratives such as *La Sylphide* and *Giselle* where the male heroes pursued female spirits of nature in search of an ideal. The feathered female figure who appears to haunt the space in *Carnets* could be likened to the Romantic ballet spiritual creatures in her potential for flight and possible symbolism of freedom.(Video clip of *Carnets*)

The reappropriation of travel metaphors for feminism

In a discussion of feminism and postmodernism Connor(1989) suggests that this interest in spaces marked as feminine can be 'understood as an attempt to retrieve control, to reterritorialize' and the result may be that feminism may find itself 'not as the vibrant voice of postmodernism, but,...,merely a part of speech within it'(p.231). This is a possible danger if the ways in which travel and mapping metaphors used in postmodern discourse are not recognised as gendered and hence positioning women in particular ways. However, although relationships between feminism and postmodernism, as Wolff(1990), Rosa Lee(1987) and others point out, can be notoriously problematic, there is nevertheless an appeal for feminism of the deconstructive and destabilising elements of postmodernism. Wolff(1993) concludes her article on travel metaphors by stating that her critique should not be read as a ban on or condemnation of such metaphors but rather as a situated analysis. She proposes the reappropriation(her emphasis) rather than the avoidance of such metaphors. Such a reappropriation is, in her words, 'a good postmodern practice which both exposes the implicit meanings in play, and produces the possibility of subverting those meanings by thinking against the grain'(p.236). Connor(1989) states that various forms of subcultural study - some of the most 'extended and representative' of which are 'to be found in feminist cultural theory' - 'explore the possibilities of inverting conventional mappings and distributions of power'(p.229).

Donna Haraway's essay *The Promises of Monsters*(1992) can be seen as an example of Wolff's proposed reappropriation of travel metaphors since she exposes and subverts the meanings in play and is thinking 'against the grain'.(5) Haraway states that the essay will be a 'mapping exercise and travelogue through mindscapes and landscapes of what may count as nature in certain local/global struggles'. The purpose of the exercise, she states, is to write theory that will 'produce not effects of distance, but effects of connection, of embodiment and of responsibility for an imagined elsewhere'(p.295). One result of this is to see 'nature' as constructed. Haraway states 'we must find another relationship to nature besides reification and possession....In this essay's journey toward elsewhere, I have promised to trope nature through a relentless artifactualism'(p.296). By artifactualism she means that nature is constructed like an artifact. It is <u>made</u> as fiction and fact.

An alternative form of travel and travel or mapping metaphors suggested in Haraway's 'journey to elsewhere' is the idea of 'networking' resulting from 'affinities'. In an earlier essay Haraway(1990) proposes this to address the fluid, multilayered and fragmentary nature of subjects. She states 'I prefer a network ideological image, suggesting the profusion of spaces and identities and the permeability of boundaries in the personal body and in the body politic'(p.212). This concept of a network ideological image also privileges seeing from more than one perspective over the single penetrative masculine gaze. *Ellis Island* suggests a 'profusion of spaces and identities' by its foregrounding of the nationalities of the immigrants using signs such as close-ups of stereotypical national dishes - spaghetti(Italy), potatoes(Ireland), etc. *Cross-Channel* subverts or negates notions of distance and suggests connections and networking through the rapid editing cuts in the film from the group of females to the group of males and the many spatial conjunctions of the two separate groups, which increase in proximity as the film progresses, for example, from the male cyclists cycling under a railway bridge over which the train which presumably carries the women is crossing, to the male performers becoming workers on the cross-channel ferry on which the women are passengers, to the two groups sharing the same beach and eventually, all going to the same party. Both *Ellis Island* and *Cross-Channel* also suggest the 'permeablility of boundaries in the personal body and the body politic' that Haraway mentions. They do this by exposing the constructed nature of gender(and also ethnic identity in the case of *Ellis Island*) showing that those personal body boundaries are not fixed but permeable, and by revealing the power invested in such constructions as they are associated with certain kinds of activity or passivity. In this sense identity is 'mapped onto' the body rather than seen as essentially located within it (Desmond,1993). This use of 'mapping' provides another example of re-appropriation of the metaphor.(6)(Video clip of *Ellis Island*)

Conclusion

When the dance films considered here are reviewed in the light of these theories, it is proposed that some pieces namely *Carnets*, *La Deroute, Land-Jäger* and *A Mossa*, because of the gendered nature of their subject-matter and its treatment, reinforce androcentric worldviews. They do this by presenting 'transparent' views of space and women from a masculine perspective, rather than revealing situated pictures of places. They also privilege a penetrative, masculine gaze which objectifies sometimes using the controlling, rationalising geometry of mapping. The results reinforce constructions of landscapes as inanimate and available for possession, nature as reified, passive and feminine and journeys and travel as active masculine pursuits in search of an ideal self. By doing this these texts mask or hide the politics and power differentials of different kinds of travel. For example, the powerlessness of the migrants of *Carnets* and *La Deroute,* I would argue, is completely eclipsed by the 'beauty' of the filming and choreography. Whereas *Ellis Island* and *Cross-Channel* present clearly identifiable places rather than anonymous spaces, <u>situate</u> the performers in them, and, through self-reflexive filming and choreography, show 'otherness' to be constructed rather than 'natural'. By working against the grain in this way, they re-appropriate the metaphors and subvert the more masculine and androcentric readings of travel and mapping.

Endnotes

1. It is important to recognise that the power invested in travel discriminates in different ways and that, as well as gender, race, class, sexuality, nationality and other factors all also have a bearing, but the focus here is on gender.

2. Lyotard(1979 transl.1984) for example, sees modernity as a mode of production and postmodernity as a mode of information.

3. A sub-category of 'nomadic subjectivity' could be the 'cultural nomad', a term employed by Searle(1983) to describe the neo-expressionist painter 'travelling the deserts of both time and space, stopping off at the occasional oasis of art, truth and beauty to conduct a little amateur archeology and grave robbing. Part anthropologist, part tourist, part cunning thief. For looting read "reclaiming"'(p.39). See also Peter Wollen's(1993) essay 'Into the future: tourism, language and art', which catalogues different phases in the 'looting' of other cultures by artists.

4. Briginshaw, V.A. <u>Dancing Dicks: a case in point(e)</u>, Unpublished paper & Daly, A. Classical ballet: a discourse of difference in <u>Women & performance</u> Vol.3 No.2 1987/88 pp.57-66.

See also Franko(1994), who's concept of 'geometrical dance' in his article, 'Double Bodies. Androgyny and power in the performances of Louis XIV' can be compared to mapping metaphors in choreography. He describes 'geometrical dance' as that 'in which texts and visual symbols were formed by large group patterns....bodies were given over to the strategic project of royal self-representation. They performed geopolitical configurations...destined to overwhelm the spectator'. Franko quotes Foucault stating '"geometry belongs to oligarchy since it demonstrates proportion through inequality"'(1971:20). He continues 'geometrical dance is fundamentally strategic: its choreography subsumes the performer in a spatial project'(p.72).

5. Another example of re-appropriation of travel metaphors is apparent in the first section of Suzanne Moore's(1988) essay 'Getting a bit of the other - the pimps of postmodernism'. She reappropriates the travel metaphor to describe the flirtation of some postmodern theorists with 'otherness' and feminine subjectivity. She states 'these days...its much easier for us all to travel - through strange places and other cultures. We try to be polite to the 'natives' and then return with anecdotes about how well we got on with the people. No, we weren't like those other tourists, we really got the feel of the place. We buy a piece of 'otherness' and bring it home to put on the mantelpiece. We didn't steal it, we bargained for it in the marketplace...in their language. We were kind and cautious. Colonisation is a cruel word for such harmless holidays'(p.100).

6. Another similar example of re-appropriation of the mapping metaphor is evident in Chambers'(1987) article, 'Maps for the metropolis: a possible guide to the present' where he states: 'our bodies...provide another temporary map on which to observe how the signs and histories of style, social position, sexuality and race traverse a surface in common.'(p.14)

<u>References</u>

Berger, John <u>Ways of Seeing</u> BBC Books, London, 1973.

Bertens, Hans <u>The Idea of the Postmodern A History</u> London & N.Y. Routledge, 1995.

Bird, Jon et al. <u>Mapping the Futures</u> Routledge, London, 1993.

Birkett, Dea Have guilt, will travel <u>New Statesman and Society</u> 13 June, 1990, pp.41-42.

Burgin, Victor 'Geometry and Abjection' in Fletcher, John & Benjamin, Andrew (eds) <u>Abjection, Melancholia and Love: the work of Julia Kristeva</u> London: Routledge, 1990 pp.104-123.

Chambers, Iain Maps for the metropolis: a possible guide to the present Cultural Studies Vol.1 No.1 1987 pp.1-21.

Chaney, David The Cultural Turn Routledge, London, 1994.

Clifford, James 'Traveling cultures' in Grossberg, Nelson & Treichler(1992).

Colomina, Beatriz(Ed) Sexuality & Space Princeton University Press, 1992.

Connor, Steven Postmodernist Culture, an introduction to the theories of the contemporary Oxford, Basil Blackwell,1989.

Desmond, Jane Mapping identity onto the body Women and performance #12 Vol.6 No.2 1993 pp.103-126.

Diprose, Rosalyn & Ferrell, Robyn Cartographies Poststructuralism and the Mapping of Bodies and Spaces Allen & Unwin, Australia, 1991.

Docherty, Thomas(Ed) Postmodernism A Reader London: Harvester Wheatsheaf, 1993.

Featherstone, Mike 'Global and local cultures' in Bird et al. (1993).

Franko, Mark Double Bodies. Androgyny and power in the performances of Louis XIV The Drama Review 38,4(T144) Winter 1994 pp.71-82.

Grossberg, Lawrence et al. Cultural Studies Routledge, London, 1992.

Grosz, Elizabeth Bodies-Cities in Colomina(1992).

Haraway, Donna 'A manifesto for cyborgs: science, technology, and socialist feminism in the 1980s' in Nicholson(1990).

Haraway, Donna 'The Promises of Monsters: a regenerative politics for inappropriate/d others' in Grossberg et al (1992).

Harvey, David The Condition of Postmodernity Oxford: Blackwell, 1990.

Huyssen, Andreas Mapping the postmodern New German Critique No.33 Fall 1984.

Irigaray, Luce Interview in Les Femmes, La Pornographie, L'Erotisme eds M.F.Hans, G. Lapouge, Paris p.50.

Jackson, Peter 'Towards a cultural politics of consumption' in Bird et al. (1993).

Jameson, Frederic 'Cognitive Mapping' in Cary Nelson & Lawrence Grossberg (eds) Marxism and the Interpretation of Culture Urbana & Chicago: University of Illinois Press, 1988, pp.347-57.

Jameson, Frederic Postmodernism or the Cultural Logic of late Capitalism London, Verso,1991.

Kent, Sarah (1984a) Feminism and Decadence Artscribe No.44.

Kent, Sarah (1984b) Art and Artifice:Changing Attitudes Artscribe No.45.

Lee, Rosa Resisting Amnesia: Feminism, Painting and Postmodernism Feminist Review No.26 Summer 1987.

Lyotard, Jean-Francois The Postmodern Condition Manchester: Manchester University Press, 1979 transl. 1984.

Massey, Doreen Flexible Sexism Environment and Planning D: Society & Space 1991 vol.9 pp.31-57.

Massey, Doreen 'Power-geometry and a progressive sense of place' in Bird et al. (1993).

Massey, Doreen Space, Place and Gender Cambridge: Polity Press, 1994.

Moore, Suzanne Getting a bit of the other - the pimps of postmodernism in Chapman, Rowena & Rutherford, Jonathan(Eds) Male Order: Unwrapping Masculinity London: Lawrence & Wishart, 1988 pp.165-192.

Morris, Meaghan 'Future Fear' in Bird et al (1993).

Mulvey, Laura Visual Pleasure and Narrative Cinema in Screen Vol. 16 No.3 pp.6-18.

Nicholson, Linda J.(Ed) Feminism/Postmodernism N.Y. & London: Routledge, 1990.

Patton, Paul 'Nietzsche and the body of the philosopher' in Diprose & Ferrell(1991).

Probyn, Elspeth. 'Travels in the postmodern: making sense of the local', in Nicholson(1990).

Rose, Gillian Some notes towards thinking about the spaces of the future in Bird et al. (1993).

Searle, Adrian 'Past and Present' in Artscribe 43 October 1983.

Wolff, Janet Feminine Sentences Cambrideg: Polity Press, 1990.

Wolff, Janet On the Road Again: Metaphors of Travel in Cultural Criticism <u>Cultural Studies</u> Vol.7 No.2 1993.

Wollen, Peter Into the future: tourism, language and art in <u>Raiding the icebox</u> London: Verso, 1993.

<u>Fig. 1</u> <u>Details of Dance Film/Video examples</u>

<u>Title</u>	<u>Date</u>	<u>Creator(s)</u>	<u>Production</u>
Ellis Island	1981	Meredith Monk	USA
Carnets de Traversée, Quais Ouest	1990	Johanne Charlebois & Harold Vasselin	France
Land-Jäger	1990	Stefan Schneider	France/ Germany
La Deroute	1991	Rodrigue Jean & Tedi Tafel	France/ Canada
A Mossa	1992	Jacques Patarozzi & Jacques Malaterre	France
Cross-Channel	1992	Lea Anderson (choreographer) Margaret Williams (director)	England

DANCE, GENDER AND MUSIC VIDEO:
CHALLENGING THE BORDERS OF DISCOURSE AND DESIRE?[1]

Theresa Jill Buckland
University of Surrey

This paper is concerned with pointing up possible directions in which to pursue research into aspects of dance and gender representation, specifically that of women, in music video. At this present stage of study, my focus has been on examining the existing literature on music video rather than with the kind of ethnographic research which I advocated as being so necessary in a recent publication (Buckland, 1993: 51-79). I hope, nonetheless, from my current position of conducting work in progress 'from the armchair' to provide some slightly contentious or, at least, ambiguous material for discussion.

The emergence of the music video since the early 1980s has been accompanied by a plethora of scholarly literature on its form, aesthetics, politics and social function. Interestingly, despite the high profile of dancing in music video, few articles have addressed themselves specifically to this phenomenon in any detail. Perhaps this should not surprise an audience of dance scholars, given that the music video has predominantly been studied either by those versed in film and media studies, or by those approaching the music video from perspectives of sociology and cultural studies.[2] In comparison, the field of dance studies has so far been relatively mute on the subject of music videos.

On reading through the literature on music video, there is occasional evidence of these non-dance specialists commenting upon structured movement. Of particular note are Kobena Mercer's insights (1986) into the impact of Michael Jackson's dancing in his study of Thriller and Andrew Goodwin's more wide-ranging reflections (1993: 68-70) on music and movement in relation to the performance of pop music and the music video in his book, Dancing in the Distraction Factory.

It is not my intention to berate scholars trained in other disciplines for their apparent lack of interest in the patterned movement which occurs in these videos; indeed, some of the few observations that have been made are arguably more stimulating precisely because those thoughts have not been shackled by what the discipline of dance studies might consider worthy of the appellation of dance.

The lack of writing on dance and music video emanating from the field of dance studies is reflective of a more general paucity of dance literature which focuses on contemporary popular culture. This is more properly true of British dance scholarship than that of North America.[3] In a number of respects, this neglect of contemporary popular dance whether on street, stage or video, is indicative of the comparative youth of dance studies as a university discipline, particularly in Britain.[4] Not only are fewer scholars involved in dance study, but questions of artistic value allied to scholarly acceptability have militated against the early inclusion of popular culture in a discipline which has been constructed as the study of high art forms. Caucasian derived theatre dance forms still predominate in British curricula of dance in higher education.

In the wake of Bourdieu and Foucault, we can ourselves be legitimated in commenting on the exclusionist tactics employed, certainly in England, in the formulation of dance studies as a discrete discipline. Strict borders have been drawn up, working from a canonical base of European and North American high art, to establish academic credentials. The selection of 'texts' to study in the academy has up to now undoubtedly focused upon the culturally more valued theatre art forms such as ballet and contemporary dance. Furthermore, much of the theoretical literature in British dance scholarship has constructed dance studies as the consideration of dances as finite art products, whereas in popular culture the production of a 'text' to be reproduced may or may not be a key characteristic. With a stronger base in academia and theoretical inroads being made from anthropology and cultural studies, there are now signs of a broadening in the formulation of the discipline of dance studies. Happily, those borders between academic discourses are being eroded. There may indeed be a shift towards considering dancing as social production as well as dances as art. Indeed, dance studies may emerge as a late twentieth century interdisciplinary space in common with other more established fields of study. I believe this to be vital when looking at the phenomenon of dancing as popular culture where modernist tendencies towards purism and specialism in the production of expressive practices are less relevant. This present consideration of dance on music video does follow an art model, of approaching the phenomenon as a discrete text, as I noted earlier, but this should not preclude future considerations of dance and music video from a more anthropological perspective.

A number of articles have been devoted to examining the high incidence of sexist representations in the music video of the early 1980s. Vincent, Davis and Boruszkowski noted in 1987 that in their sample of 110 videos over half depicted women as less than human and concluded that this portrayal was little different from that of women in other media forms. Two years later Vincent noted an increasing equality in the representation of women on music video (Vincent, 1989), yet speaking of much the same period, Bradby (1993: 157) opined that

> disturbingly traditional representations of women have been recycled in 'live' and sampled performances.

Certainly until the 1980s, rock music was a male preserve with creativity, technological competence and authorship seen as lying almost exclusively within the male domain. Where women were allowed on stage they frequently provided further emotional dimension through their bodies, either as back-up singers or else as dancers. In many respects this traditional division—men create and play whilst women decorate and display—continued in mainstream music until the appearance of such as Madonna, Cyndi Lauper, Sinead O'Connor and K D Laing. One only has to look at the camera work on old British TV pop music programmes, such as <u>Top of the Pops</u> to recognise the male control of the camera lens as close-ups of thighs, mouth, breasts and hips predominate. In the 1960s and 1970s, men are dominant singing and playing instruments whilst the women are rarely central to the creation and performance of the text, but appear, literally dancing in the margins. Where the male pop singers are not noted for their dancing skills—the verbal text and mastery of the musical machine are all important—dancing women are employed to attest to the masculine virility of white rock. As Bradby (1993: 156-7) notes, the borders of a traditional dichotomous alignment are maintained—men with technology, culture and language—women with the body, emotion and nature. All-female groups such as Bananarama, of course, famously reversed this objectification of women with their scantily clad posse of male dancers. Indeed, this 'heterosexual balance' has been a mainstay staging device of a number of male and female solo singers of the 1980s.

Frequently, in further collusion with the myth of authenticity so dominant in popular music production until the 1980s, this staging of a performance is transferred to music video and replication of performance conventions are transmitted via the videos of pop music artists. But this, of course, is not always the case. Music videos are of no single type. Gow (1992: 50-65) has perhaps provided the most useful categorization in his sixfold division into: anti-performance, pseudo-reflexive, performance documentary, special effects extravaganza, song and dance number and enhanced performance. Dancing and structured movement cut across all these categories and may occur in all of these to a lesser or greater degree. The song and dance category—incorporating those music videos based upon the Hollywood musical—obviously include more dancing. Examples include Janet Jackon's <u>Alright</u>, Paula Abdul's <u>Cold Hearted</u> and Michael Jackson's <u>Bad</u>.

Where alternative images of women are presented on music video tends to be in the work of solo female artists. Lewis (1993: 129-30) points to the phenomenon of punk in the late 1970s and MTV in the early 1980s as being instrumental in providing access for women in the pop music industry. Access has not removed the struggle for control over authorship over their image and music, however, and image frequently remains in the ascendancy in any critical reviews. Witness the abundance of ink spilt upon Madonna. Only feminist music scholar McClary (1990) can honestly be said to have engaged with Madonna's music rather than her image. Yet since a major dimension of dance is visual, I will continue this concentration upon image and turn to a selected consideration of how female artists use space and their bodies on video.

The music video, like film and television, offers musicians an enhanced and more versatile space in which to present interpretations of their work. In general, the more well-known the musician, the greater control he or she is able to exercise over their own image. They may not only select favoured directors and producers but also choreographers. Cyndi Lauper, interestingly enough, exercised a strong control throughout her 1983 version of <u>Girls just want to have fun</u>, remaining adamant that she did not wish to be portrayed as a sex object (Shore 1984: 167). The opening shots of the video in which Lauper exuberantly occupies the street space, dancing with a devil-may-care attitude, careless of who is watching, with no inviting address to the camera, asserts, according to Lewis (1993: 137), a woman's take-over of traditional male territory—the street. Certainly the space of the street for leisure and pleasure is an established male gendered space—girls on their own or in groups are expected either to move purposefully through them, never to linger and certainly not to dance on their own. Such action is tantamount at least to inappropriate behaviour, at worst to being thought a prostitute. Lauper's exaggerated dance movements suggest a confidence and control of her own body, not so much <u>in</u> the space as <u>claiming</u> the space. Most film images of young people dancing in the street are either of mixed groups or, perhaps more prevalent, that of gangs of boys—such as the Jets and Sharks in Robbins's choreography for the filmed musical, <u>West Side Story</u>. Pleasure in this music video of <u>Girls just want to have fun</u> is equated with moving joyously and rhythmically to music and with claiming both public and domestic space. Lauper moves from street to home as she leads her girlfriends in a file dancing through the city streets, not only usurping the space of workmen—those traditional harassers of women in the street—but by her bodily example, encouraging them to follow her (Lewis 1993: 137).

Although choreographed by Mary Ellen Strong, it was Lauper who persuaded these actual workmen—they are not professional extras or dancers—to join in. Gow (1992: 60) has another interpretation of this appearance of amateur dancers in <u>Girls just want to have fun</u> which differs markedly from Lewis's feminist analysis. He instead perceives these dancers as non-threatening in relation to Lauper's dancing ability. A dance scholar might reflect upon the gendered aesthetics of movement and posture. It is interesting to consider Lauper's dancing in this video. Certainly she flaunts the borders of gendered female pop dancing by occupying a large kinesphere and injecting an energy which is so intense that it approaches parody; yet, she never draws attention to her own body by being self-regarding. In fact the element of exuberant fun, by dancing in a manner not to be looked at, is arguably present in most of the dancing on the video. [Videotape example.]

In Lauper's 1994 version, she further challenges the borders of what constitutes 'woman' by including transvestites within her line up of girls who just want to have fun.

The question of who is entitled to express and control images of sexual desire is particularly relevant in the music videos of Madonna, Tina Turner and, latterly, Janet Jackson. In Turner's 1984 <u>What's love got to do with it?</u>, the singer confronts the popular association of lone woman in the street as prostitute by dressing in tight, short dresses and high heels. Arguably, however, her confidence in moving thorough the street space, occupying centre stage, meeting the gaze of men in the video and pushing groups of them aside, establish her as in control of her own body and space. In Pat Benatar's <u>Love is a battlefield</u> of 1983, this female take-over of male space is even more explicitly choreographed in the danced fights between the female singer and dancers against men in the bar and street.

This demonstration of female camaraderie, as expressed through dance, is highly apparent in Janet Jackson's 1994 <u>You want this?</u> Here there is clear taunting of men by presenting female bodies as objects of sexual desire, but the women maintain the control. In <u>You want this?</u>, Jackson and her female friends provocatively dance in front of two young male travellers, enticing them, if they dare, to take up their sexual offer, through the lyrics, dress and movements. Bared midriffs, swivelling hips and provocative gazes are picked up by the camera angles before the young women leave the two hitchhikers and jump in their cars. Moving out into the traditional male open space— that of the desert—freewheeling—normally depicted on film as a male pleasure—they come across the men walking and drive them off the road.[5] If the roles were reversed, this scene, as the women's cars circle the men, would undoubtedly be viewed as one of sexual harassment. The dancing which ensues when they leave their cars is in a much different style to that previously employed by Jackson, whose choreographers include fellow pop music artist, Paula Abdul and street dance choreographer, Anthony Thomas. Instead of the drilled narrow vertical kinesphere of <u>Rhythm Nation</u> of 1989, Jackson presents a more traditional female image to the pop music industry.

Indeed the poster advertising this new album, <u>Janet</u>, from which 'You Want This' is taken is indicative of the ambiguities of image and desire. When asked in a recent interview[6] whether her poster for the new album, which depicts herself semi-naked, arms raised, with a pair of male hands covering her breasts, owed anything to the need to compete with Madonna, Jackson appeared vaguely surprised and was emphatic in her denial that this might be the case. Yet very obviously this is a new sexual image for Jackson, inviting male desire. The provocative dancing, legs apart, rotating crotch and aggressive invitations to view the female body, are however denied to the men.[7] Ultimately, the women position the men as losers—lost in the open space, with no access to those traditional male appendages—fast cars and beautiful women. [Videotape example.]

It is not only, however, particular female pop artists who have traversed the borders of what is traditionally regarded as appropriate dance code behaviour. In some videos by Hammer and C&C Music Factory, for example, men and women often dance the same material with as much energy and verve as each other. Their scanty dress may appear as sexual provocation, but the often identical dressing in C& C Music Factory's dance troupe serves to underline the less sharply demarcated gender divisions of the more recent dance club scene (see Bradby 1993: 168). Some parallels exist in rave where dancing is de-gendered, non-display and 'child-like' in its free-flow use of energy and shape.[8]

It is clear that gender and dancing on music video is neither a fixed state of affairs nor one which offers consensus. There are tendencies towards the projection of images of dancing women which differ from those of the past,[9] but there are clearly ambiguities of response. There may be a challenge for us in terms of scholarship in crossing the borders of what we consider to be dance studies in order to engage with the literature from other disciplines. There are also challenges in coming to terms with what we as consumers desire in our reading of dancing women. Much work needs to be undertaken more precisely on the movement codes and structures employed and how these relate to other codes of movement action in relation to gender and culture. Ultimately, how we read these dancing women perhaps all depends on whether we perceive Madonna as subversive postfeminist or unwitting compliant fixed in patriarchal vision.

Notes

1.   A more extended version of this paper was given as a keynote paper, 'Aspects of Tradition and Renewal in Dance and Music Video', Nordisk Forum for Dansforskning Conference, Stockholm, 5-8 January 1995.

2.   For a frequently cited example of music video analysis from the perspectives of film and media studies see Kaplan (1987); a useful reader which brings together articles from mainly sociology and cultural studies is Frith, Goodwin and Grossberg (1993). Goodwin (1993) presents a sustained consideration of music video which locates the form and its production in relation to the pop music industry and addresses the music video and postmodernism debate.

3.   The term 'popular dance' is a problematic and often falsely oppositional one, particularly within the paradigm of postmodernism. Nonetheless, the social dancing of nonprofessionals and practices of the 'commercial' theatre have received less attention in dance scholarship. Many of the movement systems derive from Afro-American dance culture, especially in the music video. Key examples of scholarly historical studies of popular black dance are Stearns and Stearns (1968), Dixon-Stowell (1988) and Hazzard-Gordon (1990). Contemporary popular black dance culture is less well represented but see Friedland (1983) and Fine (1991). Folklore, sociology and, to a less direct extent, anthropology have provided the dominant academic frameworks for the study of contemporary popular dance in Europe and America.

4.   From 1995, the University of Surrey will become the first university in Europe to offer postgraduate courses in popular dance in its MA Dance Studies programme.

5.   Parallels with the film Thelma and Louise are evoked.

6.   The O Zone, 31 March 1995, BBC 2.

7.   Some of the movement vocabulary employed here incorporates standard Afro-American steps such as the Butterfly and may be viewed as part of Jackson's desire to appeal more directly to a black audience as her hairstyle in this video suggests. I am grateful to Jean Johnson Jones and Thea Barnes for this reference.

8.   See McRobbie (1994: 168), Melechi (1993: 33-34), Rietveld (1993: 52-54) and Bradby (1993: 165).

9.   This is particularly noticeable in the music videos of black female rap artists. See Irving (1993) and Roberts (1994).

Bibliography

Bradby, B. 1993. Sampling sexuality: gender, technology and the body in dance music. Popular Music, 12, 2:155-76.

Buckland, T.J. (with Stewart, E.) 1993. Dance and Music Video: Some Preliminary Observations. In Jordan, S. and Allen, D. (eds), Parallel Lines: Media Representations of Dance, pp. 39-79.

Dixon-Stowell, B. 1988. Popular Dance in the Twentieth Century. In Emery, L. F., Black Dance From 1619 to Today. London: Dance Books, pp. 339-66.

Fine, E.C. 1991. Stepping, Saluting, Cracking, and Freaking: The Cultural Politics of African-American Step Shows. TDR, 35, 2:39-59.

Friedland, L. 1983. Disco:Afro-American Vernacular Performance. Dance Research Journal, 15, 2: 27-35.

Frith, S., Goodwin, A. and Grossberg, L. (eds). 1993. Sound and Vision. The Music Video Reader. London: Routledge.

Goodwin, A. 1993. Dancing in the Distraction Factory. Music Television and Popular Culture. London: Routledge.

Gow, J. 1992. Music Video as Communication. Popular Formulas and Emerging Genres. Journal of Popular Culture, 26, 2:41-70.

Hazzard-Gordon, K. 1990. Jookin'. The Rise of Social Dance in African-American Culture. Philadelphia: Temple University Press.

Irving, K. 1993. "I Want Your Hands On Me": building equivalences through rap music. Popular Music, 12, 2:105-21.

Kaplan, E.A. 1987. Rocking around the Clock: Music, Television, Postmodernisn and Consumer Culture. London: Methuen.

Lewis, L.A. 1993. Being discovered: the emergence of female address on MTV. In Frith, S., Goodwin, A. and Grossberg, L. (eds): 129-51.

McClary, S. 1990. Living to Tell: Madonna's Resurrection of the Fleshly. Genders, 7:1-21.

McRobbie, A. 1994. Shut Up and Dance: Youth Culture and Changing Modes of Femininity. In McRobbie, A., Postmodernism and Popular Culture. London: Routledge.

Mercer, K. 1986. Monster Metaphors—Notes on Michael Jackson's Thriller. Screen, 27, 1: 26-43.

Melechi, A. 1993. The Ecstasy of Disappearance. In Redhead, S. (ed): 29-40.

Rietveld, H. 1993. Living the Dream. In Redhead, S. (ed): 41-78.

Redhead, S. (ed). 1993. <u>Rave Off. Politics and Deviance in Contemporary Youth Culture</u>. Aldershot: Ashgate Publishing.

Roberts, R. 1994. "Ladies First": Queen Latifah's Afrocentric Feminist Music Video. <u>African American Review</u>, 28, 2:245-57.

Shore, M. 1984. <u>The Rolling Stone Book of Rock Video</u>. New York: Rolling Stone Press.

Stearns, M. and Stearns, J. 1968. <u>Jazz Dance. The Story of American Vernacular Dance</u>. New York: Macmillan.

Vincent, R.C. 1989. Clio's consciousness raised? Portrayal of women in rock videos, re-examined. <u>Journalism Quarterly</u>, 66:155-60.

Vincent, R.C., Davis, D.K. and Boruszkowski, L.A. 1987. Sexism on MTV: The portrayal of women in rock videos. <u>Journalism Quarterly</u>, 64: 750-55, 940-41.

'Purism' versus 'Theatricality': A Re-reading of the Position of Minimalist Theatre Dance in Relation to Modernism and Postmodernism

Ramsay Burt. De Montfort University, Leicester

In 1966, Yvonne Rainer described some of the experimental dance pieces created by artists associated with the Judson Theatre as minimalist. In the 1970s this dance work began to be called postmodern, slightly before this term started to be associated with developments in post-structuralist and cultural theory. Some confusion has subsequently surrounded minimalist dance pieces like Rainer's Trio A, Steve Paxton's Flat (1964) and Satisfyin Lover (1967), and Trisha Brown's Inside (1966). Should they be seen as postmodern in the sense in which that term has come to be understood during the 1980s and 1990s, or as an instance of formalist reductionism characteristic of late high modernism? In this paper I aim to do a little good house-keeping. Focussing on Rainer's Trio A, (as it would take a longer paper than time allows to extend the argument to cover other works), I shall show that minimalist dance, in crucial ways, decisively contradicts the tenets of high modernism as they were articulated in the mid 1960s. With this qualification, I shall therefore argue that the minimalist dance of the 1960s should be seen as postmodernist and not modernist.

That there has been some debate about minimalist dance has undoubtedly been due, at least in part, to the existence of three useful resources: Sally Banes' film of Yvonne Rainer's Trio A from the piece The Mind is a Muscle revived by Rainer herself as a solo for the camera in 1978; Rainer's own essay 'A quasi survey of some "Minimalist" tendencies in the quantitatively minimal dance activity amidst the plethora, or an analysis of Trio A' written in 1966; and Michael Fried's essay 'Art and objecthood', first published in 1967 which discusses minimal sculpture. Rainer's essay starts with a chart which compares minimal dance with sculpture, while some of the sculptors who collaborated and performed with Rainer in the 1960s are mentioned in Fried's essay.[1] Fried and Rainer's essays were both published in the book Minimal Art: A Critical Anthology of 1968. More than one dance scholar[2] has linked these two essays, taking Fried's dictum 'The success, even the survival of the arts has come increasingly to depend upon their ability to defeat theatre' as a useful statement with which to characterise the aesthetic position of early postmodern dance. They have thus assumed that Fried's concept of 'theatre' could be applied to the 'theatrical' elements of theatre dance as they define them – elements like costume, illusionistic decor, mimesis, characterisation, narration. Minimalist dance, in their view, is modernist. It purifies itself by eliminating these 'theatrical' elements and devices as part of its progressive quest for the modernist ideal of pure, abstract dance. In 'Art and objecthood', Fried clearly believes that for art to survive, it needs to engage in a process of progressive purification. However, to develop this type of purist reading of minimalist dance, is to misinterpret Fried's essay. Fried explicitly denounces minimalist (or literalist as he calls them) tendencies in the arts as deviations from what he believes is all that is valuable in the modernist tradition. Fried, in fact, uses the term 'theatre' in his discussion of spectatorship and aesthetic appreciation to distinguish between the untheatrical way the spectator traditionally has appreciated high cultural products and what Fried considers to be the misguided theatricality of the situation in which the spectator is made to view minimal art.

In this paper I shall show that Fried's attack on minimalism is a defence of a model of aesthetic appreciation predicated upon the autonomous individual subject, a concept which had its origins in the philosophy of the Enlightenment. One of the catch phrases of postmodern theory in the 1980s was 'the death of the subject'. I shall argue that what was postmodern about the dance of Rainer and others in the 1960s, and what links their works with that of later postmodern choreographers, is the way all these challenge the position through which the spectator addresses theatre dance, exposing the partial and provisional nature of gendered subjectivity.

While I do not agree with Fried's judgements about minimal art, his scrupulousness and the rigour with which he develops his theoretical position in 'Art and objecthood' make it an invaluable document through which to study the art of its period. In it, Fried contrasts the modernist welded sculpture of David Smith and Anthony Caro, with the minimal sculpture of Carl André, Don Judd, Robert Morris, Tony Smith and others. Fried states that a welded modernist sculpture by Caro comprises a number of different elements juxtaposed together which achieves an artistic wholeness through the 'mutual inflection of one element by another' (1969: 137). The spectator is able to look at it from a detached, objective point of view because of the piece's quality of autonomy and completeness. A minimal sculpture, however, requires the spectator to see it as art in order for it to become art. Following Robert Morris' statements about the gestalt properties of minimal sculpture, Fried points out that appreciation of such work depends upon the spectator's awareness of the relationship between his or her body and the sculptural object. This minimalist sensibility is theatrical, according to Fried, because 'it is concerned with the actual circumstances in which the beholder encounters the literalist [Fried's term for minimalist] work' (ibid.: 125). He supports this contention by quoting Robert Morris who said that whereas in previous art what is to be had from the work is strictly located within it' the experience of minimalist art is 'of an object *in a situation* – and one that, virtually by definition, *includes the beholder*' (ibid. Fried's emphasis)

Fried's view of aesthetic appreciation and theatricality has its origins in eighteenth-century philosophy. In the introduction to his later book <u>Absorption and Theatricality: Painting and the Beholder in the Age of Diderot</u>, published in 1980, Fried states that he is using the term 'theatricality' in his discussion of eighteenth-century painting in the same way as he had used it thirteen years earlier in the essay 'Art and objecthood'. Fried uses the term 'absorption' to describe what he considers the untheatrical relationship between artwork and spectator defined in the eighteenth century by Kant and Diderot and, in Fried's view, central to the western tradition. Fried points out that Diderot's discussions of the effects of tableaux in painting and on the theatre stage are almost interchangeable. Both present action in which the participants are absorbed in what they are doing – as if there were a fourth wall separating actors (or the figures in the painting) from the spectator. This, for Fried, is untheatrical because it makes no direct address, but allows the beholder to exercise her or his judgement from a detached, objective position. It is this ability to freely exercise rational judgement that is characteristic of the Enlightenment. Kant, in his <u>Critique of Pure Reason</u> proposed that:

> The touchstone whereby we decide whether our holding a thing to be true or mere persuasion is therefore external, namely the possibility of communicating it and of finding it to be valid for all human reason. (quoted Habermas 1992: 108)

This ability to make critical, reasoned judgements was one which the enlightened citizen could exercise in the newly emergent liberal public sphere. It is generally recognised that what distinguishes this eighteenth-century view of a citizen's involvement in the public sphere from the Greek model of democracy is the modern concept of the citizen as autonomous reasoning subject.[3] It is this reasoning subject, in Kant's view that makes judgements. In his <u>Critique of Judgement</u>, Kant proposed that the spectator judges works of art with a disinterested disposition – i.e. from a detached, value-free, common sense point of view. Common sense, in this view, is what every rational subject agrees upon. It is this notion that the subject is autonomous and rational, and that common sense is an unproblematic norm that has been challenged and undermined increasingly during the twentieth century. It is in this context that Fried's opposition to what he calls the 'theatricality' of minimal art should be seen. Rather than allowing the spectator to remain detached and exercise her or his free, independent judgement, the minimal sculpture engages the spectator so that she or he can no longer be sure whether or not their response to it is, to use Kant's words, 'true or the result of mere persuasion'. Minimal art positions the subject in such a way as to problematize its coherence.

Suzanne Moore has summed up, with clarity and wit, contemporary feminist concerns about subjectivity:

> It is no longer so easy to talk of the individual or the self as an autonomous and coherent unity but instead we have come to understand that we are made up from, and live our lives as, a mass of contradictory fragments. (...) Feminists began [in the 1970s] to try to unravel the construction of gendered subjectivity – how we acquire the social characteristics associated with masculinity and femininity – not out of a desire to read lots of complicated books on psychoanalysis, but so that we might find out how we could construct ourselves differently. In other words, to unmake the processes which we feel are oppressive we first have to understand how they work and why they feel so powerful. (Moore 1988: 169-70)

One area in particular in which this feminist work on the psychological construction of gendered identity has been carried out is film theory. Laura Mulvey, in 1975, exposed the voyeuristic codes of mainstream Hollywood cinema that privilege the male gaze and objectify female performers as erotic spectacle.[4] Marianne Goldberg has argued that Rainer's 1985 film <u>The Man Who Envied Women</u> takes Mulvey's view to its logical conclusion by refusing to show the visual image of the female protagonist Trisha. Trisha, played by Trisha Brown, speaks off screen about the break-up of her relationship with Jack the eponymous man who envies women, and who also teaches psychoanalytic theory to film students. Goldberg argues that Rainer exploits Trisha's marginal position outside the visual frame 'as a way to gain a female presence that bypasses voyeurism' (Goldberg 1987/8a: 101). In a different essay Goldberg proposes that the structured way in which the dancers in Rainer's <u>Trio A</u> turn their gaze away from the audience breaks 'the movement phrasing that historically identified woman as object of display' (Goldberg 1987/8b: 11). While it might seem anachronistic to attribute such a motive to Rainer in 1966, almost a decade before the publication of Mulvey's essay, there is nevertheless evidence that Rainer was beginning to think along these lines. In a programme note for <u>The Mind is a Muscle</u> in 1968, Rainer wrote:

> If my rage at the impoverishment of ideas, narcissism, and disguised sexual exhibitionism of most dancing can be considered puritan moralising, it is also true that I love the body – its actual weight, mass, and unenhanced physicality. (Rainer 1974: 71)[5]

Rainer, however, goes on to deny that there is any link between her political commitments and her choreographic concerns: 'Just as ideological issues have no bearing on the nature of the work, neither does the tenor of current political and social conditions have any bearing on its execution' (ibid.). But then, paradoxically, she makes another vivid juxtaposition of the two, when she describes her

> state of mind that reacts with horror and disbelief upon seeing a Vietnamese shot dead on TV – not at the sight of death, however, but at the fact that the TV can be shut off afterwards as after a bad Western. My body remains the enduring reality. (ibid.)

It was through pedestrian and task oriented movement that Rainer presented the enduring reality, for her, of the body. This sort of minimalist choreographic material challenges and disrupts the experience of aesthetic appreciation which Fried holds dear. If, however, old notions of subjectivity have been disintegrating, how has minimal art positioned the subject differently? One way of answering this question is by looking at the area of the subjective experience of time.

In Kantian philosophy, the subject's knowledge of the world includes knowledge of its position in space and time. Time is one area which Fried uses to distinguish between the way minimal and modernist sculptures situate the spectator. Viewing a modernist sculpture is, for Fried, a rarefied experience:

> It is continuous and entire presentness, amounting, as it were, to the perpetual creation of itself, that one experiences as a kind of *instantaneousness*: as though if one were infinitely more acute, a single infinitely brief instant would be long enough to see everything, to experience the work in all its depth and fullness, to be forever convinced by it. (1969: 146. emphasis in the original)

Confronting a minimal sculpture, Fried points out, is far from instantaneous. Several minimal sculptors stress that this experience persists in time: Fried quotes Tony Smith – 'We can't see it in a second, we continue to see it' – and Morris – 'The experience of work necessarily exists in time'. Fried points out that the minimalist 'preoccupation with time and the duration of experience' (ibid.: 145) conflicts with the position from which one appreciates modernist work. David Michael Levin has endorsed Fried's notion of the timeless immanence of modernist art and extended it to a discussion of Balanchine's choreography. Describing a particular phrase in one of Balanchine's duets, Levin becomes rhapsodic about the way it appears that the dancers' 'substance has magically evaporated' and their bodies turned 'into a purely abstract structure, itself becoming, within this literally time-less phenomenon, a purely pictorial structural line' (Levin 1983: 137). The experience of presentness thus takes on a suspiciously metaphysical and transcendental character in both men's essays. Fried ends his with a plea 'We are all literalists most or all of our lives. Presentness is grace' (ibid.: 147).

The one moment in her 'Quasi-survey...' where Rainer gives in to rhetoric is where she discusses the very qualities in ballet that Levin valorises. One suspects here that Rainer is partly drawing on her memories of performing in James' Waring's company.

> Like a romantic, overblown plot this particular kind of display – with its emphasis on nuance and skilled accomplishment, its accessibility to comparison and interpretation, its involvement with connoisseurship, its introversion, narcissism, and self-congratulatoriness – has finally in this

decade exhausted itself, closed back on itself, and perpetuates itself solely by consuming its own tail. (1974.: 66)

One area in Trio A where Rainer's practice radically differs from the conventions of ballet and modern dance is in the way she deals with time. When, for example, the dancer pushes her or himself up from the floor, which happens more than once in the piece, this is done with clarity and economy of effort, but the action is allowed to take its own time. The dancer is clearly not getting up within four counts so as to be able to initiate the next phrase at the beginning of the next bar. There are no pauses between phrases, or at least an attempt is made to eliminate them. The smoothness of the continuity through which pauses are eliminated is aided by the fact that, as Rainer herself says, within the series of individual phrases 'no one part ... is made any more important than any other' (1974: 66). And she concludes: 'The irony here is in the reversal of a kind of illusionism: I have exposed a type of effort where it has been traditionally concealed and have concealed phrasing where it has been traditionally displayed' (ibid.). The effect of all this is that the work is experienced in time in a very different way to more traditional dance performances.

What is at stake in the difference between Rainer's and Fried's views is the question of how the subject is positioned in the field of time by aesthetic experience. The mundane, everyday world is one in which time is money and managers expect their employees to organise themselves and carry out their tasks efficiently. Outside work there is never enough time to carry out all one's familial and or social responsibilities. From this dominant, western point of view, those who live their lives to a different time scale are distinctly threatening. The western subject projects its anxiety about time onto these Others by stereotyping and discriminating against those who make it feel insecure including bag ladies, peasants, natives and lunatics. Julia Kristeva states that linear, objective 'clock-time' is the time of male subjective experience.[6] Woman as the Other to male subjectivity is associated in the male imagination with the unconscious and with the cosmic, cyclical rhythms of the female body and the womb. Death, for the subject, represents the end of 'clock-time'. 'Great Art' too functions as the Other to this male, subjective experience of 'clock-time', not in the form of a terrifying exposure to the cosmic and infinite, but naturalised and commodified as an instantaneous glimpse of timeless grace. This is how Fried views modernist sculpture and Levin views modernist ballet. Rainer felt passionately that the terror of death should not be ameliorated through commodification as TV news footage. Similarly, in her choreography, by insisting on the actual time the actual physical actions take to be performed she was in effect refusing to allow the spectator to enjoy a reassuring and distanced aesthetic experience of timelessness and grace that could be shut off afterwards as after a bad western. Her theatre dance would not play Other to male subjectivity.

My contention therefore is that postmodern dance pieces like Trio A take as their starting point modern dance's failure to convince us of the coherence of the subject. To start from the inside out (Humphrey) and to believe that movement never lies (Graham) is to hold that there are no dark corners to subjectivity – that everything within the subject can be utterly and transparently represented. Some of the most resonant examples of recent theatre dance have addressed those areas of subjectivity that are most troubling to patriarchal norms –particularly in terms of gender, race and sexuality. What I have tried to show, with the help of Michael Fried's rigorous and scrupulous essay are ways in which Rainer and, by implication, other the dance innovators associated with the Judson Theatre were also addressing the aesthetic implications of acknowledging the problematic nature of the construction of subjectivities.

In The Mind is a Muscle, Trio A was performed in slightly ragged unison by three dancers (hence Trio) while wooden slats were regularly dropped from some height onto the stage floor. I would have liked to end this paper by simultaneously showing three videos of Sally Banes' film whose history of copying and recopying has left each with a different pattern of snow and jumpy tracking, while myself standing on the table dropping wooden slats onto the floor. That way I might have demonstrated that Trio A was not a dry exercise in formalist reductionism but an exploration of radically new relationships between performance and beholder; but there isn't enough time and anyway the floor is bound to be carpeted. There is a danger of overlooking, and even of forgetting altogether, the denaturalising and destabilising elements within Trio A and works like it. But it is in these elements that links can be identified with the deconstructive orientation of much recent postmodern cultural practice.

FOOTNOTES

[1] The works of Carl André and Robert Morris are discussed in Fried's essay. Both appeared on stage in pieces by Rainer and others in the early to mid sixties. Morris appears to have known Rainer well as early as 1960 when both did a summer course with Anna Halprin in San Francisco and lived with her during the 1960s. André contributed one of the objects used in Rainer's <u>Carriage Discreteness</u> (1966) – see Rainer 1974: 303.

[2] Sally Banes in the introduction to the first edition of <u>Terpsichore in Sneakers</u> and Roger Copeland in 'Theatrical dance: how do we know it when we see it if we can't define it?' have both used Fried's quotation to discuss post-modern dance, while David Michael Levin in 'Balanchine's formalism' has used it to develop an account of modernism with reference to Balanchine's choreography. Levin also sees Rainer as a modernist. See Banes 1980; Copeland 1986; Levin 1986.

[3] For further information on the history of subjectivity see Forrester 1987.

[4] 'Visual Pleasure and Narrative Cinema' written in 1973 and first published in <u>Screen</u> vol. 6 no 3 1975, and more recently in Mulvey (1989).

[5] Performance at the Anderson Theatre, New York, April 1968.

[6] I am referring not to Kristeva's essay 'Women's Time' of 1979 but to the earlier chapter 'Without time' from her book <u>Des Chinoises</u> (translated as <u>About Chinese Women</u>) written in 1974. See Kristeva 1977.

REFERENCES

Banes, Sally. (1980) <u>Terpsichore in sneakers: postmodern dance</u> Boston, Mass: Houghton Mifflin.

Copeland, Roger (1986) 'Theatrical dance: how do we know it when we see it if we can't define it?' in <u>Performing Arts Journal</u> 26/27: 174-84.

Forrester, John. (1987) 'A brief history of the subject' in <u>ICA Documents</u> 7: 13-16

Fried, Michael. (1969) 'Art and objecthood' [first published 1967] in Battcock, Gregory. (ed.) (1969) <u>Minimal Art: A Critical Anthology</u> London: Studio Vista. 116-47.

Fried, Michael. (1980) <u>Absorption and Theatricality: Painting and the Beholder in the Age of Diderot</u> Berkeley: University of California Press.

Goldberg, Marianne (1987/8a) 'The body, discourse and <u>The Man Who Envied Women</u>' Women and Performance 3(2) 97-102

Goldberg, Marianne (1987/8b) 'Ballerinas and ball passing' <u>Women and Performance</u> 3(2) 7-31

Habermas, Jürgen. (1989) <u>The Structural Transformation of the Public Sphere: An Inquiry into a Category of Bourgeois Society</u> London: Polity Press

Kristeva, Julia. (1977) <u>About Chinese Women</u> London: Marion Boyars.

Levin, David Michael. (1986) 'Balanchine's Formalism' in Copeland & Cohen, (eds.) (1986) <u>What is Dance?</u> Oxford: Oxford U.P.123-44

Mulvey, Laura. (1989) <u>Visual and Other Pleasures</u> London: Macmillan

Moore, Suzanne. (1988) 'Getting a bit of the Other: The pimps of Postmodernism' in Chapman & Rutherford (eds.) <u>Male Order</u> London: Lawrence & Wishart. 165-192

Rainer, Yvonne. (1968) 'A quasi survey of some "Minimalist" tendencies in the quantitatively minimal dance activity amidst the plethora, or an analysis of <u>Trio A</u>' in Rainer (1974).

Rainer, Yvonne. (1974) <u>Work 1961-73</u> Halifax: The Press of the Nova Scotia College of Art.

Wollen, Peter. (1993) <u>Raiding the Icebox: Reflections on Twentieth-Century Culture</u> London: Verso.

STORIES OF THE BALLETS:
narratives, metanarratives and women in performance in the music hall ballets 1884 - 1915

Alexandra Carter
Middlesex University

A key, albeit problematic, characteristic of feminist and cultural theories is the notion of femininity as a construct which acquires meaning through a variety of discourses. Such discourses are produced in mutually reinforcing modes such as the written, visual, aural and kinetic. This paper examines the relationship of dance to the discourse of performance. It offers a case study located in the late Victorian/Edwardian era, when ballet in London was presented as the major attraction at the rival Alhambra and Empire palaces of varieties in Leicester Square. Over one hundred and forty new productions were staged throughout the period but, despite its popularity and the longevity of the era, the majority of dance historians have accommodated the tension between the appearance of a 'high art' form in the context of popular entertainment by trivisalising or ignoring its existence.

Although some of the 'arrangers' of the ballets were women, the works were produced under the dictates of an all male management for a predominantly male audience. Furthermore, each new ballet entered into the wider public domain through the writings of male critics and journalists. An activity undertaken primarily by women was, therefore, produced, mediated and circulated by men. The conflict which arises from such a disjunction remains unresolved for, not only do women's voices remain silent, but their bodies' 'pre-existing meanings, as sex object, as object of the male gaze, can always prevail and reappropriate the body, despite the intentions of the woman herself' (Wolff 1990 p.121). This paper does not address the dancers' own intentions or motivations, because their voice is not public; it is not their self-image which has become reified as social and artistic 'fact'.

The following exposition focuses on the narratives of the ballets and the dancers' roles within those stories, rather than on the dance components.[1] With the exception of the Romantic era, when only one of the two predominant styles of the period, the 'supernatural' ballet, is often misleadingly used as the only paradigm for illustrating the congruity between the stories of the dance and the spirit of the times, little work has been undertaken on this aspect of analysis. And yet, as Du Plessis claims, conventions such as plot and character interpret rather just depict experience. They can never be, therefore, 'neutral, purely mimetic or purely aesthetic' (1985 p.2). Accepting her stance that 'narrative in the most general terms is a version of, or a special expression of, ideology: representations by which we construct and accept values and institutions' (p.x), analysis of the stories of the ballets has the potential to reveal their hegemonic role in society.

The subject matter of the ballets, treated in narrative form[2], mirrored but did not question the political and social concerns of the age. Miller (1994 p.5), acknowledging Althusser's theories of ideology, claims that the narrative form 'privileges unity, coherence and resolution, while eliding or disguising contradictions.' The ballet disguised contradictions both within their texts and in relation to society itself; in its acknowledgement of social class differentiation, imperialist ideology and rigid gender roles, the ballet endorsed rather than challenged the *status quo*.[3]

It may be argued that the subject matter of the works was the dancing itself, enshrined in spectacle. As <u>The Times</u> asserted, the plot

> is a matter of supreme indifference to an audience who only requires that the stage shall be filled with brightly dressed groups of pretty and graceful dancers. (anon., 1884 p.4)

This comment, in itself, is significant in relation to its attention to the physical attributes of the dancers. However, whilst the narrative may have appeared to have been of secondary or of no importance, the ballets presented not just pretty girls in static isolation, but women who adopted specific identities in named roles and 'acted' according to the framework of the narrative. In broad terms, the subject matter of the ballets can be categorised into traditional themes that dealt with aspects of nature and the supernatural and the topical works that were based on contemporary events or interests. Historical times and foreign locations were common as were sub-themes such as romance, the tussle between good and evil and the moral dilemma.

The presentation of the supernatural was, and still is, a characteristic of the ballet genre; for many people, the two are synonymous. The cultural climate of the late nineteenth century accommodated scientific and technological change with an interest in spiritualism, ghost hunting and fairies at the bottom of the garden. As such, the incongruity of presenting traditional stories such as <u>Aladdin</u> (Alhambra 1892), <u>Ali</u> <u>Baba and the Forty</u> <u>Thieves</u> (Alhambra 1894) and <u>Cinderella</u> (Empire 1906) was not particular to the ballet, for 'the acceptance and rapid growth of fairyland as fit subject matter for literature, painting and the stage is one of the most remarkable phenomena of nineteenth century culture' (Booth, M., 1981 p.36). In the ballets the appearance of the supernatural was part of an excuse for colour, spectacle and fantastical costumes.[4] It infiltrated the ballets in legend, fairy story and mythology. Minor goddesses mixed with mortals, though the one authentic goddess from the Greek pantheon who was missing was Athene, goddess of wisdom. (Although it is possible to overstate the significance of this omission, it is, perhaps, an unsurprising one in the light of how contemporary writers perceived the intelligence of the ballerina.)   Many of the topical ballets did not neglect the crucial role of a fairy. Even the Klondyke gold fields (<u>Alaska</u>, Empire 1898) had a Fairy Good Fortune.

The world of the supernatural also served another purpose in terms of how the ballerina was presented, for it was she who danced the significant supernatural role and it was a role of moral agency. As such, she was distinguished by her quite literal other-worldliness and also by her goodness.   She was, even in her supernatural roles, generally untroublesome.

Benign nature is also untroublesome, and it was the natural world which provided one of the most common themes for either the substance and/or the setting of the ballets. Again, such thematic material is part of tradition, particularly from the Romantic era, but it also accorded with a resurgence of interest in Romanticism in the other arts. As Hennegan (in Teich and Porter, 1990 p.200) suggests, by the 1890s the countryside itself had so changed with depopulation and mechanisation, had become so tamed out of accord with poetic sensibility, that 'with tremendous thoroughness, the Decadents set about repopulating the English landscape' with nymphs and satyrs. In a period which saw so many developments which were to revolutionise social life and attitudes, the presentation of ballets concerned with flowers and fauna was not, therefore, so out of touch with the times as may first appear for they reflected not just the conventions of the ballet genre but also the psychological concerns of the period.

The significant feature of how dancers were presented in the pastoral ballets was their depiction not just as people populating country or garden scenes but how they constituted the 'scenery' itself. However, the image of dancer-as-flower in the ballets and in painting signified more than just opportunities for colour and spectacle. Dijkstra suggests that

> the 'pure' woman, the woman who, with her passive, submissive imitative, tractable qualities, seemed to share... all the features characteristic of the plant life of the domestic garden thus came very generally to be seen as a flower herself.
> Dijkstra, 1986 p.16

One central motif of *Art Nouveau* design was the presentation of women and flowers or fauna in a symbiotic relationship. In the ballets, women represented not only the natural phenomenon of flowers but also insects, butterflies and birds.[5] In pastoral characters such as a Dryad (Alhambra 1908) or Water Nymph (Empire 1912) women presented a complex image of the natural world to which men had access. These images had erotic connotations for it was 'the eroticized body of woman ...(which)... became the late nineteenth century male's universal symbol of nature and all natural phenomenon.' (Dijkstra, 1986 p.86).

A theme or a location which provided the excuse for many ballets was that of the internationally exotic. With world communication and travel becoming easier and knowledge of distant lands more accessible, these international ballets reflected contemporary interests such as the Francophilia of the *fin de siècle*. As ex-colonials, many of the audience would have been well-travelled and to others the world had become a smaller place, in mind if not in their experience.[6] The dancers usually represented national characters who were exotic, other-worldly and very far removed in both appearance and in movement from the reality of Victorian or Edwardian womanhood. Nautch girls, Eygptian slaves, Spanish dancers, odalesques and gipsies all contributed to the world of fantasy. Historical ballets fulfilled the same function. Although supposedly dealing with a more 'real' world than that of mythology and the supernatural, works located in different times and different places were similarly based on a romanticised and idealised view of the world and its inhabitants.

In seeming contrast, one of the most common themes of the ballets was that of the up-to-date or topical subject.[7] These comprised works which reflected contemporary interests such as seaside holidays (By the Sea , Empire 1891) and On Brighton Pier, Empire 1894) and the popular press (The Press, Empire 1898) ; those which referred to important events, notably Victoria's Jubilee (Under One Flag, Empire 1897) and Edward VII's

Coronation (<u>Our Crown</u>, Empire 1902), and the patriotic or military ballet (<u>Our Army and Navy</u>, Alhambra 1889; <u>Soldiers of the Queen</u>, Alhambra 1900). What is of interest, is what the ballets ignore as well as what they address. One of the most topical issues, particularly during the 1890s, was the question of the emancipation of women and the resultant disturbance of patriarchal structures. However, only one ballet has been found which explicitly acknowledged the public fight for women's suffrage.[8] That such issues were avoided in the ballets is demonstrated in a review of <u>Bluebeard</u> (Alhambra 1895) which suggested with apparent relief that

> elsewhere, 'Bluebeard' might be converted into a story of a
> woman's perilous search for knowledge, and the ultimate
> emancipation of the submerged sex. At the famous house in
> Leicester Square ... the famous story is treated with respect.
> anon., 1895b p.440

Such a statement reveals that there was a consciousness of women's search for new roles in life but these roles were not depicted on stage. As the ballet did not offer any direct critique of political issues, it would be expected that the contentious topic of the place of women in society would similarly not be seen as suitable subject matter. What was also avoided was any representation of the New Woman. This phenomenon, the term for which was created in the 1890s, is reflected in novels such as George Gissing's <u>The Odd Women</u> .[9] However, in the ballets she is conspicuous by her absence. For example, <u>The Sports of England</u> (Empire 1887) neglected to show the new athletic prowess of women but celebrated male sports such as cricket, football and boxing even though, ironically, the roles were played by women dressed as men.[10] Even if the New Woman took on the persona of the Amazon in painting, for 'she was in real life and art ... perceived as Amazonian in many ways' (Casteras, 1982 p.173) the ballets which presented Amazons, as a surprisingly large number did, negated their traditional warrior-like qualities.[11] No *première danseuse* appeared to be cast in such a potentially powerful role and for the *corps* who were, it provided an opportunity for shining costumes and spectacular stage formations. The sight of a massed *corps* of Amazons in burnished armour could have been chilling, but any possible powerful collectivity in these roles was subverted by the plot of the ballets in which they appeared to be totally ineffectual. They appeared for display, to be seen and not to act. It is also interesting that, of over twenty works which had a female name as the title, only one (<u>Cleopatra</u>, Empire 1889) appeared to deal with a real woman. Most were concerned with fictional or mythological women; the lives of real women, past or present, were not presented on stage.

Unlike in the legitimate theatre where the plays of Ibsen, Shaw and Pinero were beginning to present new images of women, the ballets in their essential conservatism made little reference to the changing roles, status or even the reality of women in society. On the contrary, the dancers' roles in these topical ballets, particularly in the patriotic works, reinforced traditional concepts such as peace and victory as female. Whether the dancers were dressed as the military, countries of the Empire or the Union Jack, they were symbolic. They symbolised Britain's power in the Empire; her military glory and her role as keeper of the peace.[12] One of the main constructs by which the dancers presented these ideals was through a device as common in the ballets as in the visual arts, that of personification.

The casting of 'spirit of', 'goddess of' or 'fairy of' was given to principal dancers in all kinds of music hall ballets. These roles were personifications of nature, artefacts, human virtues and achievements. The Spirit of the Wheatsheaf (The Reaper's Dream, Empire 1913); Spirit of Happiness (All the Year Round, Alhambra 1904) and Goddess of Genius (Inspiration, Alhambra 1901) were a few of many examples. Modern concepts were embodied in roles such as the Spirit of Mechanism (Sita, Alhambra 1894) and the Goddess of Progress (Entente Cordiale, Alhambra 1904). Warner (1985) discusses how the Victorian mind was able to build newfangled superstructures on allegorical conventions; the incongruity of such a concept as, for example, a 'Spirit of Mechanism' was not particular to the ballet.[13]

In the stories, these spirits did not relate to 'male' characters but were independent entities. As they presented abstract qualities or ideas they were agents rather than recipients of events, immune from human passions and foibles. As such, they were part of the long tradition of idealised allegorical womanhood which became one of the characteristics of the culture of the period.[14] Stubbs (1979 p.xi) discusses how the role of women as the 'moral centre' of society can be perceived in novels. In the ballets, the spirit or goddess role was also the moral centre of the narrative and it was a role which was given, almost always, to the ballerina.[15]

These personifications, however, were not limited to concepts of the 'good' but also embraced the opposite. Human vices were portrayed in roles such as the Spirit of Gambling (The Girl I Left Behind Me, Empire 1893) and the Spirit of Vanity (Femina, Alhambra 1910). What is of interest, is that with very few exceptions, human vices were portrayed by men or by travesty performers. As Warner (1985) points out, as the feminine gender had a monopoly on virtue, the masculine gender was used for its opposite. In the ballets, it meant that the image of the female dancer remained untainted and her idealisation was uncorrupted. However, images which present women as uncorrupt, morally virtuous and essentially 'good' in character can be as negative and confining as any more malevolent representation.

One facet of misogynist imagery in the arts of the period was the casting of women as seductresses but, if the ballet ignored changes in the status of women, it also ignored the potent *femme fatale* image.[16] Although seductions were a part of some scenarios, these appeared to be low key events.[17] It is interesting to note that one of the most popular stories depicted in the arts of the period, that of Salome, was never used as serious subject matter for any of the ballets presented at the Alhambra or the Empire though, tellingly, it was burlesqued in the Alhambra's Sal! Oh! My! (1908). It was as though the depiction of such a woman, so powerful in her sexuality, could not be accommodated on the music hall stage.

Romance was a sub-theme in many works and in several it constituted the main plot, but the actual living-or-dying fate of the heroines was not dependent on the men in their lives. Unlike their destinies in works of the earlier part of the century, few, if any, ever died for love. When a heroine's fate did depend on a man, in accordance with Victorian sensibilities it tended to be in the far more mundane respect of marriage.[18] Nearly every ballet which involved an element of romance ended happily.

The reason why romance played a common but low key role in the music hall ballet is obvious: there were very few male dancers to complete the partnership. The fact that the 'male' lead was played *en travesti* meant that, although the convention was accepted, there could be no significant love relationship. Even when there was a romantic hero he tended to be played by an actor. In neither case were there possibilities for romantic and certainly not passionate dance duets.[19] When a love scene was depicted it was acted out in mime. Guest (1958) relates how Genée found her mimed love scenes with Santini distasteful because of the pervading smell of garlic. Other male roles were played by character dancers who tended not to be cast as partners of the ballerina, for to have done so would have undermined her status.[20] No love relationship on stage interfered with the love affair between the dancer and the audience. When George Edwards, the Empire manager, was asked why Genée never had a partner, his reply was, 'don't you see, dear boy, that every man in the audience is her partner?' (Guest, 1958 p.50).

The hierarchical nature of any ballet company and the conventional narrative structure of the works has traditionally been based on a differentiation of roles between principals and other dancers. The ballerina sometimes appeared on programmes not in a named role but simply as '*Première Danseuse*' which established her as a separate entity even from the story of the ballet itself. In contemporary criticism, although words like 'charming' and 'vivacious' abound there is little sense of the real personality of the dancer emerging for her roles rarely allowed for individually expressive interpretation. Such a depersonalisation is inherent in the genre but was further emphasised by the fact that the powerfully expressive roles were played by the travesty performers, whose business was mime and dramatic action.

The fantasy world of the ballets, established by their supernatural subject matter, exotic locations and distant or mythological times was embodied in the stage persona of the ballerina. As a personification, representation of nature, picture of innocence and guilelessness or agent of morality, she was, in an unreal world, an even more unreal figure.[21] She remained, however, quintessentially female in character, actions and looks.[22]

The *corps* were far less rarefied than the ballerina; they were mundane, of this earth and, furthermore, their appearance *en masse* acted as a foil to her individuality. The differentiation in their dance vocabulary was endorsed by their respective roles and agency in the narrative. However, all dancers, whatever their role, served to please the eye and offered fantasy or the most pleasurable stories of reality. The music hall had to attract a large, paying audience in order to survive. Any 'virulent misogyny' (Dijkstra, 1986 p.viii), common in the visual arts, would have disturbed the complacency of the audience by undermining their notions of Victorian and Edwardian womanhood. On the contrary, the stories of the ballets and the roles played by the dancers endorsed the metanarratives of patriarchy. They accommodated the tensions between the binary symbolic constructs of femininity by presenting a singular, idealised, other-wordly ballerina and a collective, worldly *corps*. But whatever their status in the narrative, woman as fairies, as jewels, as decoratively exotic, as essentially 'good' did not disturb the *status quo*; the composite world of the ballet effectively presented a 'Fairyland of Fair Women'. [23] As such, the music hall ballet obliterated the tensions in society arising from women's struggle for personal and political emancipation. Artistic narratives and patriarchal metanarratives merged as one on the music hall stage and the sexual psyche of the era was made manifest in the body of the dancer.

NOTES

1.   The method of categorising subject matter (what the ballets were 'about, related to or concerned with', Hodgens in Adshead 1988 p.77) and dancers' roles comprised noting an impressionistic account of recurrent themes gleaned from a wide variety of sources and then listing each ballet in these categories. The surprising degree of congruency between my impressions and the formal analysis could be explained by the tendency for formulaic productions; although the formula changed   over time, certain patterns were still evident. See Guest (1992) for a choreochronicle of ballets at both venues.

2.   The term 'narrative' is used here to describe the general story line. Licensing regulations prohibited narrative theatre in the music halls but the ballet, most probably because it did not used the spoken word, was not classified as narrative theatre.

3.   See Walkowitz (1992) for a claim that other aspects of music hall performance, particularly those by women, did challenge the *status quo* with regard to gender divisions in society.

4.   The supernatural also served a purpose as escapism, as Symons so tellingly reveals in his review of <u>Titania</u> (Alhambra 1895): 'it is as fantastic and unreal and impossible as even I could wish for ... I go to see a ballet in order to get as far as possible from the intolerable reality of the world around me. ('A.S.', 1895a p.77)

5.   Although there were male performers in the music hall ballets none appeared to be cast in these roles of natural phenomena.   The difficulty of conceiving a male dancer as a flower or butterfly reveals the gender specificity of such images. In exceptions such as Bluebird in <u>Sleeping Beauty</u> (Petipa 1890) and Nijinsky's Rose in <u>Le Spectre de la Rose</u> (Fokine 1911), the 'femininity' of the roles is subverted by the bravura virtuosity of the dancing.

6.   Booth (1929 p.142) describes how a large number of patrons were home from the colonies. These men, 'wherever they fore-gathered in cities of Africa, Asia and America would bid one another goodbye with a 'See you at the Empire one day when we're back in town.'

7.   These topical themes were not particular to the British ballet ; Manzotti's <u>Excelsior </u>(La Scala 1881) included the building of the Suez Canal and the invention of the electric telegraph. However, the topical ballet was not necessarily favoured by the artists who worked on them. The Alhambra composer Jacobi, asserted that 'the sort called 'up to date' is inevitably vulgar.' ('A.S.', 1895a p.77)

8.   This was Elise Clerc's <u>On the Heath</u> (Alhambra, 1909) which had a suffragette in the cast, though it is not possible to ascertain how that role was treated. Described in the programme as a 'new revue divertissement', the ballet does not appear in Guest (1992 Appendix A) although the work did include a *premiére danseuse* and full *corps de ballet.*

9.   Casteras (1982 p.146) notes that also in painting 'the New Woman is remarkably rare, if not conspicuous by her absence.'   However, she was much caricatured in sketches and cartoons of the period, particularly in <u>Punch</u>. A few individual artists in the music hall did acknowledge suffrage issues in their acts (see Holledge, 1981 p.81).

10.   Lady cyclists were depicted in <u>On Brighton Pier</u> (Empire 1894) and hunting, an acceptable activity for women, was shown in <u>High Jinks</u> (Empire 1904).

11.   Works which presented Amazons in the cast included <u>Dilara</u> (Empire 1887) and the Alhambra ballets <u>Antiope</u> (1888); <u>The Handy Man</u> (1900); <u>Femina</u> (1910) and <u>The Dance Dream</u> (1911).

12.   See Warner (1985) for a discussion of such imagery. She points to how, during the nineteenth century, 'Britannia, the personification of the constitution, fades before Britannia as the might of Britain ...(this figure)... achieves widest currency ... in the 1890s at the zenith of Victorians' imperial faith and enthusiasm.' (Warner, 1985 p.48)

13.   There is a relationship here between the themes of the ballets and the modernist ethos. There is also a common factor between the ballet and modernism in the fine arts, for Lisa Tickner (inaugural lecture, Middlesex University, 1993) notes that in modernist iconography there is an astonishing rarity of any image of the 'modern' woman.

14.   These agents of morality were not only spirits or goddesses but also comparatively more earthly creatures. An odalesque (<u>The Debutante</u>, Empire 1906); a gipsy queen (<u>Salandra</u>, Empire 1890) and young girls in several ballets (<u>The Girl I Left Behind Me</u>, Empire 1893); <u>Sita</u> (Alhambra 1894) all display fidelity to their ideals and were epitomes of correct moral behaviour.

15.   Dijkstra (1986 p.4) argues that 'the expulsion of the middle-class woman from participation in practical life had become a fact; women had never been placed on a more lofty pedestal. An apparently insuperable plateau had been reached in her canonization as a priestess of virtuous inanity.'

16.   See, for example, Harrison (1979); Casteras (1982) or Dijkstra (1986) for analyses of the *femme fatale* image in the visual arts. The misogyny embodied in these images was linked, by Jung, to 'the first changes which were taking place in the status of women from 1870 onwards.' (McMahon, 1985 p.8)

17.   Even when Genée played the odalesque in The Debutante (Empire 1906), a 'good' temptress who uses her body to please the sultan in order to save her lover, the authenticity and potential allure of the character was undermined by the wearing of a long ballet skirt.

18.   In a few ballets the heroine was due to meet, before rescue, an unspecified but not deadly fate at the hands of a demon, pirates, brigands or a rajah (The Alhambra's Nadia, 1887; Algeria, 1887; Zanetta, 1890 and the Empire's Cecile, 1890). Such stories occurred during the early period of the music hall ballets. It could be tentatively speculated, though further detailed research would need to be undertaken, that this was a minor way in which the ballets reflected the growing emancipation of women in that they no longer needed rescuing so dramatically.

19.   Those ballets in which passion was a potential element tended to be based on pre-existing, well known tales such as Orfeo (Empire 1891); Don Juan (Alhambra 1892) and Carmen (Alhambra 1903 and 1912).

20.   Whilst there may have been a hint of romance between character dancers or other soloists as a tangential aspect of the plot, it would appear that in very few works were the *corps* or *coryphées* allowed to participate in any significant romantic role. One notable exception was the Apache Dance (A Day in Paris, Empire 1908) which achieved some notoriety. Described as a duet which depicts the passion of the man for the girl 'he strangled and threw about' (MacQueen Pope in Guest, 1992 p.137) the brutality of the piece appears to have touched the collective misogynistic psyche.

21   Although she appears to be referring to the Romantic and neo-Romantic ballets, Wolff (1990 p.136) claims that 'the roles created for women in the classical repertoire - fairies, swans, innocent peasant girls ... collude in a discourse which constructs, in a medium which employs the body for its expression, a strangely disembodied female.'

22.   When Genée appeared *en travesti* in The Bugle Call (Empire 1905) 'it was not a part that appealed to all her admirers' (Guest, 1992 p.124). Although her performance remained essentially feminine (Morrison in Guest, 1958 p.75), by dressing as a boy, Genée had presented a far more ambiguous image.

23.   'The Classical Ballet: a Fairyland of Fair Women' was the title of an article on the ballet. (Findon,B.W. 1911 The Play Pictorial Vol. XVIII June p.75)

SELECTED BIBLIOGRAPHY

Adshead, J. (ed) 1988 <u>Dance analysis: theory and practice</u> London: Dance
    Books

anon. 1884 The Alhambra <u>The Times</u> 23 December p.4

_____ 1895 The new ballet at the Alhambra <u>The Sketch</u> 7 August p.77

_____ 1895 Notes from the theatres <u>The Sketch</u> 25 December p.440

Booth, J.B. 1929 <u>London town</u> London: T. Werner Laurie

Booth, M.R. 1981 <u>Victorian spectacular theatre 1850 - 1910</u> London:
    Routledge Kegan Paul

Casteras, S.P. 1982 T<u>he substance or the shadow: images of Victorian
    womanhood</u>   New Haven: Yale Centre for British Art

Dijkstra, B. 1986 <u>Idols of perversity: fantasies of feminine evil in *fin de
    siècle*</u> culture Oxford: Oxford University Press

Du Plessis, R.Blau 1985 <u>Writing beyond the ending: narrative strategies of
    twentieth century women writers</u> Bloomington: Indiana University
    Press

Guest, I. 1958 <u>Adeline Genee: a lifetime of ballet under six reigns</u> London:
    A. & C. Black

_____ 1992 <u>Ballet in Leicester Square</u> London: Dance Books

Harrison, F. 1979 <u>The dark angel: aspects of Victorian sexuality</u> London:
    Fontana

Holledge, J. 1981 <u>Innocent flowers: women in the Edwardian theatre</u>
    London: Virago

McMahon, D. 1985 The feminist mystique <u>Dance Theatre Journal</u> Vol.3:4
    Winter pp.8-10

Miller, J.E. 1994 <u>Rebel women: feminism, modernism and the Edwardian
    novel</u> London: Virago

Stubbs, P. 1979 <u>Women and fiction: feminism and the novel 1880 - 1920</u>
    Brighton: Harvester

Teich, M. & Porter, R. 1990 *Fin de Siècle* <u>and its legacy</u> Cambridge:
    Cambridge University Press

Walkowitz, J.R. 1992 <u>City of dreadful delight</u> Chicago: University of Chicago
    Press

Warner, M. 1985 <u>Monuments and maidens: the allegory of the female form</u>
    London: Picador

Wolff, J. 1990 <u>Feminine sentences: essays on women and culture</u>
    Cambridge: Polity Press

ABSTRACTION AND HYSTERIA: THE PLACE OF
THE BODY IN AMERICAN NON-LITERARY THEATER

Roger Copeland
Oberlin College/USA

The buzz words in my title, "abstraction" and "hysteria," are borrowed from a very unlikely source, R.P. Blackmur's 1958 essay, "The Swan in Zurich," a wonderfully eccentric attempt to pin down the distinctly American quality of Balanchine's choreography for The New York City Ballet. I've taken the liberty of transposing Blackmur's terms into a very different context, that of American non-literary theater—the work of theatrical ensembles such as The Living Theater, The Open Theater, and The Wooster Group—a world that at first glance appears to be far removed, indeed light years away, from ballets like "Agon" or "Concerto Barocco." But in the final analysis, Blackmur's real focus is the American body in American culture—so in that sense, it's perhaps a little less surprising that language coined to describe the style of The New York City Ballet might also apply, mutatis mutandis, to the work of say Richard Foreman's Ontological Hysteric Theatre.

This is a going to be a fairly long presentation: so I think it may behoove me to begin with a brief summary of the argument. I'll attempt a definition of the term "non-literary theater" and then I'll share with you some videotape excerpts from prime examples of American non-literary theater in the 1960's. We'll look first at what might be called a "theater of the body," as exemplified by the work of The Living Theatre, The Open Theatre, and The Performance Group. This is work that emphasized bodily/choreographic imagery, non-verbal sound, environmental staging, a celebration of "unmediated presence," and various strategies for promoting the physical interaction of performers and spectators.

Conventional wisdom would have us believe that this work marked a decisive break with the "realistic" drama of the 1950's and the tradition of method acting we associate with Lee Strasberg and The Actor's Studio. But I want to propose an unacknowledged continuity between the two: For the "method"—as practiced by say, Marlon Brando or James Dean—also assigned a privileged place to physical gesture of a distinctly "non-literary" sort. Thus both method acting and the overtly non-literary theater of the 1960's reflect something fundamental about American culture and its deep anti-verbal biases.

But as we move from the 1960's to the 1970's, the place of the body in American non-literary theater begins to change. With the emergence of the immensely influential Robert Wilson, we encounter visual spectacles which tend to replace "bodily" imagery with "painterly" imagery. (In other words, a non-literary tradition which relied almost exclusively on the expressive power of the performer's unadorned body and voice gives way to a much more "spectacular," decor-dependent theater of surrealist dreamscapes.) And the marginalization of the performer's body is greatly exacerbated in the 1980's and 1990's with the emergence of work by Richard Foreman, The Wooster Group, and Mabou Mines, work that no longer believes in the sort of "pure" unmediated physical presence of the performer's body so celebrated by experimentalists in the 60's. What we find instead is a theater of technological "mediation" where we have no direct or privileged access to the physical presence of the actor. (For example, the performers in recent pieces by Mabou Mines and Richard Foreman frequently wear microphones, not for the conventional purpose of amplification, but so that their relationship to the audience is clearly "mediated.")

Work which relies heavily on mediation by "media" tends to greatly diminish the centrality of the performer's body. But this in turns leads to a paradox that invokes the key terms in my title: In many pieces by The Wooster Group, Richard Foreman, and sometimes even Robert Wilson, there are occasional (but "hysterical") eruptions of frenzied physical activity. Blackmur in his great study of Balanchine and The New York City Ballet, wrote

> We Americans have the technique to bring something to performance so well that the subject is left out....(The result is) both abstract and hysterical; we throw away so much and make so much of the meager remainder. We make a great beauty, which is devastated of everything but form and gait.[1]

He goes on to describe Balanchine's women as follows:

> There were all those beautiful legs and no one in the company who could walk except Diana Adams and none but her with a proper face. All the rest of the girls made up a ballet of pinheads...(They) had no faces and no legs that were inhabited. Some kind of sex was missing here—the tenderness—the predatoriness—the sexuality itself. The sense of American hardness was reinforced with the sense of American abstractness: as if Lincoln Kirstein's boys and girls danced in organized abstraction fits.... If there was unity in their dancing it was the American unity which is achieved by cutting away; unity by privation or deprivation.[2]

What I plan to argue is that the steadily increasing "abstraction" of the human body—in effect, the "repression" of the body in the theater of the 1980's and '90's—results in those volcanic eruptions of physical hysteria that I alluded to a moment ago. (Indeed, we may be witnessing something akin to what Freud called "the return of the repressed.")

It's no coincidence, I don't think, that the 1980's were the decade in which the words AIDS and cyberspace both entered our vocabulary. Nothing has done more to exacerbate a deep seated fear of the body than Acquired Immune Deficiency Syndrome. And nothing has done more to facilitate our retreat from the body than the concept of cyberspace, which promises us a liberation from all of the constraints that the body has traditionally imposed. In the words of William Gibson, whose 1984 novel <u>Neuromancer</u> introduced much of the key terminology, those who continue to live the life of the body in the age of cyberspace are mere "meat puppets" (not a term of endearment). And hovering somewhere between the twin specters of AIDS and cyberspace is the remarkable re-emergence in the past five years of an interest in—indeed a literal belief in—the existence of angels, those bodiless creatures who have always lived in the Biblical version of cyberspace and who, in plays like Tony Kushner's <u>Angels in America</u> may or may not be the source of our deliverance. Daniel Boorstein, well over twenty years ago, referred to the rise of instantaneous electronic communications as the "angelization" of information; so perhaps it's not so far fetched to suggest that Angels have come to America in the bodiless medium of cyberspace.

Well... before we waft away into the heady ethers of The Empyrean, let's return to the more workaday business of defining what we mean by "non-literary theater." Eric Bentley once argued that "A Drama Not Verbalized Is a Drama not Dramatized." Language, according to Bentley, must always be central to drama. No doubt it is—to drama. But not always to <u>theater</u>. (Needless to say, this hardly comes as news to a dance audience. But theater audiences, especially over here, are much more wedded to the word.) By contrast, beginning in the 1960's, much of the most adventurous theatrical activity in the United States has moved in non-literary directions. The play, in other words, is not always the thing.

The non-literary theater I want to focus on produces works that neither issue from nor leave behind a text (or at least, not a text that possesses the status of dramatic literature, a printed entity that can be read, understood, and enjoyed as a art work in its own right independent of performance.) Granted, you can argue—as Gide once did—that all dramatic texts are merely pre-texts for production. But some texts are at best blueprints (or even afterthoughts) whereas others possess literary merit in their own right.

The tradition that I'm going to focus on first, the work of theatrical collectives like The Living Theater, The Open Theater and The Performance Group (work that's bodily, choreographic and highly visual) emerged during that most non-verbal of decades, the 1960's, when the very concept of print culture, as demonized by thinkers like Marshall McLuhan, was very much under attack. Of course, this was also the decade in which the North American avant-garde discovered the rantings of Antonin Artaud, one of whose rallying cries was "burn the text." Artaud argued for a theater that exists only on the stage, that has no prior existence as a verbal outline to be fleshed out in production. Artaud's belief that language invariably domesticates and misrepresents reality found a ready and willing audience in the 1960's. This after all was the decade in which Lyndon Banes Johnson routinely referred to the napalming of Vietnamese villages as "limited duration protective reaction air strikes"—an all too familiar example of language debased into governmental euphemism, language that concealed rather than revealed what was actually happening. But the 60's critique of language went much further and cut much deeper. In Norman O. Brown's immensely influential book <u>Life Against Death</u>, language is characterized as inherently neurotic, a principle source of all those discontents that Freud associated with civilization. Language itself—whether written or spoken—was widely regarded as abstract, bloodless, impersonal, a barrier against "real" feeling, and politically suspect in that it was thought to be the chief tool by which the prevailing culture transmitted its values. According to this line of reasoning, we think the way we do because we speak the way we speak. In Peter Handke's extraordinary theater piece from 1968, <u>Kaspar</u>, the title character becomes indoctrinated into the prevailing culture as he learns language. And at the end of the play, Handke concludes that Kaspar has been <u>sentenced</u> to reality, that his view of the world is implicit in the <u>sentences</u> he now speaks.

Let's look at some slides of the body-based work that dominated American experimental theater in the 1960's: (Moments from The Open Theater's <u>Viet Rock</u>, The Living Theater's <u>Antigone</u> and <u>Frankenstein</u>, The Performance Group's <u>Dionysus in '69</u>...) Even the most cursory glance at these slides suggests that this non-verbal "Theater of the Body" marked a very clean break with the text-based theater that dominated the American stage in the 1950's during the heyday of playwrights like Arthur Miller and Tennesse Williams, of directors like Elia Kazan, and acting teachers like Lee Strasberg of The Actor's Studio.

But as I've already suggested, it's my belief that the movement toward non-literary theater in the U.S. wasn't entirely a product of the 1960's, but was in fact the culmination of forces that lie deep in the American psyche. Americans have always been uncomfortable with genuine eloquence. We tend to prefer the heartfelt gropings of inarticulate sensitivity; and we assume that verbal facility and authentic feeling are somehow at odds with one another. Think of those gawky, mumble-mouthed Frank Capra heros (Mr. Smith, Mr. Deeds, played by actors like Jimmy Steward, Gary Cooper) who are pitted against the silken smoothies who speak with forked, but velvety tongues. Or, in what is sometimes referred to as "real life", consider the political career of a truly articulate public servant like Adlai Stevenson.

Here then is the first component of my argument: I want to suggest that the very same theatrical impulse that culminated in non-literary theater also informed what we think of as America's chief contribution to the art of acting: the so-called "method" as employed by Brando, James Dean, and Montgomery Clift, those paragons of inarticulate sincerity, actors for whom bodily tics, mumbled monosyllables, and primal screams are considered infinitely more expressive than spoken, scripted text. Let's look at some videotape of what is indisputably the most famous moment in the history of American acting: (Brando screaming "Stellaaaaaaa....") That of course is from the 1952 Elia Kazan film of A Streetcar Named Desire. Note, in that scene, as Kim Stanley caresses Brando's back, you could almost be looking at a dance by Martha Graham....the body is that important. And of course it makes sense that America was rapidly gaining a reputation as the dance capital of the Western world during the very period of time we'll be focusing on. And speaking of dancers and choreographers like Graham, note the physical contractions in the body of James Dean in his screen debut in 1954 in Kazan's East of Eden. This is the great, great scene in which Dean plays the moody, insecure and inarticulate son of a stern, moralistic Bible-quoting figure played by Daniel Massey. Dean is desperate to win his father's affection. And with the best and most generous of intentions, he's gotten involved in a bean-growing, money-making scheme to earn back the cash his father lost when his lettuce crop failed. Here's what happens when he tries to give his self-righteous father the money as a birthday present: (Note the tortured expressiveness of Dean's body, and also the importance of sounds that never quite get articulated verbally.)

Now, let's leap from the 50' to the 60's, from film to theater, and from East of Eden to just a bit West of Eden: the lower W. side of Manhattan to be more specific, where The Open Theater is performing a production about the Garden of Eden called The Serpent in 1968. "Getting oneself back to the Garden" was a major obsession of the 1960's: and The Serpent was The Open Theater's retelling of the story of Genesis. The Biblical fall from grace was here reconceived as America's fall from grace in the early '60s, centered around the moment at which we seemed to lose our collective innocence as a culture, the assassination of John F. Kennedy. Now, note the way in which The Open Theater represents the assassination: They don't show slides of the famous Life Magazine photo enlargements of key frames from the 8 mm Zapruder film (which Oliver Stone re-created in such doting detail in his film "JFK"). Instead, the actors physically and choreographically embody the key frames, with each corresponding to numbers that are shouted out, at first chronologically, then in reverse order, then randomly. The sequence that we're going to look at is a particularly pure example of what Jerzy Grotowski had already labeled "poor theater", not of course poor in the sense of being bad, but poor in the sense of not relying on the technology of the "rich" theater (no slides, film, video, or even recorded sound effects), but emphasizing instead what actors can accomplish without any sort of technical support, relying only on their unadorned bodies and voices. Let's look at the sequence....

Significantly, one of the definitions of modernism that becomes most familiar in the 1960's is the quest for purity of medium, the desire to purge one's chosen artform of everything that seems extraneously to its underlying medium. And here—as in Grotowski's so called poor theater—what is deemed essential is the physical presence of the actor. Joe Chaikin, the founder of The Open Theater and the director of this production of The Serpent, even wrote a book called The Presence of the Actor. This emphasis on presence, on the physical here and now, is even more evident in the next sequence I want to show from The Serpent: the creation sequence in which we see Adam and Eve come to life and discover one another and the creatures in the garden "as if for the first time." You'll also see the serpent and the tree of knowledge evolve at the end of this sequence—again all of this represented through a highly physical/choreographic use of the body. Now it's true...there is spoken text in The Serpent: it's even written by a major playwright, Jean Claude van Itallie in collaboration with the company members, but it never becomes primary. It always underscores the physical expressiveness of the actors rather than the other way around.

It's significant, I think, that The Serpent was subtitled "A Ceremony"—not a play or even a theater piece. "Ceremony" has quasi-ritualistic connotations, and this reminds us that one of the recurring obsessions of non-literary theater in the sixties was the desire to emulate the key characteristics of ritual: its physicality, its non-verbal sound, its sacredness, its participatory inclusion of the whole community. One definition of unmediated physical presence is the potential for actual physical contact between performers and spectators. And that very same year, 1968, the pieces being performed by The Living Theater attempted to eliminate any physical or psychological barrier between audience and performer. This is no where more evident than in their production of Paradise Now, in which the actors directly confront, caress, cajole, and harangue their audiences. Let's look at a few minutes from a performance of Paradise Now in Brussels....

One of the most ambitious re-examinations of the relationship between ritual and theater occurs within the context of The Performance Group's production of Dionysus in '69. This is a radically revisionist adaptation of Euripides' The Bacchae, a play that depicts the way in which ritualistic, Dionysian worship is first established in ancient Greece. This production embodies some of the fundamental differences between theater and ritual, reminding us that our word "theater" derives from the Greek word "theatron" which means "seeing place", a reference to the special architectural provisions a theatrical space makes for spectators. Ritual by contrast is never a mere "spectacle." Ritual creates a space in which no one is a passive onlooker. In the scene we're going to look at, the character Pentheus has attempted to voyeuristically peer in on, from a distance, a Dionysian ritual that like all true rituals, was never intended to be watched by detached spectators. And once the Dionysian revelers realize that there's a voyeur trying to transform them into a theatrical "sight," they hunt him down and devour him. Norman O. Brown's book Love's Body, published in 1966, contains a pertinent quotation: Brown writes that

> The Garden of Eden is polymorphism of the senses...active interplay; and the opposite of polymorphous perversity is the abstraction of the visual, obtained by putting to sleep the rest of the life of the body...like the spectator in the traditional theater.[3]

Note too, in the sequence we're going to look at, the way in which the production utilizes the entire space of the performance area to envelope the audience in the action, denying them a detached vantage point or "seeing place" (theatron).

What we've just witnessed might be thought of as the revenge of ritual upon the theater. But as the 60's gave way to the 70's, this sort of physically-based, participatory, pseudo-ritualistic work began to beat a rather hasty retreat. In fact, it's remarkable how quickly this work lost its avant-garde cachet and began to look dated. This is partly attributable to the cultural backlash against the 1960's and its utopian aspirations that had begun to gather steam by the early 70's. (Certainly there's no quest more Quixotic than the attempt to replace theater as we know it with ritual as we like to imagine it.) But another factor, equally significant, was the emergence of a much less bodily form of non-literary theater in the work of Robert Wilson. You need only glance at these slides of moments from "Deafman Glance," "Einstein on the Beach," or "A Letter to Queen Victoria" to appreciate the ways in which Wilson's theater differs from the non-literary traditions we've just been examining. This is a theater of spectacular scenic landscapes inspired by surrealist painting. A quick glimpse at an excerpt from Robert Wilson's 1976 collaboration with Philip Glass, <u>Einstein on the Beach</u> will immediately establish how far we've traveled from the "poor theater" tradition of <u>The Serpent</u>, <u>Paradise Now</u>, or <u>Dionysus in '69</u>.

Wilson's theater can often seem dreamy and ethereal. As we just saw, there's a tendency for objects to float or to dissolve magically into thin air. So you may be wondering: What happens to all of that physical, bodily energy that I traced back to Brando and Dean? It's instructive to see what happens in <u>Einstein....</u> Toward the end of the "space machine" sequence we just looked at Wilson himself performs a spastic, disjointed dance that seems to erupt out of nowhere with little or no warning. As we'll see in due course, in the work of Richard Foreman and The Wooster Group, the role of the body becomes simultaneously peripheral and hysterical. These Dionysian eruptions of physical activity will increase in intensity as the live human body becomes less and less central to non-literary theater in the late 1970's and 1980's.

As we shift our focus from the 1960's to the '70's and '80's, let's compare and contrast two productions, precisely twenty years apart, emblematic of their respective decades as well as of the immense chasm that separates the 1960's from the 1980's: The Living Theatre's "Paradise Now" ('68) and Richard Foreman's "What Did He See" ('88). The former is often regarded as a quintessential affirmation of live, unmediated <u>presence</u>. Its most notorious sequence, "The Rite of Universal Intercourse," was also its most representative. Julian Beck and Judith Malina describe it as follows: "The actors gather near the center of the playing area. They lie down together on the stage floor, embracing. Their bodies form a pile, caressing, moving, undulating, loving. They are breaking the touch barrier...If a member of the public joins this group, he is welcomed into the Rite."[4]

Twenty years later Foreman's production was intent upon <u>constructing</u> barriers, not eradicating them (or, perhaps more precisely, objectifying otherwise invisible barriers). Here the performer/spectator relationship was "mediated" both aurally and visually. A transparent, Plexiglas wall separated the audience from the performers. The actor's voices were heard "indirectly," filtered through microphones and speaker systems—but not for the conventional purpose of amplification. The performance took place in an exceedingly intimate space. That thin sheet of Plexiglas notwithstanding, there was no conventional reason to amplify the actors' voices. Indeed, the space was <u>so</u> intimate the one could virtually read the actors' lips. No, this mode of technological mediation was there to mediate, not to amplify or to allow for some sort of hypernaturalism or whispered intimacy. (The body mikes by the way were unabashedly and rather gruesomely visible, taped to the actors cheeks like IV needles that had missed their marks.)

On one level, it seems to me that artists like Foreman are simply acknowledging the fact that, like it or not, technological mediation has become an inescapable part of our lives. Most of what claim to know about the world is now acquired vicariously or second hand. We rely on television, radio, or the internet to inform us of the public events that shape our collective consciousness. Here's one of the great photographs of the 1980's: Ronald Reagan addressing the 1984 Republican Convention from his hotel room, several blocks away from the "live" event.

But ironically, there's no reason to believe that "being there" is always preferable to the omniscient detachment provided by advanced technology. Certainly we've all had the experience of watching on television as a governmental official arrives in some distant land. Given the sophistication of video technology, it's not uncommon for the news anchor in New York or Washington to have a better view of who's getting off the plane than the poor "eye witness" reporter there on the ground.

But how does this apply to live performance? Well, what's at stake here is nothing less than all of the traditional claims about what constitutes the "essence" of theater. Let's run one of the most familiar versions of this argument up the flagpole and see if it still flies: What <u>is</u> unique about the theater? What can happen there that can't happen at the movies, or in literature, or while standing before a painting or a work of sculpture? Until recently, the answer—no matter who provided it—almost always had something to do with the fact that it's live and unmediated, that it can put us in the <u>presence</u> of other living, breathing human beings. Sure, the movies can cut instantaneously from Brooklyn to Moscow. They can fill the big screen with close-ups of objects too tiny to register in the most intimate loft; they can pan past vistas too vast to be contained on the deepest opera house stage. But they can't rival the face to face encounter of actor and audience that constitutes the theater's unique glory.

That at least is the traditional (if rather middlebrow) argument. This was also the point at which the middlebrow and the modernist met. (Modernism here being defined as an effort to strip each medium to its "essence", jettisoning anything in the art work deemed extraneous to that essence.) If the essence of the medium is defined as "presence" then the theatrical modernist will re-affirm this ancient wisdom with a vengeance. The late '60's work of The Living Theatre may have flaunted the possibilities of live, unmediated presence a bit more aggressively than a play by Thornton Wilder, but neither would have taken issue with this time-honored conception of what makes the theater unique.

A recent advertisement for The Denver Center Theatre Company reads in part "Not available on videocassette, compact disc, album, sixteen millimeter, eight millimeter, video disc or eight track...The Magic of Live Theatre." (A minor scandal ensued some years ago when it was revealed that Liza Minelli was lip synching to her own prerecorded voice during a particularly strenuous song and dance routine in the Broadway musical <u>The Act</u>.) And those who wax nostalgic about Broadway's golden age often argue that the sort of amplification—and unintended mediation which is now routine in so many theaters—amounts to nothing less than a fall from grace.

Let's look at several examples of what might be called "mediated presence" in the non-literary theater of the 1980's: Lee Breuer's and Mabou Mines' <u>A Prelude to Death in Venice</u> (1979) depicts a character whose relationship with the outside world is doubly mediated: Bill Raymond speaks through a ventriloquist's dummy whose only contact with other characters is over the telephone. The telephone, by the way, becomes a major icon in theater work of the 1980's.

In The Wooster Group's <u>Route 1 and 9</u> (1981) two white actresses dial telephone calls to what sound like actual restaurants, and—in broad, Amos n' Andy accents—claim they want to order fried chicken for a birthday party. We have no way of knowing whether these conversations are live or prerecorded (and for that matter, we don't know whether those on the other end of the line are unrehearsed employees of an actual restaurant or actors impersonating them). But in any event, the quality of the sound we hear is unmistakably mediated, as if we'd picked up another phone extension or tapped into the line. In other words, the voices that we hear no longer pretend to be directly or immediately "present" to us. (Let's look at this sequence on videotape.)

Laurie Anderson's talk-song parable "New York Social Life" is about life lived entirely on the telephone. And much of her work explores the unintended irony in Ma Bell's insistent urging that we use the telephone to "reach out and touch someone". (Anderson is particularly fascinated by the ways in which communications technology, which purports to bring us closer together, as members of a "global village," actually increases our sense of social isolation.)

In the concert sequence we're going to look at, Anderson not only uses the telephone, she also speaks into what she calls a "vocoder," an electronic filter that transforms her light, flat voice into a variety of vocal personae that include a deep, throaty rasp. The resulting Is-it-Live-or-is-it-Memorex uncertainty creates an ambiguous form of presence that seems both spontaneous and pre-recorded at the same time.

Well, we can look back nostalgically at the ideal of unmediated presence. But one thing is certain: The balance between what we glean about the world directly through our senses and what we absorb vicariously through the media has been forever tipped in the direction of the latter. (And to assume that a few hours of "live" theater will somehow restore a healthy sense of "being there" is naive and self-deceptive.) The on-going critique of theatrical presence is also valuable in so far as it reminds us that no experience (no matter how "live") is entirely unmediated. The "copy theory of knowledge" was invalidated long ago. The innocent eye never existed. Furthermore, the idea that the theater's "liveness" is—in and of itself—a virtue, a source of automatic, un-earned moral superiority to film and television, is sheer bourgeois sentimentality.

I've been struck in recent years by the number of "live" events that merely simulate an experience whose original version appeared on film or tape. Let's look, for example, at a medley from the smash hit production, now playing on Broadway of The Who's rock opera Tommy. What you're about to see is, in essence, a live simulation of MTV. Quite unintentionally, it makes us realize that most of what we experience today is never really immediate. In fact, a practitioner of deconstruction would probably point out that the word "immediate" contains within it the word mediate.

But mediation notwithstanding, the body is not so easily ignored. To return to R.P. Blackmur's terminology, the other side of "abstraction" is "hysteria." And this is no where more evident than in those hysterical dance sequences that erupt in almost every production of The Wooster Group. Here is the counterpoint to the mediated phone sequence we saw earlier in the group's production of Route 1 and 9: This is their scandalously raucous recreation of an Afro-American vaudeville routine from the 1940's. But given the fact that this Pigmeat Markham routine has been re-created by white performers in blackface, it too remains in some sense mediated.

So what becomes of the body in this brave new world of mediation and simulation? It seems to me that our attitudes toward the body and physical presence are trapped between two extremes: the fear of physical contact engendered by HIV and the promise of safe, simulated sex in the virtual reality of cyberspace. Clearly, we live in an age that longs to escape the afflictions of the flesh. AIDS provides the central metaphor in the most celebrated American theater experience of recent years, Tony Kushner's Angels in America. Here, in the conclusion to part I, a physically emaciated AIDS victim is visited by an angel, a creature without a body and perhaps, just perhaps, the source of our deliverance...The messenger has arrived.[5]

Endnotes

1. R.P. Blackmur, "The Swan in Zurich," (1958), reprinted in Roger Copeland & Marshall Cohen, editors, What Is Dance? (New York: Oxford University Press, 1983), 357

2. Ibid, p. 360

3. Norman O. Brown, Loves's Body (New York: Vintage Books, 1966), 121

4. Judith Malina and Julien Beck, Paradise Now (New York: Random House, 1971), 74

5. Some portions of this talk appeared in my essay, "The Presence of Mediation" (TDR, 34, 4, T128, Winter 1990, pp 28-44.)

Bibliography

Joseph Chaikin, <u>The Presence of the Actor</u> (New York: Atheneum, 1972)

Margaret Croyden, <u>Lunatics, Lovers, and Poets: The Contemporary Experimental Theatre</u> (New York: McGraw Hill Book Co., 1974)

Clement Greenberg, <u>Art and Culture</u> (Boston: Beacon Press, 1961)

Jerzy Growtowski, <u>Towards a Poor Theatre</u> (New York: Simon and Schuster, 1968)

Peter Handke, <u>Kaspar and Other Plays</u> (New York: Farrar, Straus, and Giroux, 1969)

E.T. Kirby, <u>Total Theatre</u> (New York: E.P. Dutton Co., 1969)

Marshall McLuhan, <u>The Guttenberg Galaxy</u> (New York: New American Library, 1962)

Theodore Shank, <u>American Alternative Theater</u> (New York: Grove Press, 1982)

Lawrence Shyer, <u>Robert Wilson and his Collaborators</u> (New York: Theatre Communications Group, 1989)

ISADORA DUNCAN AND THE "DISTINCTION" OF DANCE

Ann Daly
University of Texas at Austin

By the turn of the century, when Isadora Duncan began her dance career, the "dancer" was implicitly female, with little distinction between the trained ballerina, the entertaining skirt dancer, and the moonlighting factory-worker-cum-chorus-girl. She was constructed as a highly paid, empty-headed—and probably blonde—soubrette of ill repute. Subject to the whims of the novelty-hungry audiences through the theatre manager, she was hired and fired largely on the basis of her looks. Audiences clamored for the likes of Lola Montez, with her convulsing spider dance, and Little Egypt's shimmying hootchy-cootchy, and "The Naked Lady" herself, Ada Isaacs Mencken. They flocked to see Lydia Thompson and her British Blondes.

But by World War I, in large part due to Isadora Duncan,[1] dance had been transformed from entertainment into "Culture," at least in New York.[2] Duncan reimagined the form and content of dance as an aesthetic object and convinced an audience of its legitimacy as a "high" art.[3] She created a "taste" for dance, and, furthermore, made it a matter of "good taste."

Duncan managed to accomplish what historian Lawrence W. Levine has described as the "sacralization of culture." This process of sacralization endowed arts such as opera, Shakespeare, symphonic music and visual arts "with unique aesthetic and spiritual properties that rendered it inviolate, exclusive, and eternal. This was not the mere ephemera of the world of entertainment but something lasting, something permanent."[4] Culture became synonymous with the European products of the symphonic hall, the opera house, the museum, and the library, now seen as veritable temples, "all of which, the American people were taught, must be approached with a disciplined, knowledgeable seriousness of purpose, and—most important of all—with a feeling of reverence."[5]

How, in less than two decades, did Duncan gain this reverence for dance in America? By deconstructing and reconstructing it as a practice of high, white, western Culture for the privileged classes of northeastern cities. She used strategies of difference and exclusion, exploiting the conventional distinctions between high and low and appropriating the legitimacy of established European practices and discourses.

Taste, according to French sociologist Pierre Bourdieu, is not disinterested; rather, it is rooted in social origin and in education. As an arbiter of taste, Culture is not just reflective, but also productive. That is to say, it is not just "the state of that which is cultivated," but also "the process of cultivating."[6] This process of cultivating—which, similarly to Levine, Bourdieu calls "cultural consecration"—confers "on the objects, persons and situations it touches, a sort of ontological promotion akin to a transubstantiation."[7] By inscribing into perception and practice a "distinction" (difference that produces hierarchy) between the sacred sphere of legitimate, or high, Culture, and the mere vulgarity of entertainment, Cultural practice thus fulfils a social function, whether conscious or not, of legitimating social and specifically class—difference. In this talk, I want to identify the strategies that Duncan employed in order to establish the distinction of dance and then consider their social implications.

Strategies of Distinction

Bourdieu conceives of society as being organized into "fields," each of which is a structured and structuring system of social relations with its own logic. Any field, including that of Culture, has its own economy, so to speak, in which capital—economic, social, educational, symbolic—must be accumulated in order to advance or dominate in that field. The strategies for accumulating such capital and for gaining legitimacy, or distinction, are regulated by the field itself. These predisposed strategies, a generative constellation of tacit, internalized, embodied principles and practices, are what Bourdieu calls a field's *habitus*. These unwritten rules are learned not explicitly, but implicitly, through practice in the field. Although the general contours of the *habitus* are shared by each player in the field, each individual, having come from a different background and thus occupying a different position within the field, have a slightly different *habitus*.[8]

Duncan internalized the *habitus* of the Cultural field early in her life, although much of her childhood was spent in poverty and on the outskirts of polite society. Duncan's parents, Joseph Charles and Mary Dora Duncan, apparently divorced shortly after the birth of their fourth child, Angela Isadora.[9] Without support, the 30-year-old divorcee had to eke out a living for herself and her children by selling knitted goods and giving music lessons.

The Duncans' poverty was compounded by a considerable fall from social grace. Before the divorce, the Duncans had been a respected San Francisco family. Joseph C. Duncan was a poet, art connoisseur, and a cunning businessman. The suave and cultured man had been a lifelong poet and an accomplished journalist. He founded both the Safe Deposit Company, of which he was primary stockholder, and the Pioneer Land and Loan Bank of Savings, of which he was secretary and manager. Duncan's bank ran into trouble. He attempted to keep his bank afloat through some shady dealings, but it collapsed, nonetheless, in October 1877. Accused of forgery, embezzlement, and grand larceny, Duncan ignominiously fled the charges but was eventually found. After four inconclusive trials, the charges finally were dismissed, on a technicality.

Despite—or because of—the poverty and the social stigma of jail and divorce, the Duncans clung to their artistic aspirations. For Isadora, it substituted for formal schooling. Their living room functioned as a salon, where Mother played piano; Aunt Augusta, in shorts, recited *Hamlet*; and Isadora, of course, danced. On the wall hung a reproduction of Botticelli's *Primavera*, which she later would transform into a dance.

The family's last two years in California, however, were spent more comfortably, back in San Francisco. The clan's private theatricals expanded into a barn theatre. For several years, the family enjoyed a better standard of living. They gained some reputation among the town's better families for the dancing school run by Isadora and her older sister, Elizabeth. Accompanied by her mother, Elizabeth also had taught at exclusive girls' schools, bringing the family to the edges of, but hardly inside, high society.

Without any educational, social, or economic capital, however, Duncan's acceptance into the domain of Culture was largely unlikely, especially since dancing itself held no currency in that realm. But Duncan learned, at a young age, about the intimacy between class and taste, between social and artistic prestige. Denied the illusion of meritocracy that inheres in a comfortable middle class upbringing, Duncan became a remarkable master of the signs and emblems of dominant taste, and she used that practical knowledge to gain distinction for her art.

With the nineteenth-century sacralization of culture, the arts had become implicated in class status. The Duncans, with Joseph at their head, established class status not just by virtue of his income but also by virtue of his publicly-demonstrated aesthetic mastery. When the Duncans, sans Joseph, lost all their money and their social position, they endeavored to maintain and, later, to increase status through their refined Cultural sensibilities. Those evening salons functioned not merely as self-amusement but as the private performance of class. Duncan dealt with the considerable anxiety of her changing childhood fortunes by a flagrant lifelong disinterest in the management of money and thus a denial of its importance; she displaced the definition of class from money to art. If class brought Culture (as the nouveau-riche took great pains to demonstrate), then could not Culture bring class?

The usefulness of Bourdieu's scheme to an analysis of Duncan's elevation of dance as an American art form is its attention to the ways an artist constructs distinction/difference, in both practice and in the perception of that practice. Using Bourdieu's model, we can look at how Duncan made specific choices in pre-existing, intersecting fields: how she strategically engaged economic, social, intellectual, and well as Cultural institutions and practices.

Duncan's choices consistently aligned her dancing with upper-class, white Euro-America. Dancing was considered cheap, so she associated herself with the great Greeks, who deemed the art noble, and she associated herself with upper class audiences, by carefully courting her patrons and selecting her performance venues. Dancing was considered mindless, so she invoked a pantheon of great minds, from Darwin to Whitman and Plato to Nietzsche, to prove otherwise. Dancing was considered feminine, and thus trivial, so she chose well her liaisons and mentors—men whose cultural or economic power accrued, by association, to her. Dancing was considered profane, so she elevated her own practice by contrasting it to that of "African primitives." The fundamental strategy of Duncan's project to gain Cultural legitimacy for dancing was one of exclusion. In order to reinvent the idea of the "dancer," that is to say, to make her kind of dancing a matter of good taste, within the existing Cultural field, Duncan employed the dominant logic of difference along a number of axes, and used it to construct distinction. Effectively, she elevated dancing from low to high, from sexual to spiritual, from black to white, from profane to sacred, from woman to goddess, from entertainment to art.

Except for a very early vaudeville turn in Chicago and the ill-fated season at Frohman's Criterion Theatre in 1908, Duncan refused to perform in theatrical venues. Rather, she positioned herself, both literally and symbolically, in high-priced opera houses and concert halls mostly in northeastern urban centers, allying herself with symphony orchestras such as Walter Damrosch's, whose cache was already established. In one of her boldest moves, she dared to appropriate the canon of great symphonic works, notably with Beethoven's Seventh Symphony in A Major.

But before Duncan ever got to the point of public performance, she was cultivating—and being cultivated by—wealthy women, whose patronage was an important factor in the establishment of Culture at the turn of the century. Duncan's early drawing-room performances in Chicago, New York, and Newport were sponsored by the likes of Mrs. Dodge and Mrs. Nicholas Beach, whose afternoon soirées attracted attention from the most well-known society reporters.

Similarly, when Duncan later returned to New York from Europe, her reputation was based in no small measure on her reported associations with the European cultural, intellectual, and social elite. The imprimatur of elite patrons—kings and capitalists—gained Duncan an aura of economic leisure and social pedigree.

Social capital, Bourdieu explains, encompasses a number of culturally, economically, politically, and sexually useful personal relations. Duncan overcame the disadvantages of being a woman by associating herself—sexually, socially, artistically, and intellectually—with well-placed men such as Edward Gordon Craig and Paris Singer. Walter Damrosch's eager collaboration was especially important to Duncan's early artistic reputation in America. And, of course, Duncan was not shy about dropping names—Wagner, Rodin, Haeckel, Nietzsche, Schopenhauer, Darwin. I am not saying that Duncan consciously chose male associations because of their gender *per se*, but rather that, given the sexually divided social, cultural, and intellectual fields at that time, the almost exclusive dependence on men (aside from her early patronesses) was a logical—and effective—means of increasing her capital.[10]

Duncan's most successful strategy in sacralizing dance was "Greece," a symbolic matrix whose set of signifiers cut across the aesthetic, economic, intellectual, and social fields. It was embedded not only in her flowery prose, but also in her dancing—the stories, the costumes, the movement vocabulary—and the grand manner of her lifestyle (her clothing, as well as her widely publicized trips to Greece). By invoking the classical ideal, Duncan effectively displayed her education and refinement. The Hellenistic practices also presupposed a certain class of spectator: not the likes of the *Variety* reviewer who mocked the artistic pretension of "the celebrated classical dancer," but rather an educated viewer reared on classical literature and philosophy.

In the Greeks, Duncan constructed an origin for her "Natural" dancing, as opposed to ballet, which she described as physically, aesthetically, and morally deforming. No doubt genuine in her stance, Duncan was, nevertheless, capitalizing on a preexisting discourse. Even before Duncan ever trod the boards, cultural and intellectual leaders were interested in reclaiming dancing as something more than mere "amusement," which implied a lack of social import or, worse, moral degeneracy. Duncan galvanized discourses that had already been established by American and Continental intellectuals, who had begun to make quite serious inquiries into the nature and status of dancing. Although it was generally agreed that dancing was in serious decline, authors recounted its past glories and called for its "renaissance."

The Social Origins/Effects of Modern Dance

I have argued elsewhere that Isadora Duncan offered her American audiences a means of imagining themselves in the radical process of transformation.[11] For artists and intellectuals, she did embody in her dance practice a revolutionary ethos. It also needs to be said, however, that, for the upper class, she reproduced a seemingly apolitical, disinterested Platonic "Beauty." And, later on, for her middle-class "audiences," who experienced Duncan mostly second-hand, in the press and through imitators, she represented taste and breeding. Without dismissing the very real subversive meaning of her dancing for some of her audience, we also must recognize that Duncan's project was no less about cultural legitimacy than it was about aesthetics. And that this aesthetic practice was produced by and, in turn, continued to reproduce, social differences.

Duncan's idea and use of Greece was really about the aesthetic of a "Natural" body. It was not a willful flight from high culture, off to some pre-civilized utopia. Neither was it a Whitmanesque celebration of the common folk, despite her genuine love for the poet's earthy vision. Duncan emphasized the noble over the savage; her model, after all, was the Nike of Samothrace, not Pocahontas. This "Natural" body, the foundational trope from which she theorized both her aesthetic and social agenda, was the artistic transformation of Nature into Culture. It was artless artifice. And "Nature" was only "Nature" when it was thus ennobled[12]; otherwise, it remained base primitivism. For Duncan, the "Natural" body is a "civilized" body. She wanted to establish dance as "civilized," which she did, at least in part, by establishing its essential difference from the "primitive savage" she saw as manifesting itself in the African-rooted social dances of the early teens.

Duncan was specifically interested in appropriating the roots of *western* (white) Culture, with the Greeks. The Egyptians, she said, were origin of an-*other* (black) race.[13] As for ragtime and jazz, whose popularity provided her with fierce competition during her second set of Amercan tours, she scornfully dismissed them on many an occasion as "this deplorable modern dancing, which has its roots in the ceremonies of African primitives."[14]

In literal and metaphorical terms, the popularity of modern dancing threatened Duncan's social vision of unity and harmony. She railed against the uncontrolled character—the presumed *chaos*—of ragtime and jazz, because it symbolically threatened the moral order of civilization, which was precisely that moral *order* engendered by Duncan's first principle, the harmonious ideal of "Nature" that she had gleaned from the Greece of Winckelmann and Botticelli and from the monism of Ernst Haeckel. According to Haeckel, God inhered within the singular web of the cosmos.

Although a large part of Duncan's appeal was her seeming spontaneity (and she fed this illusion, that her dancing was improvised on stage), Duncan's dancing was far from wild. Her movement style had a decided sense of flowing, unhurried gentility. Compared to what she described as the "spasms" or "paroxysms" of Africanist dances, she embodied a spontaneity tempered with the unspoken, unquestioned control that marked good breeding. This particular bodily hexis (to borrow Bourdieu's term for embodied dispositions of belief)—ease borne of effortless control—was that of the upper class.[15]

By constituting a "Natural" body as the basis for dance practice, Duncan effectively removed from it any vulgar requirement of *labor*, which would have smacked of the working class; instead, it could be imbued with an aura of the innate—of good taste, which is, by definition, effortless. Something that ballet, constituted as it was by its demanding technique, could not claim. Since the popular perception of the ballet dancer was collapsed into that of untrained chorus girls, its social position was associated with lower class women who turned to dancing as a means of making a living. Thus, even though ballet could claim the history of kings, it still required and connoted work.[16] On or off stage, Duncan always aligned herself with leisure, luxury, and ease—never with necessity. "When in doubt," she often said, "always go to the best hotel."[17]

This is not to say, however, that Duncan was a calculating aristocrat. She was hardly unsympathetic toward the American masses; in her late career, after encountering the Soviet experiment, she claimed them as her true audience. Inhering in Duncan's art was a curious tension between the desire to legitimize dance as an aesthetic object through a strategy of exclusion, and the desire to spread dance as a social practice through a strategy of inclusion.

Nevertheless, when Duncan was denouncing African primitivism, or invoking Nietzsche, or constructing herself as a Greek goddess, she was producing and reproducing the social divisions between high and low. By operating strategically within the structures of the upper class, she was developing an audience and thus a "taste" for her art that drew upon and reinforced its distinction from all others—blacks, immigrants, the poor, the uneducated, the middle class. Bourdieu calls this effective social exclusion "symbolic violence: a symbolic means of perpetuating social difference in an age when overt violence has become unacceptable."[18]

Approaching Dance as Social Practice

Founded, at least in part, as a rebellion against ballet, the genre of American modern dance has long been approached by dance historians as embodying a democratic ethos. If ballet was about the subservience of the self to a male, European, aristocratic tradition, then modern dance was about the discovery of the self through a female, American, democratic experiment. A Bourdieu-modeled analysis of Duncan's practice, which looks closely at the social and historical bases of that Cultural production, yields a different, more complex story.

In order to gain legitimacy for what would later become institutionalized as American modern dance, Duncan engaged strategies whose ideological sources and effects were at odds with the democratic reputation that modern dance has come to enjoy.

Rather, I have argued here that modern dance in America was constructed from and for high Culture, that is to say, white, western, male Culture.

For the study of modern dance as social practice (rather than just aesthetic object), Bourdieu offers a theoretical and analytical framework which offers a plausible alternative to the two extremes of cultural interpretation. It offers us a way to see that Duncan was neither a "genius," forging new practices out of thin air, nor a passive function of her cultural context. Yes, Duncan's choices and strategies were delimited by the institutions and practices of her day, but they were choices, nonetheless. Bourdieu posits the artist as occupying a relational, potentially changeable position in an equally changeable field. Thus we can recognize the social structures and practices through which Duncan negotiated her art while also acknowledging her agency. And vice versa. We can recognize her agency and still credit the social structures which gave rise to that agency.

Such an approach to dance as social practice could push the field of American early modern dance scholarship past its focus on individual figures and their work and facilitate inquiry into some of the larger, under-investigated questions, such as: Why was modern dance founded by women? Was it or was it not a subversive practice? Subversive of what? What were the origins and effects of its bodily hexis in other fields? What was the nature of its patronage by colleges? How did it spread geographically? What were the meanings of its Americana phase in the 1930s? How and why was it institutionalized? By what means did ballet and modern dance struggle for predominance? Isadora Duncan's own struggle for distinction is merely the beginning, rather than the end, of an inquiry into the cultural production of modern dance in America.[19]

Notes

1.   Ruth St. Denis and, to a lesser extent, Loie Fuller and Maud Allan also pioneered modern dance. Unlike Duncan, however, St. Denis often performed in vaudeville venues. Fuller and Allan spent most of their careers in Europe, as did Duncan, but had much less of an impact in America.

2.   For the purpose of distinguishing between "culture" in the anthropological sense, and "Culture" as high art, which is the subject of this essay, I will capitalize the latter. In keeping with the tenets of a socio-historical analysis, I will also capitalize words (such as Beauty and Nature) as they were intentionally and meaningfully capitalized by Duncan and her contemporaries. Occasionally, I will place such words in quotation marks, as a way of marking the gaps in belief between Duncan's day and our own.

3.   Duncan's style of dancing was used in American pageants, too. Duncan was good friends with pageantry movement leader Percy MacKaye; it was most likely out of personal friendship than admiration for pageantry (she disdained amateurs) that she agreed to a cameo appearance in his *Caliban*, in 1916. On pageantry, see David Glassberg, *American Historical Pageantry: The Uses of Tradition in the Early Twentieth Century* (Chapel Hill, NC: University of North Carolina Press, 1990); Naima Prevots, *American Pageantry: A Movement for Art and Democracy* (Ann Arbor, MI: UMI Research Press, 1990); Dorothy J. Olsson, "Arcadian Idylls: Dances of Early Twentieth-Century American Pageantry," Ph.D. diss., New York University, 1992.

4.   Lawrence W. Levine, *Highbrow/Lowbrow: The Emergence of Cultural Hierarchy in America* (Cambridge: Harvard University Press, 1988), 11.

5.   Ibid., 146.

6.   Pierre Bourdieu, *Distinction: A Social Critique of the Judgement of Taste,* Richard Nice, trans. (Cambridge: Harvard University Press, 1984), 11.

7.   Ibid., 6.

8.   On *habitus*, see *The Logic of Practice*, Richard Nice, ed. (Stanford: Stanford University Press, 1990), 52-79; *Distinction*, 169-225. On field, see *Logic*, 122-134. The first half of *Logic* provides a coherent description of Bourdieu's overall project. On the cultural field in particular, see *The Field of Cultural Production*, Randal Johnson, ed. and intro. (New York: Columbia University Press, 1993).

9.   Because of the San Francisco earthquake and fire in 1906, in which city records were destroyed, there is no birth record available on Duncan. Her baptismal record at Old Saint Mary's Church, however, indicates that she was born Angela I. Duncan on May 26, 1877. The middle initial "I" is presumably for Isadora, shortened to "Dora" when she was a child. Although Fredrika Blair (*Isadora: Portrait of the Artist as a Woman* [New York: Quill, William Morrow, 1986]) identifies Mrs. Duncan as Mary Isadora, all other records (including Isadora's birth certificate) and biographies from primary sources refer to her as Mary Dora; however, as with her daughter, "Dora" may have been short for "Isadora."

10.   On the feminist appropriation of Bourdieu's work, see Toril Moi, "Appropriating Bourdieu: Feminist Theory and Pierre Bourdieu's Sociology of Culture," *New Literary History* 22 (1991), 1017-1049.

11.   See Ann Daly, "Dance History and Feminist Theory: Reconsidering Isadora Duncan and the Male Gaze," *Gender in Performance: The Presentation of Difference in the Performing Arts* (Hanover, NH: University Press of New England, 1992); "Done Into Dance: Isadora Duncan and America," Ph.D. dissertation, New York University, 1993.

12.   Although today "Nature" is set in opposition to "Culture," in Duncan's day the two were elided; the former was used as a justification for the latter by avant-garde artists.

13.   Isadora Duncan, *The Art of the Dance*, Sheldon Cheney, ed. (New York: Theatre Arts, Inc., 1928), 92.

14.   Ibid., 126.

15.   "Practical belief is not a 'state of mind,' still less a kind of arbitrary adherence to a set of instituted dogmas and doctrines ('beliefs'), but rather a state of the body" (Bourdieu, *Distinction*, 68). "Bodily hexis is political mythology realized, em-bodied, turned into a permanent disposition, a durable way of standing, speaking, walking, and thereby of feeling and thinking" (Bourdieu, *Distinction*, 69-70). See Bourdieu, *Logic*, 52-79; Bourdieu, *Distinction*, 169-225.

16.   The sub-field of dance in the American cultural field shifted, with the tours of Anna Pavlova in 1910 and Diaghilev's Ballets Russes in 1916 and 1917. As ballet took a foothold, and the display of technique came to displace Nature as the generally

accepted basis of theatrical dancing, Duncan's claim to naivete worked against her.

17.   Allan Ross Macdougal, *Isadora: A Revolutionary in Art and Love* (New York: Thomas Nelson & Sons, 1960), 222. Like many other tidbits of "documented" Duncan lore, this may be apocryphal. In this case, however, the aphorism rings very true.

18.   See Bourdieu, *Logic*, 122-134.

19.   This talk was extracted from a longer article: "Isadora Duncan and the Distinction of Dance," *American Studies*, 35, Spring 1994: 5-23.

'Perfect moments, immaculately framed': Lea
Anderson and the television text
Sherril Dodds
University of Surrey

Lea Anderson's work has been described as having a "streetwise urban chic" (Scott, 1993) which is said to appeal to a wider network of people than the traditional dance audience (Fisher,1993, Newman,1987, Burnside, 1990). One of the reasons for this degree of popularity is considered to be the way in which she draws upon, and recycles texts and images from popular culture. Whether it is in commercialising her work through the television medium, as in her Tights, Camera, Action series, or by creating a vernacular dance in which its codes and signs are to be readily consumed by the media-literate audience, Anderson is keen to exploit the popular form.

The title of this paper, "perfect moments, immaculately framed" is taken from an article by Suzanne Scott on the choreographer Lea Anderson and her two companies, The Cholmondeleys and The Featherstonehaughs. It attempts to locate the popularity of Anderson's work in its fashionable appeal and her use of television as a medium to present dance. Scott states,

> Maybe the reason Anderson's work stands up so well on television is that it allows her to improve on a reality which sometimes lets her down. In its televised form, Birthday was retitled Perfect Moment - and isn't that what television is really about, perfect moments immaculately framed and taken beyond the limitations of real time and real space into the realm of pure image.
>
> Scott, 1993

Contemporary society, which is often referred to as postmodernist or late capitalist, has also been characterised as the society of the spectacle or the media age. The two-dimensional images of television, film, billboard advertising, computers, magazines, and newspapers saturate daily life and serve as a type of collage which constructs an artificial reality or represented world (Chambers, 1986).

Jean Baudrillard (in Docherty,1993) describes the image as a sign, or simulation, which exists at a point between the real and the imaginary, yet due to its unlimited pervasiveness there is a danger that its pretence of reality becomes more real than the real. One of the most dominant forms of image reproduction is the ubiquitous television set through which our network of communication increasingly operates. Unlike high art, the images and events of television are not unique artifacts, but may be rapidly distributed through a series of electronic circuits. Notions of uniqueness, permanence and artist's subjectivity give way to transience, multiplicity and anonymity. In allowing her work to be simultaneously reproduced thousands of times over, Anderson is placing it in the realms of accessibility and commercialism rather than hierarchy and elitism.

It must be noted that there are other choreographers who use television as a means of making their work more accessible to a wider public, however unlike Anderson they do not necessarily explore the medium in ways which are characteristic of postmodernism. It is this relationship between postmodernism and the television text that forms the focus of this paper. In order to demonstrate various facets of this relationship, the aim is to examine Anderson's television dance piece, <u>Perfect Moment,</u> but firstly it would be useful to consider the television medium in a little more detail.

Initially television was believed to be a `window on the world' which would `relay' everyday events and experiences directly to the television screen without any ideological mediation. Even with fiction based programmes, more traditional television uses such devices as linear narrative, authentic costuming and decor, and cause and effect plots to centre the reader and give her an illusion of the `real world'. A number of theorists have since challenged these notions.

Baudrillard (in Docherty, 1993) asserts that the medium of television immediately dislocates its images from the real as it translates information into a fragmented and packaged commodity. A television programme does not simply consist of pointing a camera at an event and then recording it, but is a complex process of selecting, re-ordering and editing images and so the event is inevitably transformed.

It has been suggested that television is a postmodern medium in itself (Connor, 1989, Kaplan, 1988). The fleeting images are rapidly recycled and reassembled thus negating notions of authorship, and unlike more traditional high art activities, the viewer has an interactive relationship with the television medium by way of the remote control. The cultural theorist, Angela McRobbie (in Appignanesi, 1986) asserts that contemporary television refers less to the `real world' and increasingly to its own network of media images. Umberto Eco (Jameson, 1991) has characterised this as `Neo TV' which takes itself and its participants as its own subject. Television watching therefore becomes a network of self referential images which no longer involves the presence of the `outside world'.

It has also been suggested that some television no longer even attempts to create an illusion of reality. Steve Connor (1989) refers to a type of postmodern television which, "freely acknowledges the play of the visual signifier, making no pretence to be transmitting the `real'" (p156). Through the use of postmodern devices such as fragmentation, heterogeneity and open-ended meaning, a de-centred and unstable reader position is produced. Although it must be recognised that the work of Lea Anderson is an artistic product, and does not purport to be a `window on the world', it is possible to see how the postmodern disarticulation of reality is manifest in Perfect Moment.

The piece was created for television in 1992 and is loosely based on a social gathering and the preparations for it. Perfect Moment begins with a close-up shot of a piece of red silk skimming across a gravel stone surface. In more conventional modes of film and television the opening image tends to be an `establishing shot' which gives the reader a sense of where the action is situated and attempts to set the mood of the piece. In Perfect Moment the following shot does reveal the red silk to be part of a magnificent ball gown that Anderson is wearing which trails on the gravel surface of a yard and alleyway which she is walking along, yet the reader is given no additional information to suggest why she is in this particular location wearing a sumptuous gown.

The action then jumps to a close-up of a male dancer who is obviously in a studio setting. Seconds later Anderson appears in the background, still dressed in the ball gown, yet the viewer is given no idea as to how she passed from one location to the other, and there is nothing to suggest any relationship between the two except that Anderson appears in both. This sense of incoherence, continues throughout the work which radically shifts from one location to the next. Unlike more traditional forms of television which use a linear narrative, Perfect Moment uses an aleatory form. This discontinuous and fragmented structure is typical of postmodern television, and is suited to the anti-narrative nature of her work.

At one point the women dance in the yard in petticoats and boots, whilst moments later they perform on a bed of sand dressed in rubber wetsuits. Likewise, in one instance the men stride confidently across the yard in `Gaultier-inspired' kilts, and in another they are found curled up beneath the women's ballgowns. These radical shifts are representative of the way in which television allows for discontinuity within short spaces of time through the choice of channels and the presence of commercial breaks.

Not only does this fragmented form take place across the work but also within individual frames such as the opening shot of Perfect Moment when Anderson is walking down the alleyway. The juxtaposition of the opulent red gown, her shaved art school hairstyle and the everyday urban setting creates a collage effect which is jarring to the eye. The incongruity of the elements perhaps reflects the diversity of styles and images that can be seen as symptomatic of the postmodern condition.

Whereas in formalist dance the performers are designed to be `abstract bodies' in motion, in Perfect Moment the dancers adopt a number of guises or personas, yet they are not `characters' in a traditional sense. They do not display individual personalities that the spectator may sympathise with or relate to and at any one time, several of the performers sport the same `look' which perhaps highlights the postmodern death of the subject.

On one level Perfect Moment makes numerous references to the `real world', yet the use of fragmentation and incoherent signifiers tend to displace the work from any sense of reality. For example, the use of radical juxtaposition which creates images such as the pairs of dancers who kiss in wetsuits, serves to de-centre the reader. The individual signs, i.e. the kiss and the wetsuit, are clearly recognisable from everyday life, but by placing them in bizarre and unusual contexts `reality' becomes disordered and chaotic. What makes Perfect Moment so typical of postmodern television is that fleeting images of the `real world' are portrayed, but they are fragmented and eclectic.

Although the previous examples clearly reflect some of the ways in which the image operates in postmodern television many of these devices may also be used in live performance. I now want to look at some of the devices that Anderson uses to create images which may only be achieved through the television medium.

The close-up image is a filmic device which operates to a number of effects in Perfect Moment. In more traditional art forms there is a clear hierarchy between the various elements that make up the work. For instance in ballet, the music and dance are considered to be the most privileged elements, whereas decor, costume and lighting are less important and function mainly to enhance the dance spectacle. Perfect Moment is far less hierarchical; the design of the costumes or the `look' of the work are as significant as the dance content, so the close-up is often used to draw attention to one of these elements.

During the `bathroom scene' a number of the cosmetic activities are filmed at close range. This type of camera work is highly appropriate for Anderson's choreography which draws attention to elaborate detail, yet the reader becomes somewhat disorientated as her viewing of the dance is so highly manipulated. Whereas in live stage work the spectator is considered to be an autonomous subject who may freely view any area of the stage the close-up camera work in Perfect Moment creates a fragmented viewing. Although the reader is able to see the sense of preparation and ritual in the `bathroom scene' through this attention to detail, the body parts appear almost dislocated; there is no sense of a whole overview of the body, but fragments which appear in no apparent order. At one moment three couples play with each other's hair, followed by a close-up shot of a pair of hands. The spectator has no idea of who the hands belong to, what the rest of the body is doing in relation to them, and how this fits in to the overall motif.

Anderson uses camera trickery and special effects for a variety of purposes in Perfect Moment . The `bathroom scene' begins as if the reader is looking through a window masked in condensation. The hot steamy look ties in with the bathroom theme whilst it is also another example of how Anderson gives privilege to all of the components in her work. The movement can barely be seen and instead significance is given to the aesthetic effect of the steamy image. This device is also employed with the frosted glass, the fragments of mirror and the water that appears to stream in front of the camera.

It has been suggested that in postmodern society the multiplicity of two-dimensional images that construct the present results in a type of flattening or sense of depthlessness. Ian Chambers (1986), a theorist of popular culture, asserts that the very nature of image reproduction constructs a superficial front through its artificiality and seriality. Whereas some dance practitioners are concerned with motion and travelling through space, Anderson displays a predilection for static shape, the space around the body and tableau images. This creates a sense of two-dimensionality, and as several critics have noted, her choreography translates well to the television medium (Fisher,1993, Scott,1993).

In the final section of Perfect Moment it is possible to see some of the ways in which Anderson highlights the two-dimensional image. In some instances she creates a picture frame effect as seen with the strips of neon light, the fragments of glass or the border of painted brushstrokes which surround the dancers. Another example is her use of the top shot in which the camera is placed overhead. The upright television screen then constitutes a canvas and as the dancers move or roll across the floor they become a type of malleable design.

At several points throughout Perfect Moment Anderson uses a still shot, as seen with the final image, or a `freeze frame', in which the dancers are captured in stillness. This temporal breakdown adds to the sense of fragmented reality which is typical of this work. Through the use of slow motion or `freeze-frames', the dancers are no longer moving within the confines of `real time', but instead through an artificially constructed time. The result is an interrupted flow of images. This device of using `still images' also ties in with notion of "perfect moments, immaculately framed" (Scott, 1993). The image has obviously been highly constructed by Anderson and the director, Margaret Williams, to their specification, and by `halting' the image the reader is given an opportunity to contemplate a single moment. More conventional modes of television tend to rely on moving images and so this device could be said to alter the perspective with which the reader watches television. In some ways by drawing attention to these highly stylised moments, Anderson is allowing the reader to contemplate a single image in the way that a spectator regards a painting.

This final image, in which the dancers appear to be both suspended in mid-air and flattened against the screen, could not be achieved in live performance. Throughout the work, Anderson has persistently exposed television as a technological operation, and the images that she has created could not be achieved outside of it. Unlike the traditional linear narrative, the ending of Perfect Moment is not a resolution or a denouement. Instead it is almost like a summary of the whole work reflected in the collection of dancers and costumes presented, displayed and `immaculately framed'.

Bibliography

Appignanesi, L.(ed) Postmodernism: ICA Documents 4 London: ICA, 1986

Burnside, F.   British Spring Load in Dance Theatre Journal Vol 8 No 1 Summer 1990, p15

Chambers, I.   Popular culture: the metropolitan experience London: Methuen, 1986

Connor, S.   Postmodernist culture Oxford: Blackwell, 1989

Docherty, T.   Postmodernism: a reader Hemel Hempstead: Harvester Wheatsheaf, 1993

Fisher, M.   Base instincts in The List No 190, 12-25 March, 1993

Jameson, F.   Postmodernism or The cultural logic of late capitalism London: Verso, 1991

Kaplan, EA. (ed)   Postmodernism and its discontents London: Verso, 1988

Newman, B.   Lea Anderson of The Cholmondeleys in The Dancing Times Vol LXXVIII No 926, November 1987, pp130-132

Scott, A.   All the right moves in The Sunday Times 14 March 1993

TAXONOMIES OF DANCE AND POWERS OF EXCLUSION: THE CASE OF JAZZ DANCE

Mo Dodson and Terry Monaghan
London Guildhall University

Although the case of 'jazz dance' is rich in examples of exclusion, we want to concentrate initially on the most obvious of these exclusions—that based on racism. Exclusion here should be taken in its wider sense to include not only forms of physical and economic exclusion, but also those forms of exclusion that operate at the level of cognition. In this essay we will make use of the notion of 'oral culture', recently made popular by Walter J. Ong, but of course typically employed by anthropologists and ethnologists implicitly in their studies of so-called 'primitive, non-literate' societies.

The racism that we are particularly concerned with operates at the border between the oral cultures of European and African Americans, especially music and dance cultures. From at least the Eighteenth Century there were cross-border influences, imitations, parodies, fusions between white and black music and dance—although in using the terms white and black we are ignoring extremely important complexities of ethnic reality, including not only the wide variety of American Indian cultures, but also the range of different cultures that are subsumed under the rubric of 'black and white'. The white performer in black face is perhaps the most obvious example of this cross-border activity, and this black and white minstrelsy became one of the most popular forms of entertainment in the Western hemisphere for nearly a century, from Thomas Rice to Al Jolson. Al Jolson's world-wide popularity still demands an explanation, and it seems incredible that his popularity was not deemed at the time of sufficient political incorrectness to require a sustained commentary regarding its eccentricity. The depressingly obvious conclusion is that it was not eccentric.

One of the dilemmas facing historians of American popular and oral culture is the decision that they are forcefully invited to make about their own ethical and political position on this cross-border or cross-over activity between dominant and subordinate cultural groups in America, with 'black' and 'white' being the main terms in this debate: is the cross-over justifiable in terms of a fusion rationale, or does it represent cultural theft on the part of whites, and ideological submission on the part of African Americans (often by default, as in the case of the use of European languages)?

This dilemma is particularly acute in the case of the historiography of jazz music and dance. The term jazz is itself intensely debated and fought over by historians and practitioners: should it refer, for example, to non-theatrical dance only? If applicable to theatrical dance, should it be used to cover theatrical dance that does not use jazz music? What indeed is jazz music? (see Stearns 1959, 1968, L. Jones 1963: Hazzard-Gordon 1983; Crosby 1993; Jones, IV 1995).

This issue intersects with the related one of the transition of jazz dance from a participant, oral cultural form (the term 'social' is often confusingly applied to this type of dance, even though it may often have a ritual, religious or ceremonial function) to a spectacular, theatrical and commercial form. Quirey and Holmes (1971), Howe (1988), Crosby (1993) and Dodson (1989; 1990) have all argued that changing the context of performance from one of ontological objectification to that of theatrical image-making radically alters the form and meaning of the dance (in Benveniste's terms, the enunciation determines that which is enounced) and the experience of the dancers. Finnegan (1992) has discussed various ways in which audience participation can be incorporated into performance studies, and Grau (1994) has analysed in detail the way in which the context of performance of a ritual dance not only determined the particular meanings of a particular performance, but also the ways in which this performance helped to construct and rearrange social relations. Blacking has argued a similar position in a variety of contexts (eg 1976; 1977).

The transition from extreme participation or orality (though the two terms are by no means synonymous in all contexts) to the extreme of commercial theatre as practised in the modern metropolis is often long and subtle. African Americans who danced in a vernacular participant form were always aware of the potential for more spectacular forms, but these dancers rarely seem to have completely cut themselves off from their oral roots. The ability to articulate one's being in a public space/place that was socially impregnated, through a dance that was both proprioceptively profound as well as theatrically effective was one that most African American dancers seemed to possess as integral to their dance competence. As the dances of African Americans were taken up by the white commercial theatre, subtle changes occurred. Fred Astaire's imitations of a black 'class' dancer incorporate ironic imitations of the class dancer's perceived display of an elegant sensuality/sexuality, as well as the display of dancing skills. The irony of Astaire is not only necessary to distance a civilised white upper middle class male from the indignity of a public display of a physical movement skill that seems far too close to a public display of sexuality; the irony is also necessary because no white upper middle class male would have the opportunity to display this degree of dancing skill within the normal parameters of his culture. Astaire is bursting the boundaries of existential possibility. That he is doing so is constantly signalled by his facial expression of fixedly goofy, wry self-mockery, and his constant return, after sudden, seemingly impulsive descents into subtly awkward imitations of the black class dancers' flexible back and flexed joints moving playfully around the swinging rhythms of the music, to an erect posture regarded by Europeans as essential to the physical expression of dignity and political freedom (the Greek 'orthos' refers to this erect posture (Sennet 1994, p.49-50)). Astaire's film performances are remarkable in the skill with which they imitate the black class dancers' ability to skirt near the edge of animality without ever falling into it—a display that is already heavily ironic for the black dancer, as he knows that his white audience will expect this kind of animality from him, but will also want to be reassured that it is not really out of control—while at the same time asserting that he (Astaire) in fact is quite distant from this type of undignified display of physical pleasure. Astaire is aided in this distancing project by the obvious intent to produce a theatrically effective visual image that takes precedence over the ontological experience and articulation of the dance.

Astaire's subtle and sometimes not so subtle imitations of black dancers' supposedly uninhibited display of physical release leads in one direction to the problem of the way we perceive and think about reality through racial and ethnic stereotyping, and the way jazz music and dance has been and is used by white American culture to act as a signifier of libidinal and emotional release from the repressive forces of European 'civilisation'.

One of the most popular media presentations of jazz dance and music occurs in a cartoon film by Walt Disney: *The Jungle Book* made in 1967. In a scene set in a ruined Indian palace, a group of monkeys led by an orangutan—King Louis—plays, sings and dances jazz while they try to persuade the boy, Mowgli, to give them the secret of fire. King Louis explains, by means of lyrics in the song, that he wants fire so that he can be a 'man' like Mowgli: "I wanna be man like you." At the end of this scene, the bear, Baloo—who is supposed to be protecting Mowgli—attempts to infiltrate the band of apes by wearing a disguise that gives his sharp snout a more rounded monkey-face appearance with two halves of a coconut. He dances and sings jazz, authentically, it seems, and to the obvious delight and approval of the apes until his disguise accidentally falls off, and he is recognised as an interloper.

To us, this scene indicates that the film-makers were operating within implicitly racist assumptions about African-Americans. The initial references in themselves seem clear enough to us: King Louis the Monkey equals Louis Armstrong; Baloo the Bear equals Bing Crosby; Mowgli the Boy equals innocent (white) normality. The scene itself reminds us of, among other things, the film *High Society* in which Bing Crosby and Louis Armstrong perform jazz music together. The way in which both Bing Crosby (the Bear) and the boy (Mowgli) succumb to the rhythmic seductiveness of the jazz music by dancing while still regarding the players of the music with some suspicion is reminiscent of the entire history of popular music and dance in America, from blackface entertainer in the black and white minstrel shows, to the present. The reference to blackface in *The Jungle Book* scene is also clear to us in the disguise that the Bear wears in order to infiltrate the monkey gang. Further references that appear obvious to us are mapped over the previous references, so that: King Louis also equals gangland boss (working class) and Baloo also equals relaxed Beatnik/artist (middle class). This conflation of class with race is important to our next point which is a not uncommon one to make in this context: American and European cultures, according to a number of commentators, mark off binary distinctions between Repression and Libidinal Release; between Super Ego and Id, between Order and Chaos; between Law and Anarchy; between Regulated Normality and Unregulated Carnival; between normative plaisir and liberating jouissance; between deferred gratification and self-indulgent excess; between Culture and Nature, Mind and Body, Civilized and Savage. These binary distinctions that describe 'abstract' modes of consciousness and being are, it is said, mapped over groups of people. Thus white people, middle-class people or men become Mind, Culture, Super Ego, Law, Repression etc. Black people, working class people or women become Body, Id, Anarchy, Nature etc. In other words, groups at the wrong end of the power relation are identified with Nature, Instinct etc. Richard Dyer in *Only Entertainment* (1992, p.6) coins the term 'unruly delight' to describe the kind of uninhibited anarchic pleasure that seems to characterise certain types of 'popular culture', which, by implication, are consumed or practised typically by people in subordinate social positions.

Dyer rejects, however, a too-simple acceptance of even a Bakhtinian celebration of the carnivalesque, as for him that would ignore the socially constructed nature of this type of pleasure. This is in spite of the fact of the apparent ability of this kind of pleasure to liberate us from the socially constructed and to open the door to an ecstatic world free of ideology and free of a pseudo-unified-identity that attempts to impose a false ontological unity on the creatively schizophrenic potentiality of human existence —a world where delight explodes the boundaries of ideological repression and constriction. Dyer's caution is wise. The supposedly simple and child-like pleasure of dancing and playing jazz, apparently analogous to other biological pleasures that seem merely to require the dropping of all social or cultural codes, an unstructured free-fall into pure pleasure, is obviously not an accurate picture. That even social jazz dancing requires culturally acquired skills of a very high order is self-evident to anyone who attempts it. And yet the scene from *The Jungle Book* seems to suggest that jazz works by seducing us into dropping our cultural inhibitions and enabling us to descend into a more natural/ animal world. If this cartoon is racist, then the racism will operate not through any simple referencing, but rather by stimulating the audience into accepting these binary identifications between Culture and Whiteness and Nature and Blackness. These oppositions in turn will allow us to experience a sense of release as we succumb to the carnivalesque anarchy of the apes as they stump and flip-flop across a world that knows no dignity nor tragedy; a world where all activity is ridiculously enjoyable and enjoyably ridiculous. The punch-line here is of course the way in which this identity between Blackness and Nature and between Blackness and Animal Pleasure at once justifies the racist treatment of African Americans (in the way the cartoon portrays them as not really fully human); and also disguises the fact that this human tragedy is enacted daily (the film conveys an idea that all Black people are incapable of dignity and tragedy; in fact they go through life laughing and dancing and singing, no matter what their problems and pains, provoking from whites the response: "Gosh, I wish I could be as carefree as that! But then again, who wants to be a full-time clown?"). For a discussion of these structured binary oppositions see Anthony Wilden's *Man and Woman, War and Peace.*

This labelling of one of the most important cultural developments of the 20th century—African American popular dance and music—as primitive, instinctual, and perhaps illicitly sexual is both common, more common than many of us imagine, and yet glossed over. Rudolf Laban reveals explicitly an extreme form of racism when he writes, in *A Life for Dance*:

> They say that the white American dances Negro dances, but this is a mistaken idea. In fact, the steps are all of old-English origin and were subsequently imitated by the Negro and heightened into a virtuoso-grotesque style. The Negro has a tremendous feeling for rhythm and an inherited mobility which he has preserved from the memories, still fresh in his mind, of his ancestors' daily physical struggle with the forces of nature, and which he has brought to the northern urban life. I doubt whether the Negro is capable of inventing any dance at all. If one hopes to find any kind of Negro dance culture here, one is in for a big disappointment. A gift for dance invention as well as the higher development of the other arts and sciences seems to be the privilege of other races. The Negro adopts our dance-inventions just as he adopts our stand-up collars and top hat, and uses them grotesquely, remodelled to fit his own feelings. Where music is concerned he seems to possess an inborn talent, but only for rhythmic melodic, unsophisticated expression. The fact that the white race has re-adopted distortions for its own dances only shows the lack of taste of the robot-age, and is not a sign of a complete dearth of original ideas.
>
> Laban, 1975, p.134

Although any such quotation suffers from being isolated from its context, the mere fact of it being said at a particular moment, by someone whose influence on dance education has been so enormous, requires comment. Rather than evidence of a particular and isolated case of racial prejudice, this quotation seems to us to indicate the opposite— a much more generalized and pervasive racial prejudice among the European/American cultural elite that emerges often when least expected. In *The Modern Dance* (1936), John Martin wrote:

> The insistent thump, thump, thump of the miserable type of jazz which is dispensed by the neighbour's radio for a considerable number of hours a day must give him some pleasure though it seriously offends the tastes of the more cultivated, and is in no sense significant from an aesthetic point of view. It is built upon two rhythm bases—silence and accent— which alternate with unfailing regularity at a tempo just in excess of the normal blood pulse. The effect is hypnotic in a marked degree, and psychological in that it tends to increase the blood pulse and it produces thereby a fast stimulation. This hypnotic effect of elementary rhythm persisted and over a period of time was well known to primitive man and was used deliberately by him in the production of frenzy and licentiousness.
>
> Martin, 1936, p.40

Martin was not always so crude in his labelling of African American culture, and a few pages earlier he writes:

> Indeed the Negro musical style which we know as "blues" has had an influence outside the bounds of its own field, and the Negro form of the ubiquitous clog dance ranks as the finest development of this almost universal folk manifestation outside Spain. In the "blues" there is to be seen the germ of a creative art, as opposed to an art merely of amusement, a slave art
>
> Martin, 1936, pp.35-36

We assume that Martin is here continuing in the classical European tradition of distinguishing between the 'liberal arts' (the intellectual skills that only free citizens are capable of) and the 'mechanical arts' (the non-intellectual skills characteristic of slaves and non-citizens). This categorising of jazz music and dance as primitive, instinctual, licentious etc can be found in a variety of forms throughout the literature available. Cecil Sharp in, for instance, *The Dance* (1924 p.32) uses phrases like 'merciless tom-tom rhythm' and 'vibratory shakings of the shoulders' to describe what he called the Jazz.

Eric Hobsbawm, the eminent historian, writing under the name of Francis Newton (*Jazz Scene* 1959), takes the argument to a level that some jazz musicians and dancers have approved of: he distinguishes between popular commercial jazz music, made to dance to, and more serious jazz music made to listen to. This is essentially the distinction between Art and Entertainment, or between Fine Art (spectacular) and Popular Art (participant or quasi-participant), or, arguably, that between a Literate Culture and an Oral Culture. To approve of this categorization is to succumb to the binary oppositions that distinguish Nature from Culture, Id from Super Ego, while trying to open the hatch to some elements of the Id so that they may climb up into the Super Ego, from Entertainment or Folk Culture into High Culture.

Roger Taylor in *Art, an Enemy of the People* (1978) attempts a subtle if controversial explanation of the binary opposites deployed by both whites and African Americans in their use and practice of jazz music and dance. For Taylor, jazz was born at the interface between white power and African American attempts to deal with this power. Although the details of Taylor's analysis often slip into potentially controversial judgements, the main thrust of the method illuminates the ironies and double and triple meanings of African American culture. White culture needed, according to Taylor, not only a concept of the contemptible Negro, but also a concept of the 'orgiastic', which it imposed on aspects of African American culture. In order to survive, African Americans often deferred to these definitions of their secular music and dance as orgiastic, while working in their own meanings. The question is then, how much of the meaning of this culture is determined by white expectations? And what meaning should we attach to the notion of 'orgiastic'?

We would like to suggest a way out of this problem that still acknowledges the implicit racisms of these categories. Certain types of oral culture seem to be highly resilient in the face of general historical changes. 'Oral' dance and song are particularly notable for their resilience (Czekanowska, 1994). The reasons for this resilience are, I would suggest, two-fold: first the immense importance of oral communication to human health and happiness; and, second, the probability of a strong genetic determination of oral communication competences, as in Chomsky's positing of an inherited deep grammar for language. A recently published work on language posits a number of other human 'instincts', including the instinct to categorize the living world according to certain basic criteria—animal, plant etc. (Pinker 1995, p.420).

Pinker does not refer to music or dance in his list of possible human (or species-specific) instincts, but the late John Blacking did posit an instinct for music and dance, equivalent to that posited by Chomsky for speech (Blacking 1976). Blacking proposed that the hominid precursors to homo sapiens practised proto-music and dance, and that this practice had at least three important evolutionary consequences:

— the development of language
— the development of the ability to think within the parameters of truth, mercy, pity and justice
— the development of eye-hand coordination

> The important common denominator is how people's bodies respond to such situations, rather than the supposed mental gymnastics by which the same concepts (mercy, pity, truth, justice) may have been arrived at in different societies and cultures. If society is seen as a system of active forces in which every body is highly sensitive to other people's feelings, then mercy, pity, truth and justice can be understood as distinct feelings...so thinking may come from movement, and, especially, shared, or conceptual, thought from communal movement...essentially (inspiration) is a form of unconscious cerebration, a movement of the body. We are moved into thinking. Body and mind are one.
>
> Blacking, 1977, p.21-23

Blacking is here positing a relationship between the collective structures of dance and music, embodied literally as well as in conceptually analysable structures, and the processes of thinking within codes that are both collective and individually creative within that collectivity. The call and response, the mutuality, that music and dance embody can be found perhaps at the base both of our social and linguistic competences, starting with the primary word of I-Thou of Buber and leading out to a wider collectivity embodied in the deep grammars of language and the social discourses of culture.

If we can entertain this notion of an inherited instinct or competence for music and dance (a competence in socio-sensuous communication that verges on the cognitive in unique ways), then the 'seductiveness' of African American music and dance loses some of its susceptibility to being interpreted in the stark agonistics of contemporary cultural studies' analyses. This oral cultural practice would not just be attractive because of its position within a set of cultural oppositions between sexual release and repression, mind and body, clean and dirty and so on. No doubt music and dance can be used to articulate such oppositions, and any rhythmical movement in a culture that has associated any such activity with a forbidden sexuality will automatically tend to evoke ideologically loaded notions of sensual and sexual release. The appeal of African American music and dance could then, on the other hand, be partly attributed to its ability to preserve much of the highly sophisticated oral cultural traditions (strongly grounded in genetic tendencies) of its African originals, not to mention the other oral traditions it absorbed from both indigenous aboriginal cultures and European immigrant cultures. These oral traditions could therefore be said to satisfy profoundly human instinctual drives towards a sophisticated communality that is based on the somatic ground of our being—our bodies in relation to each other, and the genetic blueprint that determines the nature of our bodies.

The difficult fact remains, however, that two of the most popular entertainers in the history of European culture have been white men who performed in 'blackface' in theatrical contexts that at the best must be regarded as ambiguously racist—Thomas Rice and Al Jolson. It is this difficult fact that perhaps partly explains why those who have lived through the jazz age, and those who have tried to study the jazz age, find it in turn so difficult to arrive at an agreed taxonomy of what jazz music and dance is. (Crosby 1993; Jones, IV 1995; Boross 1994; Hazzard-Gordon 1983; Stearns 1959; Jones 1948; Siegenfeld 1990).

Bibliography

Blacking, J. (1976) 'Dance, Conceptual Thought and Production in the Archaeological Record ' in Sieveking, G. de G. *Problems in Social and Economic Archaeology* London: Duckworth

Blacking, J. (1977) 'Towards an Anthropology of the Body' in Blacking, J. (ed) *The Anthropology of the Body* SAS Monograph No.20 London Academic Press pp.1-28

Buckland, T. (1989) 'The Tunstead Mill Nutters of Rossendale, Lancashire' in *Folk Musical Journal* 5(2):pp.132-149

Chambers, I. (1986) *Popular Culture* London: Routledge

Courlander, H. (1963) *Negro Folk Music* New York: Crown Publishers

Crosby, J.F. (1993) *Will the Real Jazz Dance Please Stand Up* (Doctoral thesis for Columbia University)

Czekanowska, A. (1994) 'John Blacking's work as perceived by Polish ethnomusicologists (unpublished paper)

Dodson, M. (1989) 'European Social Dance' in *Edinburgh Review* 82, pp.136-138

Dodson, M. (1990) 'European Theatrical Dance' in *Edinburgh Review* 86, pp.154-56

Dodson, M. (forthcoming 1995/6) 'Taste and Virtue or the Virtue of Taste' in J. Palmer and M. Dodson (eds) *Design and Aesthetics* London: Routledge

Dyer, R. (1992) *Only Entertainment* London: Routledge

Emery, L.F. (1988) *Black Dance from 1619 to Today* London: Dance Books

Ewen, D. (1961) *The Story of America's Musical Theater* USA: Chilton Company

Featherstone, M. et al (1991) *The Body, Social Process and Cultural Theory*

Finnigan, R. (1992) *Oral Traditions and the Verbal Arts* London: Routledge

Grau, A. (1994 unpublished paper) 'Dance as part of the infrastructure of social life'

Hazzard-Gordon,K. (1983) 'Afro-American core culture social dance: an examination of four aspects of meaning' in *Dance Research Journal* 15/2 pp. 21-26 (Spring 1983)

Herskovits, M.J. (1941) *The Myth of the Negro Past* Boston: Beacon Press

Howe, M.(1988) *Shades of the Dancing English* London: Terrace Trust

Jones, IV, J.T. (1995) 'Racism and Jazz' in *Jazz Times* March 1995, pp.53-59

Jones, L.(1963) *Blues People: Negro Music in White America* New York: Morrow Quill Paperbacks

Laban, R. (1975) *A Life for Dance: Reminiscences with Drawings* London: MacDonald and Evans (translation of *Ein Leben fur den Tanz* (1935 Dresden) by Lisa Ullman)

Martin, J. (1936) *America Dancing*

Mathews, J. (1994, unpublished) 'All That Jazz' paper delivered for History Workshop Research Seminar

Newton, F. (1959) *Jazz Scene* ('Newton' is E. Hobsbawm) London: Penguin

Ong, W.J. (1982) *Orality and Literacy* London and New York: Methuen

Pinker, S. (1995) *The Language Instinct* London: Penguin Books

Quirey, B. and Holmes, M. 'An Apology for History' *Dancing Times* 1969-1971

Sennet, R. (1994) *Flesh and Stone* London and Boston: Faber and Faber

Sharp, C. (1924) *The Dance* London: Halton and Truscott Smith Limited

Siegenfeld,B.(1990) 'If Jazz Dance then Jazz Music' in *Dance Teacher Now* October 1990 pp.50-53

Stearns, M. and J.(1994) *Jazz Dance: The Story of American Vernacular Dance* New York: Da Capo Press (originally 1964)

Stearns, M. (1959) 'Is Modern Jazz Dance Hopelessly Square' in *Dance Magazine* June 1959, pp.30-35

Taylor, R. (1978) *Art: An Enemy of the People* U.K.: Harvester Press Limited

Wilden, A. (1987) *Man and Woman, War and Peace* London: Routledge and Kegan Paul

Harder, Faster, Longer, Higher -- A Postmortem Inquiry into the Ballerina's Making
Susan Leigh Foster

Here she is, a consummate embodiment of feminine ideals; a perfect blending of delicate beauty, athletic vitality, and youthful grace. Vulnerable, she exposes throat, armpit, and crotch. Yielding, she overflows into the eerily supple arch of the foot and the equally aberrant curve of the neck. Controlling, she directs the shapes of arms, legs, torso, and head. Desiring, she strains to surpass the bounds of her joints' flexibility. Costumed in a child-like leotard that emphasizes her absolute skinniness, no breasts, no belly, no voluptuousness of flesh anywhere, the geometry of her form nonetheless suggests maturity. The horizontal plane achieved by her head, the degree of angle between the legs, the straightness of the arms, with their flared, stiff fingers, the matter-of-fact expectancy of the gaze -- all suggest a professional, even rational competence. Yet the fact of such a precarious balance, achieved through the momentum of torso arching back against leg lifting up, both with such intensity that the body almost seems to turn itself inside out, conveys transcendence. She moves in ecstasy to eclipse the formal choreographic goals that guide her performance. And she accomplishes all this for us. Charged with the wantings of our many eyes, she emblazons herself in space and draws us beguilingly towards that space.

Although in this photo she appears dancing her way through the streets of New York City, as if her magical presence will revivify the city's economy through a revitalized circulation of cultural capital, she has made equally compelling appearances around the world. We have seen her wrapped differently for her roles in Swan Lake, Jewels, The Ballet of the Red Guard, center stage in the repertories of the National Ballets of Canada, Taiwan, South Africa, Cuba, the Philippines, Australia, Mexico, Brazil, Argentina. (Paloma Herrera, pictured here, immigrated to New York City from Buenos Aires.)..At times the ballerina replicates into a dozen or more sororal figures, the corps de ballet, who, although clearly inferior, aspire to dazzle the audience as she does. At times the ballerina is accompanied by a male suitor who presents her to the audience, supporting, manipulating, adoring her every movement. Yet his body does not incandesce as hers does. His manly achievements -- jumps, turns, beats -- extend but do not defy the physically possible. Her body is uniquely capable of such effortless effervescence. Her body alone houses the distortions that transform labor into effortless gesture, fleshly curves into geometric ideals, and chronic pain into transcendent joy. Her body specifically stands as the synthesis of cultural difference and a world-wide language of the heart and the senses.

A global phenomenon, today's ballet, performed live and circulated on video, has set standards of virtuoso accomplishment with which all dancers must reckon. Its pedagogical orderliness and clear criteria for excellence promise a homogenizing medium for the expression of cultural difference. Rather than expand on the issues of colonization raised by ballet's international sweep, I want here to focus on the training procedures through which that most charismatic of all balletic spectacle, the ballerina, is constructed. For, if ballet asserts an ideal physicality, it equally purveys a distinct image of the feminine around the world. The icon of the ballerina competes with the superstar images of women in film, music, and sports industries as one of the estimable forms that femininity may take. The conflation of all dance with ballet and with the feminine evident in the proliferation of paraphernalia celebrating the ballerina -- dolls, charms, trinkets, birthday cake decorations, and Christmas tree ornaments -- invests femininity with an adorable inconsequentiality. Thousands of young girls become infatuated each year with the ballerina's incomparable prettiness, and in their efforts to approximate her grace, learn to judge their bodies as irredeemably inadequate.

A powerful cultural practice, ballet builds bodies that are distinctly gendered, a claim that has been explored in the kinesiological literature on dance,[1] in biographical and auto-biographical accounts of dancers' lives,[2] and in feminist criticism by Cynthia Novack, Ann Daly, and Janet Wolff, among others.[3] Novack and Wolff, in particular, have delineated the contradictory possibilities offered up by ballet that may allow viewers to separate the gendered "messages" of the performance from the choreographic and dancerly skills through which that content is conveyed. In what follows I want to re-travel some of the territory they explore in an effort to locate additional sources of ballet's magnetic contradictoriness. I am in search of a theory of ballet's charisma that brings together the effects of training practices with dancers' and viewers' experiences of performance.

Ballet training, while it may consist initially of weekly or twice-weekly lessons, soon becomes for the serious student an every day, several hours a day commitment. Embedded at every turn in the training process are reminders that ballet is superior to all other forms of dance. Its formal and geometric concerns are thought to embody a universal aesthetics. Its choreographic elaboration of physical flexibility, strength, and plasticity exceeds the expression of grace in any other physical endeavor. Most important, it requires a degree of technical competence unparalleled in any other form. To fail at ballet is to fail at all dance. Other traditions that train the body for other aesthetic purposes do not provide alternatives but instead rank far beneath ballet as inferior systems of training. Claiming itself as supreme instantiation of dancerly competence, ballet offers <u>the</u> system capable of producing the consummate dancer

Yet this competence must be hard won for, once engaged in serious training, the ballet student begins to incur several kinds of corporeal injuries. These include meniscal dislocations, patellar fractures, ligamentous tears, muscle strains, blisters, bursitis, tendonitis, arthritis, sprains, fractures, fascitis, osteochondroses, bunions, discogenic back pain, spondylolysis, sciatica, snapping hip syndrome, delayed menarche, amenorrhea, decreased bone density, anemia, hypoglycemia, ketonuria, hypokalemia, and shin splints. Most of these physical traumas result from relentless repetition over long periods of time of exercises designed to instill in the body ballet's aesthetic ideals. Unlike the sudden and quixotic tears, bruises, or breaks that occur when the body mistakenly collides with other bodies or objects, these injuries emerge as the registering of the incompatibility between an aesthetic ideal and a physical real. Not the product of mistaken judgment or a sudden failing of strength or flexibility, these injuries are explained as resulting from over-zealous practice, bodily ineptitude, or a misunderstanding-understanding of the training system.[4] Ballet training itself is never the problem, yet, no-one in ballet dances injury free.

Aspiring ballerinas must not only excel in the training that enables them to perform the repertoire, but they must also cultivate and maintain a specific physical appearance. In order to achieve a more desirable physique, female dancers may undertake surgeries to enhance the size of the lips, the curvature of the arch, or to remove unwanted cellulite tissue. In order to maintain their sub-standard weight, stipulated as part of the contracts in many ballet companies, they engage in intentional dehydration, laxative abuse, self-induced vomiting, and extended fasting. A large number of dancers are bulimic, hurling themselves regularly into cycles of bingeing and vomiting because of the proscriptions against eating necessary to sustain their skinniness. Many verge on anorexia, and many teenagers training seriously for ballet fall into anorexic patterns that require medical assistance.

The dancer's willingness to risk injury, endure pain, and monitor her weight is rationalized by ballet's claim to superiority as a training program and performance tradition. But this claim achieves its persuasiveness through the cycles of defeat and conquest, pain and transcendence, fright and exhilaration, regimentation and dedication that classes, recitals, auditions, advancements, and competitions provide. Each of these occasions for testing a dancer's skills establishes the dancer's own agency in the artistic project. She endures paralyzing pre-performance anxiety in order to display incomparable agility; she plunges into social isolation in order to become the center of attention; she spends years in the back of the class in order to move to the front; she suffers months of physical therapy in order to make a triumphant comeback; she perseveres in the face of vicious competition in order to be proclaimed the best. Throughout her career, she supplies the determination necessary to succeed at the same time that she dedicates herself and her actions to a higher good, that of serving the Terpsichorean tradition.

Nowhere is this complexity of subjectivity rendered more vividly than in the dancer's relationship with her own mirror image.[5] For well over a century, ballet instruction has relied heavily on the mirror to calibrate the dancer's proprioceptive sense of moving with the visual appearance of that movement. The mirror-body shows the dancer discrepancies between how the movement feels and how it looks. At the same time, it represents the audience, showing in reverse image what viewers would see if the dance class were a performance. The mirror thereby transforms muscular sensation into visual symbolization tied to the palpable experience of being looked at and appraised.

Overtime, the supervised repetition of exercises in front of the mirror closes the gap between the felt-body and the mirror-body, but as the dancer comes to know the mirror-body as her own, she comes to loathe it. Only rarely does the student note out of the corner of her eye some aspect of the mirror-body that realizes the desired appearance. Most often, the body in the mirror is abjectly deficient, hideously disappointing, calling forth a need stoically to endure its despicable inadequacies. The mirror-body in the accuracy of its visual rendition of the dancing-body assumes authority to judge the dancer. It is not a mere passive reflection, but instead, an active enunciator of physical deficiencies.

Like the photograph, the mirror-body exudes an effect of the real, so much so that the dancer comes to coexist-exist with her image as though it were a partner, a body the dancer dances with. It greets her very morning as she comes into the studio for class and dances just in front of her throughout the day. Although the mirror-studio is populated with many other mirror-bodies, the dancer regards only her own image. For information about other dancers' deficiencies and accomplishments, the dancer consults their bodies not their images. The mirror-body is the private, although entirely public, projection of each individual dancer.

Very little in this relationship between dancer and mirror-image corresponds with Narcissus' predicament. The ballerina like Narcissus is fascinated with her own image, yet where he sees an image to desire, the ballerina sees an image she hates.[6] And where his concerns with his image revolve around its ephemerality and loss, hers invest the mirror-body with powerfully contradictory and authoritative responsibilities: private yet public, the mirror-body is both the dancer and the audience; it judges her in its reflection of her; it stands for everything about her yet only shows her visual attributes; it is both her own reflection but also her partner, and both the real and its representation.

Little wonder that many dancers have difficulty adjusting to on-stage rehearsals and performances where the mirror-body on which they have come to depend is absent. The stage, however, substitutes a whole new intensity of scopophilic gratification in the opportunity it affords to be viewed by many live bodies rather than one reflective body. Here, in the most concentrated structuring of visual consumption, the ballerina binds together and folds into each movement the most spectacular of contradictory images, replicating the mirror-body's enigmas and the training process itself on a grandiose scale: Beauty and athleticism, rationality and physicality, all combine in her masterful gesturings. Substantiality and ephemerality, hereness and vanishing, are performed in every shift of weight. A perpetual mutating of form, she attracts, invites, beckons and then disappears. In her, the chaos of body transmutes into geometric form. The years of bodily disciplining have refigured fleshly curves and masses as lines and circles. Pythagorean perfection displays itself at both core and surface. Bodily shapes present one stunning design after another, notable for their silhouette and also for the interiorized configuration of lines running parallel to the skeleton around which the musculature is wrapped. Via this geometry her movements turn mess into symbol.[7]

Yet, in order to achieve this agglutination of physicality and abstraction, the ballerina must violate the sanctity of the body's limits. She must push, bend, and sometimes rupture muscular and skeletal capacities for bodily shape and coordination. She must mold and align the flesh around the abstract linear core of the torso and each limb. She must also emaciate her body so as to achieve the desired balance between the corporeal and the conceptual. She must learn to do more and more -- harder sequences, faster steps, longer balances, higher legs -- with less and less body.

Success at turning the unruly, inert, and stupid body into disciplined geometry unfolds as a process that dissolves pain into a range of painful sensations, each with a distinct texture and dynamic. The dancer comes to know these feelings so intimately that they, like the mirror body, define the contours of self. She pushes into and past these painful sensations in order to restructure bodily limits. Each wrangling with muscular resistance, each coaxing of ligamentous tissue stages an encounter with what physicality has come to be. The tedium of the dancer's repeated engagements with these limits contrasts with the euphoria that occurs when she suddenly discovers that they have expanded. Each small augmentation in the repertoire of the harder, faster, longer, or higher produces exhilaration, whatever the muscle's high-pitched protest, the bone's resonant aching.

Eventually, the body's anguished responses give way to moments of clarity and lightness where corporeal capacity coincides momentarily with movement's form. Here, where the full extension of body into pose is achieved, the dancer's body reverberates with a deathlike stillness. In Paloma Herrera's pose we witness the death of the body. We see stasis, the perfect giving over of physical vitality to formal purity. We feel the body arrested at the end of its fullest effort. We hear the silence of the state where the body has fused with geometry. We apprehend the entire ten-year process that has given the body over to death through the careful transformation of fleshly reality into abstract ideal.

And then, miraculously, the dancing body revivifies. The live body extricates itself from positionedness and moves on towards the next stasis. The dancer's facial features and hands suddenly flicker in a way that animates the anorexic structure of her body and brings geometry back towards personality. The energy necessary to mobilize limbs into and through their linear coordinates surges momentarily into prominence only to deliver them into their next lifelessness. Ballet, a celebration of this dance with death, alternates between the fixedness of the body's designs and the momentum of the physicality necessary to motivate the body through those designs. And this resuscitation of physical vitality only to convey it into abstraction constitutes the final kind of violence that ballet levels at the body, the ultimate perversion of physical significance which the training process performs on the body.

Where in this landscape of sacrifice and accomplishment can the ballerina's gratification be located? Surely, it must come from more than the gaze of an adoring public, and from more than mastery over such unstable property as bodily virtuosity. Does she feel an erotic charge in the violation of bodily limits? in the consignment of the body to/the retrieval of the body from death?[8] Does she revel in the suffering that comes from being bound up in a tradition of bodily training?[9] Do the reiterations of overcoming the insurmountable suffice to keep her at it?[10] Does the persistent denial of the flesh, or the company of mirrors provide solace? Are the tiny accomplishments in every dance class sufficient reward?

The kinesiological literature generated thus far on the violence sustained by the ballerina throughout her career casts her in one of two roles: she figures either as the hapless victim of a ruthless aesthetic system, or as the uninformed, but diligent student who lacks only the modicum of nutritional and anatomical knowledge that would enable her to adjust perfectly to ballet's demands. What I have tried to choreograph here does not reject nor does it praise unquestioningly the ballet's aesthetic goals. I do not wish to speak <u>for</u> the ballerina as though the poor, deceived creature lacked the analytic skills necessary to apprehend her own victimization. Nor do I aspire to blast ballet as the sadistic site of feminine spectacle. What I hope this text may catalyze is a more critical engagement in ballet by audiences, who will no longer indulge unreflexively in their own viewing pleasures, by mothers, who will think twice and three times about what their daughters are doing at their weekly ballet classes, and by ballerinas, who may allow themselves to imagine choreographing their own desires. This multi-bodied response, as dense as the ballerina's signifiability, might just move ballet towards a more three-dimensional exchange between the bodies that watch it and those who dance it.[11]

NOTES

---

1 See, for example, Marian Horosko and Judith Kupersmith's The Dancer's Survival Manual (New York: Harper and Row, 1987); Allan Ryan and Robert Stephens' The Healthy Dancer (Princeton: Princeton Book Publishers, 1989) and their The Dancer's Complete Guide to Healthcare and a Long Career (Princeton: Princeton Book Publishers, 1988); Daniel Arnheim's Dance Injuries (Saint Louis: C.V. Mosby, 1975); L.M. Vincent's The Dancer's Book of Health (Princeton: Princeton Book Publishers, 1988) and his Competing with the Sylph (Kansas City: Andrews and MeMeel, 1979); Priscilla Clarkson and Margaret Skrinar, eds. The Science of Dance Training (Champaign, Ill.: Human Kientics Books, 1988); and Ruth Colomon, Sandra Minton, and John Solomon, eds. Preventing Dance Injuries (Reston, VA: American alliance for Health, Physical Education, Recreation and Dance, 1990).

2 These include among others Toni Bentley's Winter Season (New York: Vintage Books, 1982); Gelsey Kirland and G. Lawrence's Dancing on My Grave (Garden City: Doubleday, 1986); and Suzanne Gordon's Off Balance (New York: McGraw-Hill, 1983).

3 See Ann Daly's "The Balanchine Woman: Of Hummingbirds and Channel Swimmers" The Drama Review, Vol. 31 (1) (Spring 1987) 8-21; Cynthia Novack's Sharing the Dance (Madison: University of wisconsin Press, 1990) and her "Ballet, Gender, and Cultural Power" in Dance, Gender, and Culture, Helen Thomas, ed. (London: Macmillan Press, 1993) pp. 34-48; and Janet Wolff's Aesthetics and the Sociology of Art (London: George Allen and Unwin, 1983).

4 Misinterpretation of the training system is occasionally attributed to the teacher whose role in the training process is unfortunately neglected here. I hope to expand on the teacher's influence on the creation of the dancer's subjectivity in a subsequent essay.

5 In the analysis of the function of the mirror in dance that follows, I am moving alongside a Lacanian interpretation while also attempting to indicate the substantial complexities that the dancer's specific relationship to the mirror entails. Following Lacan one could argue that the mirror enhances the dancer's access to the realm of the symbolic articulated not through words but rather through the formal vocabulary of positions and steps elaborated in ballet training. Such an analysis would provide an important correlation between structured movement systems such as ballet and linguistic systems more typically associated with the symbolic. The mirror's actions as explored in this essay encompass not only the function of transiting the dancer into the symbolic but also into the conjectured evaluations of a collective of viewers who embody certain standards for aesthetic judgement.

6 Narcissus' predicament is complicated by Julia Kristeva through her proposal that Narcissus' mistake was simply not to recognize that the mirror image was not another person and by her equation of the image with the mother. See Tales of Love (New York: Columbia University Press, 1987) pp. 103-121. Neither of these notions seems to apply to the dance student's experience of the mirror-body. However, Kristeva does suggest that the spring into which Narcissus stares, even though maternal is like a partner. p. 113 She also emphasizes one of the important aspects of the dancer's experience in alledging that "Actually, Narcissus is not completely without object. The object of Narcissus is psychic space; it is representation itself, fantasy." p. 116.

7 Elsewhere I have argued that the fusion of flesh and geometry create a phallic identity for the ballerina which secures her magnetic appeal for male and female heterosexual viewers as well as homosexual male viewers. See "The Ballerina's Phallic Pointe" in Corporealities, Susan L. Foster, ed. (London: Routledge, 1995).

8 To answer this question in the affirmative follows from Georges Bataille's theorization of the relationship of transgression to eroticism and death. Bataille imbues any violation of boundaries with an erotic charge, and he further argues that sexual activity and death are the ultimate violations of the taboo stipulated within nature to continue living: "If we view the primary taboos as the refusal laid down by the individual to co-operate with nature regarded as a squandering of living energy and an orgy of annihilation we can no longer differentiate between death and sexuality. Sexuality and death are simply the culminating points of the holiday, nature celebrates, with the inexhaustible multitude of living beings, both of them signifying the boundless wastage of nature's resources as opposed to the urge to live on characteristic of every living creature." Erotism: Death and Sensuality. [1957] trans. Mary Dalwood. (San Francisco: City Lights Books, 1986) p. 61.

9To answer this question in the affirmative would entail an elaboration of masochistic involvement on the part of theballerina with ballet. Yet the roles of sadist and masochist as typically defined fall short of the complex subjectivity that ballet training creates. Foucault suggests a more viable framework for sado-masochism, one which may help to explain specifically the gay male interest in ballet when he observes: S & M is not a relationship between he (or she) who suffers and he (or she) who inflicts suffering, but between the master and the one on whom he exercises his mastery. What interests the practitioners of S & M is that the relationship is at the same time regulated and open. It resembles a chess game in the sense that one can win and the other lose. The master can lose in the S & M game if he finds he is unable to respond to the needs and trials of his victim. Conversely, the servant can lose if he fails to meet or can't stand meeting the challenge thrown at him by the master. This mixture of rules and openness has the effect of intensifying sexual relations by introducing a perpetual novelty, a perpetual tension and a perpetual uncertainty which the simple consummation of the act lacks. The idea is also to make use of every part of the body as a sexual instrument." Michel Foucault: Politics, Philosophy, Culture Lawrence D. Kritzman, ed. (New York: Routledge, 1988) p. 299. I can imagine various ways in which the performances of both male and female dancers onstage could be seen by gay male viewers as resonant with the evidence of a training process that conforms to Foucault's sketch of the S & M scene. I can also imagine the performance itself as setting up the possibility of viewing relations that introduce "a perpetual novelty, a perpetual tnesion, and a perpetual uncertainty." I am not sure, however, that the training process itself sets up this notion of an S & M encounter.

10 Overcoming the unsurmountable while denying the fleshly is consonant with both Puritan and Christian belief systems. The congruity between religious sacrifice and ballet trianing has been noted by many including Agnes De Mille: "The forces which impelled women to the austerity of the church operate to form the great dancer. In a strange transmutation dancing is a form of asceticism -- almost a form of celibacy." And Promenade Home (New York: Atlantic, Hill, Brown, 1956).

11 For their poly-vocal imput into these essay, I wish to thank Susan Rose and Marta Savigilano.

MODERNIST VALUES AND HISTORICAL NEGLECT:
THE CASE OF TORTOLA VALENCIA

Iris Garland
Simon Fraser University

One of the consequences of postmodern cultural theory is the consideration of voices that have been marginalized or silenced in the development of our disciplinary canons. In this presentation I will suggest one such example in the period of early modern dance, traditionally dominated by American dance pioneers, Loie Fuller, Isadora Duncan, and Ruth St. Denis. The early modern dance canon has privileged innovation and novelty, while artistry within the same genre has been devalued as imitation. Initially dismissed as imitators, Maud Allan and Gertrude Hoffman have begun to interest dance scholars but nowhere in the critical literature can one find the name of Tórtola València, a Spanish dancer born in Seville, who was an early exponent of what was then called the "classic" style. Touted variously as "The First Dancer of the Latin Race", "The Barefoot Dancer", "The Dancer of the Hypnotic Eyes", "The Queen of the Latin Dancers", "The Muse of the Poets", "Dancer of the Historical Intuition" and "The Rodin of the Dance", Tórtola València was hailed in the press as one of the famous dancers of Europe in a league with Karsavina, Pavlova, Duncan, and Maud Allan.[1] In her Catalan monograph Peypoch claims:

> Together with Isadora Duncan and the fabulous Anna Pavlova, she was an equal; absolutely comparable to Pavlova and superior to Duncan. Tórtola was considered with them as the three best dancers in the world, each with their own style, they were incomparably the best.[2]

Tórtola València was a solo dancer, who had a prodigious career between 1908 and 1930. Like her contemporaries Duncan, Allan, and St. Denis, she was self-taught, began her career in the varieties, interpreted the great music of classical composers, researched the themes of ancient cultures in museums and literature, inspired the work of numerous poets, painters, and intellectuals, and lived a very colorful life as an independent woman. The press coverage during her European and Latin American tours was enormous, and she was critically acclaimed wherever she appeared. Yet, she has been virtually neglected in dance scholarship. Why?

I propose that this neglect is due to factors in the constructs of early modern dance history which has utilized limited source material and ethnocentric bias. Further, I will examine the boundaries of Modernism in Spain and Latin America versus Northern Europe and North America to explain the success and longevity of Tórtola València's career.

Tórtola was not the first early modern dancer in her genre, but she was second to none in achieving a long, critically acclaimed, and financially rewarding career. Her publicity photographs, the titles of some of her dances, and her musical selections bear a distinct similarity to works of other choreographers of that era, such as Allan, Fokine, Duncan, and St. Denis. Titles of her dances include: *Danza Arabe, La Bayadera, La Bacanal, La Rosa, La Maja, Danza del Incienso, El Cisne, La Serpiente,* and *Salome.* Her dances were described as having a sensual tone and a religious sensibility, demonstrating a profound analysis and extraordinary intuition for capturing all the details of each theme she undertook.[3] She received numerous tributes not only from newspaper critics, but the intellectuals, poets, and artists of her day, such as Maurice Maeterlinck:

> Tórtola València is the expression of the most pure art that I have seen in
> my life. The great heroines of Greece have been resuscitated from mys-
> tery and have passed before my eyes.[4]

Over 200 poems were dedicated to her, including those by the great South Ameri-
can poet Rubén Darío, and Spanish literary giants, Ramón Valle-Inclán, and Pio Baroja.[5]
She was painted by well-known Spanish artists including Chicharro, Anselmo Miguel
Nieto, Zuloaga and Penagos.[6]

It is incomprehensible that the collected writings of well known dance writers of
her time such as Levinson and Van Vechten do not include her, nor is she mentioned in
general dance history texts such as Jowitt, Kirstein, McDonagh, Martin or the biographies of her contemporaries. Tórtola València has fallen through the cracks of history,
without even a footnote to acknowledge a triumphant career.

The chroniclers of modern dance history have been mostly American. There may
be unintentional but nevertheless ethnocentric tendencies to ignore artists who did not
significantly contribute to the development of modern dance in the United States. In
Kurtz's study of dance history curricula and texts in the United States, it is clear that
there is a hegemonic emphasis on North American modern dance artists.[7] It is true that
Germany is represented by Rudolf Laban and Mary Wigman as part of the canon, but
they have been influential in the U.S. through immigrants such as Hanya Holm, who set
up a school and a company in the early 1930's in New York. American writers of dance
books beginning with John Martin have staked a claim on the birth of modern dance as
an American phenomenon.[8] Much of the German material is either untranslated or
inaccessible, although Huxley indicates that the latter situation is changing.[9] Is it mere
coincidence that there is a direct correspondence between the nationality of the dance
writers and the dance artists who are said to have defined the period? There is a dearth
of Spanish dance writing about early modern dance, and the little that does exist is well
hidden, untranslated, and not widely distributed outside of Spain.

However, historical ethnocentric bias is only one possible factor in Tórtola's obscurity. I posit that Tórtola València's association with the mass culture venues in
Northern Europe was significant in her neglect as a serious artist. After her debut as a
Spanish dancer in London (1908) in George Edwardes' musical *Havana,* Tórtola successfully toured her solo "oriental" dances to many of the same European music halls
as Ruth St. Denis and Maud Allan.[10] She also appeared in the Munich productions of
Max Reinhardt (*Kismet* and *Orpheus in the Underworld*, 1912), as well as *Sumurum* by
Sacha Guitry which played Paris and London in 1912. However, these were the "musical comedies" and the "Varieties", hardly the venues of "high" art that Modernism
extolled. Huyssen, outlining his core of the modernist aesthetic, describes the Modernist stance as a separation of the "modernist" work from the sphere of mass culture:

> Only by fortifying its boundaries, by maintaining its punty and autonomy,
> and by avoiding any contamination with mass culture and with the signi-
> fying systems of everyday life can the art work maintain its adversary
> stance: ...adversary to mass culture and entertainment which are seen
> as the primary forms of bourgeois cultural articulation.[11]

St. Denis is not likely to have achieved her place in dance history had she stayed
in Europe on the music-hall circuit, rather than becoming a progenitor for Graham,
Humphrey and Weidman and their long line of succession. Duncan refused to perform
in the music-hall "varieties", and achieved her success in Europe as a solo concert
artist.[12] Weinzweig claims that La Argentina (Antonia Merce), a contemporary of Tórtola's
who theatricalized Flamenco dances on the music-hall circuit, did not achieve success

until she was discovered and promoted by the renowned critic, Andre Levinson, and "dissociated herself from...the Gypsies of the music-hall."[13] In German music-halls one was likely to encounter "song and dance to comedians, acrobats, snake-charmers, magicians and—after the British model—groups of women performers known as 'sisters'."[14] Lloyd describes the influence of "exoticism" prevalent in these performances on the German Brücke artists, who frequented the music-halls in search of source material to transform into their "higher art".

> In May 1912 the 'Indian' dancer Roshanava, daughter of an English colonial official, was appearing at the Eispalast in Berlin; she was followed in June by Tórtola Valéncia, 'a new Egyptian dancer who is presently enjoying huge success on the European stage'. In August 'the Egyptian snake dancer All'Aida' made her debut. It was this kind of act that inspired Ludwig von Hoffman's *Exotic Dance*, illustrated in Kunst und Kunstler in 1908....

None of these dancers' names rings a bell today, and all are lost in the limbo of entertainers for the mass culture. Elaborating on the role of these exotic performers, Lloyd cites Tórtola as an example:

> A photograph of the famous Tórtola Valéncia on a donkey in Hyde Park which appeared in the BIZ in July 1912, show how these dancers, just like non-European natives, were seen to occupy a mediating zone between the primitive and the modern: in this case she appears in a collage of photographs between 'King David of Uganda, the ruler of the powerful Central African Empire who is presently on a tour of Europe' and the Austrian military traitor, Colonel Redl.[15]

It wasn't until Tórtola debuted in Spain in 1911, that she achieved a solo concert status, due to a crusade by Spanish poets, writers, and artists, and thus came into her own as a serious artist. Her return to her native country as an established, acclaimed dancer in Europe is all the more fascinating because her birth origins have been shrouded in mystery.

Her birth certificate states she was born Carmen Tórtola Valéncia, in Seville, June 18, 1882, to Llorenc Tórtola Ferrer, Catalan; and Georgina Valéncia Valenzuela, Andalucian.[16] However, there have been intimations of an illegitimate birth, possibly involving a Spanish nobleman and at other times an Englishman. Tórtola claimed her mother was a Spanish gypsy and her father was a Spanish grandee.[17] She spoke five languages: English, French, German, Italian, and Spanish; all with an accent which compounded the cloud of doubt surrounding the authenticity of her origins. On her arrival in Madrid in 1911, she spoke Spanish poorly.[18] Her evasiveness about family manifests itself in this statement of Tórtola's: "I have nobody, not in Seville, not in London, not anywhere."[19]

An amateur biographer, Odelot Solrac, states that she was placed in the foster care of a wealthy British antique collector in Kensington when she was ten to twelve years of age, and never saw her parents again.[20] Various statements Tórtola gave to the press alter the time frame that she emigrated to England, and her previous dancing experience.[21] However, she never wavered in her claim that she never studied any dance techniques.

Tórtola's debut in Madrid on Dec. 2, 1911, was by all accounts a disaster. Her program included her "oriental" numbers, including *Danza del Incienso* and *Danza Arabe*. The Teatro Romeo was a venue for mass entertainment and a lamentable cabaret style gypsy flamenco dancer and musician performed between her numbers.[22] Accustomed to more vulgar forms of dancing and bull fights, the audience did not comprehend her *Danza del Incienso*.[23] The audience was so boisterous and unappreciative that police had to be stationed in the wings.[24] A few young Spanish intellectuals, artists, and writers were present in the theatre, and Tórtola was championed in the press by these "literati", who saw the value of her aesthetic presentation. Tomás Borrás wrote:

> But an intelligent minority, a group of artists and literary men, soon saw in the dancer, a unique, exceptional artist, and every night fought [with the philistines], and at last the intellectuals triumphed. Today the [philistines] contemplate with an amazing respect the work of the Sevillian, without arriving at understanding. But they applaud.[25]

Not satisfied with taming the unruly masses on Tórtola's behalf, these same young men wished to lure the upper class Madrilenians to see and appreciate her artistry. Spearheaded by the writer Federico García Sanchiz, the group of young artists and writers arranged a special solo concert performance on Dec. 15, 1911, under the sponsorship of the Academy of Fine Arts, the Circle of Fine Arts, the Ateneo of Madrid, and the Association of Writers and Artists.[26] The Ateneo was the *"crème de la crème"* academy of respected artists in Madrid. A select audience was invited from the cultured classes, who under normal circumstances would not attend the Teatro Romeo, and they included "beautiful and elegant ladies, and a notable representation of 'literati', artists and politicians".[27] Tórtola performed *Danza* (Chopin), *Danza del Incienso* (Bucalossi), and *Danza Arabe* (Tchaikowsky). A quartet played musical interludes of Bach, Haydn, Beethoven, and a suite of classical Spanish music between the dances; a format that Tórtola would continue in all of her future solo concert performances throughout Spain and Latin America. Initially, there was great resistance to sponsorship of the event by conservative elements in the Ateneo, who objected to a dancer, especially a varieties dancer and a woman, being included in their select circle; but again, the young artists and writers prevailed. The concert was a triumph for Tórtola. Afterwards a dinner in Tórtola's honour was given by twelve or fourteen of the "literati", including the renowned Jacinto Benavente, Ramón Valle-Inclán, and Pio Baroja. In all of her tours she made contacts with the poets, "literati", intellectuals, and artists in each city she performed. Fortified by the many tributes she received in the press from important Spanish intellectuals and artists in Madrid, she had an impressive "press-kit" which she used as credentials on her travels to other parts of Spain and to Latin America.

Why were these "literati" and artists so impressed with Tórtola's dancing that they elevated her from the Varieties to the prestigious Circle of Fine Arts and honored her as an equal at the Ateneo? I suggest that the explanation lies in the unique character of Spanish Modernism or "Modernismo", which flourished in Spain between 1875-1916, or upwards to 1932, according to some authors.[28] "Modernism" in Spain had different emphases than in the rest of Europe and North America. Although there are many strands, in Northern Europe and North America the "Modernist" project can be said to be "abstraction", beginning with Cubism. The preoccupation with exoticism was considered as the death throes of *fin-de-siècle* Symbolism and devalued by 1912. However, in Spain and Latin America "Modernismo" is synonymous with what Diez-Canado has termed "the influence of the return".[29] A return to the roots of civilization in "oriental" lands was a counter current to the rapid technological advances of the time in which Western civilization was believed to have lost contact with the knowledge based in the instincts and powers of the spirit; it was a back lash against "positivism" and rationalism, and paradoxically, a manifestation of the scientific work of Darwin and the discoveries of archaeologists.[30] Poets and literati, such as Ramón Valle-

Inclán, Jacinto Benavente, and Rubén Darío, who is credited with introducing "Modernismo" to Spain from South America, were among those who evoked the roots of past civilizations, mysticism, and idealization of "Woman". While these themes had been mined by the Romantics and Symbolists of Northern Europe, Spain, never having had a proper Enlightenment (bourgeois revolution), or Romanticism (critique of the bourgeois), embraced these ideas much later under the rubric of "Modernismo".[31] Tórtola embodied the primal essence of the female archetype situated in the lost civilizations celebrated by the Hispanic "modernistas".[32] Valle-Inclán's Mexican Sonnets are an example:

> In these ruins of palaces, of pyramids and of gigantic temples...I have seen for the first time a singular woman, an Indian servant.... She is a bronzed beauty, exotic, with the strange grace and undulation of the nomadic races, a figure hieratic and serpentine...with the double charm of priestliness and voluptuousness.[33]

Compare this with excerpts of Valle-Inclán's poem to: "Tórtola València":

> She has the graceful walk of a feline
> it is filled with profound eroticism...
> ...and coiled in her luxurious serpent's breast
> a sense of the Sacred....[34]

or his statement quoted in Tórtola's Programme notes:

> Tórtola València is a sublime harmony and the greatest living poem of all the mythologies and religions.[35]

Tórtola's successful career flourished in the Hispanic countries after 1914 until 1930, and the Modernistas had paved the way for her acceptance as a solo concert artist.[36] Except for a brief New York engagement with Ziegfield in 1917, where she had a mixed reception, she did not tour North America.[37]

During this time period "Spanish Dancing" was all the rage in European and North American popular entertainment. Spain was considered part of the exotic "other", and Spanish dance meant flamenco, castanets, boleros, seguidillas, and fandangos. Tórtola València never studied these dance forms, preferring instead to interpret the "soul of Spain" in her Spanish numbers.

Contributing factors in her descent into obscurity outside of Spain are that she never formed a company or a school, and did not leave a legacy of her techniques to be passed on to future generations. However, she made a vivid impression on those who were fortunate enough to have seen her dance, and a choreography prize in her name (Premio Tórtola València) has been established in Catalonia for the best new choreographic creation of the year.

Notes

1.   "The Sustained Rage for Dancing: The Principal Interpreters of Russian, Moorish, Classical, and Spanish Dancing", *The Tatler,* No 539. London, Oct. 25, 1911; "Dos Famosas Bailarinas: Tórtola València y Anna Pavlowa", *Nuevo Mundo: Revista Popular Illustrada.* Ano XXII: Num. 1.352. [Mexico City], Dec 5, 1919; *Die Noche,* No. 52,

Berlin, 1911 or 12 (date unclear), and various other clippings in the Tórtola València Archive, Centre d'Investigacío, Documentacío i Difusío (referred to hereafter as: CIDD), Barcelona, España.

2.   Irene Peypoch, *Tórtola València,* Gent Nostra. #30, Ed. Nou Art Thor, Barcelona: 1984, p. 3.

3.   *Ibid*, p. 7.

4.   Quoted in *La Provincia* [Lima, Peru], Nov. 2, 1929, and various other clippings in the Tórtola València Archive, CIDD, Barcelona, España.

5.   *Los Poetas a Tórtola València.* Vol. I and II: unpublished bound xeroxed collection. CIDD. Barcelona, Spain, 1952.

6.   Frances Fontbona and Luis Antonio de Vellena."Tórtola València en Su Mundo Artistico," *Una Aproximacion al Arte Frivolo: Tórtola València/Jose de Zamora.* [traduccion del Catalan al Español, Juan Carlos Mas], Coor. Andres Pelaez y Femanda Anclura. Comunidad de Madrid/Consejeria de Cultura. (Exposicion Catalag, Teatro Albeniz.) 1988-89.

7.   Sandra Kurtz, "The State of the Art: Current Practices in Teaching Dance History." *Proceedings Society of Dance History Scholars.* Brigham Young University, Provo, Utah, Feb. 1994, pp. 113-118.

8.   John Martin, *The Modern Dance.* N.Y.: Dance Horizons, 1933, 1965.

9.   Michael Huxley, "European early modern dance", in Janet Adshead-Lansdale and June Layson (ed.), *Dance History: An Introduction.* London: Routledge, 1983, 1994, p. 153.

10.   See Suzanne Shelton, *Divine Dancer: A Biography of Ruth St. Denis.* Garden City, NY: Doubleday, 1981; Felix Cherniavsky, *The Salome Dancer: The Life and Times of Maud Allan.* Toronto: McClelland & Stewart, Inc., 1991; Tórtola València Archive clippings (CIDD), Barcelona, España.

11.   Andreas Huyssen, "Mass Culture as Woman". *After the Great Divide: Modernism, Mass Culture, Postmoderism.* Bloomington: Indiana University Press, 1986, p. 54.

12.   Amy Koritz, "Dancing the Orient for England: Maud Allan's The Vision of Salome", *Theatre Journal,* 46, 1994, p. 66.

13.   Meira Weinzweig, "A 'Heart of Darkness' in the New World: Carmen Amaya's Flamenco Dance in South American Vaudeville". *Proceedings of Dance History Scholars, Fourteenth Annual Conference.* Miami, Fla., 1991, p. 182. See also, André Levinson, "Argentina", *Theatre Arts Monthly,* Oct. 1928, excerpted in Joan Acocella and Lynn Garafola (ed.), *André Levinson on Dance: Writings From Paris in the Twenties,* Hanover & London: University Press of New England, 1991, p. 96.

14.   Jill Lloyd, "Urban Exoticism in the Cabaret and Circus". *German Expressionism: Primitivism and Modernity.* New Haven, Ct: Yale University Press, 1991, p. 87, 88.

15. *Ibid*, p. 90, 91.

16. Peypoch, *op. cit*, p. 1.

17. Interview, *The Morning Leader,* [London], Apr. 26, 1912.

18. Federico García Sanchiz, *La Noche,* [Madrid], Dec. 7, 1911; ("Tórtola casi ni sabe hablar el castellano.")

19. *España Libre,* [Madrid], Dec. 6, 1911. "No tengo á nadie, ní en Sevilla, ní en Londres, ní en ninguna parte...."

20. Solrac, Odelot, *Tórtola València and Her Times.* New York: Vantage Press, 1982, pp. 1, 16.

21. Federico García Sanchiz, *loc. cit*; (Tórtola, seduced by an aristocrat, emigrated to London at age 14); Solrac, *The Life and Times of Tórtola València*, states she never danced before auditioning for 'Havana' in 1908 at age 26; however, in an interview with Emilio G. de Bustillo in *El Noticiero Universal,* Barcelona, Sept. 1917, Tórtola says she started dancing when she was very young and danced in public for the first time at age 16.

22. Tomás Borrás, "El arte de la danza: Tórtola València", *España Nueva,* [Madrid], Dec. 14, 1911.

23. *Ibid.*

24. García Sanchiz, *loc. cit.*

25. Borrás, *loc cit.* ("Pero una minoría intelligente, un grupo de artistas y literatos, pronto vió en la bailarina una artista única, excepcional, y todas las noches se daba la batalla de la que al fin salieron triunfantes los intelectuales. Cuanto á los 'serranos' ontemplan hoy con un respetuosoa somboro el trabajo de la sevillana, sin llegar á comprender. Pero aplauden.")

26. *Teatro Romea Programa*, Dec. 15, 1911. Tórtola València Archive, CIDD, Barcelona, España. ("a petición de la Academía de Bellas Artes, del Circulo de Bellas Artes, del Ateneo de Madrid, y de la associacíon de Escitores y Artistas.")

27. *El liberal*, [Madrid], Dec. 16, 1911. ("Bellas y elegantes damas, y un notable concurso de literatos, artistas y politicos, formaba el público.")

28. See Litvak, Lily, *El Modernismo,* Edición de Lily Litvak, Madrid: Taurus Ediciones, 1991; an anthology of authors who place the dates variously.

29. Diez-Canado, Enrique, "Rubén Darío, Juan Ramón Jimenez y los comienzos del modernismo en España." in Litvak, *Ibid*, p. 216.

30. Litvak, Lily, "A La Búsqueda De Los Orígines, El Rencuentro De Las Civilizaciones Asiásticas en España (1870-1913), *España 1900: Modernismo, Anarquismo, y Fin de Siglo*, Barcelona: España, Anthropos, 1990, p. 201.

31.   Paz, Octavio, "Traduccion y Metafora", in Litvak, *El Moderismo, op. cit,* pp. 100-102.

32.   Litvak, *España 1900: Modernismo, Anarquismo, y Fin de Siglo, op. cit,* p. 246.

33.   Valle-Inclán, Ramón, "Sonata de estío", quoted in Lily Litvak, "Tematica De La Decadencia En La Literatura Española De Fines Del Siglo XIX: 1880-1913", *Ibid,* p. 249.

34.   Valle-Inclán, Ramón, "Tórtola València", *Los Poetas a Tórtola València.* Vol. II: fol. 141, No. 12.747, unpublished bound xeroxed collection CIDD; Barcelona, España. ("Tiene al andar la gracia del felino; es toda llena de profundos eros...y enroscada en sus senos la serpiente, decora la lujuria de un sentido, Sagrado...")

35.   Programmes (1916-1930), Tórtola València Archive, CIDD, Barcelona, España.

36.   See Schulman, Yván A., "Reflexiones en torno a la definición del modernismo", in Litvak, *El Moderismo, op. cit,* pp. 90-92. (citing Marlo Vargas Llosa as an example, Schulman states: "the [Latin] American modernismo, with its baroque past, is prolonged and its ascendency is perceived farther than the temporal limits of its period of major flowering.") Tórtola toured Latin America with great success during 1916, 1918, 1921-25, and 1930.

37.   Her appearance in Ziegfield and Dillingham's *Miss 1917* as a "Spanish dancer" with comedians, soubrettes, ballroom dancers, and chorus girls was not an appropriate vehicle for her talents, but she performed a special matinee solo program of her "oriental" numbers that was well received by the critics; Tórtola València Archive clippings, CIDD, Barcelona, España.

Bibliography

Acocella, Joan and Lynn Garafola (ed.), *André Levinson on Dance: Writings From Paris in the Twenties,* Hanover & London: University Press of New England, 1991.

Cherniavsky, Felix. *The Salome Dancer: The Life and Times of Maud Allan.* Toronto: McClelland & Stewart, Inc., 1991.

Fontbona, Frances and Luis Antonio de Vellena. *Una Aproximacion al Arte Frivolo: Tórtola València/Jose de Zamora.* [traduccion del Catalan al Español, Juan Carlos Mas], Coor. Andres Pelaez y Femanda Anclura. Comunidad de Madrid/Consejeria de Cultura. (Exposicion Catalag, Teatro Albeniz.) 1988-89.

Huxley, Michael. "European early modern dance", in Janet Adshead-Lansdale and June Layson (ed.), *Dance History: An Introduction.* London: Routledge, 1983, 1994.

Huyssen, Andreas. "Mass Culture as Woman". *After the Great Divide: Modernism, Mass Culture, Postmoderism.* Bloomington: Indiana University Press, 1986.

Lloyd, Jill. "Urban Exoticism in the Cabaret and Circus". *German Expressionism: Primitivism and Modernity.* New Haven, Ct: Yale University Press, 1991.

Koritz, Amy. "Dancing the Orient for England: Maud Allan's The Vision of Salome", *Theatre Journal,* 46, 1994.

Kurtz, Sandra. "The State of the Art: Current Practices in Teaching Dance History." *Proceedings Society of Dance History Scholars.* Brigham Young University, Provo, Utah. Feb. 1994.

Litvak, Lily. *El Modernismo.* Madrid: Taurus Ediciones, 1991.

Litvak, Lily. *España 1900: Modernismo, Anarquismo, y Fin de Siglo.* Barcelona: España, Anthropos, 1990.

Los Poetas a Tórtola Valéncia. Vol. I and II: unpublished bound xeroxed collection. CIDD. Barcelona, Spain, 1952.

Martin, John. *The Modern Dance.* N.Y.: Dance Horizons, 1933, 1965.

Peypoch, Irene. *Tórtola Valéncia,* Gent Nostra. #30, Ed. Nou Art Thor, Barcelona: 1984.

Shelton, Suzanne. *Divine Dancer: A Biography of Ruth St. Denis.* Garden City, NY: Doubleday, 1981.

Solrac, Odelot. *Tórtola Valéncia and Her Times.* New York: Vantage Press, 1982.

Weinzweig, Meira. "A 'Heart of Darkness' in the New World: Carmen Amaya's Flamenco Dance in South American Vaudeville". *Proceedings of Dance History Scholars, Fourteenth Annual Conference.* Miami, Fla., 1991.

Tórtola Valéncia Archive, Centre d'Investigacío, Documentacío i Difusío (CIDD). Institut del Teatre. Barcelona, España. [press clippings, programmes, visual material, etc.]

TEXT AND THE DANCING BODY IN THE WORK OF
ROSE ENGLISH AND LAURIE ANDERSON:
THE DIVA OF PERFORMANCE ART AND THE TECHNO ICE-QUEEN

Jools Gilson-Ellis
Dartington College of Arts

This paper is an analysis of the practise of two contemporary women perform-ance artists who use written texts in relation to the dancing body; Rose English and Laurie Anderson. I will be focussing on English's *The Double Wedding* (English; 1991) and Anderson's *Home of the Brave* (Anderson: 1986). My thesis is that the uses of written text in relation to the dancing body, in the practise of these two women, enables their work to develop meanings that are more difficult to articulate within practise that does not question its own disciplinarity. Both of these women are en-gaged in interdisciplinary art practise, although this is importantly different in process and production. I will be seeking to describe the dancing body as an integral part of both these women's practise, and to argue for an analysis of written/spoken text that imbricates the dancing body in verbal discourse, and shifts the range of possible mean-ings.

The Double Wedding is a quest for the double wedding of its own title. It is already a doubling of pairs before the performance begins; a doubling of closures. As a title, it appears simple, direct, and one implicitly expects there to 'be' what it an-nounces. But there is no 'double wedding' beyond the attempt to retrieve it. In re-peated reminiscences, frequently verging on the nostalgic, the cast try to summon some aspect of this originary double wedding, yet everyone remembers it differently, forgets parts, speaks of different versions. The loss of a single coherent, locatable meaning, and the endless hope for its retrieval, has marked some of the most important twentieth century theoretical work. For Derrida such a meaning was the 'transcenden-tal signified', the still figuring of full meaning, and meaning in language was always the antithesis of the achievement of this; endless play, deferral, disruption[1]. For psychoa-nalysis, and for Lacan in particular, the loss of coherent, locatable meaning is a charac-teristic of the psychic subject herself, who is always split, and yearning for the loss of originary oneness (the semiotic/the Real)[2]. In *The Double Wedding*, transparent truth is marked as an illusion, and mirrors this search for identity—which is always incomplete. Truth feigns presence—is a bad actor. English stages *The Double Wedding* as 'theatre,' self-consciously revelling in its conventions of mimesis. By doing so, English places these questions over the nature of meaning within a practise which has a troubled relationship to the real/Real (transparent/objective reality and Lacan's notion of Full Being). Mimesis describes a version of performance which distinguishes the actor from her role/the original from the staged fiction. In *The Double Wedding*, English blurs these distinctions, as well as foregrounding them. In her opening monologue, English prom-ises "To take (us) beyond belief" (English 1991; 3) This is the language of the ringmas-ter whipping up awe; the hyperbole of music hall, but we are already beyond belief—there is no artifice here that does not want to reveal itself as well as seduce us. The slips and starts and forgettings in *The Double Wedding*, are not 'really' so, but are written and rehearsed as this, and only 'pretend' to be 'real,' participate in the conven-tions of theatre at the same time as disturbing them.

The Double Wedding is a performance filled with doubles; there are two hypno-tists, two cameramen, two members of the Fake Adagio, two nebulae, two viscera, and two members of the True Adagio. I am interested here in the parallel pairs that make up the Fake and the True Adagio. English purposely uses the term 'adagio' which refers to a slow, often lyrical dance, usually between a man and a woman, and often including spectacular lifts, as the hinge for her naming of these pairs. The Fake Adagio are involved in endless discussion, about the nature of their dance. At different points, neither of them are quite sure they are even in the show at all. They talk much more about dance than they actually dance. The True Adagio, in contrast, simply present their ice dance. Situated at the finale of the performance, the True Adagio, perform a stunning duet on a circle of ice. This pair are 'really' Olympic ice-skaters; Paul Askham and Sharon Jones, they never speak, are named as 'True,' and, so the implication goes, are somehow originary. The Fake Adagio, in contrast, don't quite make it; they are disruptive, frequently make false starts, get depressed and fail to appear. The irony here is that The Fake Adagio are both 'really' dancers; Nigel Charnock and Wendy Houston. Both Charnock and Houston have worked extensively with DV8[3], and Charnock in particular is well-known both as an accomplished dancer, and for the extremes of physicality in his own work and in his work with DV8.[4] English wryly refers to this when she introduces him within *The Double Wedding* as 'overenthusiastic.' "He is overenthusiastic," she says, "but it is just an act." (English 1991; 5) 'Really,' English suggests, Charnock feigns extreme physicality, it is a frippery, a mask. *Real* exhaustion, *real* risk, the catching of flying bodies, repeated falls; English cunningly places this practice in the realm of theatrical convention, where characters ask each other "Were you really writing then, or pretending to write?" (English 1991:18), and whole casts use glittery pipes they never light.

The following speech is spoken by Charnock at the end of Act One, as English passingly refers to The Fake Adagio as "re-creating the great adage from the original production" (English 1991; 37), in fact half of this adagio (Charnock) is obsessing about dance discourse, whilst his partner (Houston) continually falls asleep;

> ### The Fake Adagio/The Dew
> It's not just that I'm tired of dancing. It's not just that I'm physically tired. It's that I'm mentally exhausted. I've been thinking about dance so much recently that I've worn myself out. I'm tired of talking about dancing. I'm tired of watching dancing. I'm tired of dancing dancing. I'm tired of reading about dancing. I'm tired of listening to dance. I'm tired of anticipating a dance. I'm tired of the after effects of a dance, the residue. I'm tired of the preparation to dance. I'm tired by the lack of preparation. I'm tired, I'm exhausted by my own stamina! The thought of my own energy wears me out! Even the idea of recovering from my dance fatigues me. I feel mortified! Mortified by my own exhaustion!
>
> (English 1991; 38)

Here the crisis is that an overload of verbal discourse on the dance has somehow cancelled out the possibility of the dance itself and yet we know this is a dancer who speaks this; we know he dances, even as he verbally refuses this here. It is as if, all this chatter is 'too much,' overwhelms the dance. Having said this, I do not think that English is arguing for silent, unthinking dance, rather she draws attention to the disciplinary demands we place on art practise. English disturbs the borders we keep dear, even as we dismantle them. Charnock recently ventured into television, playing a character dying of Aids in *Closing Numbers*.[5] One might assume that participating in TV realism would be a less physical option, than Charnock's usual performance work, and yet Charnock had to diet radically to achieve the body of someone about to die of AIDS. Mimesis cutting into flesh. English's performance always wants to reveal as well as seduce, television realism is only interested in seduction; wants us to confuse this sign of a dying fragile body with one that is 'really' dying. This is a strange feigning, but perhaps only if one knows of Charnock's astounding strength, else we are seduced.

Charnock's partner, Wendy Houston, has a different relationship to the real/Real in *The Double Wedding*. Whilst Nigel talks and talks, she slips into sleep, although this is, no-doubt, feigned sleep. Here, not only does she not speak, but she does not even figure in consciousness. Houston is both inside a structure of conscious discourse (*The Double Wedding* itself) and outside of it, (as a character sleeping, and configured as Woman, who always cannot be seen or heard within the marked Symbolic Order). Towards the end of *The Double Wedding*, in the Lido scene, Houston enters as a showgirl, high-kicking between sentences, in a parody of Buzby Berkeley extravaganzas. When English demands to see the whole Lido Scene again, everything runs smoothly, except that Houston fails to appear, and the row of characters (including Charnock) gesture endlessly in their white suits, towards the place of her expected entrance. Peggy Phelan in her landmark work *Unmarked* (Phelan 1993), says; "(w)ithin the realm of the visible, that is both the realm of the signifier and the image, women are seen always as Other; thus, *The Woman* cannot be seen. Yet, like a ubiquitous ghost, she continues to haunt the images we believe in, the ones we remember seeing and loving" (Phelan 1993: 6) Phelan argues for such 'active vanishing' as a means of achieving political power, and here English plays on these ideas by linking the theatricality of the missed entrance, with the impossibility for women to 'enter' an economy of the visible in their own right at all; *The Woman* has always already missed her entrance.

In a show which is bursting with doubles, a character called The Figment is conspicuously without a partner. The seduction of traditional narratives from pantomime to Hollywood film, to classical ballet suggest that his partner is Rose, the central harridan, who is also without a partner, but sustains such a central role in the performance that her lack of a pair is less conspicuous. She also introduces herself at the beginning as "alone, totally alone, but in the company of consorts" (English 1991; 2). The Figment is a curious kind of hero. He has long hair, wears black tights and dances on black pointe. His 'part' in the production is always deferred; "The seventh person to appear in this story is the figment" says Rose "...(h)e is elusive and evasive but comes into his own in the second act when he makes himself known to me," (English 1991; 6). Even his name links him with fabrication, with something made-up, or pretended. As the last character to be hypnotised by Rose at the beginning of Act One, The Figment says that his 'part' in *The Double Wedding* "...involved a lot of dancing which was much more my cup of tea... It was as if we were doing it at the same time as we were thinking it." (English 1991:15). Such a description of the experience of dancing, elides the processes of choreography and rehearsal and shifts the dance into a 'pure' expression of thinking; as if this were the originary dance, the re-call to a dance that was 'complete' expression. At the beginning of Act Two, The Figment dances with the two Viscera, who dance ballet, and are well-skilled. Once the Viscera stop, The Figment continues with a solo. On pointe and using the vocabulary of the ballerina, the effect is more than a little humorous. He stops the dance, and says immediately; " So. Rose, how's it going" (English 1991; 42). This colloquialism after dancing ballet, gestures towards the closed nature of certain traditional art practices, such as classical ballet. Such that to speak at all would be quite radical, but to speak such chatty colloquialisms to the heroine, combines elite and vernacular cultures in the body of one performer, a characteristic of postmodernism. Rose has a hero in her show, but he's almost not there, looks ridiculous, and doesn't know his discipline when he dances it.

The two female ballet dancers referred to as The Viscera, parallel the two acrobats known as The Nebulae. These are another doubling of pairs, and are conspicuous in their displays of skill, performed by non-speaking bodies. English names them in oddly contrasting ways, 'viscera' referring to the intestines, 'nebulae' to a diffuse mass of interstellar dust or gas. Both are nouns of words commonly used as adjectives, visceral meaning 'affecting the viscera', or 'intensely emotional', and *nebulous* meaning 'lacking definite form or limits/unclearly established.' These namings are placed at the opposite ends of vigorous presence; one 'in the guts' and the other so diffuse its presence is vague and unclear. That both these pairs are skilled physical practitioners makes these namings all the more curious. That the ballerinas are 'The Viscera' may be some wry comment on the roles available to women within classical ballet. Such a project involves achieving tininess and lightness, through years of rigorous training, and physical pain. The dancing of The Viscera is light, sweet, and pretty—it does not *look* gutsy, but its achievement required guts. The Nebulae on the other hand, are far from light and sweet and pretty. Their arching spinning bodies reveal their physical training in a way that classical ballet seeks to conceal it. Additionally, classical ballet is usually closed within a narrative structure, and though there are physical feats, the seduction is that these are part of a particular 'role', and its expression. In circus or cabaret, feats are themselves revealed as the focus of the performance. Both forms are altered irrevocably by being imbricated in the Rose English text. Both are unmarked by spoken text in a performance noisy with verbal play.

English ends Act One with a monologue in which she says, "...you just have to be tremendously tenacious and hang on for dear life in the face of fiction. " (English 199 1: 41) After she says this, one of the nebulae flies in, hanging by her teeth and spinning from a 'sanga bisz.' In this context of staged interrogations, we are primed to ask questions ("...you get what you interrogate for" [Phelan 1993; 125]); the shifting of boundaries shifts the resonance of this woman's silent spinning. Unmarked by spoken discourse, her spinning body drills a fissure in the arguments over the nature of the real/Real. She is 'really' hanging from her clenched mouth, like a circus version of Wonderwoman, she spins unbearably, hangs on (literally) for dear life. Not only does this spinning woman remain unmarked by written/spoken text, but the very act (and it is 'an act') of suspending her body weight from her clenched teeth, means that there is no room for speaking. Quite literally, a metal plug is in her mouth; she clasps her teeth around it. Her open mouth would end the spectacle. This is a marvellous and uncomfortable juxtaposition of discourses. Her body achieves the implied perfection of ballet, and does not touch the ground at all, but the effort of transcending the stage floor means that she cannot speak, is mute in the face of fiction.

* * *

I think of Laurie Anderson's mouth, and of the nature of fiction. Three things. A close-up of her face with dark glasses obscuring her eyes, clenched fists beating her head, as she beats the sound is amplified, at the end she opens her mouth and snaps her teeth shut several times—it echoes. A grin from *Kokoku*, teeth clenched, a light in her mouth that shines through her teeth. An absent mouth from the video of *Sharkey's Day*; a thin circle with nothing inside it, a triangle shape for her nose and two buttons for eyes. I think of the spinning nebula, gritting her teeth to spin freely. But these mouths here underscore rather than obscure the possibility of speaking, even as the possibility of full speech eludes them. They are used as epilogues/wry comments on spoken text/as costume. Anderson's performing body seems porous; light and sound rush through it, video techniques erase it, but she always has agency, is at the centre of all her performances and transforms her body as a site from which to speak, make sound, dance, as a place where the body and technology itself are sometimes confused.

Anderson's dancing body opens her film *Home of the Brave*.[6] Her body in silhouette moves wildly, to a regular funky beat. She plays on her own two-dimensionality; in wide seconds, she swoops, wriggles, presents her palms to us, finds right angles at knees and elbows. In front of 30 foot of blue glow, Anderson's body dances like a shadow- marionette. As she dances, the title of the piece HOME OF THE BRAVE appears high on this screen in square upper-case. This small body, this vast screen, this regular beat and these words invoke an epic beginning. Here technology is smooth, wants to conceal its own complexity. As Anderson draws the bow across her violin, so lights draw up and reveal her wearing a lycra face mask. When she speaks it is through the vocoder which lowers her voice an octave. This female body is effaced first by shadowing, then by mask and subsequently by altered voice. The effect of these layers of concealment is a curious kind of drag, not quite masculine, certainly not feminine, she becomes a kind of friendly 'creature.' Moving further downstage, Anderson begins a sort of techno-prologue, in which she introduces the numbers 'one' and 'zero' to her audience. This meditation combines comments on the colloquial references of being 'number one', with versions of lyrics in digitalised series of ones and zeros. This combination mirrors the mixtures of signs resonant in the body of this woman; the confusion of technology with this woman's body. Here, Anderson appears to share English's delight in dressing up, but whereas English in *The Double Wedding* froths up her staged showgirl femininity, wears big heels, shining silver and carries a wand. Anderson wears only a white suit, and the tight mask, and speaks in baritone. Technology, not sequins construct this body, and its wires, modems and obsessive digitalising are concealed, and revealed by Anderson.

What I am interested in here is the ways in which Anderson imbricates the body in her spoken and sung text. Jessica Prinz[7] argues that Anderson's shifting of voices in her texts, and vocal range via the vocoder, undermines the hegemony of any one position. This is an important point, but I do not think that Anderson's shifting subject position is ever easily locatable as masculine/feminine, or visual/verbal. The altered voice which Anderson herself refers to as 'the voice of authority' is itself constructed by technology, in the same way that her performing body is, and these are the same concerns that haunt her texts; the ordinary body in the face of technical overload. Anderson's work is a more troubling metonymy than Prinz would argue. Perhaps one of the reasons for this is Anderson's use of simple text, and branded colloquialisms, cliches that bore us, and haunt us with their loneliness and familiarity. This branded nature of capitalist culture extends to gesture as well as text. At the end of *Kokoku*, Anderson's text finishes with:

> We're so pretty,
> Shake our hands,
> Shake our heads,
> Shake our feet.
>
> We're so fine
> The ways we live
> The way we shake.
> We're so nice.[8]

As Anderson finishes saying this, the sibilant at the end of 'nice' forms into a grin with clenched teeth, and a light inside her mouth makes her teeth glow. The stage lights slide to blackout, such that this red grin hangs in the darkness, with the word 'nice'. Such a vocal and visual gesture is double-edged; reminds us of endless commodities, and of a lost imagined time when nice meant 'nice'. The inside of this performing body glows. Technology is coming, it seems to say— *'Nice'.*

Laurie Anderson and Rose English might seem like vastly different performance artists; the diva of performance art and the techno ice-queen, but their involvement in the construction of meaning via performance, shares a similar project; an on-going refusal of closure, and of traditional author-ity.

The whole of *The Double Wedding* is a play between the presence of the multiple signifiers that make up the chatter of retrieval, and the absence of a retrievable core. This is true for meaning at the level of the sentence (according to Derrida) as well as at the level of the playtext. The traditional view of the author as the source of meaning, casts the author herself in the role of transcendental signified. Such an author is here staged: English stands beyond 6 foot, glimmering in her silver frock. This author strives for profound and full presence, by being *here*, visceral, seductive, gorgeous and hilarious before us, and this makes her lack of author-ity even more profound. This is clever, for all its play at accident and mistake. English stands before us, gesturing at every cliche of passionate presence, and yet she and her whole performance signify absence, lack, loss. *The Double Wedding* signifies closure, closure intensified, and yet in the unfolding of its performance, it is only endless deferral; at its 'end' everyone promises not to marry each other.

Anderson achieves a similar open-endedness, this time not by masquerading at full presence, and the search for it, but by gesturing only at fragments. Anderson's texts are monologic; all verbal discourse is sited in this one female body. In this work the most prominent presence besides Anderson herself is the free play of technology — of projected image/slides/film/animation, and of sound — synthesiser, violin, synclavier, or the alteration of her voice by the vocoder, and Anderson is not always distinguishable from this equipment. These elements achieve a free-play of signifiers. Free because there is little attempt at semantic closure. Meaning is gestured towards, tonal, unsettling, not demanded, pointed at and expected. In Anderson's work there is no striving towards a central kernel of meaning. It is as if she quietly acknowledges the futility of such a project. The play of simple language, uneasy use of visual and verbal cliche, clash in us who recognise them and fail to recognise ourselves. 'HELLO', 'WE ARE EXPERIENCING DIFFICULTIES', 'ACTUAL SIZE' rush towards us on Anderson's screen. Here absence is multiple; a repeated haunting Her role as author is problematised by her shifting narrative position, her range of voices. If we presume she is the source of meaning then we are quickly un-done. Here there are dialogues, hanging sentences, voices that speak as low as men do Where is her author-ity?

* * *

I sit with Robert in New York. Grief sleeps in his face, as if he had been made up to look older. This was my father, he said. He tells me about Laurie and about working with her. He tells me that she's really happy with Lou Reed, who told her father when he met him that he was more famous than her. Robert says it was the right thing to say. He calls me the next day and says "I spoke to Laurie today." Laurie and fathers seem to haunt me. At the Lincoln Centre, where I have learnt bureaucracy by heart, I overhear the pages repeating to newcomers; 'These stacks are closed'. I am given the wrong file by one of the pages, and inside is one small yellow newspaper clipping, which says "ACTRESS DIES AFTER 5-STORY LEAP, Miss Lauri Anderson, twenty-three years old, of 115 East Eighty-sixth Street, died in Mt. Sinai Hospital early yesterday morning of injuries which she received when she jumped from the window of a fifth-floor apartment...after appearing in musical comedies in New York, she obtained work as a stenographer." The clipping is dated Mar 25 1932. Over sixty years later, and another Laurie Anderson appears in musical comedies of her own making; sixty dollars a ticket and on Broadway. One woman and forty tons of equipment. I think of a photograph of an old man clutching a cat and smiling, and of a woman who jumped out of a window. Laurie Anderson eludes me; I try to fix her, lay out meanings, and still I leave town before she arrives. Rose English makes me tea, is kind to my nervous questioning; her enthusiasm curves its way inside her articulate sentences. These are the images I remember seeing and loving. This body right here tapping keys and speaking before you. Such dancing bodies as these shunted, cocooned and veiled by text. Peggy Phelan says; "What one can see is in every way related to what one can say" (Phelan 1993: 2) Anderson and English know this implicitly, delight in play and provocation and use the dancing/textual body to say what it is they see.

Notes

[1] For a good introduction to these concepts see; Bass, Alan, trans., 1978. *Writing and Difference*. Chicago, University of Chicago Press.

[2] For a good introduction to Lacan see; Lacan, Jacques, 1978. *The Four Fundamental Concepts of Psycho-Analysis*. New York & London, Norton.

[3] The following articles give an introduction to Nigel Charnock, Wendy Houston and their work with DV8; Constanti, Sophie, 1988. "Spring Loaded" *The Dancing Times* Mar pp. 535-536 / Constanti, Sophie, 1994. "Dance Umbrella '93" *The Dancing Times*, Jan p. 330 / Meisner, Nadine, 1990. "You must go on" *Dance and Dancers*. Oct pp. 18-19 / Peppiatt, Anthony, 1984. "Sickled Feet, Scrunched Shoulders and Sexual Stereotypes" *Dance Theatre Journal* v.2, no. 4 Winter pp. 8-10.

[4] Constanti describes Charnock as "an incurable masochist" (Constanti 1994: 330).

[5] *Closing Numbers* directed by David Cook, Film on Four 1993.

[6] There are important differences between live performance and film, and I do not intend to deal with these here, but nor do I wish to elide their significance. One of the criticisms of *Home of the Brave* was that it retained too much of the concert format, and failed to become truly 'a film', instead it mimiced a documentary style, with many shots framing the performance as if being seen from the audience These factors contributed to the critical failure of this film, but assists me in my analysis here.

[7] Prinz, Jessica. 1991 " 'Always two things switching' Anderson's Alterity" collected in *Art Discourse/Discourse in Art*. (Prinz 1991). Prinz argues that Anderson "sets up a continuous binary opposition that fluctuates between male and female without resolution and without priority...all discourses (male and female, verbal and visual) become 'other' or (alter) to each other in a way that undercuts and denies hegemony to any. Situating herself in this way 'between' the sexes and the arts, Anderson transgresses both the 'laws of genre' and gender" (Prinz 1991:135).

[8] 'Kokoku' from *Home of the Brave* (Anderson 1986).

Bibliography

Anderson, Laurie, 1994. *Stories from the Nerve Bible*. New York, HarperPerennial.

Bass, Alan, trans., 1978. *Writing and Difference*. Chicago, University of Chicago Press.

Constanti, Sophie, 1988. "Spring Loaded" *The Dancing Times* Mar pp. 535-536

Constanti, Sophie, 1994. "Dance Umbrella '93" *The Dancing Times*, Jan p. 330

English, Rose, 1991. *The Double Wedding*. unpublished.

Lacan, Jacques, 1978. *The Four Fundamental Concepts of Psycho-Analysis* New York & London, Norton.

Meisner, Nadine, 1990. "You must go on" *Dance and Dancers.* Oct pp. 18-19

Peppiatt, Anthony, 1984. "Sickled Feet, Scrunched Shoulders and Sexual Stereotypes" *Dance Theatre Journal* v.2, no. 4 Winter pp. 8-10

Phelan, Peggy, 1993. *Unmarked* London & New York, Routledge.

Prinz, Jessica, 1991. *Art Discourse/Discourse in Art*. New York.

Filmography

Anderson, Laurie, 1986. *Home of the Brave*. New York, Cinecom International Films.

Cook, David, 1993. *Closing Numbers*. Film on Four.

RHYTHM, REPRESENTATION AND RITUAL: THE RAVE AND THE RELIGIOUS CULT
Georgiana Gore
(Université Blaise-Pascal, Clermont-Ferrand)

INTRODUCTION[1]
The impulse to juxtapose two events as different in kind and context
as the British rave and the Southern Nigerian cult to the god Olokun
came from an early preoccupation with shamanistic techniques of
ecstasy and a more recent, but perhaps self-evident, realisation that
rhythm is in some way central to the mastery of such states. Since
my early days as a performer in physical theatre of the sixties and
seventies and more recently with time spent in Nigeria, I have been
exploring the ways that multimedia devices, especially sound and
movement, are orchestrated by the ritual officiant (shaman, chief
priest) to induce transformations (psychosomatic and social) in the
participants including him/herself. Central to both the rave and the
Olokun ritual cult is dancing, and dancing for prolonged periods of
time, as well an evident concern with inducing altered states of
consciousness including trance in the former and possession in the
latter.

RITUAL, LIMINALITY AND COMMUNITAS
There are a number of further parallels which may be drawn between
the two events. The most immediately evident, though one which will
not be explored substantially in this paper, is that they may be
conceived as rites of passage entailing liminality and communitas
(see Van Gennep [1960] and Turner [1977] for conventional
definitions). This is Turner's term for that form of sociality which
exists as a '"moment in and out of time," and in and out of secular
social structure, which reveals, however fleetingly, some recognition
... of a generalized social bond that has ceased to be and has
simultaneously yet to be fragmented into a multiplicity of structural
ties.' (Turner 1977: 96). Olokun worship usually requires initiation
into a cult, and initiation is a characteristic form of rite of
passage (see Van Gennep 1960: 65-115), a process usually veiled in
secrecy and involving some form of journeying, literal or symbolic.
Secrecy and journeying also typified the rave of the eighties in that
the venue and means of access were not revealed to participants until
a few hours before its beginning. To the urban young, the rave
perhaps constitutes a space of liminality and potential communitas,
in which habitual personae and roles as defined by family and work
are shed every weekend.

THE RAVE
The rave first came to public notice in 1988, dubbed the 'Second
Summer of Love', when ingenious promoters took over empty fields or
disused warehouses or hangars. These were last-minute operations
veiled in secrecy and designed to elude the police. Late at night,
ravers in carloads hovered around phone booths at motorway service
stations and awaited the tip-off which would give the location and
directions for access to the venue. This nocturnal quest was
rewarded with non-stop dancing to the latest Acid House music, a
British derivative of American House music.

House music evolved in the eighties when disc jockeys (DJs) began to
manipulate creatively the record tracks that they played by using

principally two techniques: seamless mixing so that the music never stopped, and the layering of sounds, including voice-overs. The new musical instrument became the turntable and the new high priest(ess) the DJ, transformations which heralded the 'death of the singer' (to misquote Barthes' well-known aphorism). The cult and fame of the DJ turned producer/songwriter rest upon his/her skill at remixing established tracks. Witness how clubs now promote themselves and the events that they stage by advertising DJs as solo performers; the fate of a club like that of an Olokun cult is dependent on the skills of its principal officiants. Clubland is a network of competing dance venues, each with its own creative profile.

Like its forebear House, contemporary rave music is characterised by a high energy beat and driving rhythm. Melody is absent, lyrics sparse and the main concern from the DJs' point of view is the number of beats per minute (bmp); the ideal for trance dancing is said to be 180 bmp and has a 4/4 rhythm. Dancing is generally a narcissistic activity, devoid of the spectacular and the overtly sexual posturing of eighties disco. Indeed sexuality is low on the agenda while feelings of happiness, friendliness and fulfilment are valued. These are equated by some participants with a return to a more 'primitive' condition through dancing and rave culture in general, thus the references to things tribal. Is this the re-invention of a dance tradition, which passes through sixties' 'freaking-out' to connect with shamanistic techniques of ecstasy and trance?

As rave culture became established, it acquired the trappings of more commercial popular dance culture events such as club venues and annual festivals incorporating sound and light systems using the latest in digital technology. What continues though is the addiction to dancing and for some to Ecstasy, the amphetamine drug, MDMA. Ecstasy, first patented in the 1910s in Germany, and rediscoved in the late sixties as a therapeutic tool inducing empathy and friendliness, is said to put people in touch with their feelings and remove inhibitions (Saunders 1994: 36). Known as the 'happy pill' in rave culture, it has undoubtedly contributed to the rebirth of sixties ideology of 'love' and 'peace', to a rekindling of interest in things spiritual and psychedelic, as well as quite simply giving newcomers to raving the stamina to keep dancing for hours on end. One of the known side-effects of sustained dancing on ecstasy is a dramatic increase in body temperature along with raised pulse, the cause of a number of well-publicised deaths from over-heating. Club owners of the nineties have introduced the 'chill-out': a room in which ravers can relax, have a drink and enjoy ambient music, atmospheric sounds with little or no rhythm, and the latest in technologically produced visuals.

This psychedelic element in raving is currently spawning a new form of club entertainment away from the dance floor. The Big Chill is a monthly event held in a London club on Sunday afternoon and evening. Described as having the atmosphere of a 'festival come down party[,] without the dogs' (Pembo 1994: 20), this is a techno-hippy event for all the family with spaces for relaxed enjoyment of 'chill-sounds and -images', for eating to live ambient music, having a Shiatsu massage or a Tarot reading, and even exploring the wonders of Internet. If house music and raving had already challenged and transformed many of the conventions of pop and rock culture, especially that of the star system predicated on live entertainment and mass circulation of songs through the music distribution industry and the club circuit, so it may now transform clubbing into an interactive psychedelic event. Sixties' style happenings meet the microchip!

OLOKUN WORSHIP IN SOUTHERN NIGERIA

'The king of the water who surpasses the one on land' (Nevadomsky 1988: 197), thus goes one of the many praise names for Olokun, Bini god of the sea, wealth and fertility and a son of Osanobua, the creator God. Olokun worship is a common practice in Benin City, capital of the Kingdom of Benin of Southern Nigeria, since, traditionally, an altar-like shrine to the deity is created for every woman in a household. Besides these domestic shrines, there are a significant number of more elaborate ones. Furthermore, there is in Benin City at least one public shrine to Olokun, which indicates not only his popularity as provider of children, wealth and health[2], but also his importance in relation to the centralized politics of the kingdom which revolve around the divine king (Oba).

All of such shrines are constituted by an altar made of whitewashed mud on which are placed an array of objects, chosen by the devotee, including clay or mud sculptures, sometimes life-size, depicting Olokun and his courtiers under the sea. Mandatory to each shrine is a small clay pot (uru) filled with chalk, ferns and above all river water, usually taken from the river in which the devotee was ritually purified during initiation. Each shrine may become an ongoing artistic creation with objects being added, rearranged, amalgamated but rarely removed, depending on the intelligence, commitment, energy, enterprise and financial solvency of the individual worshipper.

Collective worship of Olokun (and the other Bini gods) is performed in cult associations, which usually form around a priestess, who has initiated for reasons of affliction often associated with health or fertility. There exists therefore a nexus of cult associations, each of which operates as a centre for creativity in the ritual and performing arts (Gore & Nevadomsky 1991). Each cult holds a weekly[3] afternoon dance and a seven day annual festival with two all night and several other dances. Initiation as a full priestess, as opposed to a cult member, entails a fourteen day rite of passage, during which the initiate performs during at least four all night dances and four to five other dances[4].

Dancing constitutes such an important element of worship and apprenticeship to the Olokun priesthood because it is through dancing that possession trance is achieved. Only then may divination occur, the therapeutic aspect of the priestess's craft and the test of her skills. Dancing also honours Olokun, who is said to demand beauty in all its forms, unlike the other Bini deities (Ben-Amos 1980: 46).

'Onstage' members of the cult including priests and priestesses are either seated according to rank, or form a circle in which they dance, sing and play the calabash rattles (ukuse) to exhort the solo performer in their midst. At the edge of the performing space sit the musicians - two drummers playing ema (small hollowed log drums covered in goatskin) and an egogo player (iron bell-shaped instrument beaten with a wooden stick) - and the audience. Solo performers take centre 'stage' in order of seniority with the chief priestess usually

135

coming last. During trance, steps are simple but very rapid to fast running polyrhythms, with snake-like arm movements, and include much spinning and twirling. Dancers may sing or divine at the same time. Crucial to the rhythmic manipulation of the event is the use of a goatskin fan (ezuzu) which is used by the performer to orchestrate the drummers' tempo, and to stop or change the rhythms when introducing new songs. Possession trance is the climax of the event, and the dramatic impact depends as much on the performer's skills as on the god's hold over the devotee. With jumps and shouts of 'eyo', the dancer intensifies her dramatic and technical performance sometimes dancing for up to an hour. As with raving, there is a phase of cooling down when the performer retreats backstage into seclusion, after she has made an offering to the spirit world at a nearby crossroads. It is during this stage that a performer will be informed of her prophecies, as she may well remember nothing of her trance dancing and possession!

POSSESSION/TRANCE, RHYTHM AND REPRESENTATION

Unlike with the rave where trance is achieved through the DJ's rhythmic manipulation of the whole group of dancers, the Olokun dance is a finely orchestrated event in which each participant knows his or her own role in sustaining the overall performance, as well as in assisting in engendering possession in the main performer. Apprenticeship is however a prerequisite in both contexts for achieving trance. Not only is it a question of familiarity with local contexts and conventions, but also a matter of psycho-physical training - of learning how to ride the rhythm (conceived as both sound and movement) in order to slip into different dimensions - to deterritorialize.

Rhythm may be conceived as structure on the one hand, and as noise and chaos on the other. It is the performing subject's oscillation between these two poles simultaneously present in the musical and dance structures of the event, which resolves itself in the steady state of trance or possession. So in Olokun dancing the drumming marks out repeated rhythmic themes, while the calabash rattles which are covered with a net of beads, produce a continuous whoosh of white noise. The dancing alternates between short repeated linear sequences and continuous twirling movements. In rave trance dancing a tension similarly exists between conformity to rhythmic structure and abandonment to the chaos of sinuosity in sound and gesture. Rhythm as structure represents the straightjacket of the social order; it acts as a form of discourse. Musical rhythmic themes (Deleuze and Guattari's 'ritournelle' [1980: 381-433]; Rouget's 'mottoes' or 'call-signs' [1985: 99]) operate like speech; with tonality in Nigerian languages the speech effect of drumming is evident (viz. the Yoruba talking drum). And it is when driving rhythm has forced total conformity to its discourse, when subjection to its imperative becomes absolute, that, paradoxically, the dancing subject may slip through the nodal points ('points de capiton') anchoring the subject in the chain of desire, of signification, and the scene of the unconscious to the symbolic, and may enter into trance or possession. The split or rupture in the human subject, created first during the mirror-phase and secondly through entry into the linguistic and social orders, is what enables rhythm to occupy subjectivity, thus giving free rein to the unconscious within the linguistically determined cultural parameters which constitute that unconscious. The vertigo experienced sometimes during trance is perhaps the subject's hovering on the yawning abyss, the gap or lack, created by the rupture in subjectivity. It is no coincidence, therefore, that most subjects describe the experience of possession or trance as one of which they remember nothing ie that they are not conscious.

Loss of consciousness also implies a loss identification with the spatio-visual field. As rhythm takes over subjectivity so the subject is carried beyond the realm of the specular field, first constituted during the mirror-phase, to a region of preconscious speech. For the unconscious is, we must remember, structured like a language. This must surely explain why the initiate to Olokun priesthood chooses, under trance, the attribute by which she, and her shrine shall be known.[5]

So rhythmic manipulation is more sophisticated than a simple trigger for trance. Rhythmic structure, as an articulation of the social in Bini culture, is organised differently for different gods. That is, each god has its specific musical rhythmic patterns with characteristic dance steps, creating body patterns which represent the attributes of the god in question - harmony and grace for Olokun with arm/hand movements like flowing water; aggression for Ogun, god of iron and war, with acrobatic movements; speed and lightness for Eziza, god of wind, with spinning turns and skipping movements. The performer is therefore programmed during initiation into the appropriate rhythm and movement style which will enable her to enter into the 'groove' of the god being called to perform, since the performer is the god's mouthpiece. Rhythm thus acts as a mnemonic system to evoke the kinaesthetic, a tool for literally incarnating the gods and their dicta, which are revealed in speech through possession.

CONCLUSION
Despite the correlations drawn between the rave and the Olokun cult, the differences between the two events appear to be greater than the similarities. Following Baudrillard (1988: 25), I suggest that Olokun cult performances may be described as rituals of expression or mimicry, dramatic enactments of events belonging to a stage or scene other than that which is constructed in representation. Through possession trance, Olokun rituals construct

> a body of metamorphosis, the one of a pure chain of
> appearances, of a timeless and sexless fluidity of forms, the
> ceremonial body brought to life by mythology ... as well as
> by dance: a non-individual body, a dual and fluid body - body
> without desire, yet capable of all metamorphoses - a body
> freed from the mirror of itself, yet given over to all
> seduction....
> The body of metamorphosis knows no symbolic order, it knows
> only a vertiginous succession where the subject loses itself
> in ritual sequences.
> (Baudrillard 1988: 45&47)

The rave on the other hand is a rite of passage leading nowhere. The trance dancer hovers over an abyss of nothingness, for all meaning has been erased from the event except in simulation of a double past. It is a ritual without content except for the ecstasy of pure communication when you can become 'instant friends with complete strangers' (Rave New World 1994: 20). Raving is ecstatic, solitary and narcissistic. It is a game of chance and giddiness; its trance is aleatory and dizzying. There is no performance, no stage, no play of identification and seduction, no otherness – only deterritorialization and the 'massive buzz'. To quote Baudrillard, 'deterritorialization is ... a figure of metastasis; a deprivation of meaning and territory, lobotomy of the body resulting from the turmoil of the circuits' (1988: 50).

This body that I now speak of, as if for the first time, has become the silent partner in a dance which rhythm has been leading.

ENDNOTES
1. This paper is constructed from material derived from a variety of sources including personal experience, fieldwork, informants' accounts, interviews, secondary sources etc. It should not therefore be viewed as ethnographic in the 'pure' sense of the term. I thank the following: for their unstinting help with Olokun material, Ohen Ohun'Ahwen, Juliana Akenzua, Ukinebo Ehidiaduwa, Charles Gore and Shashi Osawe; Ruth Trueman for her assiduity in gathering rave material; and Joseph Nevadomsky and Norma Rosen for their friendship. Financial assistance is acknowledged from the University of Benin's Research and Publications Committee for research into 'Traditional and contemporary methods of training Nigerian dancers and choreographers'.
2. Children are important to the Bini not only because of matters related to succession, but also because of Bini conceptions of life, death and reincarnation. An individual is born from and, at death, returns to the world of the spirits (erinmwin), the realm of the deities and the ancestors. A childless person cannot return to the spirit world, for in order to become an ancestor an individual must inevitably have descendants to undertake proper mortuary rites and so effect safe passage to the other world, as well as to erect and tend the ancestral shrine. Childlessness, conceived as the woman's fault, thus becomes a Bini 'catch-22' for the infertile; whence Olokun's popularity as a mainly female cult. Men do however initiate, and the public shrine is led by a chief priest.
3. The Bini calendar operates on a four day week.
4. I differ from Nevadomsky (1988) in my calculation of the number of dances performed by Rosen during her initiation, and believe that initiation follows a structure of events parallel to those of a priestess's annual festival, which is a 'refresher' ritual, ie a renewal of the priestess's powers and following through a re-enactment of the intitial rite of passage.
5. This section owes much to my readings of Lacan's theorizing of subjectivity (Donald 1991; Lacan 1966, 1971, 1979; Lemaire 1977), mediated by my experiences as a performer/choreographer and as an observer of Olokun rituals.

BIBLIOGRAPHY

Baudrillard, Jean (1988) The Ecstasy of Communication. New York: Semiotext[e].
Ben-Amos, Paula (1980) The Art of Benin. London: Thames and Hudson.
Deleuze, Gilles & Guattari, Félix (1980) Mille Plateaux. Paris: Les Editions de Minuit.

Donald, James (ed) (1991) Psychoanalysis and Cultural Theory.
        London: Macmillan.
Gennep, Arnold van (1960) The Rites of Passage (1909). London:
        Routledge and Kegan Paul.
Gore, Charles and Nevadomsky, Joseph (1991) 'Practice and agency in
        Mammy Wata worship in Southern Nigeria'. Paper presented at
        the African Studies Association meeting, November 1991.
        Publication forthcoming.
Lacan, Jacques (1966) Ecrits I. Paris: Editions du Seuil.
_____ (1971) Ecrits II. Paris: Editions du Seuil.
_____ (1979) The Four Fundamental Concepts of Psycho-
        Analysis. Middlesex: Penguin.
Lemaire, Anika (1977) Jacques Lacan (trans. by David Macey).
Nevadomsky, Joseph with Rosen, Norma (1988) 'The initiation of a
        priestess: performance and imagery in Olokun ritual' The
        Drama Review, 32, 2, Summer 1988: 186-207.
Pembo (1994) 'Pembo's five star clubbing' Mixmag, 2, 43, December:
        20-1.
Rave New World (1994). London: Channel 4 Television.
Rouget, Gilbert (1985) Music and Trance. Chicago: The University of
        Chicago Press.
Saunders, Nicholas (1994) 'E for Ecstasy' (1993) Eternity, 23: 36.
Turner, Victor (1977) The Ritual Process. Structure and Anti-
        Structure (1966, 1969). Ithaca, New York: Cornell
        Paperbacks, Cornell University Press.

On the notion of bodily intelligence: cognition, corporeality, and dance

Dr Andrée Grau, Senior Research Fellow Roehampton Institute

1. My approach to the study of dance is anthropological. The general aim of anthropology, it can be argued, is to describe in the broadest possible sense what it means to be human. It seeks to distinguish what derives from being human from what derives from being born into a particular group, in a particular time and place. Thus, looking at dance from such a perspective implies, in theory at least, an investigation into both the biological and the socio-cultural foundations of dance. In practice, however, greater emphasis has been laid on the latter than on the former.

Because nothing can be understood outside the cultural, historical and physical contexts that make it possible, dance is seen as a social fact made by people for other people, in the sense that it depends upon associations between people for its transmission and meaning. Similarly the body in general, and the dancing body in particular, cannot be understood as a constant amidst cultural flux. Rather, it is perceived as having a history, in the sense that it behaves in different ways at particular historical moments.

The view that reality is socially constructed is now widely accepted not just in the social sciences but in other disciplines too. Personally, however, I cannot go all the way with the social constructionists. I depart from them when, for example, they argue that, as the body cannot be known apart from specific systems of knowledge, it is not only given meaning by discourse, but it is wholly constituted by discourse, to the extent that it vanishes as a biological entity and becomes instead a socially constructed product which is infinitely malleable and highly unstable.

Foucauld, in his <u>History of sexuality</u> proposed that the notion of 'sex' does not exist prior to its determination within a discourse in which its constellations of meanings are specified. Following this argument, bodies have no 'sex' outside a discourse in which they are designated as sexed. In Foucauld's terms

> the notion of 'sex' made it possible to group together, in an artificial unity, anatomical elements, biological functions, conducts, sensations, and pleasures, and it enabled one to make use of this fictitious unity as a causal principle, an omnipresent meaning; sex was thus able to function as a unique signifier and as a universal signified (1984:154).

I have no problem with that. This notion is indeed useful, for example, to argue against the idea that the natural body is the basis on which individual identities and social inequalities are built, or to support the argument that gendered identities are fractured, shifting, and unstable (indeed the division sex-gender used in the social sciences becomes highly challengeable from such a perspective) but I cannot quite come to term with this idea of a vanishing body, as I do not think one can ignore people's experiences of their bodies. I agree that the body is shaped and perceived through discourse, but it is not reducible solely to discourse. Although cultural processes and social relations do shape the body, the body itself, as a physical component of human agents, provides a basis for these social relations and cannot be reduced to an expression of them. The body is both receptor and generator of social meanings.

Human beings are affected by both biological and social forces. Human evolution has provided us, for example, with species-specific capacities for such phenomena as language, intellect and imagination, upright stance, tool making and manipulation, and extended childhood and parenting. Bodies are not just social constructions. They are also biological entities. It is through our bodies that we make contact with the entire spatiotemporal world that surround us. As Marcel Mauss argued in 1935, the body is at the same time the original tool with which human beings shape their world, and the original substance out of which the human world is shaped. The position of our body in space, the amount of space we occupy, the spatial distance between us and objects, for example, are all existential givens of which we have unverbalised tacit awareness. Human cognition is a holistic phenomenon which involves perceiving, thinking, feeling, and acting in the world and each cognitive domain shapes the others. What we perceive triggers thoughts and feelings and suggests possible actions. At the same time, how we think, feel and act shapes our perceptions.

Biology, one can argue, sets parameters within which history moves. To ignore the biological foundations of dance, to fence off the social from the biological, in my view, can only succeed in impoverishing history. One must not forget, however, that the participation of history and biology is not symmetrical. As Connel argued in his discussion of patriarchy :

> Historicity implies a historical process, a social dynamic. Biology enters the constitution of the major categories of patriarchy; but [it enters] a social dynamic. There is such a thing a biological dynamic, i.e. organic evolution. But the space of historical transformation is vastly greater than that, and dominates its effects (1983:60).

An approach looking at dance as a category which is both biological and social, looking at the dialectic between the two, could provide a starting point for going beyond the limitations of both naturalistic and social constructionist views. Such an approach, however is not easy. Any discussion of a biological foundation of dance, because of its universalist tendency, not only is unfashionable today but seems to go against the grain of most recent theory.

2. My work in the anthropology of performance has been greatly influenced by the late John Blacking. I worked with him from 1976 when I first met him to the time of his death in January 1990. When I first met him he had just published his rather controversial article 'Dance, conceptual thought and production in the archaeological record' on the subject of dance and evolution. In it he argued that 'the evidence of the forms and functions of music and dance in different societies can throw considerable light on relationships between [human beings] biological evolution and cultural development' (Blacking 1976:5). This idea remained with him for the rest of his life and resurfaced on regular occasions in different forms. In an interview given four months before he died, for example, he reiterated his belief that 'the origins of culture are to be found in music, in dance, and in performance' (Blacking 1990:199). Because dance is contained within the body, one can argue that, with song, it is the most elementary artistic process. Blacking believed that they were 'a special kind of exercise of sensory, communicative and co-operative powers that is as fundamental to the making and remaking of human nature as speech' and that they 'can be understood as primary adaptations to the environment; with them, [humankind] can feel towards a new order of things and feel across boundaries' (1987:60). (see Grau 1995, in press, for a detailed discussion of Blacking's argument)

To me these ideas are important even though Blacking got a lot for flack for them because so much of his argument was unsubstantiated and speculative. It was this aspect of Blacking's work, I believe, which made Drid Williams, for example, argue that his approach to human movement and dance was as diametrically opposed to hers, as Newton's laws of motion are opposed to quantum mechanics! (Williams 1986:177)

A major aspect of my work has been to find empirical evidence for something I intuitively felt was on the right track. My aim has not been to prove Blacking's right. That's irrelevant. The process of exploration itself, however, is, significant and it may open up new kinds of knowledge, even if the original premises prove to be unworkable (see Grau 1993 for a general discussion of Blacking's approach to dance).

3. Having worked in a number of non Western societies the logocentricity underpinning so much of recent theoretical thinking disturbs me. I am uncomfortable, for example, with statements such as Derrida's that 'from the moment that there is meaning there are nothing but signs. We think only in signs' (1976:50, quoted in Dissayanake 1992:217) and I agree with Dissayanake when she argues that 'contemporary knowledge about the brain, about child and animal behavior, or human mentality in cross-cultural perspective (...) makes this assumption at least debatable (Dissayanake 1992:217). There is no doubts that post-modern, post-structuralist theories could only have emerged in hyperliterate societies (it is no accident that many of the more extreme proponents of postmodernism are literary critics). Hyperliteracy has permeated most of contemporary Western thoughts, producing an almost obsessional preoccupation with language, particularly the relationship between language and thought, and language and reality. There is nothing wrong with that, indeed the pursuit is worthwhile, but again I would agree with Dissanayake when she argues that

> I doubt that many philosophers spend much time doing mechanical repairs. And it seems obvious that they do not stay at home with young children either, or they could never have come up with their assumption that you cannot think, you cannot have meaning and experiences, except in terms of language. Look at the toddler who has only a tiny vocabulary, yet can figure out (think) how to solve problems with her toys (which shape goes where in the puzzle, which ring goes on the spindle), how to quietly drop her peas on the floor so she can have a cookie, how to engineer a second or third good-night kiss (1992:216).

Infants transmits clear messages without verbal language. They are fully competent in using alternative, non-verbal modes of communication. Although they have to acquire the language and cultural conventions of their societies, infants are nevertheless fully equipped with their own 'supra-culture' which transcend the limitations of time, space and cultural convention. Blacking called these "angelic qualities". Through our research work, respectively among the Venda of Southern Africa and among the Tiwi of Northern Australia, Blacking and I felt that these non-verbal modes were later used by older children and adults in self-consciously structured forms of music and dance. Not only did these allow them to communicate 'spiritual' reality but also to relate to it. If this was the case among the Tiwi and the Venda, we argued, could not music and dance then be taught in such a way in our society too, so that it would help children to develop their angelic qualities through the exploration of non-verbal, 'performative' modes of thought?

I realise that I am going into deep water and that, to some, it may sound preposterous. Yet thinking of some of today's theoretical discourse, I cannot help being reminded about some aspects of positivist science, which claimed, for example, that a single scientific method can be used to investigate all domains of reality, including human life and which assumed that if other people describe the world differently from the scientific observer, their perception was in some way distorted.

4. There is no doubt that there are also many contemporary thinkers who are uncomfortable with contemporary propositional, sentence-based philosophy. They are asking, in Thomas Csordas' words, why not 'begin with the premises that the fact of our embodiment can be a valuable starting point for rethinking the nature of culture and our existential situation as cultural beings?' (Csordas 1994:6). In the final part of my paper I will present a number of approaches, within a variety of fields such as philosophy, psychology, anthropology, and education, which may lead us one day to a better understanding of the biological foundations of dance.

4.1 George Lakoff and Mark Johnson (Lakoff and Johnson 1980; Johnson 1987), for example, recognise the importance of "embodied" imagination when they demonstrated how many of the metaphors which structure our experiences are derived from bodily-based image schemas such as containment, balance, and force. These patterns are constrained by the logic of bodily experience and are projected metaphorically across various domains of experience. When we speak, for example, of someone being 'upright', as enjoying a high 'standing', or 'falling' upon hard time, our oppositional concept of 'up' and 'down' arises out of our bodily experience of verticality.

Although people differ in individual metaphor-making and metaphor-recognising abilities, language itself is full of hidden metaphors which allow us to understand and experience one thing in terms of another. Metaphors, then, become a basic mode of understanding, not just expressive of knowledge but constitutive of knowledge.

4.2 Contemporary neurophysiologists describe the activity of human thought more broadly as an activity which involves the transformation of represented information from one form to another. Their way of thinking about thinking not only accounts for abstract rational thought but also acknowledges that other quite normal but nonverbal transformation can be considered as kinds of thoughts. Howard Gardner, for example, has proposed a theory of multiple intelligence, giving a list of seven different types of intelligence: bodily, musical, linguistic, logical-mathematical, spatial, inter- and intra-personal (Gardner 1983). Every individual possesses all of these mental capacities, and under normal circumstances each of these intellectual regions will develop to some degree, as most domains of activity require the joint mobilisation of many intelligences.

Spatial thinking, for example, is an important mode of thought for all living creatures. Although space is largely visually perceived, even with our eyes closed we are aware of the muscular, kinaesthetic feeling of our position in space, whether, for example, we are vertical, tilted, or resting horizontally. Spatial awareness is so ingrained in our psyche , so much part of our being-in-the world that we are rarely aware of the degree to which we perceive and act in our everyday lives on the basis of concepts of objects, persons, and events that are in large part constructed out of spatial features and relations.

Each socio-cultural environment will provide different encouragement and support towards different types of intelligences. In our Western science-oriented world, for example we have implicitly absorbed biases in our word definitions. The term intelligent, for example, is reserved for talking about rational-logical thinking. 'Skilled' or 'talented' rather than 'intelligent' would be used for people with excellent knowledge and control of their bodies. A student of mine at the London Contemporary Dance School told me recently that when her ballet school merged with the local grammar school to provide a broader education for its students, the dance students were systematically put with the low achievers in class, even though they often ended up top of the class (see also Healy 1993).

Western dancers may have a much more developed spatial intelligence than non-dancers, but this awareness tends to be limited to their immediate space, whilst in many Australian Aboriginal societies, including Tiwi, dancers are physically aware of their whole geographical environment, as they regularly have to "face" sacred places which may be miles away. Furthermore, I have discussed elsewhere (Grau 1992, 1993, 1994, and in press) how among the Tiwi a complex cosmology and an extraordinarily complicated and abstract kinship system are taught, experienced, and reinforced through dance. Bodily intelligence is part of everyday Tiwi reality and David MacKnight's comment that among the Lardil of Mornington islands 'the best dancers are the best intellectuals' (1994) can be applied to the Tiwi as well.

Although Western societies have for centuries manifested the tendency to think of thinking as rational, orderly, critical thinking, and to believe that abstract concepts can only be elaborated, learned and taught in an intellectual way, it is important to realise that this type of thought is really only one kind of mentation, and that its predominance is by no means universal.

4.3 The anthropologist Paul Conerton proposed the notion of "body memory". In his approach he distinguished between two types of social practice: 'incorporating practice' and 'inscribing practice' (Connerton 1989:74-75). A smile, a handshake, for example, are incorporating practices in the sense that they are messages people send by mean of their own current bodily activity. The transmission occurs only during the time that their bodies are present to sustain that particular activity. The information imparted by these actions can be conveyed intentionally or unintentionally. Under incorporating practices Connerton distinguishes between techniques of the body which includes gesture repertoire shared by a social group, proprieties of the body which includes the rules defining 'proper' behaviour, and ceremonies of the body, practices through which individuals display their social status.

Inscribing practices, on the other hand, Connerton argues, are practices which do something to trap and hold information, long after the human organism has stopped informing. The alphabet is a typical example of an inscribing practice. It is a practice which exists by virtue of a systematic transfer from the temporal properties of the human voice to the spatial properties of the inscribed marks. A dance score then, in Connerton's term, would be an inscription, but the dance, when performed, an incorporation.

Connerton also asserts that the transition from an oral culture to a literate culture is a transition from incorporating practices to inscribing practices.

4.4 In education, teachers inspired by Rudolf Steiner put great importance on the body. Just as in the system there is no separation between the artistic and intellectual realms, similarly there is no separation between the intellectual and the bodily. When children encounter writing at about the age of seven, for example, the body is involved as a way of learning. The teacher takes them through the gestures and movements of the vowels and consonants using Eurythmy, the system of movement developed by Rudolf and Marie Steiner in 1912 (individual letters have specific gestures attached to them). Children are also made to walk the letters on the floor. The teacher also pays special attention to breathing as 'healthy breathing' is believed to serve as a foundation for balance between activity and rest, waking and sleeping, giving and receiving, all important for the development of healthy individuals.

At the age of 9-10 when children are seen to encounter a new self-consciousness, specific exercises are introduced to meet and foster this process. Instead of working in a circle, for example, children are made to stand on their own, away from the security of the circle, they also learn to move backward in order to feel where they are through their whole body. Eurythmy also helps to retain a living quality in subjects which demand abstract thinking, such as when geometry appears on the curriculum. Forms are experienced through the body, geometrical exercise become progressively more complicated and lead not only to increased spatial awareness, but also to the ability to visualise and carry out an intention with precision. These exercises are used because they are said to develop the adult's capacity for clear and mobile thinking.

Becoming aware of the attitude towards the body in Steiner education made me want to enquire further into other fields under the broad umbrella of anthroposophy, the term used to refer to Steiner's views of the human condition. I was particularly interested in anthroposophical medicine and in its application in conjunction with curative eurythmy and with what has been called "neurological reorganisation", a recent therapy starting to develop techniques which are seen to regenerate the nervous system, going against the belief that once cells are destroyed or damaged, the nervous system can not be regenerated. When I interviewed a curative eurythmist during my stay in Switzerland last December I was told that there is a whole trend not only in Switzerland, but in France, and Germany too where such techniques are beginning to be utilised within mainstream allopathic medicine, because of the physical results observed.

5. At the moment in my research I am just exploring different avenues about body and intellect and I must say the task is rather daunting since so many fields overlap, and

each one of them has a vast literature. Yet I feel that the work may be significant, even if it is not fashionable. If we can show that through movement brains cells can be regenerated and made to work again, that abstract thought can be developed and encouraged trough movement, then Blacking's argument that if a society fails to take full account of the place of dance in the definition of human being, and so limit people's opportunities for dance or dance-like communication, it could deprive individuals of necessary ingredients of normal psychic development takes another meaning.

In addition, intelligence in general, and bodily intelligence in particular, need to be investigated in our days where not only racism and racial prejudice, but also racist theories are cropping up again. Although crosscultural studies of cognition have demonstrated unequivocally that many so-called intelligence tests say more about Western ethnocentric presuppositions about meaning and rationality than about the intelligence of people in different socio-cultural systems, these tests continue to hold an incredible power, both in popular thought with organisation such as Mensa, and in academic circles with the publication of books like The Bell Curve last year by the American psychologist Richard Herrnstein and political scientist Charles Murray, which argues among other things that black people have on the whole a lower intelligence than white people. I believe that any work counteracting such insidious influences is important.

References:
Blacking, John
1976   Dance, conceptual thought and production in the archaeological record. In Sieveking, G., Longworth, I. and Winston (eds) Problems in economic and social archaeology. London: Duckworth.
1987   A common sense view of all music Cambridge: Cambridge University Press.
1988   Dance and Human Being: strengthening children's individuality and angelic qualities for adaptation to cultural convention. Proceedings of the Dance and the Child conference, London: Roehampton Institute.
1990   Interview with Keith Howard, translated into French, published under the title 'Un Homme Musical: Entretien avec John Blacking', Cahiers de Musiques Traditionelles. 3:187-204.
Connel, Robert
1983   Which way is up? London: George Allen & Unwin.
Connerton, Paul
1989   How societies remember Cambridge: Cambridge University Press.
Csordas, Thomas ed
1994   Embodiment and experience: the existential ground of culture and self. Cambridge: Cambridge University Press.
Dissayanake, Ellen
1992   Homo Aestheticus: where art comes from and why. new York: The Free Press
Foucault, Michel
1984   History of Sexuality, an Introduction. vol I. Harmondsworth: Penguin
Gardner, Howard
1983   Frames of mind: the theory of multiple intelligence. New York: Basic Books
Grau, Andrée
1993a   Gender interchangeability among the Tiwi. in Thomas Helen (ed) Dance, gender,and culture. London: Macmillan.
1993b   John Blacking and the development of Dance Anthropology in the UK Dance Research Journal 25(2):21-31.
1994   On the acquisition of knowledge: teaching kinship through the body among the Tiwi of Northern Australia. Paper presented at the European Association of Oceanists, Basel Conference, Knowing Oceania: Knowledge and Identities
in press (a)
            Dancers' bodies as the repository of conceptualisations of the body, with special reference to the Tiwi of Northern Australia. Proceedings of International Association for Semiotic Studies, Fifth Congress, 1994 - University of California, Berkeley. The Hague: Mouton

in press (b)
> Dance as part of the infrastructure of social life. <u>Festchrift for John Blacking</u> (working title) Berlin: World of Music.

Healy, Katherine
1993   Expanding minds. <u>Dance Now</u> 2(4):10-17.

Macknight, David
1994   Untitled paper on dance among the Lardil of Mornington Island presented at the fourth Goldsmiths Anthropology of Dance Colloquium "Reflections on the Body".

Mauss, Marcel
1935   Les techniques du corps. <u>Journal de psychologie normale et pathologique</u> 32:271-293

Williams, Drid
1986   (Non) anthropologists, the dance, and human movement. in Bob Fleshman ed. <u>Theatrical Movement: a Bibliographical Anthology</u> Metuchen N.J & London: The Scarecrow Press.

BORDER ART, BORDER TOWN:
LOS ANGELES DANCES ON THE EDGE

M. A. Greenstein
Art Center College of Design, Scripps College

Los Angeles is a border town. Unlike its sister city San Diego, which straddles the political rims of the U.S. and Mexico, L.A., in her overwhelming geographic expanse and youth, her seductive Pacific Coast clime and her celluloid persona, gives rise in mythic proportions to the opposing forces of life and death, anonymity and instant fame, destitution and Hollywoodesque abundance. Called a "heteropolis" by Charles Jencks, the city of the "simulacra" by Jean Baudrillard, L.A. is redundantly surrounded by bourgeois fantasy communities.[1] It is, in a word, a Wildean city in which life does imitate art, where an artist is pressed to create a star image before he or she creates a work of art. In this matrix of duplicitous and virtual realities, one finds historical seeds of artistic innovation and political rebellion—Ruth St. Denis, John Cage, La Raza, the Watts Riots. Revolt and transform are the watchwords (or verbs as it were) for the L.A. artist. Breaking with tradition in L.A. is as natural as an earthquake. Perhaps art does imitate life after all.

In L.A.'s virtual spaces where the real meets the unreal, where tradition meets "the now," one finds a border aesthetic developed by contemporary Los Angeles choreographer and dancer Frank Guevara.[2] Recognized as the innovator of the first Latino modern dance company in Los Angeles, Dance Theatre of East L.A., Guevara is part of a new generation of L.A. border artists who challenge the mono-cultural hegemony, that is to say, "white" and "modernist" hegemony that has held sovereign rule over the Los Angeles fine art dance aesthetic.[3] While hardly unified in their terpsichorean views, this new group, which includes Guevara, Turkish born, hyperdance artist Mehmet Sander and Japanese born, Butoh inspired Oguri, turns kinesthetic inquiry into a cultural critique of bourgeois rationalism and cultural domination. Guevara, age thirty, is currently building an expressive dance theater vocabulary of "masculine movement" which at times, incorporates a hyperdance aesthetic emphasizing athleticism, physical risk and endurance and at other times, lays stress on the sheer emotional dimension of the male psyche.[4] His choreographic themes typically focus upon the border issues of being a homosexual marginalized by a homophobic Latino community, and being a Latino or "brown" person historically marginalized by the dominant Anglo or "white" community.[5]

Before I go on to talk about Guevara and his work, allow me to show a brief video clip of *Reto*, a duo that premiered at the Nosotros Theatre in Hollywood in December 1994. Guevara commissioned Los Angeles tango artists Alberto Toledano and Loreen Arbus to choreograph the work, which in the video is danced by Guevara and his company member Bogar Martinez.[6] According to Toledano, *Reto* means "challenge" with a sense of defiance and though it does not bear direct evidence of the hyperdance aesthetic, it remains for Guevara, a "technically hard piece" to perform.[7] [Show video.]

To speak of Guevara's border aesthetic as it pertains to *Reto*, I would like first to pose the following questions: "What is Latino modern dance? What does it mean to look "Latino" on stage? What is "masculine" dancing? And on what ground of social existence are these questions raised? In other words, how should one read Guevara's urbane dancing, inspired as were, by the European packaging of Argentine tango, created in spite of his lack of support from the L.A. Latino community? Will we see a psychological metynonomy of border identity or a collapsed metaphor of the cultural betwixt and between? Does the concept of "masculinity" infer liminality, if one is Latino and gay?

Founded in 1992, the name of Guevara's company "Dance Theater of East L.A" and the fact that Guevara frames it as "Latino," is telling of the semantic layers of awareness the artist maintains in determining his artistic persona and his border aesthetic in the eyes of the Los Angeles press. That is to say, positioned by the press to distinguish his non-"Anglo" artistic identity, Guevara re-appropriated the most often used press label "Latino," a general category of Latin and Central American heritage that subsumes Mexican, Guatemalan, Puerto Rican, Costa Rican and so on under its heading.[8] By doing so, he consciously rejected the more politicized label "Chicano," a slippery, multi-valent term which often denotes the ethnic identification preferred by the Mexican-Americans who possess "a non-Anglo image of [themselves]."[9] More pointedly, "Chicano" (and "Chicana") infers the self-reflexive awareness of one's Mestizo or "hybrid," pre-Columbian, indigenous and European lineage and typically implies one's political consciousness of La Raza. La Raza, the popular Chicano battle cry of 1960's, is the twentieth-century grassroots revolution dedicated to resolving the plight of socio-economic and geo-political self-determination among Mexican-Americans in the U.S.[10]

At the time I interviewed him, Guevara described himself as "not a Latino doing Latino art, but a human being, making human being art." This is not the echoing cry of the Chicano artist who must assert difference in a time of monocultural assimilation but rather the resounding voice of the 1990's young, Latino artist who is trying to create art during a chilly season of "multiculturalist" overload, an artist who does not deny the political circumstances of Latinos in the U.S. but who is attempting to rethink the place of Latino nationalism in art. The artist himself raises the question of what "ethnic" category he and his work should be placed. Though both of his parents were born and raised in Mexico, his maternal grandparents were Spanish; his paternal grandfather was Argentinean and paternal grandmother, who still lives in Mexico, is a "full-blooded" Aztec. Guevara notes further that his father was brought up in a home that followed Aztec traditions. Guevara, the artist, was born and raised in East L.A., a flatland ecology that defines L.A.'s downtown urbanity, the inland edge of the L.A. suburban, metropolitan sprawl. Today East L.A. remains the primary Mexican barrio in Los Angeles county.[11]

Despite his indigenous ancestry, which again for some L.A. artists would be political and psychological grounds for claiming their Chicano ethnicity, and in spite of his consistent use of Spanish titles and obvious address of Chicano subject matter in some of his works, Guevara resists the totalizing aesthetic of Chicano nationalism.[12] This is an artist who spent his primary school years dancing folklorico as a member of a touring troupe, and claims that by the time he was twelve, he was ready to move on from "dancing about burritos." At that point he began to study ballet and modern dance at the local East L.A. community center, Plaza de la Raza.[13] I should point out that in light of his rejection of folklorico, it is rather ironic that Guevara discovered the world of European and North American fine art dance at Plaza, one of the few non-profit institutions devoted to promoting contemporary and folkloric Mexican heritage in "Los Angeles," Spanish for the city of "the angels." Today, Guevara expresses his contempt for folklorico in *Cuerpo Marcado*, a work that criticizes the choreographic cliches of Mexican sombreros and zarapes, cliches that unconsciously symbolize the not so subtle racism embedded in the self-preserving movement to embrace "La Mexicanidad"—the ideological return to "native" pre-Columbian Mexico.

The folklorico image is not the only essentializing masquerade in which Guevara refuses to engage.[14] He is equally vehement about resisting the enclosing, stereotypic fey image of the male dancer, cultivated in part by the Euro-American ballet and modern tradition and projected onto him by his own homophobic Latino community. He claims the homophobic fear is so great that he has been denied both financial and artistic support from the Latino quarter.[15]

Consequently, both issues, that of being perceived as "brown" by a white culture and being seen as "gay" by a straight, Latino population, converge on the topic of masculinity, an issue which drives Guevara to conceive of dances like *Reto*.[16] Is *Reto*, with its smokey cool tribute to Argentine tango, a study of two upper-class men about to engage in a hot, erotic affair?; a portrait of the psycho-social complexities of being male and Latino? Guevara sees *Reto* as a work that both explores the upper-class, male dominion of dancing and critiques the traditional "Butch" behaviors Latino men initiate in forming relationship, behaviors that typically signify the suppression of feelings to avoid the display of weakness.[17] As one might expect, "weakness" here reads as the unconscious binary signifier, "feminine." Inspired by the waltz scene in the public television production of Evelyn Waugh's *Brideshead Revisited*, *Reto* allows Guevara, once a lower-middle class kid from an East L.A. barrio, the opportunity to fantasize about upper-class male entitlement, even if one is gay. In this case, the aristocratic privilege of the homosexual male translates into the leisure of a man dancing tango with another man, the freedom to express desire and gamesmanship in the dark, secret dwellings of a male supper club. It is a piece, Guevara claims, that he could never present to a L.A. Latino audience.

Why the self-censorship? Or is it a censoring of the self? And which of Guevara's selves is censored? Which self, in *Reto*, takes up the "challenge" and "defiance" of Latino homophobia by personifying an "educated, well to do," virile, Latino male? Guevara mentions Jose Limon dancer and teacher Anthony Balcena, with whom he studied at Plaza in the early '80's, as being responsible for modeling the epitome of the "masculine dancer." According to Guevara, Balcena had successfully cracked the "feminine" body code of lyrical, lean male dancing by bulking up to project the image of a "strong, powerful male" and was capable also of showing a range emotions on stage. In *Reto*, one sees Guevara's interpolation of Balcena's "masculine" motif in his taking on the traditional male tango role: a strong, hunky, elegant body that dons roguish Ralph Lauren apparel; a taut, urbane body that cunningly pursues his object of desire; a seductive body that hungers and never relents.[18]

And yet, by performing an European-influenced version of an Argentine tango, Guevara thickens the plot of this mini-ethnography, for the tango he performs is, according to political theorist and dance scholar Marta Salvigliano, the colonized tango of the early 1900's. As a dance of the lower-class made popular in the rapidly changing, urbanized Buenos Aires, the tango became an exoticized, romanticized *"Other/Otra,"* the raw, Argentine export that once delighted and scandalized otherwise repressed, European upper classes in France and England and then returned to its home of origin to be celebrated by the bourgeois and upper-class Argentineans.[19] That Guevara would choose the colonizer's tango on which to ground on his perceptions as a gay, Latino, North American male, is to say that his projection of Latino masculinity through tango dancing necessitates an inverted doubleness in thinking. The tango embrace, as Salvigliano points out, is the iconographic embrace of physical, social and political bodies. In its tight grip, one sees the heart of colonized, Argentine class, gender and race conflicts, those being a series of lower- and upper-class power plays between dark and light-skinned, heterosexual males performing machismo for each other, not necessarily for the female partner. In other words, in its early inception, tango, as a game of machismo, was not directed specifically to playing the game of heterosexual love but rather to enact the brute power of "true maleness."[20] In fact as Salvigliano shows, early forms of tango, as a province of black "homosociality," were said to be performed as male couple dances; the introduction of females into the couple dance signified a Romantic degeneration of the macho cult.[21] In *Reto*, Guevara's gay tango lovers subvert the Romanticized, heterosexual embrace all the while attempting to escape the straightjacket of the femme male, that tight-fitting, modern, homophobic projection of the bourgeois, Latino macho; at the same time, they desire to slip into the performative skin of the Latino "masculine" ego-identity still normatively organized relative to that of the performative, upper-class Anglo—ironically, the same tactic employed by lower-class, heterosexual, black or dark-skinned Argentineans who sought to compete for the womanizing machismo power commanded by wealthy, white and "straight," tango dancing, European males. In other words, Guevara's perception of Latino masculinity describes a threshold of performed identity, where the contradictions of Latino maleness and "machismo" become magnetized into a coherent shape of border identity relative to the hybrid culture in which the identity is made—in this case, Mexican, Argentinean, European, North American, gay and class-stratified.[22] Guevara's hombres dance on the razor's edge of performative masculinity and performative homosexuality because both performative images are manufactured on the L.A. borders of Latino heterosexual fantasy and are caught in the discursive web of re-imagining the bourgeois Latino male. What better way to challenge oneself than to be tangoed by the Other's other?[23]

Notes

1.   Charles Jencks, *Heteropolis: Los Angeles, the Riots and the Strange Beauty of Hetero-architecture* (Academy Editions, London, 1993); Jean Baudrillard, *Amerique*, (Paris: Grasset, 1986) and *Cool Memories* (Paris: Galiliee, 1987).

2.   Inspired by the informal discussions I've had with self-proclaimed "border artist" Guillermo Gomez Pena about his writings and performances, and after working through the intellectual premises of Victor Turner's concept of liminality, I presently use the term "border aesthetic" in a positive sense to qualify the "in-between" and sometimes transitional nature of hybrid or culturally-mixed artistic perceptions. See Guillermo Gomez Pena *Warrior for Gringostroika*, (St Paul, Minn.: Graywolf Press, 1993) and Victor Turner, *From Ritual to Theatre, the Human Seriousness of Play*, (New York: Performing Arts Journal, 1982).

3.   The body of this paper is based primarily on an in depth, personal interview with Guevara conducted at his home in North Hollywood, California on February 5, 1995 (audio tape recording). Also see Jan Breslauer, "F-O-L-K Is a Four Letter Word," *Los Angeles Times*, Calendar section, (December 11, 1994) 4, 98.

4.   Approximately a year ago, *Los Angeles Times* dance critic Lewis Segal published an article describing "hyperdance" as a "timely metaphor for survival in an age of disaster." Here he named Guevara and Sander among the L.A. choreographers who make physical risk the object of their aesthetic desire. See Lewis Segal, "Dance to the Edge," *Los Angeles Times*, Calendar section, (March 6, 1994) 8-9, 78-79.

5.   I base my use of the term "Anglo," on the Latino and Latina slang for a "Euro-American" or "white" person. Though the popular Latino perception of Los Angeles as an "Anglo town," is grounded upon past census readings and employment records, a recent census study conducted by the Los Angeles Cultural Affairs Department suggests a reversal in domination, at least demographically speaking. To be specific, the study projects asserts that by the year 2000, the total number of white individuals inhabiting southern California, will decrease from the 1970 average of 75% to the projected figure of 43% of the population. Whites moving out of area? Hardly. Rather, the study suggests that 39% Hispanic, 10% Asian, and 8% African-American peoples

will make up the dominating population of California's "golden coast." See *Our Many Voices: A New Composition*, (Bank of America, Los Angeles, 1991).

Also, one may note above, the use of the term "Hispanic," the current U.S. federal, homogenizing, assimilationist term, denoting anyone claiming Spanish heritage. To wit: According to the 1990 U.S. Federal Census of Population and Housing, persons of "Hispanic origin" total 1,370,476 in Los Angeles City. No numbers were given for persons of specifically Mexican heritage. See the U.S. Department of Commerce, Bureau of Census 1990, Summary Tape File 3A, CD ROM.

6.   *Reto* was performed to audio-taped music composed by Enrique Santos Discepolo. Guevara gave choreographer Toledano carte-blanche to choose the music and title for the work in addition to the choreographic responsibilities. The idea for *Reto*, however, is Guevara's (Guevara, personal interview, 1995).

7.   Alberto Toledano, telephone interview, 10 April 1995; Breslauer, 98.

8.   I say "re-appropriated" to suggest that the L.A. press, specifically the *Los Angeles Times* was hardly responsible for generating the legitimizing awareness of non-Anglo ethnicity. Rather as *Times* dance critic Lewis Segal pointed out to me, it is more the case that the press responds to the self-generated community discussion concerning self-identified ethnicity. Lewis Segal, personal interview (April 12, 1995).

9.   Ruben Salazar, "Who Is Chicano? And What Is It the Chicanos Want?," *Los Angeles Times*, part 2 (February 6, 1970), 7.

10.   See Glora Anzaldua, *Borderlands: The New Mestiza = La Frontera* (San Francisco: Spinsters/Aunt Lute, 1987); Francisco E. Balderrama, *In Defense of La Raza, the Los Angeles Mexican Consulate, and the Mexican Community, 1929 to 1936* (Tucson: University of Arizona Press, 1982); Juan Gomez-Quinones, "Toward a Concept of Culture," in *Modern Chicano Writers: A Collection of Critical Essays*, edited by Joseph Sommers and Tomas Ybarra-Frausto (Englewood Cliffs, New Jersey: Prentice Hall, 1979); Armando Rendon, *Chicano Manifesto*, (New York, Macmillan, 1971).

11.   Since the 1920's, East L.A. has been defined as L.A.'s Mexican-American "barrio" or quarter, the demographic result of people fleeing the violence of the Mexican Revolution and settled communities facing encroaching land development. Here one finds the historical roots of "pachucos," the zoot-suiters who faced racial and economic discrimination in 1940's and a strong camp supporting the urban, chicano farm workers' movement. At present, East L.A. is home to middle and lower-middle class, Mexican-American families and as the seat of Mexican culture in Los Angeles, its community constitutes the largest Mexican population outside of Mexico. See Richard Griswald del Castillo, *The Los Angeles Barrio, 1850-1890,* (Berkeley: University of California, 1979); Ralph H. Turner and Samuel J. Surace, "Zoot-Suiters and Mexicans" in *Racism in California: A Reader in the History of Oppression*, edited by Roger Daniels and Spencer C. Olm (New York: The Macmillan Company, 1972), 210-19; Zena Pearlstone, *Ethnic L.A.,* (Beverly Hills: Hillcrest Press), 53-60.

12.   A good example of Guevara's address of popular Chicano subject matter is *Mojado* (1994), a work that expresses the plight of border crossing Mexican farm-workers. For a discussion of Chicano iconography see *Cara, Chicano Art: Affirmation and Resistance*, exhibition catalog, (Wight Art Gallery, University of California, Los Angeles, 1991).

13.   Guevara's parents first enrolled him at age five in folklorico dance classes and were not pleased with their son's change in artistic direction. That is to say, to reject

folklorico was tantamount to rejecting one's familial heritage and by implication, choosing to enter fully into "Anglo" culture. At age seventeen, Guevara was "kicked out" of his parent's home for selecting modern dancing as life-long career (Guevara, personal interview, 1995).

14. In using the term "masquerade," I am thinking of Harold Brod's recent effort to distinguish between the anti-essentialist discussions that framed masculinity in terms of gender role, gender performance and gender masquerade. See "Masculinity and Masquerade," in *The Masculine Masquerade: Masculinity and Representation*, edited by Andrew Perchuk and Helaine Posner, (Cambridge, MA: The MIT Press, 1995), 21-30.

15. When questioned about the Latino participation as financial patrons, Guevara maintained that predominant support came from L.A.'s gay, white community (Guevara, personal interview, 1995). At this point, there have been no statistical analyses conducted to discern the ethnic or class distinctions in patronage.

16. During our conversations, Guevara used the term "brown" interchangeably with "Latino " (Guevara, personal interview, 1995).

17. *Reto* is not the only work in which Guevara explores the emotional contradictions of being Latino and male. Compare for instance *Hombres*, a 1994 work choreographed in the same year as *Reto* and performed by Guevara and Martinez on the same bill at the Nosotros Theatre.

18. *Reto*'s co-choreographer Alberto Toledano claimed that Guevara had handed him a list of descriptive terms including "seductive," "strong," and "not-feminine" to help him construct the dance. In addition, Guevara commented that in the last five years, he has purposefully scaled up his physique rather than down to insinuate power and strength as a homosexual male among straight Latino males. When I asked him about the significance of the scaled down physique, he related it to the performance of "feminine" movement qualities, inferring a nineteenth century ballet idiom—serpentine movement, "lyrical," "flowing lines and spirals."

19. See especially Chapters Three and Four in Marta Savigliano, *Tango and the Political Economy of Passion*, (Westview Press, 1995).

20. See Chapter Two in Salvigliano (1995), especially pages 40-48.

21. Alberto Toledano maintains the tango evolved out of the "milango," a dance originally performed by men as a dance of machismo, a dance of true maleness (telephone interview, 1995). Salvigliano argues for a messy state of tango historiography but substantiates Toledano's claim by noting the milango influence and by adding that with the tango embrace, comes the complicated story of a machismo dance signifying "love and sensuality." She notes that the early tango choreographically carried both heterosexual and homosexual inferences. See Salvigliano, 32-47, 158-163; also see photo on page 147.

22. In speaking about performed gay identity, I refer the reader to Judith Butler's *Bodies That Matter: On the Discursive Limits of "Sex,"* (New York, Routledge, 1993).

23. I extend acknowledgements to my colleagues Sue Spaid and Eugenia Butler for their editorial comments, to Alberto Toledano for his historical perspective on tango and to Frank Guevara for taking the time to speak candidly with me about his work.

Breaking Down the Barrier of Habit:
An Interdisciplinary Perspective on the Ideas of F.M. Alexander and the Theory and Practice of Dance

Michael Huxley, Martin Leach, and Jayne Stevens
De Montfort University: Leicester

The three of us are colleagues in the same University.[1] We have had an interest in the Alexander Technique and dance; have researched it and, in the case of two of us, taught and applied it, for some 14 years between us. We come from different backgrounds—choreographer and dancer, Alexander teacher, dance historian—and our work also encompasses anatomy and theatre. Border Tensions has given us the opportunity to use and celebrate this diversity and this is a first result of our collective endeavour. What we have found in our research is the possibility of opening up new fields of enquiry. We believe this to be in the spirit of the conference; we think it healthy for dance; and we identify this approach as characteristic of the Alexander Technique.

F.M. Alexander did not write specifically about dance.[2] However, many of the underlying concerns that seem to be raised about dance are problems which he suggested ways of dealing with. We believe this to be demonstrable in theory and in practice. For this paper we take Alexander's consideration of habit as our focus and we argue for a re-appraisal of his ideas and Technique as applied to current dance practice.

We begin with a historical relocation of Alexander's work within a dance context. We then identify habit as a limiting factor in dance training and education. Finally, Alexander's analysis of habit and its applicability to dance is examined.

Our enquiries have led us to a consideration of two main periods— 1888–1941 and 1964–the present. The first being the one during which Alexander developed his Technique and published his findings. The second being the one when his work came to be recognised as having an applicability for dance.

The dates of publication of Alexander's four main books—1910, 1923, 1932, 1941[3]—also bracket an important period in the development of early twentieth century dance, where many attempts were made to set out 'theories' of dance and movement. Many of these are well known— those of Duncan, Jaques-Dalcroze, Laban, Mensendieck, Meyerhold, Schlemmer, Todd, for instance.

The basis for early European modern dance was published from 1910 onwards.[4] Laban, for instance, published books in 1920 and 1926.[5] However, his books in English do not begin until much later, 1947.[6] In the United States, at the same time, theories were being worked out which would have a major impact on American modern dance much later—particularly those of Mabel Elsworth Todd who published books in 1929 and 1937.[7]

Alexander developed his Technique in Australia in the last decade of the last century.[8] He moved to London in 1904 and first published his ideas in pamphlets between 1906 and 1909.[9] His first book, <u>Man's Supreme Inheritance,</u> followed in 1910. It contains many of his main ideas, particularly that of use, and an identification of the role of habit.[10] By his third major book, <u>The Use of the Self</u> published in 1932, he had both laid out the foundations of his Technique and described how he had arrived at it.

As far as we know, Alexander did not visit mainland Europe professionally during this period. However, he did make extensive visits from London to the USA. He went to New York in 1914 for a period of 4 years and then made regular, extended visits to New York and Boston until the mid 1920s.[11] During these visits he taught his Technique at Columbia University, NYC, as did his brother, A.R.Alexander.[12] At this time John Dewey, the pragmatist philosopher and educationist, was Professor of Philosophy at Columbia and Chair of Teachers College. He had lessons with Alexander from 1916 onwards. He provided an introduction to the second edition of <u>Man's Supreme Inheritance</u> (1918), read the manuscript of his second book, <u>Constructive Conscious Control,</u> (1923), wrote an introduction to this and to the second edition of Alexander's third book, <u>The Use of the Self</u>.[13] He recognised the validity of Alexander's ideas, and in one of his own books, <u>Human Nature and Conduct,</u> (1921) made extensive reference to them, especially Alexander's notion of habit.[14]

Dance at Columbia at this time, under the tutelage of Gertrude Colby and Bird Larson, was dynamic and progressive.[15] Margaret H'Doubler took her MA at Teachers College in 1916 and taught there part time before returning to Wisconsin, where she established her renowned dance programme.[16] Mabel Elsworth Todd was another faculty member and she published the syllabus of her anatomy course in 1929. This became the basis for her much cited book <u>The Thinking Body</u> (1937).[17]

Alexander's fourth book, <u>The Universal Constant in Living</u> was published in 1941. There were new editions of his earlier books in 1946 and the eighth edition of <u>Constructive Conscious Control</u> was reprinted again in

1955, [18] the year he died. The 1960s saw the start of publication of books by teachers who had been trained by Alexander, marking the beginning of a second period of development. Lulie Westfeldt published in the States in 1964. [19] This was closely followed by Edward Maisel's digest of Alexander's writings (1969), and Wilfred Barlow's book, in England, in 1973.

There is very little to be found in the dance literature about the Alexander Technique until the mid 1960s. [20] In the year 1967 to 1968 Judith Leibowitz published 'For the Victims of Our Culture: the Alexander Technique' in <u>Dance Scope</u>. [21] She extolled the Alexander Technique's virtues, but began by regretting that it had only become 'well known' over the last three years. In the following year, 1968, in London, Jane Winearls published a new edition of her book, <u>Modern Dance: the Jooss-Leeder Method</u>. She extended her first edition, adding four chapters including one by Gerald Wragg [22] which referred to, and drew heavily on, some of Alexander's main terms. [23] In this edition there is very little to suggest why she included it, but in her semi-autobiographical book, <u>Choreography</u>, (1990), she describes her four great influences as having been Laban, Jooss, Leeder and Alexander. [24]

Contemporaneous with these developments was an emergence of approaches that built on other earlier foundations. Todd's <u>The Thinking Body</u> was republished by Dance Horizons in 1968, followed by the exposition of 'Ideokinesis' by her pupil, Lulu Sweigard in 1974. Laban's theoretical work of the published period 1920–1966 [25] was developed by a number of his pupils: of relevance for this paper is Bartenieff's analysis of 1980. [26] Bonnie Bainbridge Cohen's Body–Mind Centering was developed in the 1960s and 1970s and her New York School opened in 1973. [27]

The renewed interest in the Alexander Technique, that started with Leibowitz, has continued. In the thirty years between 1964 and 1994 at least thirty books on the Technique were published, many within the last five years. [28] There has been a steady and growing interest in the Technique expressed by dancers and dance teachers. A number of respected dancers have acknowledged the Alexander Technique as part of their 'training', for instance, Randy Warshaw and Stephen Petronio. [29] Remy Charlip, Eva Karczag, Joan Skinner and Mary Fulkerson have acknowledged it in print, as has Miranda Tufnell. [30]

Hardly any of the books written on the Alexander Technique mention dance, except in passing. [31] There have been attempts to detail its benefits to dance: some, informal accounts by teachers in <u>Contact Quarterly</u>; [32] others, more extended accounts of the technique's applicability, in <u>Kinesiology and</u>

<u>Medicine for Dance</u>.[33] There has been one substantial and notable account of the applicability of the Alexander Technique to dance training, by Richmond in 1994, published in the States in <u>Impulse</u>.

There has, however, to date, been no published systematic examination of the use of the Alexander Technique in dance. This does rather parallel the situation with books on the Alexander Technique itself, where the majority derive from a particular teacher's view of what the technique is.[34] Written for perceived audiences and with a particular focus, they might be seen as limited academically, and limiting in scope. Their purpose is not the technical exposition of procedure. The major exception is Frank Pierce Jones' analysis and account (1976).[35] Alexander's ideas <u>are</u> difficult to talk about and to understand. He himself was not always happy with his written explanations and asked Dewey (amongst several others) to read the manuscript of his second book.[36] However, Alexander's texts will yield up their meaning on close analysis combined with practical instruction in the Technique.

We will now consider in some depth the relationship between dance and what Alexander had to say.

The recent interest in the application of the Alexander Technique to dance has accompanied changing aesthetic and choreographic concerns[37] but it has also been part of a recognised need to apply scientific principles and knowledge to dance pedagogy (Bird et al. 1979; Oliver 1993 a & b). It has been part of the impact of dance science and somatics[38]; as such it has most frequently been associated with the latter and with body therapies. It has been seen as therapeutic despite the originator's insistence that it was neither a therapy nor contained by the term 'body'. Nevertheless dancers have found it useful in, for example, improving efficiency of movement, correcting posture, rehabilitating and preventing injury and conferring longevity of career. Many dancers who have trained as Alexander teachers have done so following an injury, trauma or impasse. Consequently, the Technique's relationship to the essential practice of dance is frequently seen as merely remedial or corrective. Much literature concerning the Technique and dance focusses on affirmations by dance practitioners of its benefits. Testimonies to the achievements of the Alexander Technique, however valid, tend to obscure detailed consideration of its theoretical and practical relationship to dance theory and practice.[39]

Most of what has been written relates the Alexander Technique to technical practice, rather than to creative practice, choreographic process and performance. We have, in our work, been concerned with all of these but, in line with the literature, begin with a consideration of technique as a basis for further discussion.

Dancers need techniques which are reliable and strategic in matching choreographic possibilities and human capacities. Most technical teaching, and even more so learning, shapes the dancer. It develops patterns of coordination which are firmly established through practice and on which the dancer as performer can rely. Dancers need technical responses which are immediate and dependable. For many this means a technique which is described as operating as unconsciously as habit or even instinct.

Vaganova, for instance, says of basic principles of classical ballet: 'The correct setting of the body, the full control of it, once mastered ... becomes a habit' (1946, 1969:12). Put another way, as Pavlova is quoted as saying, 'perfect your technique, and then forget it' (Shook 1978: xi). In modern dance also technique is said to become, in Graham's words, 'so ingrained by proper training as to seem instinctive' (1941:46). Here too Shawn [1939] sought 'an instrument that will respond almost unconsciously - a perfect and effortless instrument of [his] will' (quoted in Hutchinson Guest 1988:ix). Even non-traditional methods of dance practice, though frequently more dialogic, with more emphasis on exploration and less on uniformity, involve recourse to the same mechanism and recognise this in a number of ways. Joan Skinner talks of dancing experienced on 'a level underneath conscious decision-making or control' (Skura 1990:13) and Bonnie Bainbridge Cohen of reaching ' a point where we become conscious and then we let it go' (Stark Smith 1981:6) When the operation of technique no longer requires any conscious attention to feedback, we would say, it becomes habitual.

There is no doubt that significant degrees of skill can be achieved and for some such methods work well. However, other practitioners, artists and educators have found themselves compromised. For example, a dancer who trained in the Bournonville school felt herself well prepared for work with New York City Ballet but not for ' the variety of repertory' demanded by American Ballet Theatre, the company she subsequently joined.[40] Similarly, Meyer reports that modern dancers trained in one school had difficulty adjusting to another's choreography (1966, 1970:368).

These experiences also illustrate current research which indicates that, if skill is a pre-determined pattern, then the dancer, to benefit from practice, must be trained in the exact technique to be used in performance (Ryan & Stephens 1987:19; Plastino 1990:26). Researchers in the field of skill acquisition know that performance which is highly skilled 'may also become rigid in the sense that it cannot be adjusted to meet changing circumstances' (Welford in Gregory 1987:716). Fokine, in 1916, complained of the 'very few dancers who can walk and run about naturally' (Steinberg 1980:23). Fifty years later when Cunningham restaged <u>Summerspace</u> for the New York City Ballet, Tomkins reports that 'marvelously trained as Balanchine's dancers were, they found it extremely difficult to move in the large, sweeping manner that is <u>natural</u> [our emphasis] to the Cunningham company, and they could not do everyday things like running without making them seem slightly artificial' (1968, 1970:272).

Non-traditional approaches seek to avoid some of the disadvantages that the repetition and specialised vocabulary present in most traditional approaches appear to create. However, they too recognise the necessity of practice in learning (Fortin 1993:95). Despite calls to 'embrace as wide a range of physical expressions as there are human emotions' a repeated emphasis on easiness, softness, smoothness and gentleness, as is common for example, means that, to quote Myers, [the] 'right way of moving is often characterised as stressless, strainless and tensionless whereas wrong movement is often thought of as forceful, rugged and vehement.' (1991/2:18).

In learning dance technique therefore, the dancer may paradoxically be learning how to restrict herself. Hanya Holm said, 'A walk is of no value unless it is of the nature that you can change it .... If you can follow only one pattern which is very thoroughly ingrained in you, then you have closed the doors to all of that which is expressional' (Sorell 1969:180). We recognise that there are exceptional practitioners. Their plasticity and versatility allow them considerable freedom or it is exactly their idiosyncratic, individual style which makes them successful. These are however exceptional and it is our experience that many practitioners feel that they have been as much restricted by technical training as by the lack of it. Young people, particularly those who wish to choreograph, are wary of much dance training precisely because they see it as limiting.

The dance community has recognised as much for many years. An approach which allows for traditional dance skills together with versatility, individuality and spontaneity has long been sought. In 1965 Eric Hawkins talked of training the 'dancing instrument, without limitations and personal eccentricities' (1965:45). Concerns such as this led to speculation, of which renewed interest in the Alexander Technique was a part, that it might be possible to achieve, in the late Bonnie Bird's words, 'the perfect body training that would produce a dancer that could then be imprinted like paper by any style' (Bird et al. 1979:45).

However, the dancer entering the dance studio is not, even if she ever had been, a tabula rasa. She is unique and complex. By the time she first takes up dancing she has formed all manner of ideas, beliefs and ways of doing things. These she brings to her dance practice, whether technical or creative. The way in which she approaches dance will not only be in accordance with the way in which she approaches any other activity of life, we argue, it will be <u>determined</u> by the way in which she approaches the rest of her life.

This, then is where the dance historian and dancer and dance teacher find themselves. How, then, can Alexander's ideas take us forward?

Alexander called just this way in which the human organism engages in activity 'use', and use became a key concept in the explication of the Technique he discovered.[41] Whether dancing, performing, choreographing or sitting listening to a presentation such as this we are, whilst we live and breathe, using ourselves all of the time. We are constantly engaging ourselves in activity. <u>Any</u> activity in which we engage involves both (so called) physical and (so called) mental faculties. If we consider sitting it can be seen that without a skeletal structure and musculature there is nothing to sit up or sit up with. Without neural activity that same skeletal structure and musculature is completely inoperative.[42] Alexander was clear that use not only constituted physical and mental action but that these were inseparable. Hence his term (and book title) the 'use of the self' (1932).[43]

Alexander recognised that an individual's manner of use was largely learned and that it operated habitually. You have not always been able to sit in a chair nor I to deliver a paper. At some point we learned these skills. How learning is accomplished has been the subject of considerable research and no less debate for eighty years (Blackman in Gregory 1987:430). What is known is that we <u>do</u> learn and that doing so involves the reception of and response to information. When a stimulus is presented and a response made neural pathways in the brain are selected. Having selected these pathways, only once, the likelihood is that upon future presentations of the same or similar stimuli we will select these pathways again. Repetition thereafter serves to ingrain our response. Whereas the response, in the first instance, might have required conscious direction, it soon no longer requires any conscious attention. It becomes a learned activity that is no longer directed consciously. It becomes habitual.

Moreover, this response, through familiarity, comes to feel right; not only right but natural, essential, even imperative. Alexander said, 'We get into the habit of performing a certain act in a certain way and we experience a certain feeling in connexion with it which we recognise as "right." The act and the particular feeling associated with it become one in our recognition' (1987:82). He contended that we do not tend to think about how we employ ourselves in activity, more often than not we are merely doing things in the only way we know how, and in ways which feel right to us.[44]

So the problem is not merely that a dancer, having mastered a set of appropriate technical responses, has difficulty letting them go to master a different technique; it is that the instrument, her own self, is habitual. Any technique will be built on the foundations of an habitual, overall manner of use—a constant factor in all our activity. Moreover, Alexander maintained that the quality of an individual's overall use influences performance in any sphere of activity.[45] Skills, such as posture and coordination, which are fundamental to dance have been learned or acquired from an early age and in accordance with an established quality of use. We learn such fundamental skills as how to sit, stand, walk and talk at an age before we can be instructed in the best ways of doing these things. The flexibility and plasticity of the instrument we have means that any slight imbalance anywhere in the system will unbalance the whole.[46] The likelihood is, therefore, that we learn to do things with, using Alexander's term, misuse. That is we establish ways of doing things which do not maintain perfect balance and coordination. For Alexander a bad habit was one which involved misuse.

For dancers bad habits are those that limit conformity to the technical axiom.[47] The acquisition of bad habits is commonly attributed to poor teaching and it is recognised that such habits are difficult to eradicate. Dealing with their prevention in early training or their correction later concerns many writers on practical dance technique. Some recognise that verbal correction invariably does not solve technical problems. Many dancers experience the paradox that they can not always direct what they intend, that their thoughts and ideas do not always resolve into the results they desire. Force of will may be called upon to discipline the body (Weiss in Cunningham 1951, 1982:7; and Cohen, R 1986:14, 52) and much could be said about the conflict in which the dancer then engages and what this regime of discipline engenders. Corrections achieved may be costly in that initial problems may be disguised and further, potential problems created (Oliver 1993b:68). Traditionally, dancers may be rejected as untrainable (Cohen, R. 1986:24).

A less traditional response to the general problem is to expand the dancer's curriculum to provide more information and a range of experiences and viewpoints upon which she can draw. These might include experience of different technical styles and approaches rather than a narrow training in one specific technique; alternative movement systems, body therapies and conditioning, and anatomical studies. Many dancers and choreographers do now come from just such eclectic and diverse backgrounds. These may be useful in many respects. However, if they do not recognise the extent and influence of the individual's underlying manner of use and have an effective way of reaching it then fundamental, habitual modes of thought and action, established over many years, continue to be brought to bear.

Historically, these problems have been seen and some solutions proffered. 'Change' recognised Sweigard 'is possible only through the enormous task of recoordinating the neuromuscular pathways responsible for habitual balance and movement patterns' (1974:5). Ideokinesis, the method which she developed, uses mental activity, the 'concentration on mental imagery, without ... voluntary movement', [to] 'recondition neuro-muscular action patterns in the body' (1949, 1970:362).

Sweigard's work, as previously mentioned, was based on that of her teacher, Mabel Elsworth Todd. There are similarities between the work of Todd and that of Alexander. These are more notable within their analyses of the problem than in the practical solutions they proffered. The employment of imagery, that is 'visualisation of an imaginary situation,' (Sweigard 1949, 1970: 362) as developed from the work of Todd by Sweigard and others is not found in Alexander's own exposition.[48] The use of imagery in recoordination and dance teaching generally is, as yet, little researched. Hanhrahan and Salmela (1990) in their work on the efficacy of imagery in some dance learning question the evidence to support the widespread appeal of its employment amongst the dance community. Though Todd (1929) and Sweigard (1949, 1970) recognise, for example, that interpretation of images differ and readjustments to balance and coordination produce unfamiliar feelings they do not give the same prominence to the influence of habitual modes of thought and action as Alexander does. [49] If, an habitual manner of use, as previously mentioned, feels right it is unlikely that a dancer will do what feels wrong, uncomfortable, unnatural or impossible (as a truly different response would feel). This is particularly so when much emphasis is placed upon the reassurance of sensation and feeling in much dance practice. The dancer will, therefore, interpret instructions, images and visual cues within her own terms. She will, as we teachers and choreographers require her to, make the movement her own. The relationship between the ideas of Todd and Alexander and the continued relationship between the practice of Alexander's Technique and the use of imagery in dance is an area of research in which we are currently engaged and which has been more closely focussed by the work we have done on this paper.

Alexander contended that specific habits cannot be dealt with without dealing with general habits of use as a fundamental prerequisite.[50] Without changing this general manner of use no amount of extra techniques or therapies will deal adequately with any of the specific problems of habit that may have been recognised. 'To change habitual reaction permanently' he wrote, 'it is necessary to change the manner of use of the self that is associated with it.' (1986:94).[51]

If the dancer can learn to become aware of her habitual misuse and learn how to choose not to respond in her old way then she has the possibility of putting something new, and <u>consciously directed,</u> in its place. In practice learning to circumvent habitual misuse is a lengthy process. However, an Alexander Teacher, by practical assistance and instruction, can help to bring about a fundamental re-coordination and re-direction of use. Alexander said, 'Even when I have explained to a pupil why this difficulty has arisen in his case, and he understands the reason for it "intellectually", he will need ... considerable encouragement and practical assistance in order to be enabled to make the experience of gaining a given end by means of a use that is new and unfamiliar to him (1932, 1985:82). The teacher can help to bring about the improvement which the dancer needs in order to begin her discoveries. Within the period of a three year undergraduate programme, for instance, significant progress can be made and demonstrated.[52]

Alexander recognised that the individual's fundamental manner of use is difficult to reach. Our experience of applying the Alexander Technique to dance and dance education confirms the approach which Alexander took to solving his own problems of performance (1987). That is, use must be tackled in everyday activities before it can be tackled successfully in performance. Whilst the dancer's use in the rest of her life remains unchanged, it will constantly militate against any fundamental change in her dance practice. Ideally an improvement in her general manner of use would be gained prior to her embarking on any dance training. In practice these go hand in hand. The dancer must be helped to see the inseparability of her everyday activities and her dancing. She can then be encouraged to work on technical problems as they arise everywhere in her life, outside and inside the dance studio. When sufficient experience of a new way of going about things generally has been achieved it becomes possible to apply this new use more specifically to dance.

Throughout this process the dancer is learning to prevent her habitual misuse and direct a new use of herself. However, she is not simply replacing one habit with another.[53] Even if a new manner of use is the most advantageous that can be achieved the fact that it operates habitually will be a limiting factor.

This is an overlooked and misunderstood feature of Alexander's work. He was clear that his technique was to enable conscious direction of all activity. That is to enable us to learn to direct at will what we want, rather than to be bound by our habits; old or new, good or bad. New and improved use if operated habitually will continue to be, in Alexander's own words, a 'stumbling-block to rapid adaptability, to the assimilation of new ideas, to originality' (1946:55). Only when the direction of ourselves is conscious can we free ourselves of the limiting influence of habit and protect ourselves from the potential limitations of newly acquired skills becoming habitual.

For the dancer or choreographer there is an obvious need for the recognition of the centrality of habit in the problems of dance practice and of the importance of conscious control as a means of escaping from its boundaries. Any style, choreographic or technical, ossified into habitual solutions will mean that new ideas will tend to be drawn into the orbit of the old and consequently stifled. The Alexander Technique therefore has a place in dance practice at least as a means of freeing the dance practitioner from habit. It may not be possible to produce "highly skilled dancers [but] without any rigid style imprint in their bodies' (Fortin 1993:97) but it should be possible to produce highly skilled dancers who have, and are skilled in operating, a capacity to change. Change is an essential part of dance and so dance practice should have the capacity to embrace and facilitate it.[54]

Alexander's radical approach to re-education presented alternatives to learning based on habit and typified by repetition, replication and imitation which thereby prevented openness, change and creativity. Some seventy years after he (and Dewey) were at work these ideas have come to the fore again in current debates about curriculum design and in particular in relation to dance (Hanstein 1990).

To conclude, Alexander was contemporary with a number of key figures in twentieth century dance. Many dancers have sought a means of improving their practice. Paradoxically, it was Alexander who had a Technique which provided a means to do so. It was not recognised by dancers at the time, although some other contemporaries, particularly Todd, on close reading, reveal ideas which are similar to Alexander's and which may be unwittingly unacknowledged. The relationship between the Alexander Technique and dance has not always been made clear. However, the problems identified by dancers and commentators are precisely those which, when analysed in terms of Alexander's concepts of habit and use, are amenable to solution.

His Technique was discovered in the last decade of the nineteenth century but, when considered from the standpoint of this paper, can be seen to have a clear relevance in the last decade of the twentieth. It should be clear that the Technique cannot be simply added to dance training but, at least in terms of Alexander's solution to habit, is central to dance training and education. The Alexander Technique provides a radical re-education for the individual and a wherewithal to break free of habit. It provides choice, a means to break down the barriers of habit and transform our own dancing.

[1] De Montfort University: Leicester, formerly Leicester Polytechnic. Michael has been teaching dance history there since 1980, Jayne has been teaching dance technique and choreography since 1983. Martin has been teaching the Alexander Technique since 1992. His predecessor, Sue Davies, first started teaching the Technique there on a regular basis in 1985 after it had been introduced by Brian Door.

[2] He did not write about dance per se. However, he was critical of methods of physical education which were popular at that time and which have certain similarities with dance training. See especially <u>Universal Constant in Living</u> (1941).

[3]<u>Man's Supreme Inheritance</u>, <u>Constructive Conscious Control of the Individual</u>, <u>The Use of the Self</u>, <u>The Universal Constant in Living</u> respectively.

[4] Set out in, for instance,
Jaques-Dalcroze (1912, 1920; 1930),
Schlemmer (1924, 1961),
Braun (ed.) (1969) <u>Meyerhold on Theatre.</u>
Mensendieck (1931) <u>It's Up To You</u> is the main English language text, but there is an earlier, untranslated German text, Mensendieck (1919) <u>Körperkultur der Frau: praktisch hygienische und praktisch asthetische Wink.</u>

There are various commentaries on aspects of theory at this time, the most recent being Daly's 'Isadora Duncan's Dance Theory' (1994) which also begins to contextualise the period.

[5] Laban (1920) <u>Die Welt des Tänzers</u> (The World of the Dancer), unpublished translation (1966) by S. Goddard, courtesy of G. Curl.
Laban (1926) <u>Choreographie</u> (Choreography) unpublished translation (1966) by S. Goddard, courtesy of G. Curl.
Laban (1926) <u>Gymnastik und Tanz</u> (literally Gymnastics and Dance) unpublished translation (1966) by W. Brooks, courtesy of G. Curl.

[6] Laban and Lawrence (1947) <u>Effort,</u> although this was predated by the lesser known, limited, publication, (1942) <u>Laban/Lawrence Industrial Rhythm and Lilt in Labour.</u>
Laban (1948) <u>Modern Educational Dance.</u>
Laban (1950) <u>Mastery of Movement on the Stage.</u>

[7] Todd's theories were first published in Boston in 1920 and 1921. They were extensively laid out in her published syllabus of 1929 before being developed for her main publication of 1937.

[8] 1888-1898.

[9] Three of these (1906, 1907, 1909) were specifically about "respiratory re-education". The second of which, (1907) The Theory and Practice of a New Method of Respiratory Re-education, appears in the 3rd Edition (1946) of <u>Man's Supreme Inheritance</u>. The other pamphlet, (1908) Re-education of the Kinesthetic Systems (Sensory Appreciation of Muscular Movement) Concerned with the Development of Robust Physical Well-Being was reprinted in the 1st Edition (1910) of <u>Man's Supreme Inheritance</u>.

[10] (1946:20, 52, 54, 55, 122, 136, 137).

[11] Alexander's visits to the States are documented in some detail in Jones (1976).

[12] Albert Redden Alexander (1874-1947), F.M Alexander's brother, learned the Technique from him in Australia, developed it with him, came to London, visited the U.S.A. extensively and stayed there. He taught F.P. Jones, amongst others. See Jones (1976) for one of the few acknowledgements of his work.

[13] Dewey (1918) 'Introductory Word', Man's Supreme Inheritance.
Dewey (1918) 'Reply to a Reviewer of Man's Supreme Inheritance'.
Dewey (1918) 'Another Letter from the Pen of Professor John Dewey', May 27, 1918.
Dewey (1923) 'Introduction', Constructive Conscious Control of the Individual.
Dewey (1939) 'Introduction', The Use of the Self.

[14] Republished as 'The Barrier of Habit'. The importance that he attaches to Alexander's analysis of habit is summed up: 'The medium of habit filters all the material that reaches our perception and thought' Dewey (1921,1978:71).

[15] Described in Spiesman (1960) and celebrated by Kraus (1969:131-3), a later Professor of Education at Teacher's College.

[16] Where she wrote and published (1940, 1957) Dance: a Creative Art Experience.

[17] Todd first published in 1920 and 1921.Her syllabus, The Balancing Forces in the Human Body was published privately in 1929 whilst she was at Teachers College. The Thinking Body is an expanded version of the earlier text. There has, to date, been no examination of the relationship between her ideas and Alexander's. However, there is sufficient similarity in the use of a cluster of terms such as 'psychophysical', 'position of mechanical advantage', 'sensory appreciation' and 'habit', along with detailed mechanical descriptions, to warrant further research into provenance. For instance, Alexander used all these terms as early as 1910 (in the first part of Man's Supreme Inheritance): 'psychophysical' (1910, 1946:10 et. seq.); 'position of mechanical advantage' (1910, 1946:52 et. seq.); 'sensory appreciation' (1910, 1946: 53 et. seq.). Todd's first paper was in 1920.In the following year she begins to favour mechanical 'disadvantage' rather than her earlier term mechanical 'misadjustment'. There is also extensive reference to habit (1920; 1921 and 1929) that requires further comparison. Alexander first referred to habit, within the totality of his consideration, in detail, in (1910, 1946: vii et. seq.).

[18] Alexander (1946) Man's Supreme Inheritance, 3rd edition.
Alexander (1946) Constructive Conscious Control of the Individual, 8th edition, reprinted in 1955.

[19] The year before she died.

[20] Dance & Dancers included an article which identified interest in the technique by Holmes in 1963. In 'Relieving the Tensions' the author admitted that he was not an authority on the subject, neither had he wanted to write the article in the first place.

168

[21] Leibowitz trained as an Alexander teacher with Westfeldt, was co-founder of the American Centre for the Alexander Technique and a teacher at the New York Juilliard School.

[22] Wragg is credited as co–founder of The Jane Winearls Studio in London [1962] where he taught 'movement coordination'.in an undated pamphlet <u>The Jane Winearls Studio,</u> London. Winearls took up a post at the University of Birmingham in 1965.

[23] 'A technique for performance' (1968:162-8). Winearls' second edition, on close reading, reveals attributions to Alexander by both Wragg and Winearls herself, but although both refer to Alexander by name, neither refers to his 'Technique'.

[24] 'Rudolf Laban illuminated, Kurt Jooss inspired, Sigurd Leeder enlightened and F. Matthias Alexander integrated a life that would have been impoverished without the richness of dance' (1990:113).

[25] Laban (1920; 1926; 1948; 1950; 1966), Laban and Lawrence (1947). Choreutics, first drafted in 1939 was finally published, posthumously, in 1966.

[26] Bartenieff, and Lewis's (1980) <u>Body Movement: Coping With the Environment</u> is drawn primarily from Laban's work, but is wide ranging in its other sources, and includes a small acknowledgement to Alexander's ideas.

[27] Described in, for instance, Bainbridge Cohen (1982; 1987; 1988).

[28] Some are by teachers trained by Alexander; some by teachers trained by them and and some by others. The latest being Macdonald (1994). A full listing will be found in a bibliography to be published in Huxley (forthcoming). In addition there were many pamphlets privately published by Alexander Schools and Associations.

[29] Initially in their biographical details in programmes for Trisha Brown Company (1983).

[30] See Charlip (1981; 1986), Pierpont (1980), Crow (1985), Skura (1990), Fulkerson (1978;1982; 1987), Tufnell and Crickmay (1990).

[31] For instance, in Macdonald (1994) testimonials are given by people from various professions and pastimes including "dancing", where Madeleine White extols its benefits, particularly its remedial ones, for ballet dancers. Conable and Conable (1991/2:114–117) include a chapter entitled 'If you're a Dancer'.

[32] See, for instance, Caplan (1985), Charlip (1981), Crow (1985; 1988), Rosenthal (1981).

[33] Especially Eddy (1991/2), Myers (1980; 1991/2), Myers and Horosko (1989), Oliver (1993a,b).

[34] With the exception of books like that of Hodgkinson (1988), a populist account by a journalist.

[35] Jones' <u>Body Awareness in Action: A Study of the Alexander Technique</u> has the most academically oriented bibliography.

[36] Dewey said, amongst other things:
'The principle and procedure set forth by Mr. Alexander are crucially needed at present. Strangely, this is the very reason why they are hard to understand and accept. For although there is nothing esoteric in his teaching, and although his exposition is made in the simplest English, free from technical words, it is difficult for anyone to grasp its full force without having actual demonstration of the principle in operation. And even then, as I know from personal experience, its full meaning dawns upon one slowly and with new meanings continually opening up' (1923, 1987;xi).

'The principle or theory of Mr. Alexander and the observed consequences of its operation have developed at the same time and in the closest connexion with each other. Both have evolved out of an experimental method of procedure. At no time has he elaborated a theory for its own sake' (ibid xiv).

[37] See, for example, Novack (1990). Some of these concerns are referred to later. Others invite further research.

[38] According to Myers (1991/2), somatics is a term popularised by Thomas Hanna, editor of <u>Somatics Magazine: Journal of the Bodily Arts and Sciences</u> in the late seventies. The term refers to things pertaining to or affecting the body.

[39] One must assume that it would be possible to find equal numbers who would attest to how much the Alexander Technique, as taught them, did not benefit their dancing significantly.

[40] Lisa de Ribere in Berardi et al 1992/3:12.

[41] He detailed his idea of use in his first book (1910), expanded on it in his second (1923);and titled his third book (1932) <u>The Use of the Self</u> after this central concept.

[42] Magnus (1924). Unpublished translation courtesy of B. Door.

[43] Much more could be said about Alexander's concept of use than time or space here allows. It will be considered in more detail in future papers.

[44] "This led me to a long consideration of the whole question of the direction of the use of myself. 'What is this direction,' I asked myself, 'upon which I have been depending?' I had to admit that I had never thought out how I directed the use of myself, but that I used myself habitually in the way that <u>felt natural to</u> me. In other words, I like everyone else depended upon 'feeling' for the direction of my use" (1985:35).

[45] 'It can be demonstrated [that] the influence of the manner in which we use ourselves is operating continuously either for or against us in every moment of our lives' (Alexander 1986:8).

[46] Basmajian and Luca (1985).

[47] This applies whether the axiom be a tradition, its development, the originator's style, efficiency, economy or safety.

[48] Though it is employed by some Alexander teachers.

[49] Alexander contended that, "The pupil's conception of what his teacher is trying to convey to him by words will be in accordance with his (the pupil's) psycho-physical makeup. In this sense it can be truly said that a pupil hears only what he wants to hear, because what he wants is decided by the standards fixed by his present habits" (1987:79).

[50] 'Satisfactory general use is essential to satisfactory specific use' Alexander (1987:134).

[51] There is a great deal to be said (and experienced) about this process. Space and time here does not allow us to deal with factors other than those directly relevant to habit. Factors which are not dealt with in any detail in this paper include, in Alexander's terms, sensory appreciation, primary control, direction, inhibition, means whereby and end gaining.

[52] The three year B.A. (Hons) in Performing Arts: Contemporary Dance programme at De Montfort University enables students to study dance and the Alexander Technique in the relationship to one another that this paper begins to describe. Students can, if they so wish, take modules in Alexander Technique for Performers in each year of their course, alongside modules in Dance Practice, Contemporary Choreography and Performance.

[53] Conable & Conable (1991/2:114) point out that dancers frequently gain an 'Alexander habit'.

[54] This is not generally the case. See Oliver (1993a & b) and Stephens (1987:16-50).

REFERENCES

Alexander, F. M. (1906) Introduction to a New Method of Respiratory Vocal Education, London: Balliere.

—— (1907) The Theory and Practice of a New Method of Respiratory Reeducation, London: Balliere.
       reprinted in Alexander,F.M. (1946):188–205.

—— (1908) Re-education of the Kinesthetic Systems (Sensory Appreciation of Muscular Movement) Concerned with the Development of Robust Physical Well-Being (pamphlet), London.
       reprinted in Alexander, F.M. (1910): 185–189.

—— (1909) Why We Breathe Incorrectly (pamphlet), London.

—— (1910) Man's Supreme Inheritance, London: Methuen.

—— (1912) Conscious Control in Relation to Human Evolution in Civilization, London: Methuen.

—— (1918) Man's Supreme Inheritance: Conscious Guidance and Control in Relation to Human Evolution in Civilization, revised, 2nd edition, London: Methuen; New York: Dutton.
       incorporates Conscious Control (1912)

—— (1923) Constructive Conscious Control of the Individual, London: Methuen; New York: Dutton.

—— (1932) The Use of the Self: Its Conscious Direction in Relation to Diagnosis, Functioning and the Control of Reaction, London: Methuen.

—— (1939) The Use of the Self: Its Conscious Direction in Relation to Diagnosis, Functioning and the Control of Reaction, 2nd edition, London: Chaterson.

—— (1941) The Universal Constant in Living, New York: Dutton.

—— (1946) Man's Supreme Inheritance: Conscious Guidance and Control in Relation to Human Evolution in Civilization, 3rd edition, London: Re-Educational Publications.

—— (1946, 1955) <u>Constructive Conscious Control of the Individual,</u> 8th edition, 2nd reprint, London: Re-Educational Publications.

—— (1985) <u>The Use of the Self: Its Conscious Direction in Relation to Diagnosis, Functioning and the Control of Reaction,</u> 4th edition, London: Gollancz.

—— (1986) <u>The Universal Constant in Living,</u> Long Beach, Calif.: Centreline.

—— (1987) <u>Constructive Conscious Control of the Individual,</u> 8th edition, London: Gollancz.

Bainbridge Cohen, B. (1982) 'The Training Problems of the Dancer', <u>Contact Quarterly</u> **VII**(3/4): 9–15.

—— (1987) 'The Action in Perceiving: Movement as the First Perception', <u>Contact Quarterly</u> **XII**(3): 22–26.

—— (1988) 'The Dancer's Warm-Up Through Body-Mind Centering', <u>Contact Quarterly</u> **XIII**(3): 28–29 + 32–33.

Barlow, W. (1973) <u>The Alexander Principle,</u> London: Gollancz.

Barlow, W. (ed.) (1978) <u>More Talk of Alexander: Aspects of the Alexander Principle,</u> London: Victor Gollancz.

Bartenieff, I. and Lewis, D. (1980) <u>Body Movement: Coping With the Environment,</u> New York: Gordon & Breach.

Basmajian, J. V. and De Luca, C. (1962, 1985) <u>Muscles Alive: Their Functions Revealed by Electromyography,</u> 5th edition, Baltimore: Williams & Wilkins.

Berardi, G. et al. (1992/3) 'Professional Goals and Personal Needs: Excerpts from the "Finding Balance" Seminar', <u>Kinesiology and Medicine for Dance</u> **15**(1): 1–14.

Bird, B., Jarrell, J., et al. (1979) Some Considerations of Technique, <u>Dancing and Dance Theory,</u> V. Preston-Dunlop (ed.) , Sevenoaks, Kent: The Scorpion Press.

Braun, E. (ed.) (1969) <u>Meyerhold on Theatre,</u> New York: Hill and Wang.

Caplan, D. (1985) 'The Alexander Technique: the use of conscious control in the prevention and treatment of dance injuries', <u>Contact Quarterly</u> **X**(3): 31–32.

Charlip, R. (1981) 'Bone Meditations', <u>Contact Quarterly</u> **VII**(1, Fall): 21–32.

——(1986) 'Now Thyself: First Instalment', <u>Contact Quarterly</u> **XI**(1): 23–34.

Cohen, R. (1986) <u>The Dance Workshop,</u> London: Gaia Books.

Conable, B. and Conable, W. (1991/2) <u>How to Learn the Alexander Technique: a Manual for Students,</u> Second revised and enlarged edition, Columbus, Ohio: Andover Road Press.

Crow, A. (1985) 'Interview with Eva Karczag: two Alexander teachers talk', <u>Contact Quarterly</u> **X**(3): 33–38.

——(1988) 'Awareness and Choice: a look at F.M. Alexander's "inhibition and direction"', <u>Contact Quarterly</u> **XIII**(2): 27–28.

Cunningham, M. (1951, 1982) 'The Function of a Technique for Dance', <u>Contact Quarterly</u> (Spring/Summer): 5–7.

Daly, A. (1994) 'Isadora Duncan's Dance Theory', <u>Dance Research Journal</u> **26**(2, Fall): 24–28.

Dewey, J. (1918a) 'Introductory Word', in Alexander,F.M. (1918) <u>Man's Supreme Inheritance,</u> 2nd edition: v–xvii.
     reprinted in Alexander, F.M. (1946) 3rd edition:xix–xxi.

——(1918b) 'Reply to a Reviewer of <u>Man's Supreme Inheritance</u>', <u>New Republic,</u> 55. in Alexander,F.M. (1918) <u>Man's Supreme Inheritance,</u> 2nd edition: xviii–xx.

——(1918c) 'Another Letter from the Pen of Professor John Dewey, May 27', in Alexander,F.M. (1918) <u>Man's Supreme Inheritance,</u> 2nd edition: x–xxii.

——(1921,1930) <u>Human Nature and Conduct,</u> New York: Henry Holt.

——(1921, 1978) The Barrier of Habit, <u>More Talk of Alexander,</u> W. Barlow, (ed.) London: Gollancz:69–73.
     first published in Dewey, J. (1921)

——(1923) 'Introduction' in Alexander, F.M. (1923) <u>Constructive Conscious Control of the Individual</u>
    reprinted in Alexander, F.M. (1987) 3rd edition:xi–xviii.

——(1929) <u>Experience and Nature,</u> New York: W.W. Norton.

——(1939) 'Introduction', in Alexander, F. M. (1939) <u>The Use of the Self,</u> 2nd edition,   reprinted in Alexander, F.M. (1985) 3rd edition:7–12.

Eddy, M. (1991/2) 'Overview of the Science and Somatics of Dance', <u>Kinesiology and Medicine for Dance</u> **14**(1, Fall/Winter): 20–28.

Fortin, S. (1993) 'When Dance Science and Somatics Enter the Dance Technique Class', <u>Kinesiology and Medicine for Dance</u> **15**(2, Spring/Summer 1993): 88–107.

Fulkerson, M. (1978) 'An Interview Between Mary Fulkerson and Members of the New Dance Collective', <u>New Dance</u> (7): 12– 14.

——(1982) <u>A Move to Stillness,</u> Theatre Papers, Dartington: Dartington College of Arts.

——(1987) 'In Interview with Peter Hulton and Richard Allsopp of Theatre Papers', <u>New Dance</u> (40): 20–21

Graham, M. (1941, 1980) A Modern Dancer's Primer for Action, <u>The Dance Anthology,</u> C. Steinberg, (ed.), New York: Plume:44–52.

Gregory, R. L. (ed.) (1987) <u>The Oxford Companion to the Mind,</u> Oxford: Oxford University Press.

H'Doubler, M. (1940, 1957) <u>Dance: a Creative Art Experience,</u> Wisconsin: University of Wisconsin.

Hanrahan, C. and Salmela, J. H. (1990) 'Dance images: Do they really work or are we just imagining things?', <u>Journal of Physical Education, Recreation and Dance</u> **61**(2): 18–21.

Hanstein, P. (1990) 'Educating for the future: A post–modern paradigm for dance education.', <u>Journal of Physical Education, Recreation and Dance</u> **61**(5): 56–58.

Hawkins, E. (1965) Pure Poetry, in <u>The Modern Dance: Seven Statements of Belief,</u> S. J. Cohen, (ed.), Middletown, Conn.: Wesleyan University Press:39–51.

Hodgkinson, L. (1988) <u>The Alexander Technique and How it Can Help You,</u> London: Piatkus.

Holmes, A. (1963) 'Relieving the Tensions', <u>Dance and Dancers</u> (June): 47–49.

Hutchinson Guest, A. (ed.) (1988) <u>Shawn's Fundamental of Dance,</u> London: Gordon and Breach.

Jaques-Dalcroze, E. (1912, 1920) 'Rhythm as A Factor in Education', <u>The Eurhythmics of Jaques-Dalcroze,</u>3rd edition, London: Constable.

——(1930) <u>Eurhythmics, Art and Education,</u> F. Rothwell (trans), C. Cox (ed.), London: Chatto & Windus.

Jones, F. P. (1976) <u>Body Awareness in Action: A Study of the Alexander Technique,</u> New York: Schocken Books.

Kraus, R. (1969) <u>History of the Dance in Art and Education,</u> Englewood Cliffs, New Jersey: Prentice-Hall.

Laban, R. (1920) <u>Die Welt des Tänzers,</u> Stuttgart: Walter Seifert.

——(1926) <u>Choreographie,</u> Jena: Diederichs.

—— (1926) <u>Gymnastik und Tanz,</u> Oldenburg: Gerhard Stalling.

——(1948) <u>Modern Educational Dance,</u> London: Macdonald & Evans.

——(1950) <u>Mastery of Movement on the Stage,</u> London: Macdonald and Evans.

—— (1966) <u>Choreutics,</u> London: Macdonald & Evans.
    Part I written in 1939. Published posthumously.

Laban, R. and Lawrence, F. C. (1942) <u>Laban/Lawrence Industrial Rhythm and Lilt in Labour,</u> Manchester: Paton Lawrence & Co.

—— (1947) <u>Effort,</u> London: Macdonald & Evans.

Leibowitz, J. (1967/68) 'For the Victims of Our Culture: The Alexander Technique', <u>Dance Scope</u> **4**(1): 32–37.

McDermott, J. J. (1973) John Dewey: a Biographical Sketch, <u>The Philosophy of John Dewey,</u> ed. J. J. McDermott, Chicago: Chicago University Press.

Macdonald, G. (1994) <u>Alexander Technique,</u> London: Headway.

Magnus, R. (1924) <u>Körperstellung,</u> Berlin: Springer.

Maisel, E., ed. (1969) <u>The Philosophy of the Body: The Essential Writings of F. Matthias Alexander including Articles on the Alexander Technique,</u> New York: University Books.
    republished 1974 as <u>The Resurrection of the Body</u>.

Matt, P., H (1991/2) 'Ideokinesis: Integrating the Science and Somatics of Dance', <u>Kinesiology and Medicine for Dance</u> **14**(1, Fall/Winter): 68-77.

Mensendieck, B. M. (1919) <u>Körperkultur der Frau: praktisch hygienische und praktisch asthetische Winke,</u> Munich: F. Bruckmann.

——(1931) <u>It's Up To You,</u> New York: Mensendieck System Main School.

Meyer, R. (1966, 1970) Freedom Through Discipline, <u>The Dance Experience: Readings in Dance Appreciation,</u> M. H. Nadel and C. G. Nadel, (eds) New York: Praeger:366–369.

Myers, M. (1980) 'Body Therapies and the Modern Dancer: The Alexander Technique', <u>Dance Magazine</u> **LIV**(4, April): 90–94.

—— (1991/2) 'Dance Science and Somatics: a Perspective', <u>Kinesiology and Medicine for Dance</u> **14**(1, Fall/Winter): 3–19.

Myers, M. and Horosko, M. (1989) 'When Classes are Not Enough: Body Therapies', <u>Dance magazine</u> (July): 47–50.

Nadel, M. H. and Nadel, C. G. (eds) (1970) <u>The Dance Experience: Readings in Dance Appreciation,</u> New York: Praeger.

Novack, C. J. (1990) <u>Sharing the Dance: Contact Improvisation and American Culture,</u> Madison: University of Wisconsin Press.

Oliver, S. K (1993a) 'Case Study: The Alexander Technique as an Intervention in Lower Back Dysfunction in a Dancer', <u>Kinesiology and Medicine for Dance</u> **15**(2): 80–87.

Oliver, S. K (1993b) 'Lower Back Injuries in Dancers and the Alexander Technique', <u>Kinesiology and Medicine for Dance</u> **15**(2): 65–79.

Pierpont, M. (1980) 'A Conversation with Remy Charlip', <u>Dance Magazine</u> **LIV**(4, April): 92.

Plastino, J. G. (1990) 'Incorporating Dance Science Into Technique Class And Performance Training', <u>Journal of Physical Education, Recreation and Dance</u> **61**(2): 26–27.

Richmond, P. G. (1994) 'The Alexander technique and dance training', <u>Impulse,</u> Champaign, Ill. **v.2**(no.1. Jan.): 24-38.

Rosenthal, E. (1981) 'Alexander Technique: Notes on a Teaching Method', <u>Contact Quarterly</u> **VII**(1, Fall): 14–19.

Ryan, A. J. and Stephens, R. E. (eds) (1987) <u>Dance Medicine. A Comprehensive Guide,</u> Chicago: Pluribus Press.

Schlemmer, O. (1924, 1961) 'Man and Art Figure', <u>The Theater of the Bauhaus,</u> W. Gropius,(ed.), Middletown, Conn.: Wesleyan:17–32.

Shook, K. (1977, 1978) <u>Elements of Classical Ballet Technique,</u> London: Dance Books.

Skura, S. (1990) 'Releasing Dance: interview with Joan Skinner', <u>Contact Quarterly</u> **15**(3): 11–18.

Sorell, W. (1969) <u>Hanya Holm: The Biography of an Artist,</u> Middletown, Connecticut: Wesleyan University Press.

Sorell, Walter, (1951) <u>The Dance Has Many Faces,</u> Cleveland & New York: World Publishing.

Spiesman, M. C. (1960) 'Dance Education Pioneers: Colby, Larson, H'Doubler', <u>Journal of Physical Education, Recreation and Dance</u> (January): 25–27.

Stark Smith, N. (1981) 'Living Anatomy of Vision: Interview with Bonnie Bainbridge Cohen', <u>Contact Quarterly</u> **VI**(2): 4–9.

Steinberg, C. (ed.) (1980) <u>The Dance Anthology,</u> New York: New American Library.

Stephens, R. E. (1987) The Etiology of Injuries in Ballet, <u>Dance Medicine. A Comprehensive Guide,</u> A. J. Ryan and R. E. Stephens, (eds) Chicago: Pluribus Press:16–50.

Sweigard, L. E. (1949, 1970) Psychomotor Function as Correlated with Body Mechanics and Posture, <u>The Dance Experience: Readings in Dance Appreciation,</u> M. H. Nadel and C. G. Nadel, (eds) New York: Praeger:358–365.

——(1974) <u>Human Movement Potential: Its Ideokinetic Facilitation,</u> New York: Harper & Row.

Todd, M. E. (1920) 'Principles of Posture', <u>Boston Medical & Surgical Journal</u> **clxxxii**(26, June 24): 645–649.
        republished (1977), New York, Dance Horizons.

——(1921) 'Principles of posture, with special reference to the mechanics of the hip joint', <u>Boston Medical & Surgical Journal</u> **clxxxiv**(25, June 23): 667–673.
        republished (1977), New York, Dance Horizons.

——(1929) <u>The Balancing Forces in the Human Body,</u> New York: Privately Published.
        republished (1977), New York, Dance Horizons.

—— (1931) 'Our strains and tensions', <u>Progressive Educ. Mag.</u> (March):

—— (1934) <u>The First Principles of Body Balance,</u> pamphlet, republished (1977), New York, Dance Horizons.

——(1937, 1968) <u>The Thinking Body: a Study of the Balancing Forces of Dynamic Man,</u> Repub., New York: Dance Horizons.
        first published in 1937 by Paul B Hoeber, first Dance Horizons republication 1968 with a Preface by Lulu Sweigard.

—— (1977) <u>Early Writings 1920–1934,</u> New York: Dance Horizons.

Tomkins, C. (1968, 1970) An Appetite For Motion, <u>The Dance Experience: Readings in Dance Appreciation,</u> eds M. H. Nadel and C. G. Nadel, New York: Praeger. 257–292.

Tufnell, M. and Crickmay, C. (1990) <u>Body, Space, Image: Notes Towards Improvisation and Performance,</u> London: Virago.

Vaganova, A. (1946, 1969) <u>Basic Principles of Classical Ballet: Russian Ballet Technique,</u> trans.A. Chujoy, repub. of second (1953) edition, New York: Dover.

Westfeldt, L. (1964) <u>F. Matthias Alexander: The Man and His Work,</u> Connecticut: Associated Booksellers.

White, M. (1993) 'Ballet and the Alexander Technique', <u>Dance Gazette</u> (213, June): 46-47.

Winearls, J. (1968) <u>Modern Dance: The Jooss – Leeder Method,</u> 2nd edition, London: A&C Black.

Winearls, J. (1990) <u>Choreography: The Art of the Body,</u> London: Dance Books.

Wragg, G. (1968) 'A Technique for Performance' in Winearls (1968:162–168)

TENSIONS IN THE DEFINITION OF COMMUNITY DANCE

Linda Jasper
Community Dance and Mime Foundation

Community Dance is the fastest growing dance profession in the UK. It currently employs an estimated 250 practitioners, and membership of the Community Dance and Mime Foundation (CDMF) stands at over 500. From its recent beginnings in 1976, with the establishment of three posts, this profession has established itself as a 'growing concern'.

In 1993, the Arts Council published *Community Dance: A Progress Report* (Peppiatt and Vennor, 1993) in which an argument is made for a wider and more inclusive definition of the community dance worker, defining workers by what they do rather than by job title or funding. So, by what is in effect *self* selection, Community Dance workers are people who work primarily, for example, as educationalists, choreographers or free-lance dancer/teacher/animateurs. Community Dance work crosses over the borders of education, youth and community, dance company education, therapy, community building, performance, and recreation and leisure.

This wider definition leads to consideration of the underlying connections between these practitioners and raises the question of what defines Community Dance practice. CDMF has addressed this issue, working with its members and the Executive committee to identify the common principles that underpin the work of this diverse profession.

An allied area of debate in the dance world is whether Community Dance should be distinguished as separate from other dance practise, or be included within all Dance fields. This inclusive/exclusive debate is one that has been presented through the Community Dance magazine *Animated* and Arts Council reports. This paper will explore the question of whether Community Dance can be positioned as a separate entity within the dance world through the comparison of the policies and practices of Community Dance with those of other sectors in the wider dance field.

Roots

In order to see where an organisation is positioned it is useful to examine where its origins lie. The emergence of Community Dance in the late 1970s had three influences: (1) the adoption of American contemporary dance in the late 1960s and the growth of a professional company and school; (2) the Laban-based educational dance provision in the education sector; and (3) the Community Arts movement. Each are discussed below.

The importation of American contemporary dance

In my opinion, this was the most important influence in the first phase of Community Dance development. Significant in the Arts Council's funding of the first animateur posts was the need to create audiences for the national and regional contemporary companies that sprang from the Contemporary Dance Trust and the subsequent 'new dance' development (e.g., EMMA, Cycles, Spiral, Extempory, New English Dance Theatre). All these companies took on a range of educational activities as well as the creation and performance of new work.

In the 1980s when regional dance companies were closing due to lack of audiences, resources and funding, there was a growth in animateur posts. The regional arts boards started to invest in animateur posts as revenue funding to companies was withdrawn. Many companies saw the new animateur posts as a cheap substitute for proper funding of their work. The main reasons for the demise of the regional companies were that the regional audiences could not sustain a local company, and that venues preferred to bring in a range of dance performance work, not necessarily that based in their region. As one reason was poor audience figures, the Arts Council and Regional Arts Associations saw the first animateur posts as a means of developing a dance culture and infrastructure in the UK for contemporary dance. In the light of this, it is interesting to note the origins of the first three posts: in Cardiff, with Molly Kenny; in Ellesmere Port, Cheshire, with Veronica Lewis; and in Swindon, with Marie McClusky.

The demise of the Welsh Dance Theatre in 1975 after two years of operation generated an animateur post based at the Sherman Theatre, Cardiff. Molly Kenny was appointed in 1977, and developed the post into the Rubicon Dance Project. In a paper for the Welsh Arts Councils seminar on Community Dance, which took place in November 1982, Faith Wilson (Dance Officer, Welsh Arts Council) outlines the reasons for developing a Community Dance post after the demise of the company:

> That it was necessary to engage in some form of direct initiative was inevitable in a country with little or no history of professional dance (though Wales does, of course, possess a vigorous folk dance tradition, and like anywhere else in the UK, there were private dance teachers of Ballet offering the usual syllabus-based classes), but the Panel now had to give close consideration to the appropriateness to Wales of such initiatives.... The panel resolved to work from a 'grass roots' level in the hopes that a tradition for it would grow organically over a period of years.
>
> Wilson, 1982, p12

Wilson goes onto argue the importance of dance activity for its own sake rather than just for professional artistic development. But the primary reason stated for the initiation of the animateur post was to develop a supportive culture for future professional dance work.

Veronica Lewis's post, later to become Director of Cheshire Dance Workshop, was established from a successful dancer-in-residence placement initiated by the Gulbenkian Foundation, then chaired by Peter Brinson, creator and director of Ballet For All. This project has always had direct links with the professional dance world, providing opportunities for the local population to access the dance of the mainstream companies. Particularly of note are the epic annual performances that bring together professional and amateur dancers.

The Swindon project grew out of a different root, the Community Arts services within the Thamesdown Borough's Leisure and Arts Department. Dance was one arts activity recognised within the structure, having been developed voluntarily by Marie McClusky, a local private dance teacher who had a professional dance training and had been a student at London School of Contemporary Dance. Presenting performances and the development of professional artists, particularly through the Foundation Course, has been an ongoing focus for the project.

Therefore, at the beginning, due to the Arts Councils and Regional Arts Associations' involvement, the animateur posts were closely associated with main stream dance companies and thereby theatre dance forms.

Educational dance

The establishment of educational dance was influential in the second wave of dance animateurs. In the first Arts Council of Great Britain evaluation in 1985, 56% of these were found to have had teacher training as well as dance training. The teacher training courses in dance were well established by the 1970s, and many animateurs took this training into the field. The Laban-based courses presented an analytical movement model which could be applied across a variety of contexts. It also meant that many animateurs were qualified to teach in state schools, and consequently there was an emphasis on working in education and within the local advisory structure. For example, as Scilla Dyke did in Suffolk.

Community Arts movement

The notion of every one being an artist—cultural democratisation and the democratisation of culture (Kelly, 1984)—was revealed in the Community Arts movement's practice of broadening the definitions of who could produce art, in which context and for what purpose. Particularly influential for Community Dance was the use of pedestrian movement (also introduced through the New Dance movement). The recognition of the 'everyday' in art making was thereby translated into a movement and gesture vocabulary that did not require a long and highly skilled training. This philosophy, of Community Arts, coupled with the accessibility of contemporary dance and educational dance techniques and methods, was the basis for Community Dance work.

Developments

The starting point for the original three posts was for the reasons of audience creation and education, but it can be seen that other functions became important as the work developed. All Community Dance projects, even the ones with clear professional dance company links, developed a range of activities through addressing the practicalities and opportunities of managing and interacting with people in community-based projects. The second generation of posts in the early 1980s, usually had links with professional performance artists written into their brief, but as new posts were formed a wider focus for the work emerged. Community Dance projects were initiated and funded by youth services, community services, and social services as dance could be seen as a potential medium for the delivery of objectives other than those involved with audience development.

Present State of the Profession

In order to position Community Dance in the wide variety of dance work, it is important to identify in more detail the people who work in the field and the work that they do. The people who deliver the work are mainly highly educated in the medium of dance. A survey of workers was undertaken by Christopher Thompson in 1988, to which there was a high response rate of 63%. One of the questions, on education and training in dance, revealed the following:

183

All had completed some course of higher education. For all but 8 this had included formal training in Dance.... For 23% the main subject in their higher education course was Dance, for 53% it was Dance and Teaching.

Thompson, 1989, p5

Asked about their work, respondents to Thompson's questionnaire gave the following as high priorities:

- Making the experience of dance available and accessible. 62% rated this a high priority. 57% rated it as top priority. Only 2 people gave this a low priority.

- Developing and encouraging the practice of dance as a creative and expressive activity.

- Using dance as a resource for education in its widest sense.

- Offering dance particularly to minority or disadvantaged groups and to those with learning difficulties or special needs.

They gave as low or fairly low priorities:

- Offering pre-vocational dance training.

- Offering access to dance as a means of developing fitness and general well-being.

- Creating a dance information and resource network.

- Asked if they wish to bring about radical change, 43% rated this a low priority. (Only 15% rated it highly.)

The work objectives might prove to have similar concerns but the areas in which the workers practise are wide and do not display the same cohesiveness. This is clearly displayed in the list of activities published *Community Dance: A Progress Report* (Peppiatt and Vennor, 1993). Most Community Dance workers see access to dance itself as the primary reason for their work. It is therefore understandable that criticism has been levied at the Community Dance movement for being 'ameliorative' rather than 'radical', to quote Chris Thompson's model (1994). This model describes three distinct positions in Community Dance practise: alternative, ameliorative and radical. Thompson suggests that although projects might embrace different aspects in their diverse programmes, in the main the work falls into the 'ameliorative' area.

Perhaps it could be argued that it is difficult to be 'radical' or 'alternative' when posts are funded by state quangos, managed mainly by public-sector employees and the workers have received a traditional dance training and/or education. Can it be really possible within these restraints to present a radical approach to dance development?

Community Dance Policy

Consideration has to be given as to where the profession is in the middle of the 1990s. The Community Dance and Mime Foundation's statement on policy is as follows:

Community Dance is the application of dance by a professional in a specific place for a particular group of people. It offers participants a wide range of educational, recreational and aesthetic benefits. It can improve fitness, develop social and communication skills, body awareness and coordination and enable participants to learn about other art forms and cultures.

CDMF, 1994, p2

What is clear from this statement is the openness of interpretation of the process, content and context. The only thing that is clearly addressed is that the participant within the group becomes the focus and also that dance is referred to its widest forms, that is, not just as an art form. It also suggests a strong educational focus in the work. What is not explicit in the policy statement is the intention to be 'radical', or to offer an 'alternative' vision for dance work. The socio-political nature of the work associated with the Community Arts movement is one that needs to be explored in terms of Community Dance. The question is, how far can it be positioned within this work?

Community Arts

Some Community Dance posts are positioned within Community Arts teams, such as the Cambridge animateur post and the Valley and Vale project in Wales. Other posts, even though not directly involved with Community Arts teams, share the name 'community.' Therefore, it could be argued, the two movements are associated in the arts world. It is useful to look at how the work that Community Arts workers do is characterised.

In the 1991 NAMS document, *Community Arts* (Corner, 1991), the foreword contains mission statements for the work:

There is no longer time for, nor relevance in, the old arguments for "democratisation of culture" or "cultural democracy".... With education and outreach officers in virtually every established arts organisation we need not here concern ourselves with widening access to the accepted forms.... We will argue instead that one woman's transcendency is another woman's mundaneness; that the experience of the banker from Knightsbridge watching the Royal Opera is no more transcendent than that of the forklift truck driver from Brightside watching Sheffield Popular Theatre.

Corner, 1991

These statements give the spirit of the Community Arts teams that have developed over the past thirty years, as the radical alternative to mainstream 'high art'. However, in another publication, *Community and Public Policy*, a much broader view of Community Arts is presented. In their chapter, Lola Clinton and Andrew Glen (1993) classify community arts activities into four main types: (1) amateur and cultural arts; (2) access to arts; (3) professional arts activities; and (4) arts as a socio-political tool.

These types take the definition of Community Arts into embracing the widest range of activities possible, maybe reflecting a policy stance which is not threatening to politicians and funding bodies. These four activities can be matched to the range of activities carried out under the title of Community Dance. In embracing the whole range of participatory activities, it could be said that the Community Arts movement is now defining itself in the broader and less radical terms of the Community Dance movement. Perhaps this is a sign of the change brought about through responding to the accountability and monetarist culture of the 1980s.

Education

The Community Dance policy stated above has an obvious educational direction. One could ask how it differs from the objectives of an educationalist working in a school or college. What is different is the explicit interest in the subject knowledge base as an art form in the formal education sector.

> The 'Dance as art' model championed within education—performance, composition and appreciation—which has become firmly established in the last ten years has taught pupils to learn the skills of dancing, to create and perform in dances, and, through watching their peers and professional artists, to learn to respond, enjoy and make discerning judgements.
>
> CDET et al., 1990

The National Curriculum document, which includes dance as part of the PE curriculum (as published in January 1995), embraces the full range of dance activities, but the 'dance as art' model is still the one examined at GCSE, A Level and usually at tertiary level. (In addition, the focus of BTEC examinations in performing arts is clearly on preparing the individual for employment, which is an instrumental view of education, different from the aims of Community Dance.)

Youth and Community Services

Youth and Community Departments have been traditionally supported and managed through the Education departments of Local Authorities, and some support dance work. The aims of the youth and community curriculum are geared towards personal development and social education. The medium of dance is used for the delivery of social education objectives, unlike education, which emphasises knowledge of the form itself. The emphasis on the individual can be easily situated within the stated Community Dance policy. The main difference in the youth and community application lies in the specific focus on a young section of the population (14-22 years).

Dance Company Education

The number of dance companies with education units and policies and funding for educational work is increasing. One can see that the distinction between their work and that of animateurs is sometimes blurred, and their relationship can be one of tension, especially with reference to access to dance and mainstream dance companies' involvement with Community Dance. In the Community Arts policy (Corner, 1991), the company dance education units are not seen as Community Arts workers. But in the wider definitions described by Clinton and Glen (1993) they would be included. Whereas many animateurs might have dance company promotion in their briefs, there are many who are not working in this area. Company education workers often work with local animateurs to establish relevance to local needs, but their work lies solely in exploring the relationship between the artist and the audience.

Leisure and Recreation

The exercise of the body, particularly in women-dominated associations like the KFA, League of Health and Beauty Exercise and Margaret Morris Movement is another sector which is sometimes included in Community Dance. The common factor is an emphasis on physical fitness and well-being. While this might be a part of Community Dance activities, as can be seen in Chris Thompson's research, it has a low priority for most animaters.

In this sector, the work often leads to dance events such as the choreographed events at the Albert Hall, choreographic competitions and, of course, social networking through the classes. The difference in approach lies in its curriculum, which is usually prescribed from a central governing body so that safe exercise, rather than dance, can be delivered to all. In contrast, CDMF's policy states the intention to adapt dance forms to particular groups' needs.

Dance Therapy

The Dance Therapist uses dance as a medium for individuals to work on particular problems or difficulties. Community Dance workers might work with people in, or outside, institutions who are receiving therapy; they see their application of dance in this context to be at the most 'therapeutic', but they do not prescribe outcomes. In fact, many Community Dance workers see therapy as potentially patronising, taking the view that people receiving therapy need access to the same experiences that others have, rather than 'special or 'therapeutic' activities solely for them. Community Dance workers have involved themselves with groups of people who are disadvantaged and at the edge of society because they tend to be people who have been historically denied access to dance.

Distinguishing Factors of Community Dance Practice

Penny Greenland, Director of Jabadao, draws a middle ground between therapy and Community Dance activity, called "community building" (Greenland, 1993). She sees Community Dance workers as able to make a difference in their lives and the lives of the clients through the work. She cannot understand why Community Dance practitioners have chosen to draw upon Western theatre dance rather than the 'authentic' dance movement of the body to express the individual's own feelings and ideas.

This middle ground she describes as:

1. True communities offer people an environment in which they can grow stronger, more powerful and more effective.

2. True communities can be built through people's commitment to each other and to the struggle for 'personal disarmament'.

3. Dance is the most direct medium of human communication we possess; it allows us to express things that otherwise we could not express and to know things that we otherwise could not know. It is a powerful tool for community building.

These are distinctive working principles that seem directly to address the concept of dance as a medium for community development, and in particular the individual within the community. These working practices could not be particularly mistaken for dance in other contexts. In an interview, Greenland made clear her distance from other Community Dance practitioners: "Asking my opinion about what's happening in mainstream dance is like consulting the tomato-grower's association" (Ings, 1993, p2).

Most Community Dance workers do not work in this way, however. They are more concerned with dance itself and the proliferation of the notions of "dance for all," which leads them into the concept of education in and through dance. This is a way of working that can be indistinguishable from dance teachers/leaders in other sectors. Animateurs see dance itself as the liberating force for personal change. Taken to its logical end, the work of Jabadao and other community projects of this kind, which are attempting an 'alternative' approach in applying dance to make a change in the lives of individual practitioners, is where Community Dance practice is distinctive from other dance work. The principles that other Community Dance workers adhere to are shared with other dance professionals and could be described as good educational practice.

Of course Community Dance programmes address different aspects of the work at different times. It could be argued that to develop and serve a wide population there needs to be a wide approach to the delivery of dance. For example Penny Greenland's approach to the work might be said to be solely 'alternative', whereas Marie McClusky's programme might be addressing a range of needs which move across and into various sectors. Its very adaptability and breadth is probably the reason for Community Dance's proliferation and sustainment, whereas most of the Community Arts teams working within a 'radical' sphere of activity from the 1970s have disappeared.

Distinctive in Community Dance, in comparison to other educational practices, is the *context* in which it takes place and the *self-definition* of the workers. If the context is 'radical' enough, then the effects can be revolutionary for the individuals concerned in gaining access to a previously elusive activity, and in changing notions of who can dance what forms of dance. Examples of this would be a ballet class with senior citizens in the social club, or a contact class including adults with learning difficulties in the adult training centre. However, even though the context is 'radical', the working practices themselves are usually about access to the dance forms and not about using the medium to challenge the status quo.

The self-definitions of some Community Dance workers are also a distinguishing factor. Many CDMF members see themselves primarily as artists who possess additional skills which enable them to work within the community. This is particularly evident in Greenwich Dance Agency's Community Dance policy which refers to Community Dance workers as 'artists'. The work they do is seen as affecting mainstream dance, through the creation of new choreography, the widening of the kinds of spaces used for performances and the challenge to how dance is perceived and managed in the UK.

An often quoted example of the evidence of Community Dance artists' effect on the mainstream is CanDoCo, a professional dance company that employs disabled and non-disabled dancers,. It was created by Celeste Dandeker (a former LCDT dancer injured during a performance in the 1970s) and Adam Benjamin (non-disabled dancer/teacher). The fact that the company has been acceptable to the dance establishment and to audiences is said to be the effect of the broadening of the boundaries through Community Dance practice.

I believe that the influence of Community Dance in this area is difficult to quantify without reference to the other influences on society at this stage of the 20th century: for example, the legal changes in the rights of people with disabilities, demographic shifts in the population, and, in mainstream dance, the development of site-specific work and the influences of new dance and postmodern dance, to name but a few.

For me the clearest distinguishing feature is not necessarily in the practice, but rather in the purpose of the job or the post the person is appointed to. One of the most obvious differences of the work of Community Dance workers is their overall mission of 'spreading the word' about dance. Their programme builds a dance culture throughout an area, involving as many people in dance as possible. Projects are seen as stepping stones to realise the further ambition of dance available to all. This is in the end what distinguishes the Community Dance worker from a teacher, Community Arts worker, youth worker, lecturer or choreographer, that s/he is paid to develop a dance network, dance industry or dance culture for a particular geographical area/region.

Inclusive/Exclusive

Having tried to establish the boundaries of Community Dance I now address the opportunities and threats for the work in integration and segregation from the other dance professions. There are problems with retaining a separate title for what can be seen to be an activity that crosses many sectors. Sue Hoyle, questioning the use of the term Community Dance when she was Dance Director of the Arts Council of Great Britain, said in an interview: "What we have been calling Community Dance is integral to the whole culture of dance." She goes onto say that through using a separate term "the work is not simply localised but marginalised" (Ings, 1994, pp2-3). There is a general problem with being separatist in that it can be seen as second rate not as important as work in other fields. Fergus Early states that Community Dance principles have now pervaded the whole of the dance community, and hence by implication does not need to be distinguished separately (Ings, 1992).

So, what can be the reasons for keeping a separate term? If posts exist with the intention of working towards 'dance for all', encouraging a range of practices based on the common principles of the centrality of the participant's experience in the dance activity, then this seems to be worth maintaining. Certainly, there needs to be much research done in analysing and disseminating different models of practice in order to develop working practices and continually update training courses for the profession.

Conclusion

Within a harsh funding climate, it would be difficult to ensure that an area of work survives that is not commercial, or directly to do with the development of professional dance workers/artists, if it does not have a clear identity of its own. Educational work in informal settings for the purposes of personal growth, pleasure and/or community building which is not geared towards the acquisition of skill for employment, is difficult to support financially in this harsh funding climate. I believe that if the work was to be subsumed under amorphous professional and educational dance umbrellas, then it would not be sustained or developed. For these reasons the keeping of a separate title for Community Dance is paramount in the discussions about the future of the work and the organisation that serves it.

References

CDET, NATFHE, NDTA, and SCODHE. (1990). *Dance in the school curriculum* [promotional leaflet].

Clinton, L. and Glen, A. (1993). Community arts. In Butcher, H et al., *Community and public policy*. Community Development Foundation and Pluto Press.

Community Dance and Mime Foundation. (1994). Policy statement on community dance. In CDMF, *First annual report.* Leicester: CDMF.

Corner, L. (ed.) (1991). *Community arts: discussion document.* London: ACGB, National Arts and Media Strategy.

Greenland, P. (1993). Community dance and community building, *Dance and the Child International*, 2.

Ings, R. (1992). Early days. *Animated*, Autumn, pp 2-4.

Ings, R. (1993). Tomato growers in the dance world? an interview with Penney Greenland about the Jabadao and the power of dance. *Animated*, Summer, pp 2-5.

Ings, R. (1994). An interview with Sue Hoyle. *Animated*, Winter, pp 2-3.

Kelly, O. (1984). *Community, art and the state: storming the citadels*. London: Commedia.

Peppiatt, A. and Vennor, K. (1993). *Community dance: a progress report.* London: Arts Council of Great Britain.

Thompson, C. (1989). *Survey of community dance activity: outline paper for the Dance Education and Outreach Committee.* London: Arts Council of Great Britain.

Thompson, C. (1994). Dance and the concept of community. *Dance and the Child International*, 3.

Wilson, F. (1982). *Welsh Arts Council seminar on community dance* [conference pack].

Bibliography

ACGB, National Arts and Media Strategy. (1991). *Education and the arts: discussion document.* London: Arts Council of Great Britain.

Brinson, P. (1991). *Dance as education: towards a national dance culture.* London: Falmer Press.

Glick, R. (1986). *The dance and mime animateur movement: a national evaluation.* London: Arts Council of Great Britain.

Jasper, L. (1994). *Community dance—vision 2004.* Unpublished paper written for CDMF Executive.

Matarasso, F. (1994). *Regular marvels.* Leicester: CDMF.

Thompson, C. (1989). Community dance: what community...what dance? In *Young people dancing: an international perspective* [conference proceedings], Vol III, London: DaCi, pp 88-98.

IMAGINARY HOMELANDS: CREATING A NEW DANCE LANGUAGE

Shobana Jeyasingh
Shobana Jeyasingh Dance Company

I have called my paper "Imaginary Homelands." This will probably be the only paper in this conference which has as its starting point a tube of shaving cream. This particular one was my gift to my brother and it bore the legend "Mysore sandalwood shaving cream," and since our childhood home was not a million miles away from Mysore I thought it was a rather well chosen little gift. On receiving it, my brother rather unsubtly, I thought, started reading the small print. "But it says made in England," he exclaimed in a rather accusing tone of voice. In fact, the same tone of voice he used to reserve for me when I was found cheating very mildly in Monopoly. So there you have a living everyday example of "border tensions" as two supposedly mutually exclusive territories encroached on each other's terrain, producing a wail of dismay at the loss of authenticity and integrity. Strangely enough, my brother's personal history seems to have prepared him superbly for the kind of commercial and historical entanglements that called the shaving cream into being. He has lived a thoroughly modern urban life in cities in Sri Lanka, India, Malaysia and Britain. He now lives in Antwerp with a German wife and is part of that international community of computer professionals whose culture brooks no limits of geography.

Salman Rushdie in an essay he calls "Commonwealth Literature Does Not Exist" says: "If history creates complexities, let us try not to simplify them." However, despite the multiple compass points of modern urban life, there are areas where a simpler mythical version seems to be preferred. You notice this in many areas and I suppose an area that immediately springs to mind is politics. In politics, definitions of national identity are often a denial of the sort of complex present in favour of some nostalgic, eternal and much purer past. Advertising, that ultimate myth-making machine, for example, makes easy fictions whether they be of ideal families or exotic holidays. These are, I think, all symptomatic of a refusal to see the changing borders raging all around. In fact, that exotic country that you are about to visit is just like the one you have left, caught in that fine arbitration between past and present for various historical reasons. This refusal to see or to be allowed to see does not come about in a haphazard manner; rather it follows established patterns of power and discourse. The advertiser obviously wants to sell you his holiday, the politician wants the supreme power of all, to shape the story of the past—what we call history—in order to shape your present. One such established discourse is that between the East and the West. What we really mean is the "colonised" and the "coloniser" and the unequal power relationship between them. I do not really have the time to go deeply into the whole area of this particular power structure, and there are people who are much better qualified than I who have done so. I can mention Edward Said's book *Orientalism*, which deals with this whole area in great depth, as do the writing of Paul Gilroy, Homi Bhabha, and Salman Rushdie.

So I can only talk about my personal experience in this area. In fact, whenever I hear the phrase "East-West collaboration" used about what I do I have a very strange sensation. It is a sensation of being a baby wanting to be born but being pushed back into the uterus, of not being allowed to be born. "You cannot come out," says the midwife. "Not as a common or garden British choreographer you can't, specially if you don't have any particular mission. Yes, you *can* have a mission—I mean to update Bharata Natyam. You can come out if you want to give voice to non-western cultures or to oppressed minorities or Indian women or Third-World issues. You can be a social ambassador, but not just a choreographer. You can come out if you make perhaps a colourful dance about arranged marriages, told entirely through hand gestures, of course. And this is very important—before you actually perform it, you have to explain each one because, of course, each one has a specific meaning and .... What? You mean you want to work with a white composer? That will be a 'cross-cultural collaboration.' Never mind that he lives next door to you in Stamford Hill. But, of course, if *he* wants to work with *you* that will be different, that will be 'influenced by world music and his rich eclecticism.' And what do you mean 'West-East collaboration'? That just never happens. No, no, *we* engage in deeply ironic postmodern quotations but never collaborations, so in you go."

I find this kind of experience as a citizen of a country where I want to be born, where I am labouring to be born, to be deeply undemocratic. I think it is very undemocratic to be prescribed your areas of concern, the issues that you want to deal with as a choreographer and as an artist. So I suppose what I reject about these categories is perhaps the best prologue to talking about what I do or what people like myself do. Central to these frustrations is not that I resent being an ambassador, because I think all dance work is representative of its maker's life and concerns and I think in that way all artists are ambassadors to their own private countries. I think what gets me is the sheer inaccuracy of the country I am supposed to be representing. The country I represent, I admit, is difficult to chart. It is definitely not India, especially that fictional incarnation of India as a place entrenched in deep spiritual and cultural certainties, if that exists. It is difficult to chart the landscape of this country for the simple reason that it is being created and imagined even as we board the train. The journey and the destination are one and that is home. As Marina Warner says in her book *Managing Monsters*, "Home lies ahead in the unfolding of the story in the future, not behind waiting to be regained." So, Ithaca and Penelope are not things that you know and have left behind, but Ithaca and Penelope are very much things that you are creating and inventing all the time. There is nothing particularly radical about what I say about this dynamic, ideal home. I think it is the experience of most city dwellers, of anyone whose life is different to their parents'. This is true whether you live in Bombay, London, Singapore, or Toronto or anywhere else. Those of us who have been part of the great post-war migrations are only an extreme example of this imaginary home making. In fact, Homi Bhabha says in his book *The Location of Culture*, "The truest eye may now belong to the migrant's double vision." Perhaps that is why the Booker Prize is won again and again by the Rushdies and the Ondaatjes and the Ishiguros—by those who illuminate the dynamism of journeys, the constant packing and unpacking, the constant loss and recovery and loss again. Those who illustrate a pattern of belonging that is multi-dimensional. However, this experience of "unhomeliness" is not to be confused with "homelessness." Rather, I think to these artists their unhoming has been a source of immense creative activity. I remember my first reading of *Midnight's Children,* a novel at once extremely Indian and extremely English, which reminded me simultaneously of Sterne and of the *Arabian Nights*: magical and real at the same time. (Reading it was the closest I got to sitting on a box of firecrackers!) It is also no surprise, I think, that Marina Warner in her last Reith Lecture where she talked about British national identity does not invoke Churchill or Shakespeare but Derek Walcot—a man of mixed parentage who is content to forget the injuries of history and "the vain search for one island that heals with its harbour and a guiltless horizon where the almond shadow does not injure the shade." Obviously what he finds joyful is that "there are so many islands," as he says, and he defines his theme like this: "The arrows' flight to a target whose aim we will never know." Late 20th century living, whether lived in Bombay, in London or in that imaginary homeland of the Diaspora, which is where people like myself belong, has made Captain Kirks of us all.

Choreography 1991-1994

I shall start first with *Making of Maps,* which I made in 1991. I suppose the first thing I thought about when I made *Making of Maps* was the question of heritage. One of the things that I found very frustrating about East-West collaborations and cross-cultural ventures was that they seemed to prescribe to me a very static view of my own heritage. For me, my heritage is a mix of David Bowie, Purcell, Shelley, and Anna Pavlova, and it has been mixed as subtly as a samosa has mixed itself into the English cuisine in the last 10 years or so: impossible to separate. But it is surprising how to many people my heritage could only be things Indian.

About two years ago I asked Richard Alston to make a piece for my dancers, and he chose the music of Purcell. In one of the reports that I got from the Arts Council observers was the comment, "The dancers are now dancing to *our* music, Purcell. It's is wonderful that they have made it their own." What I think the person did not know or did not care to know was that someone like myself from the age of 12 in my school assembly in Malaysia heard nothing but Purcell. So, for me, Purcell, like Shelley, like David Bowie, is not "the other"—it is part of my heritage. And in dance terms Rukmani Devi *and* Merce Cunningham are also part of my heritage. So, *Making of Maps* really started in a way as a process of inventing my own heritage. One of the first things I did was to commission two composers to make the music. One, Alistair Macdonald, who lived in Birmingham, and the other R.A. Ramamani, who lived in Bangalore. (Both cities begin with a B and that seemed a reasonably good reason!) One of the images that I had for *Making of Maps* was someone sitting in a room and playing different cassettes and different CDs into their machine or sitting in front of a radio and twiddling the knob. It seemed to me that one of the things that characterised the way my peers and I lived was the amazing accessibility and openness of the universe which was there for the taking. Through technology, we could actually twiddle the knob of a radio and go from Beijing to London or play on our music machines cassettes of classical Indian music, Andean music, Malaysian music, or English music. I also wanted sounds of everyday life, of station announcements, of church bells because, again, as Homi Bhabha says in his book, "The recesses of the domestic space become sites for history's most intricate invasions." So that was the kind of logic behind this work *Making of Maps*.

When I started *Making of Maps*, obviously I had to also look at what I did with the dance language. The dance language that I was given was Bharata Natyam and the reason *why* is rooted in certain historical events. The reason I learned Bharata Natyam was a direct result of the British presence in India. One of the movements in India which led to Independence came to be known as the "Self-Respect Movement." I suppose when the psyche of a country has been bashed around for over 100 years, one of the things that actually happens when you want to break free is that you begin to re-evaluate and re-find your own culture. The struggle towards political independence was paralleled by our stuggle for cultural credibility against the predominance of Greece and Rome. Therefore, for my parents, who were typical of their generation, it was important that their daughter learned Bharata Natyam, the classical dance of India. The idea was that by doing that we kept faith with something ancient and precious about Indian culture. In fact, as I grew up and started reading about the history of Bharata Natyam, I found that its antiquity was only half the story. It had suffered a great neglect and was rediscovered and rejuvenated in the early decades of this century—a process in which even Anna Pavlova had a part to play. It is a far more interesting and a more subtle story than sometimes one is led to believe.

The advantages of a classical dance language are its strength and its power to communicate with sureness and confidence—and its objective technique that you can fit your body into. The things that I wanted to change were the rigidity that is there in lots of classical dance, the almost mechanical quality. You work very hard to attain a kind of virtuostic quality for no other reason except to be virtuostic, and I think in a way classical dance also has this feeling of a kind of impersonality which did not suit me. I wanted in some ways to introduce a strain of idiosyncrasy to balance this non-personal feeling, and I suppose, most importantly, it did not offer me those domestic spaces where those historically intricate moments happen. So we as a company looked at vocabulary, and I also looked at the composition because I think in a way in *Making of Maps* more things happen in the area of composition than in the area of vocabulary, although obviously both cannot but be interconnected. Often, when one simplified the dance language—because obviously it started off as solo dancing and it has an immense density of structure but within one body—if one wanted to unpick that structure from the individual body, then one found that in fact one had to compensate by compositional layerings. Otherwise, you just ended up with something extremely flat and one dimensional.

In the area of emotion, the floor seemed to beckon me in a very passionate manner. It is a very logical thing actually for a Bharata Natyam dancer to think about the floor. Bharata Natyam takes the body from the erect standing position and it wants the dancer to turn out at the hips and then lower the body along the central median into a demi-plié. Eighty percent of the dance is actually done that way. The depth of plié is a very important part of Bharata Natyam. It is a dance which very much obeys the pull of gravity. It is very aware of the floor, but the way it actually relates to the floor is very contained, very formal. I wanted to make the dancers roll on the floor and embrace it in a much looser way than doing Bharata Natyam footwork. One of the things that I know, being a Bharata Natyam dancer, is that because it is quite a cerebral, quite an academic dance language, Bharata Natyam dancers become great experts at marking. It was good to have a movement which was outside the normal terminology of Bharata Natyam and which could not be marked. I think the formal qualities which I like about Bharata Natyam are still there in *Making of Maps*. The whole way I think about space and about bodies in space and their relation to time is very influenced by the formality in Bharata Natyam.

In the work *Romance ... with Footnotes*, I was trying to see how much emotion I could get out of formal movement. For me touch was something that I played around with my dancers because, again, we come from a solo tradition where the body is extremely self-sufficient. It is also very much in command of the space that it performs in. With each piece that I make, I try and go further—to go further into an emotional relationship which the dancer has with the space around or with the person with whom they are dancing. *Romance* starts off with certain iconic positions which are there in Indian dance, and I have tried to change them and give them much more of an incidental feel, a much more friendly feel.

Raid, which we are touring at the moment, is based on a game that is played in the streets of India and Birmingham and Glasgow, called "Kabbadi." I suppose it is the sheer perversity of the game really that interested me because although there are two teams, the "raiding" is done by a single raider who runs into the opponents' territory and takes on the entire team singlehandedly. Just to make life more difficult, all the time they are in the enemy territory they have to hold their breath and chant "Kabbadi, Kabbadi" to prove that they are holding their breath. While they are holding their breath they have to try and touch one person on any part of their body and then run as fast as they can back home. Once they have actually touched somebody, all seven of the opponents can tackle the raider, piling on top of them and holding them down until they lose their breath. So the raider just seems to have an incredibly difficult time of it all. The other thing that intrigued me was that even though it was a game of territories the border line was there for crossing. It was crossed and re-crossed the whole time and all the interesting things happened when the raider actually crossed and went over to the other side. While they were in their home ground nothing much dynamic happened at all. I find sport an interesting area because with all this talk about East and West, sport is one area where post-colonial discourse does not seem to happen. People are quite happy for Linford Christie to be extremely British as long as he is winning, and I sometimes wonder whether if Linford Christie were a choreographer or a painter, whether his ethnic origins would be more of an issue.

Raid is a piece about two territories, and because I am called Shobana Jeyasingh, people assume that these two territories must be East and West. In fact, they are not. They are sport and dance. I suppose the prosaic and the poetic. One of the things that I had in mind when I choreographed it was something that I had read a very long time ago in that book *A Hundred Years of Solitude* by Gabriel Garcia Marquez where he goes from describing something very, very ordinary, a scene in somebody's kitchen, to then looking out of the window where he says "and then there was a rain of marigolds." I thought it was really a brilliant way of one territory very slowly going into another with perfect credibility. In my own humble way I also wanted to go from the kitchen into that rain of marigolds.

(Here followed a practical demonstration by a dancer from the company who illustrated examples of the invented dance language used by the company. Videos were used to show examples from all the dance works discussed. Then there was a question and answer period.)

Question: What type of things do you do in the studio with your dancers? Can you describe the process?

SJ: The process actually changes from piece to piece and from year to year because I don't have a permanent company. In fact, each year there is always a change to the people in the company so in a way a lot depends on who the people are. For example, for this particular piece *Raid* we started by watching lots of videos of the game and looked at the rules of the game and the type of movements. On the whole, I suppose I am quite a directive choreographer in that I have a picture in my head when I come to the studio of roughly what I want to do and where I want to go. With this particular company that I am touring with at the moment there have been more instances of me handing phrases which the dancers actually developed or played around with. We would look at it and see whether it would fit or not. Obviously, one of the things that characterises the way I work is that all the dancers are trained in Bharata Natyam so that gives us a common language as far as things in that area are concerned. However, when the movement is personal and invented, we do not have that common terminology and have to make up our own.

Question: I am curious how you take from that traditional vocabulary.

SJ: It is really trial and error. Sometimes I have an image in my head of what it could look like and then I ask the dancers to try something. I use improvisation in a way as a process of communicating rather than as a way of getting vocabulary out of the dancers. So sometimes I set up a particular problem or a particular thing to solve and by doing it I hope they understand what I want them to do. It might not actually be what they have been doing, but it is a way of showing the road which I want to take—which I often do in the studio.

Question: Do you see yourself in the future seeking a new, third language, say, designating a movement so that this is movement number 1. Not so much finding a terminology as a movement vocabulary, so that you could say to your dancers, "Do movement number 1 or movement number 2."

SJ: I think it's difficult when you make contemporary dance work actually to find that way of signalling because it changes from year to year. If I put a name to it, then I'll be doing what I'm trying to get away from. Because when you put a name to it, that's when you make it rigid. In some ways it's good to be rigid, I'm not saying it's all bad — but that it would be the problem because one year I might want to call it X and the next year I might want to call it Y. Very confusing for the dancer.

Question: What sort of audience comes to your performances?

SJ: I don't think there is a particular kind of audience. Certainly, when I make work I don't actually think of a particular audience, I don't think, "This is for Indians," or "This is for non-Indians." I make dance for a dance audience and I think the people who come to The Place, for example, where we normally perform for longer seasons, are a mixture and very typical of London.

Question: What strikes me about your audience is that some South Asians who live in London come to see it, but not as many as I personally would always hope.

SJ: South Asians are a small minority in Britain, so I suppose that proportionately even if one South Asian came to my performance, it would still be a huge number — out of an audience of 250.

Question: Have you shown this particular material in India?

SJ: This is a question many people ask me. I wonder why! No, I haven't taken it to India. The British Council might take it to India as part of British dance. I don't see an immediate and amazing relevance between what I do and India to be quite frank. I think it will be intriguing to show it in India, and it will be intriguing to show it in Australia where we are going to do it next year. As I was saying, I don't see what I do as "Indian dance influenced by the West" because for me both India and the West are not static things. It is not like being a carpenter, taking a bit of East and a bit of West and sort of putting a few nails together and there is the product. I think in a way history has already made these East/West conversations and I just reflect what is there. We have taken our work to Europe and to North America and people who live in cities, people whose lives are a mixture of things, would find something to look at. I think mixtures attract mixtures.

Question: In Indian film music, there are all kinds of influences; they have Mozart's 40th Symphony or popular songs, for example. Do you think that the ritual and general nature of the history of Bharata Natyam is one of the reasons why people, Indians in particular, think it's so sacrosanct, not to touch it or tamper with it?

SJ: I think it goes back to what happened in India in the 1930s and 1940s. I think it has to do with those political reasons why Indians such as my parents felt that in dance and music one had some image of India which they wanted to hold very precious. Obviously, to recover Bharata Natyam took a lot of effort by various people, so there is a very natural inclination to conserve. But when one has the confidence that comes out of that conservation—and I'm saying that it's a very important process—then the next step is to say, "Well, actually, now that I'm sure and free, I need to take a step forward." I'm not saying that Indians have a very specific culture and therefore they won't find the relevances. I'm saying the opposite, actually. I'm saying that in cities in India, as you say, there is an amazing mixture of influences. So I think Indians are not any more particular than anyone else in any other country where there is also a mixture of past and present, of juggling various elements. We're all jugglers now.

Question: I think it was very interesting that you invited Richard Alston to make a piece on your company. Would you be interested in making a piece in another classical medium, like ballet?

SJ: I made a piece for the National Youth Dance Company which had students from Rambert, London Contemporary Dance School, and Laban. There were people there, especially from the Rambert School, who had a lot of ballet training. It was something that I enjoyed very much. The piece that came out of it, *Janpath,* has had three revivals, so I think it is a piece that has been fairly successful. I also made a piece for Ludus Dance Company, an educational dance company in Lancaster. So, I *am* interested. I hope that in the future, the prejudice that if you are an Indian choreographer you've got to deal with matters Indian will change. Because I think choreographers, no matter what they do—the divide could be between classical and contemporary—the skill and the craft of choreography, like mathematics, is universal. If it's a serious profession (like being a computer professional!), I think it has to cross those boundaries of race, and I look forward to a time when it will.

"They've done me, they've robbed me, but, thank God, I'm the champion still!" Clog Dancing in the Victorian Music Hall

Caroline Kershaw (Royal Holloway and Bedford New College, University of London)

Clog dancing, like many areas of popular culture remains comparatively undocumented. Although a common act, lasting throughout the whole music hall period, it has been written out of music hall history, dismissed as an un-noteworthy, peripheral activity.

In this talk, I will summarise the sites of tension created by cultural disputes of class, regionality and gender and demonstrate how these tensions led to the ideological and political control and suppression of clog dancing in the Victorian music hall. I will concentrate my study on the form of clog dancing generalised as Lancashire[1] with its emphasis on display and competition rather than other forms such as minstrel or team clog acts.

By the early nineteenth century, when Britain was in the hold of the industrial revolution, the clog was the predominant item of footwear in all areas of heavy industry such as mills, mines, iron foundries and in occupations requiring protection from damp or heat conditions. Clogs were therefore found in the main urban industrial regions and soon took on a symbolic significance embodying the nation's labouring class. Rooted in an underlying fear of revolution by the workers, to a capitalist society the clog also had associations of immigration, squalor, poverty and disease.

In 1854 Elizabeth Gaskell highlighted the increasing rich-poor divide. In *North and South* [2]the clog is symbolic of the struggle between capital and labour when it is literally hurled across the divide between workers and employer. The clog also found a place in the literature of the cotton famine in the poems and autobiographical accounts of Stephen Laycock and others.[3] Although to the workers the clog was a cheap and comfortable necessity, representative of work, warmth and survival, to the middle-classes associations of hunger and revolt had been established.

To allay these fears, a hegemonic form of social control exerted itself seeking to confine the clog to its working environment and attaching to it a stigma of social shame. In Lancashire for example, clogs were either banned or shunned from ideological sites of cultural negotiation: schools, churches, town halls, dances, exhibitions, Volunteers' reviews. The law was also enforced, suppressing clog fighting, forcing it to go underground. Known as the 'Lancashire way of fighting' or in dialect 'purring' or 'puncing', these fights though often spontaneous , were usually organised as a vehicle for betting and consisted of men stripped to their underwear and clogs, kicking each other into submission. Baines in his *History of the County of Palantine* states that judges declared clogs "unfit for human beings to wear and only fit for the uncivilised in some outlandish district"[4] a statement implying an analogy between the industrial workers of urban Britain and uncivilised beasts occupying marginal territory.

The origins of clog dancing are obscure. Steps were created and transmitted by demonstration through generations of families and pupils. It is suggested that Lancashire clog dancing originated in the cotton mills as the operatives stepped in their clogs in time to the rhythms of the power looms. Certainly surviving steps and dances indicate an industrial influence. Pat Tracey[5] points to steps common to all dances with names such as the pick, the shuttle, the two up and two down, derived from weaving processes or components of the looms and imitative of both their actions and sounds;[6] the steps of Bill Gibbons,[7] a bargeman on the Leeds-Liverpool canal , imitated the sounds of the barge engine. There would also seem to be a considerable Irish influence with many clog dancers of Irish descent or parentage. Steps are common to Irish and Lancashire step dancing and many of the tunes used for the Lancashire clog dance are Irish. This cross-cultural fertilisation was due to the large proportion of immigrant workers in Lancashire. Almost without exception, clog dancers appear to originate from industrial occupations, immigrant or travelling communities, or families of performers. Clog dancers could therefore be viewed as existing on the peripheral borders of Victorian society.

The amateur or semi-professional clog dancer was forced into illegitimate performance in places of popular recreation, fairs, public houses or street busking, but the main performance platform, also more financially rewarding, was the illegal free and easy which defied licensing regulations eliciting the condemnation of middle-class reformers. In the early 1870's, a journalist exploring the 'Dark side of Glasgow', discovers in what he describes as a very cursory examination of the east end Glasgow Cross area of the city, nineteen free and easies within five minutes walk of Trongate alone, calculating there to be between 600 and 1000 paying visitors at each, in the course of a popular Saturday or Monday night. Describing them as morally filthy places in disreputable areas, he surmises that they can only lead youth, men and women to "the downward road that leads to shame and sorrow". Standing at an entrance "besieged with a motley, and with some exceptions, a most unsavoury-looking rabble - smoking, shouting, swearing, crushing and vociferating their orders at the top of their discordant voices", he can hear "the scraping of fiddles, the sound of the piano and the clatter of clog dancing". At another free and easy, frequented by both men and women, he discovers the majority of women to be mill girls. Clog dancing is again in evidence - "an inebriated 'lumper' whose efforts threatened to bring down the house around our ears". With the initiation of a spontaneous reel by four couples the landlord is forced to intervene to prevent a police raid.[8]

Like the performers themselves the free and easy could not cross the border into legitimate entertainment surviving only within the poorer confines of the city.

However, playbills demonstrate that the clog dancing did occur on the legitimate stage as an extension of the stage hornpipe, a performance platform in which professional actors or dancers could demonstrate virtuosity, prowess or trick or comic steps, incorporated into the main play, a pantomime, or dividing the programme.[9] The mixed bill format of programming was designed to appeal to lower-class audiences and the inclusion of the clog dance must have been a response to the rising predominance of the industrial worker. The increasing improbability of the trick feats of hornpipes and clog dances played on the audiences taste for both rivalry and suspense. A typical example from the Old Leeds Theatre in 1822 records Mr Dore's benefit, at which he danced a new hornpipe in clogs and real fetters. The following week Mr Pritchard rivalled this with another hornpipe in fetters. Mr Dore responded the week after with a hornpipe in wooden shoes, real fetters and at the same time accompanied himself on the violin.[10]

With the passing of the 1843 act, the legitimate theatre sought to distinguish itself from the saloon entertainments, seeking a higher class-specific audience, omitting elements which would attract lower-class patrons or incite disruptive behaviour. Although clog dancing persisted into the second half of the century in the provincial theatres, it now found its metier in the developing music hall.

By the second half of the nineteenth century, clog dancing was a staple and popular act in the provincial and the London music hall. But it was still confined to the almost ghettoised territory of the lower-class halls. In London, the Middlesex music hall was renowned as the domain of the clog dancer. George Belmont, clog dancer and sometime theatre manager, cited three of many other music halls in London where clog dancing could be witnessed: Pitman's, The Falstaff and the Rodney Head,[11] all situated east of the City and of small audience capacities. Both Pitman's and the Falstaff had their licences refused (1879 and 1899 respectively) forcing them to close in subsequence, and in 1885, the Rodney Head withdrew its application to renew its licence.[12] In the light of Penelope Summerfield's evidence on the licensing of small, independent music halls,[13] these closures could be viewed as a contributory factor to the suppression of working-class entertainment and indirectly of clog dancing itself.

Concentrating my studies on Manchester, London, Glasgow, and Newcastle and Teeside, areas geographically sited at the compass extremes, and all areas of rapid urban expansion and, with the exception of London, of heavy industry, I have found a consistent pattern. A concentration of clog dancing acts occurs in the lower priced halls, notably those declaring themselves to be 'for the people'. Meeting the expectations of the audiences, clog dancing became an arena for the thrashing out of regional tensions. This dynamic occurred particularly in areas which retained strong national or local identities. In Glasgow for example in 1893, a bill of entertainment at the People's Palace, a music hall situated at Glasgow Cross declaring itself to be "The working man's house in the heart of working Glasgow" and charging "popular prices", included an overture of Scottish melodies, a Scottish military spectacle - 'The Gathering of the Clans', W.C. M'Phie the Great Scottish National Vocalist and Andy Reynolds the Champion Boy Clog Dancer, Bone and Drum Soloist of the World.[14] This emphasis upon national identity would have influenced the reception of clog dancers appearing at the hall; bills for the same year included Irish, English, Scottish, female, or juvenile clog dancers and champions.

Dagmar Höher's research shows that a large proportion of audiences in urban industrial areas shared the same occupation, with the music hall acting as a centre for socialising away from their work environment. In Sheffield for example 75% of all those whose occupation was stated, worked in the cutlery trade, and in Manchester 2/5ths were textile workers.[15] To appeal to a dominant audience sector was an astute managerial move, creating an entertainment venue in which the audience confirmed its identity and relieved occupational tensions. The People's Music Hall, Manchester was an acknowledged clog dancing venue - a hall renowned for its roughness. It was a meeting place for rival gangs to arrange assignments, notably the Adelphi gang or the Ancoats Roughs (of whom we shall hear more presently). The manager, Thomas Burton, turned both occupational and local hostilities to advantage by holding competitions which pitted local rival warehouse workers against each other in a contest of their working skills , a contest in which the audience factions must have felt an emotional and personal sense of involvement, whether out of loyalty to their workplace, friends or community.[16]

Benefit organisers sought local attendance through the inclusion of local amateur clog celebrities; thus in 1864 Young Peacock the celebrated clog dancer of Pile and Co.'s Shipyard, late of Hull, made his first and only appearance at a benefit in the Theatre Royal, West Hartlepool[17] and in 1881 at the benefit of a worker from the Middleton Shipyard, East Hartlepool, the Champion of the North and the Champion of Yorkshire and Lancashire performed both solo and duo clog dancing at the Literary Institute, Wingate.[18]

Many of the processes surrounding clog dancing as a competitive form were common to various popular sports: the role of the professional trainer who often had connections in other sports, bookmakers , the use of competitors colours to facilitate betting, the model of the championship belts - identical to boxing belts, and the strict system of judging with a system of marking usually based entirely on technical precision. The audiences' appreciation of and admiration for a dancer's skill, inventiveness and personal charisma, were no doubt augmented by the incentive of high betting stakes, prize money and the value of the championship belt, all serving to heighten the suspense and personal interests in the outcome of the competition.

That tensions ran high both within the audiences and between the competitors is proven through numerous testimonies of the hostilities that occurred before, during and after competitions. Performers' clogs were slashed, laces stolen, brick dust scattered over the stage. Competitors' hostilities were thrashed out in the personal columns of both the sporting and the theatrical press. Matches were often 'thrown' with judges threatened by audience factions. Clog dancing appealed in a variety of ways to audiences; often intense levels of appreciation caused internal controversies.

But as a clog dancing craze established itself within the music hall during the 1870's and early 80's, a transforming influence began to take over the music hall industry as a whole. With the rise of the big business syndicate music halls, there was a deliberate move to unify and monopolise variety entertainment and to create an appeal of respectability in order to attract a higher class audience. A comparison of bills indicates that with few exceptions, clog dancing, whilst remaining a staple entertainment in specifically lower-class halls, was omitted from the new ' Empire' style of programme (the only exception I have discovered seems to have been triggered off by a highly publicised revival of the Championship of the World competition in

1898). Managers of small halls were increasingly forced to adhere to tightened licensing restrictions, manipulated into a position whereby acts that incited disruption of any form or were associated with immoral practices such as gambling or excessive drinking became a threat to the licence. Clog dancing with its reliance on audience division and betting now became a danger to the music halls existence as it sought to comply with regulations.

With its extreme class associations and regional or independent national loyalties, clog dancing clashed with the new style of bourgeois variety entertainment, the values of which were fundamentally rooted in support for the United Kingdom, Victoria and the British Empire. It was therefore simply suppressed.

That no conflict occurred between audiences and management can also be explained in terms of hegemony. The dominant cultural hegemony (driven by economism in the case of the syndicate music halls) substituted a new moral order of popular recreation, encouraging a supposedly rational and elevated level of cultural appreciation. Audiences either passively accepted this successful populist drive or they retreated to the struggling enclave of the lower-class music hall - which could not, in any case, remain uninfluenced by the cultural hegemony - rapidly diminishing in number towards the end of the century.

During this transitional period of music hall development, throughout the 1880s and 1890s, clog dancing began to be documented. As the music hall attracted a wider press, it could not fail to notice clog dancings' popular presence. Coverage was however restricted mainly to the satirical press, reflecting an attempt to undermine its validity as an art form or even as an entertainment. In a satirical Leeds newspaper of 1881, Arthur North cites the most notable aspect of the Prize Jig- which from the accompanying illustration appears to be a clog dance - as the "awful, painful, fearful expression of the faces of the 'artistes' as they go through with it. It is nothing so much as the expression on the face of a patient undergoing a horrible surgical operation." He describes the exit as an embarrassed, awkward sidle off the stage.[19] The journalist succeeds in distancing himself from the audience, assuming a superior critical stance in which it is impossible for him to participate in the necessary dynamic between audience and performer.

Another account *Music Hall Land* by Percy Fitzgerald (1900) also attaches shame to the dancer "it is now more a 'side-accomplishment introduced in a rather shame-faced way. It is rarely that we now see 'the old champion clog dancer' who came on so triumphantly with his broad silver belt and 'plastrons'.[20] He does not attempt to account for the inexplicable metamorphosis from proud champion to shame-faced side-show and contradicts the evidence of the provincial clog dancing competitions which were still going strong. The descriptions are negative and derogatory "lanky, rigid, curious, stolid, violent, highly monotonous" the awareness of the clog dance as a monotony, to the spectator with no critical understanding, was apparent to Arnold Bennett who describes clog dancing as "full of marvels to the connoisseur, and to the profane, naught but a highly complicated series of wooden noises of progressive difficulty".[21]

Clog dancing posed a cultural threat to the middle-classes. A low-art form which appeared to be authentically working-class, grounded in the industrial vernacular, played on the earlier fears of a labour uprising necessitating a repression of a working-class identity which could possibly lead to subversion. Both the fear and the actual suppression become clearly apparent through the study of two performers who transgressed the hegemonically imposed cultural borders.

My first example is drawn from fiction. Arnold Bennett interlinks class fear with a fear of women in a description of the female clog dancer Miss Florence Simcox, contained in *Clayhanger* .[22] The passage is also interesting for its inclusion of many of the elements of clog dancing already discussed. The year is 1872, Florence is the wife of a Lancashire comic who has sporting connections. As the champion female clog dancer of the midlands she is touring "the realms of her championship...mingling terriers, recitations and clogs." The scene described is set in a free and easy, the audience is exclusively male, 'respectably' smoking and drinking. Florence is immediately established as a sexual figure and a focus of male sexual tension by the attention to "the shortness of her red and black velvet skirts, and the undeniable complete visibility of her rounded calves". Male statuses are confirmed in relation to her own, granting the chairman a superiority over his fiancee, the landlady of the public house, but causing Florence's own husband to assume a role of servitude and humiliation. She is described in regal terms, heightening her position of superiority and unobtainability. Bennett places her in a position of tantalising sexual authority which has a profound hold over the audience. As the dance progresses Bennett's language is increasingly sexual and the increasing excitement of the clog dance becomes a metaphor for orgasm. The experience of the clog dance symbolises Edwin Clayhanger's sexual awakening, his transition from schoolboy to manhood.

But by placing Florence in the dominant sexual role, Bennett must constantly reiterate her transgression of appropriate gender roles and he does this by portraying the female clog dancer as an anomaly, emphasising the clog's associations with squalor, using it as a metaphor for prostitution. As a female clog act Florence is a "daring item" and the only one to have appeared in the respectable confines of Bursley. She overshadows the only women in the room, who shun her, made nervous by her act which they turn instinctively away from. She has the confidence to stare down any man in the room and is accustomed to being regarded by audiences, an object of mens' eyes. She is a pretty doll-like woman; with a show of bare flesh, jewels and golden ringlets she has none of the modesty or docility "that Bursley was accustomed to think proper to the face of woman". Her transformation of "that which the instinct of the artist had taken from the sordid ugliness of the people" is achieved through her physical beauty, "The clog, the very emblem of servitude and the squalor of brutalised populations, was changed, on the light feet of this favourite, into a medium of grace....the clog meant everything that was harsh, foul and desolating; it summoned images of misery and disgust. Yet on those feet that had never worn it seriously, it became the magic instrument of pleasure....putting upon everybody an enchantment." Florence disguises squalor through beauty, she is the clog-dancing personification of the vamp or temptress leading men into a world of escape. Clog dancing becomes dangerous, subversive, threatening, offering a momentary illusion of escape from the reality of misery. Through his creation of Florence Simcox, Bennett unites the ugliness of the working-class with the transgression of woman emphasising two of the dominant fears of the Victorian capitalist patriarchy.

Contrary to the impression given by Bennett, there were indeed many female clog dancers, but like Florence, they were subjected to a set of judgements based on gender roles and were not given the same status as equivalent male performers. Although they appear to have performed to the same criteria as male dancers with no differences in dancing style or competition rules, they were awarded lower prizes and achieved little renown. The ladies championship clog dancing match of 1898 excited attention in the theatrical press. When asked to comment on it, the organiser J.H Wood, initiator of the Championship of the World competition replied "Let me see. Some of the ladies will wear very costly dresses."[23] Female dancers were assessed through physical appearance rather than on their merits as competitive dancers. Although the competition attracted bets the odds were described in euphemistic terms, gambling was not a territory open to women. The many skilful female performers and champions remained on the periphery of success and earning potential due to the stereotyped confines of their gender and the incompatible symbolism of the clog.

The process of suppression is apparent when a performer of immense popularity crossed the border between lower-class and middle-class entertainment.

By the age of four Dan Leno was clog dancing as part of his family's act.[24] Whilst developing as a performer of considerable talent and range across a wide spectrum of popular entertainment styles and conventions, clog dancing was perhaps the skill at which he worked hardest. By 1880 he had won the Championship of the World, held at the Princesses' Palace, Leeds, competing against some of Britain's most renowned dancers. It was at the second contest, the following year, at Cooke's Circus in Manchester that a fierce and complicated dispute occurred. Leno apparently won the competition, but the title and belt were awarded to another dancer, Tom Ward, almost provoking an audience riot. The circumstances are now confused but would, from

Leno's account, appear to indicate fixed judging - with the assistance of the omni-present Ancoats Roughs. Leno's subsequent actions and correspondence through the *Era* reveal much about his character at that time, consistent with the challenging, competitive and combative behaviour of clog dancers.[25]

Tom Ward, addressing Leno directly, alludes to " a savage and brutal assault at Wigan" the week prior to the competition.[26] Whether Leno was himself involved in the assault is unstated, but his correspondence with Ward and four years later with the dancer John Williams is aggressive and even threatening.[27] This impression of Leno conflicts with the present image of him as the underdog 'Little Man' tragi-comic philosopher a construction resultant from a process of cultural manipulation and mythology.

Leno took to "nightly exposing the whole affair from the stage, and all concerned in it" incorporating the exposure into his act and rallying the support of audiences.[28] The 1882 match also ended in a fiasco but in 1883, Leno finally secured the Championship of the World belt. It was soon after this that the music hall performer Charles Coborn witnessed Leno's act in which he entered the stage wearing his clog dancing outfit and the silver belt and sang a song exposing the three year dispute.

"They've done me, they've robbed me, but, thank God,
I'm the champion still".[29]

On Leno's arrival in the London music halls in 1885, he was involved in another lengthy and contentious wager against John Williams. Williams' challenge was for £100 but although Leno accepted and appears to have raised £400 backing, Williams pulled out, the challenge remaining unresolved.[30] It was Leno's London debut that the biographer Hickory J. Wood[31] and other writers completely distort in order to portray Leno as a respectable celebrity of the new style music hall. Wood states that his clog dancing was received badly, the southern audience unable to relate to a northern entertainment, forcing Leno to exclude it immediately from his act, concentrating on his more successful talents as a comedian. Contrary to Wood's interpretation, *all* the contemporary reviews describe him primarily as a dancer, unrivalled in style, execution and originality. The evidence of these reviews suggests that his dancing was tremendously received by both audience and management and that it was only the middle and upper-class commentators of the west-end music hall who were unable to relate to the northern entertainment; thus what appears on the surface to be a geographical tension is in fact better viewed as a class tension. Leno ironically reverses class bias in his statement regarding the pressure that was imposed on him by the commentators: "My title was a proud one in the provinces, but London had not been educated up to it".[32] Leno's debut booking at the Middlesex music hall -a hall associated with a high level of clog dancing - was achieved on the strength of his fame as a clog dancer, Leno himself viewing his clog dance as the centre-piece of his act and it was not until the end of 1888 that Leno even began to omit the clog dance from his act . Following over three years of consistent appreciation in both London and the provinces, the critics began to pressurise Leno into abandoning his clog dance. They found the dichotomy in his act, with its comic songs followed by a serious dance disturbing and true to form criticised his dancing for its monotony and physical exertion:

"A shade of gloom used to come over him as he began it, which increased as he 'tripled' and fairly overwhelmed him as he concluded, breathless and exhausted....In the interests of mirth we would ask Mr Leno, after our Monday night's experience, to always omit his clog dance, which whatever its qualities - we know them to be great - is, after all, a merely mechanical exercise, and instead of the melancholy beat of the clog step, give us humour, which with him is not mechanical, but unforced and fresh."[33]

The critics were discomforted by Leno's serious presentation of a skill rooted in the northern factory classes. Unlike the presentation of his lower-class comic characters, over which the middle-classes were able to feel a reassuring sense of superiority, his clog dancing demanded only direct admiration from the audience, placing the performer in an exclusive controlling, and therefore superior position. The London critics and increasingly middle-class managements were not prepared to allow a music hall performer to control them by means of an indisputably lower-class language of which they had no critical or cultural understanding, and which therefore manipulated them into a loss of power. Leno struggled to maintain his identity as a dancer but was forced in the end to comply, and from then on the assertive, challenging face of Leno is subdued into submission. Although his dancing was successfully repressed in London, provincial reviews from the late 1890's show that he was not allowed to leave the stage until he had performed his championship dance.

In 1897, at Hammerstein's Olympia Music Hall, New York, Leno was hissed off the stage during one of his songs. Leno changed offstage, returned in his clogs and succeeded in winning the audience's warm applause by his clog dancing.[34] This incident, like many others demonstrates the confidence and assurance with which he controlled an audience by his clog dancing. He had successfully asserted this control at the outset of his London career, but it was only when he attempted to cross the class border within the music hall that critics, sensing disconcerting implications rooted in class tension, forced him to abandon it.

At the London Pavilion, on 20th October 1904, during what proved to be his final performance, his third item was a dance. It was stated by various sources that after prolonged bouts of insanity, he had lost his comic continuity. On this occasion he attempted to regain control of his act by dancing "with all the vigour that characterised his efforts in the days when he claimed championship honours as a step dancer". But by this time the association with clog dancing was interpreted as further confirmation of his madness, placing him in the ultimate position of loss of control . Could this apparent symptom of madness been Leno's last struggle to transgress the boundaries imposed on him by unconsciously challenging a construction of madness influenced by the increasing theatrical demarcations of the legitimate and the illegitimate?

---

[1] Nineteenth century commentators appear to have generalised British solo clog dance as Lancashire, the county predominantly renowned for its origin. Certainly examples of the clog-dance and also the closely related musical hornpipe exist to confirm the association with Lancashire: e.g.; Thomas Marsden's *A Collection of Lancashire Hornpipes old and new* , 1705 (See Inglehearn "The Hornpipe, our national dance?" NEMA: *The Hornpipe*, 1993. pp.37-50). Jerry Duke states that Tom Rice, originator of "Jim Crow" referred to his famous dance as a "Lancaster clog ". (Jerry Duke: *Clog Dancing in the Appalachians*, 1984. p.31)

[2] Elizabeth Gaskell: *North and South*. 1854. (Penguin edition, 1970. p.234)

[3] "The Wearing of Clogs in Lancashire" from a series of newspaper clippings from the *Manchester Weekly Times* (Notes and Queries), 1891. Manchester Central Library local studies collection. Q942. 7389 M79. Vol.12, pp.93,100-101.

[4] Thomas Broughton: "Lancashire Clogs". Manchester Central Library local studies collection. Newspaper Clippings F942.72 Ha7. Vol.2, p.127.

[5] Dates not given. A present day dancer from an unbroken family line of Lancashire clog dancers, Pat Tracey traces her steps back via her grandfather to the 1820's but believes them to have originated in the late eighteenth century.

[6] See Patricia Tracey: "The Lancashire Hornpipe". NEMA: *The Hornpipe* pp.15-22. (1993)

[7] Dates not given. According to Pat Tracey, Bill Gibbons was born in the late 1890's in Burscough, living and working on the Leeds-Liverpool canal where he learnt his steps as a bargeman.

[8] "The Free-and-Easies of Glasgow" and "More about Free-and-Easie" (sic.) Contained in unidentified newspaper articles on "The Dark Side of Glasgow", 1871. Mitchell Collection, Glasgow. G914.1435Q*.

[9] See J.S Bratton: "Dancing a Hornpipe in Fetters". Folk Music Journal Vol.6, no.1, pp.65-82. (1990)

[10] Playbills for the Old Leeds Theatre, 11th, 16th and 17th July, 1822. Symington Collection, University of Leeds.

[11] Letter from George E. Belmont: "Clog Dancing Reminiscences". *Era* 23rd October, 1897 p.18.

[12] See Diana Howard: *London Theatres and Music Halls 1850-1950* (1970) for licensing applications.

[13] Penelope Summerfield: "The Effingham Arms and the Empire: Deliberate Selection in the Evolution of Music Hall in London." Yeo and Yeo: *Popular Culture and Class Conflict* Ch.8. (1981)

[14] Programme for People's Palace, 22nd May,1893. Mitchell Collection, Glasgow.

[15] Dagmar Höher: "The Composition of Music Hall Audiences 1850-1900" ed. Bailey: *Music Hall: The Business of Pleasure* p.80. (1986)

[16] See newspaper clippings on the People's Concert Hall, Manchester Central Library local studies collection. F942.7 M10. Vol.10 pp.68-72.

[17] Bill: 11th February, 1864. Wood Collection, Tyne and Wear Archives. Box 963/1/3, B1982.

[18] Bill: 31st December, 1881. Wood Collection, Tyne and Wear Archive. Box 963/4/3, B11443.

[19] Arthur North: "Music Hall Types". Yorkshire *Busy Bee* 20th August, 1881, pp.8-11.

[20] Percy Fitzgerald: *Music hall Land* p.55 (1900)

[21] Arnold Bennett: *Clayhanger*, 1910 (Methuen edition 1962, p.84).

[22] Ibid. Ch. X "Free and Easy".

[23] *Variety and Variety Critic* Vol.1, no.10. 16th April, 1898. p.11.

[24] See Caroline Kershaw: "Dan Leno: New Evidence of Early Influences and Style" *Nineteenth Century Theatre* Vol.22, no.1. (1994) on which the remainder of this essay is based.

[25] See *Era*, 18th June, 1881, p.23. See also *Era*, 16th October, 1897, p.20, and 6th November, 1897, p.19; "Dan Leno and the Belt, the true story of the Clog Dancing Competition", *Dancing Times* June 1923, p.914; Whimsical Walker: *From Sawdust to Windsor Castle*, (1922) p.143; for other accounts of the contest.

[26] *Era* 18th June, 1881, p.23.

[27] For exchanges between Dan Leno, John Williams and other dancers, see *Era*, 29th August, p.23; September 5th p.23, 12th p.23, 19th pp.19 & 23, 26th p.23; 3rd October p.23; 7th November p.10, 1885 and 2nd January p.23 1886. *Sporting Life,* 16th September,1885.

[28] *Era* 18th June, 1881, p.23.

[29] Charles Coborn: *The Man who Broke the Bank: memories of the stage and music hall.* p.150 (1928)

[30] See Note 25.

[31] Hickory J. Wood: *Dan Leno* (1905)

[32] *M.A.P.* 10th August, 1901, p.142.

[33] *Era,* 29th September, 1888,p.15.

[34] *New York Dramatic Mirror*, 8th May, 1897, p.17.

Bibliography: (All publications London, unless otherwise stated).

Primary sources:
Manuscript and other unpublished material.

Empire account book, 1900-01, Farmer Collection, University of Glasgow.

Flett Tom. MS notes. Metherell collection. Newcastle.

Gaiety Theatre Account Book, 1903-1907. Birmingham Central Library.

Glasgow music hall programmes, 1850-93; 1898-99; 1900-01; 1902, Mitchell Collection, Glasgow.

MacMillan, J., "Description of Checks issued by Birmingham Concert Halls, 1850-1920", Birmingham Central Library.

Manchester music hall programmes, Manchester Central Library.

Manchester Central Library, newspaper cuttings.

Marsden Thomas. *A Collection of Lancashire Hornpipes old and new.* 1705. MS, British Library.

Metherell, C. (Private Collection). MS notes of Instep Research Team; newspaper cuttings. Newcastle.

Middlesex Music Hall, souvenir 1902, New London Theatre Collections.

Mitchell Collection, Glasgow, scrapbook.

People's Palace Museum, programmes, Glasgow.

Symington Collection, University of Leeds.

Theatre Royal, playbills 1838-9, Mitchell Collection, Glasgow.

Vaughan Williams Memorial Library, collection on step-dancing.

Walsh John (pub.) *3rd Book of the most celebrated Jiggs, Lancashire Hornpipes, Scotch and Highland Lilts, etc.* c.1731. MS. British Library.

Wood Collection, Tyne and Wear Archives.

Newspapers and periodicals

City Jackdaw (Manchester); *City Lantern* (Manchester); *Dancing Times; Era;Freelance* (Manchester); *Glasgow Evening News*; M.A.P; *Manchester Weekly Times; New York Dramatic Mirror; Sporting Life; Variety and Variety Critic; Yorkshire Busy Bee.* (Leeds).

Contemporary books and articles

Bennett Arnold. *Clayhanger.* 1910.

Coborn Charles. *The Man who Broke the Bank, memories of the stage and music hall.* Hutchinson, 1928.

Fitzgerald Percy. *Music Hall Land.* 1900.

Gaskell Elizabeth. *North and South.* First published in *Household Words*, 1854-5.

Sayce R.U. "Pattens and Clogs", *Transactions of the Rochdale Literary and Scientific Society,* Vol.xxi, 1941-43. 1942, 46-51.

Walker Whimsical *From Sawdust to Windsor Castle*, 1922.

Wood Hickory. J. *Dan Leno*, Methuen, 1905.

Secondary sources:

Books and articles

Bailey Peter (ed.) *Music Hall: The Business of Pleasure.* Open University Press. Milton Keynes and Philadelphia. 1986.

Bratton, J.S. "Dancing a Hornpipe in Fetters", *Folk Music Journal,* Vol.6, No.1. 1990. 65-82.

Duke Jerry. *Clog Dancing in the Appalachians*, Duke Publishing Co. San Francisco, 1984.

Howard Diana. *London Theatres and Music Halls 1850-1950.* The Library Association. 1970.

Höher Dagmar. "The Composition of Music Hall Audiences, 1850-1900" in Bailey (ed.) *Music Hall: The Business of Pleasure.* 73-92.

Inglehearn Madeleine. "The hornpipe, our national dance?" in NEMA *The Hornpipe.* 37-50.

Kershaw Caroline. "Dan Leno: New Evidence of Early Influences and Style" *Nineteenth Century Theatre.* Vol.22, no.1. 1994. 30-55.

Metherell Chris. *An Introductory Bibliography on Clog and Step Dance.* Vaughan Williams Memorial Library Leaflet no.22. English Folk Dance and Song Society. 1994.

National Early Music Association (NEMA) *The Hornpipe* conference papers, 1993.

Summerfield Penelope. "The Effingham Arms and the Empire: Deliberate Selection in the Evolution of Music Hall in London" in Yeo & Yeo, *Popular Culture and Class Conflict,* 1981. Ch.8.

Tracey Patricia. "The Lancashire Hornpipe". In NEMA *The Hornpipe.* 15-22.

Yeo Eileen & Stephen, *Popular Culture and Class Conflict 1590-1914: Explorations in the History of Labour and Leisure,* Harvester Press, Sussex, 1981.

The research undertaken for this essay was assisted by the Beilby Research Scholarship and the Ian Karten Charitable Fund.

Restoration or Collapse of the (Dance) Tradition?
The Case of the Dance *Tsámikos* on the Island of Lefkada, Greece

Maria I. Koutsouba

Ph.D. student, Goldsmiths College, University of London

The paper touches upon various issues such as gender, kinship, social identity, tradition and change. However, its main concern is with the ability of dance to challenge or even to eliminate boundaries of two kinds: first, theoretical ones, since dance constitutes a subject matter that can illuminate many fields of inquiry; second, practical ones, as dance performance is able to comment upon social relationships and boundaries among people.

Although I would not consider myself a connoisseur of postmodern-feminist methodology, I would like to adopt Frazer and Nickolson's ideas of such an approach, according to which (1988, pp:101) "theory would be explicitly historical, attuned to the cultural specifity of different societies and periods and to that of different groups within societies and periods". This paper is a first attempt to use these ideas in relation to folk dance, taking Greek society and Greek dance as starting points. Folk dance in Greece constitutes an important cornerstone in social life and continues to function actively within it. Thus, dance can be used as a paradigmatic example of social reality and change in Greek social structure. At this point I would like to clarify that by saying "it still functions", I do not refer to the "frozen Greek portrait" (Koutsouba,1991, p:60) that is formed by staged folkloristic performances, which is another dimension of Greek dance. I refer to dance which "is bound up with the everyday life of the people" (Raftis, 1985, p:17) and which is used as a means for socialisation in community life. It can be said that some aspects of it are also "frozen". Yet, a clear distinction between these two ideas can be made. The former is "connotative", i.e. the main focus is on the spectator, but the latter is "emotional", i.e. the main focus is on the dancer (Zografou, 1989, p:104).

The data used in this paper is part of a large ethnographic research that took place on the Ionian island of Lefkada, western Greece, during the years 1992-1994. In particular, I will examine the performance of the dance *Tsámikos* at the village fair of Karya on the island of Lefkada. More specifically, I will look at the performance given by an old man and an old woman and the recent innovation of a young woman performing the dance using male elements. This accords with Skouteri-Didaskalou (1984, p:67), who remarks that "the relationship between the two sexes must be studied not only on the basis of their previous history but also of their contemporary historical presence". Through the analysis of the three performances, I intend to define both their stylistic characteristics and their similarities and differences. Reference to the socio-historical background will then follow in an attempt to locate each of the dance styles in time and place and, most importantly, to reveal the social values that the styles transmit.

Context

In every Greek village fairs take place once a year at the name day of the saint to whom the village is dedicated. Usually, they occur in the village square. In the past, their duration used to be three days, the saint's name day falling on the middle of the three days. Nowadays, they last only two days, finishing on the name day. The last day is considered to be the more important. In the village of Karya, the fair takes place on the 10th and 11th of August. This is a very unusual period for festive activities because people fast for the 15th of August, being the feast of the Assumption of Virgin Mary. Live music in the form of instrumental ensembles *(órgana)* is one of the main characteristics of the fair. According to my informants there used to be many ensembles, six even seven. Yet, after the evolution of amplified sound these have been reduced to one or at most two, and in this latter case, one will be away from the square to prevent musical confusion. The general structure of the fair is as follows: various groups of relatives and/or friends mainly from the village or other villages will dance in turn. The order of the dance is organised according to prearranged bookings, whereby the leader of each group gives the musicians a piece of paper with his name on it. Then the musicians will call each one, following strictly the order of the booking, otherwise misunderstandings *(parexigisi)* may occur. Only one group performs at a time and no outsider is allowed to join. Usually each group participates in only one of the two or three days of the fair. This is for both practical reasons to ensure that all groups may perform, but also for financial ones, since even one performance of the group requires a considerable financial commitment.

Village fairs are opportunities to demonstrate social power and economic strength. The bigger the group, the more social power it designates. Everyone present will look critically at each performance. A group can be appreciated either in terms of dance or in terms of social respect. Appreciation will be shown by sending an offering *(kérasma)* usually beers and occasionally champagne. The duration of each group's performance can vary between one and three or four hours. This is an interesting point considering that the fair starts at about eleven o'clock at night and can go on until the next morning, when the attendance of the morning church service is obligatory for the community. The duration of the group's performance depends on two criteria: i)the number of the members of the group, and ii) the economic status of the group. This can be understood on the basis that each member of the group has to perform one or two dances and has to pay the musicians about 5.000 drachmes (almost £15) for every small section of a song in a specific dance. For example, a small group of four people might pay 40.000 drachmes (£100), while a large group of ten people might pay 100.000 drachmes (£250). Thus, the performance of many dances by a large group inevitably demonstrates economic strength. Performers may choose to give gold coins, which is considered ostentatious.

Each member of the group has its own favourite dance-song which the musicians are obliged to know. Of course, because the instrumental ensembles are few and the same for the whole island, musicians are aware of the taste of the dancers. As a result there is a mutual relationship between performers and musicians where every action, such as the choice of a particular song, becomes meaningful to the people. In this context *Tsámikos* constitutes one of the main dances of the dance repertory performed at the fair of the village Karya.

The dance *Tsámikos*

Tsámikos is not just one dance. It is rather a dance genre which has many forms in the various areas where it is performed, and can be accompanied by many different songs. It is also called *Kléftikos* from the *kléftes*, the mountain fighters during the Greek War of Independence from the Turks in 1821 (Dimas, 1976, p:36). *Tsámikos* has come to be called a "panhellenic" dance (Holden & Vouras, 1976, p:104 and Roubis, 1990, p:160), in the sense that it represents the Greek national identity. The process of receiving such a title goes beyond the scope of this paper. However, the panhellenic character of the dance and its frequent performance at Karya are the main reasons for its selection for this study.

Tsámikos is considered mainly a male dance where the primary aim is the demonstration of gallantry. With this dance, men demonstrate their skill. People usually say "the good dancer will dance *Tsámikos*" (Mazaraki, 1984 p:103). Improvisation is the main characteristic (Dimas, 1993, pp:136-138). The dance improvisation occurs mainly during the clarinet *(klaríno)* improvisation -klaríno is the main instrument for *Tsámikos*. This instrumental improvisation is called *vérso* (Mazaraki, 1984, p:103 and Tirovola, 1992, p:89). By that time the dancer usually performs on the spot *(ston tópo).* However, the fact that in many areas of Greece such as in Roumeli, Epirus, Thessaly and Lefkada, *Tsámikos* is also performed by women has been understated. Yet according to my informants, the female performance existed for over 150 years. It is true that the male and female performance differ, yet this does not change the fact that it is performed by both sexes. In particular, at the fair of Karya *Tsámikos* is a favourite dance for both sexes.

I want now to look at the male and female performance of the dance in the context of the fair at Karya to define each style. I have chosen the performance of two local old people, a man and a woman. They are around the same age and are always present at the village fair. They have been deliberately chosen so as to represent the same generation, and, thus, the same dance background. Because of their age and their dancing activity they are respected by the community. A performance of the dance by a young woman in her 30s follows. She attempts to use male variations in her performance, a very recent phenomenon in the context of the village fair.

The performance of *Tsámikos* by the old man

The old man in his mid 60s is from the village of Karya. Coming from a local "dance family", he is an important figure at the fair because of his permanent presence in it and because of his participation in all the dance activities of the village. At the specific performance he is with a group of five men and a young boy. This is the way he usually performs at the fair. His group is the last one to dance that day and the old man is the last performer of the group. He has already performed his first dance and paid the musicians once. He has left *Tsámikos* for the end. In the short interval between the two dances he drinks beer that was sent as an offering to his group. Wearing trousers and a shirt, and having a cigarette in his mouth, he starts to dance *Tsámikos* around the table with the offering on it, while other offerings have been dropped and broken on the dance floor. His son holds him with a handkerchief. He starts *Tsámikos* performing the basic motif with very small elaboratively smooth movements. This is followed by a squat on one foot and a turn to the right. Then he repeats the basic motif and after that he makes a squat, turns to the right and touches the dancing floor with his right hand. Once again he performs the basic motif. Afterwards he jumps, turns to the right, squats, kicks his foot, turns to the right again and gets up completing the basic motif. Then, he repeats the basic motif twice making a turn to the left at the end of the second motif followed by two more basic motives with a turn to the right at the end of the second one. Finally he jumps, squats, kicks his foot, turns to the left and gets up completing the basic motif. Thus, his performance consists of the basic motif, which he can perform on its own or vary with squats, turns, jumps, kicks and touching the floor. However, whenever the old man performs the variations, he incorporates them in the basic motif of the dance. Overall, he moves very little in space as he mainly dances on the spot and performs any shifting with small steps. After the completion of *Tsámikos* he has hardly done a half circle. During his performance he mainly moves on the vertical axis with very smooth movements. His body is in an upright but not open position. On the contrary, it seems that he keeps the energy in himself. The rest of the group follows in simple steps. At the end of his performance he pays the musicians again.

The performance of *Tsámikos* by the old woman

The old woman in her 60s, wearing a skirt below the knee and a shirt with short sleeves, is not from Karya but from a nearby village. However, because this particular fair is famous throughout the island, and because she has relatives at Karya, she and her family usually participate. On this occasion she performs with a mixed group in which her husband, son and daughter-in-law participate as well. *Tsámikos* is the first dance of her performance. Her son, who supports her with a handkerchief, orders the song for her and pays the musicians. The old woman starts the *Tsámikos* by performing the basic motif three times. The fourth time she embellishes it with a turn to the right and one to the left. She repeats the basic motif and afterwards she does so with a turn to the left. Two plain motives follow and then one with a turn to the left, a plain one and one with a turn to the right. By that time she accepts an offering which is passed to her by her son. The old woman continues her dancing with two motives with a left turn. She finishes by performing a plain motif and one with a left turn. Thus, her performance consists of the basic motif embellished only infrequently with turns to the right or left. She does not perform any other variation. During her performance the woman makes smooth medium steps and as a result she has performed a whole circle by the end of the dance. Despite the larger shifting, she moves mainly on the vertical axis, with an upright but not open position of her body. The rest of the group can easily perform the basic motif with her.

The performance of *Tsámikos* by the young woman

The young woman is in her 30s and she performs with a small group consisting of her husband, her father-in-law, her little son and a friend. The family is not from the village, nor from nearby ones, as the audience could not identify them. Wearing short leggings, she starts her performance by standing on her left foot and moving her right leg to the front and back of the central line of her body in a semi-circle. The movement is very small at the beginning, but gradually it becomes bigger. Then, she makes two steps and a squat, and starts jumping on both feet to the left and to the right side. After a turn to the left she repeats the jumps. Getting up on her left foot, she turns to the left and starts the semi-circles with her right leg once more, followed by jumps from one foot to the other. By that time she tries to move to the back of the circle. Yet her husband pushes her to the front to continue the dance which he has ordered and for which he has paid. She continues her dance in the same way as before with squats, turns, jumps on both feet or from one foot to the other and semi-circles with her right leg. However, she does not complete the song of *Tsámikos* this time either as she moves to the second position of the circle after some time leaving her husband to do so. By the end of her performance the young woman has hardly moved a quarter of circle as she mainly performs on the spot. Although she uses many variations, she performs them irrespectively of the basic motif of the dance, which never appeared in her dance. Moreover, she dances in very open positions, moving far away from her centre of gravity both to the vertical and horizontal axes with very intense movements that sometimes make her off-balance. Her energy is pouring out. During this performance there were no offerings.

Discussion of the three performances

The performance of a good *Tsámikos* at a village fair is based on the following characteristics: keeping good time with the music; good physical coordination; movement mainly on the vertical axis; keeping the energy internalised by maintaining the body in a closed position, remaining, however, upright. In terms of the male performance, it is a common phenomenon to have a dance group consisting only of men at a village fair. Even if there are women in the group they will leave after their performance and the men will remain. Each man of the group performs one or two dances in turn. *Tsámikos* has to be one of them otherwise the amateurism of the performer will be implied. Every man has his own favourite song for *Tsámikos*, and performs it in his own unique style. Apart from the most important characteristics of the performance the man may apply variations as he chooses. Small steps, dancing on the spot on one or both feet or even with the back, turns, squats, kicks, dancing on the top of bottles and glasses are some of the usual variations. Their combination is unique for each dancer. Because of this freedom and scope for improvisation the performance of a male dance group is considered to be the most ostentatious and extraordinary part of the fair. Smoking, drinking, breaking of bottles are all allowed in a man's performance. He is expected, however, to wear trousers and a shirt, and strong, formal shoes.

The women perform only in the presence of men who must be relatives, usually their husbands, sons or sons-in-law. A group consisting exclusively of women has never appeared in a fair, although it is common in other dance contexts. The woman of a mixed group will perform one or two dances in front of the group only after she has been invited by a close relative who must hold her hand. In the female performance *Tsámikos* will be usually the first dance. The woman is not allowed to pay the musicians or to order her favourite songs. This has to be done through the men of the group. The female performance of *Tsámikos* is very restricted. The woman can dance the basic motif and the only variation allowed is turns to the left or to the right. She dances only briefly on the spot, and when she does so, her body will remain in a straight position. As a result, she makes a larger use of space, although her steps are small. She mainly moves around the vertical axis. Smoking and breaking of bottles are not allowed. Even if there is an offering during her performance, she will drink it only if the men of the group pass it to her. It is not proper to wear trousers and sleeveless shirt; a skirt below the knee and a shirt with short sleeves is preferable. Anything beyond this will be an exaggeration and will not be well received by the audience.

The phenomenon of young women performing in a male style is very rare in the village fair. During the fieldwork the woman described before was the only exception at the specific fair. Her performance is characterised by the use of many male variations such us dancing on the spot for a long time, squats, turns and kicks. Although she uses the male variations, her performance is totally different as she dances on both axes, the vertical and the horizontal, and in very open positions using large movements which usually make her to be off-balance. Despite these innovations a number of elements from the performance of the old woman are kept. She is in a mixed group where the payment of the musicians and the order of the songs are made by the men. She does not complete her dance, but instead, she moves to the second position of the circle during the song. In addition her group is not from the village not even from the island, according to the comments of the audience. None of the local women would consider wearing her leggings and perform like her in the square of the village. Thus, she received very little attention from the people around.

Having presented and discussed the three performances certain differences have emerged. In terms of the performance these are the use of the body and space; the type and quality of movement; the performance group; the order of dancers and dances and the clothing. In terms of context these are the origins of the dancers, the reaction of the audience and the offerings. These differences inevitably imply that men and women are viewed differently in the local society. A discussion on the gender categories in Greece is then an important step to understand the three different performances.

Gender categories of the Greek society

Gender issues in relation to those of kinship hold an important position in the field of anthropology where "it is becoming a commonplace that [these two issues] should be the subjects of a unified analysis" (Loizos & Papataxiarchis, 1991, p:7). Particularly in Greece "the history of the anthropological study of gender, parallells and has influenced interest in women within the field of anthropology as a whole" (Dubisch, 1986, p:5),. since there is a large number of studies focusing on these issues. The following discussion is based on the results of these studies. Although they refer to different communities, some of the characteristics apply to the case of Karya as well.

Greek society, dominating by "androcentrism" (Herzfeld, 1986, p:232), constitutes a strict "patricentric community" (Danforth, p:159), where men and women are considered to be of a different nature. Among anthropologists in Greece "women are associated with the private, the natural, the profane and the polluting" (Danforth, 1983, p:157). The Greek woman "is identified with reference to a man" (Cowan, 1990, p:80). As a girl she is identified in relation to her father, as a woman in relation to her husband. In such a community "the roles of man and woman are restricted to a particular sphere of activities, i.e. the man is representative and protective and the woman domestic and expressive" (Campell, 1964, p:150). In particular the man is considered to be "the head of the house" in front of whom "the woman must show respect at all time" (Campell, 1964, p:151). In this social context woman always has a marginal position in the community.

If participation and leadership in dance activities is perceived as an additional indicator of overt power along with political and religious ones, as Friedl proposes (1975, pp:6-7), and bearing in mind the above social context in Greek society, then the dance performance of the old man and woman can be easily examined and identified. The free and improvised dance performance of *Tsámikos* by the man indicates his powerful social status, whereas the strict and limited one by the woman her marginality. Possibly it is on this basis that the understatement of the female performance during previous years can be explained. The village fair is then an "organised dance demonstration ... which seems to strengthen the social ties " (Loutzaki, 1984, p:62). Moreover, it is a "cultural scenario" (Schieffelin, 1976, p:3) which "reflect[s] and formalise[s] the established patterns of the prevalent social hierarchy" (Adshead, 1988, p:79). This is particularly true in the case of *Tsámikos* which is so much gender-orientated.

The question here is on what basis can the phenomenon of the young woman performing in a kind of male style be explained. This can be historically associated with the postwar period in Greece. As du Boulay states (1983, p:260) "after 1950, with an economic and cultural situation changing with increasing rapidity, ... Western ideas and values" were brought throughout the country. Processes of "modernisation and industrialisation" (Salamone & Stanton, 1983, p:118) and those of "urbanisation and migration" (Meraklis, 1989, p:92, 139 &174) took place all over Greece. The explosion of the tourist industry must also be included. Increased prosperity, exposure to new ideas, educational opportunities, career-orientation and women's liberation, are some of the results of these processes that the above writers mention. In this context gender-orientated "cultural scenarios" which were used only for reaffirmation of old relationships, to paraphrase Schieffelin, are now also used to form new ones. The delay of the appearance of these changes in the dance performance of *Tsámikos* at the mountainous village Karya of the Ionian island of Lefkada is not surprising. Social changes in the mid and late 50s "started from the urban centres and then moved to the periphery" (Meraklis, 1989, p:139). They appeared later in dance and definitely much later at the island.

But, have these social changes really taken place? And if so, how welcome are they in dance? I mentioned that the performance of the young woman not only keeps some basic elements, such as the ordering of the song and the payment of the musicians, but also, that it was not appreciated either in terms of the dance itself or in terms of the reaction of the audience. These parameters certainly reduce the significance of the phenomenon, and they can be used as an argument that, at a fundamental level, the society maintains its social structures with firmness. However, the fact that change of social gender roles is an ongoing process in the strict, gender-orientated Greek society, can been used as a counter-argument. However, how does this change affect the dance? Is it implied that with the change of the social roles the Greek folk dance and with it the tradition will collapse? I do not think there is a straightforward answer to this question, considering the unstable character of the present social condition. It is possible that dance and tradition will finally collapse. But it is also possible that they will be transformed, thus serving the new ideas. It is too early to ascertain either possibility. The phenomenon of a young woman dancing *Tsámikos* using male elements, which at present has sporadically appeared, does not indicate either collapse or restoration of (dance) tradition.

Conclusion

So far I have examined the performance of only one dance *(Tsámikos)*, by three people of different social status, at a particular festive occasion in a specific place (village Karya). I have analysed this performance and by relating it to various issues (gender, kinship, tradition and change) I have used it as a means for commenting upon social structures. Thus, I have shown that the performance of one dance is able to challenge and even eliminate boundaries among people; furthermore, that dance can also touch upon many areas of inquiry. Through this process it becomes explicit that dance is a challenging and enormous subject for study; a subject which has its own unique identity, not as a representation of society, but as an inseparable part of it.

N.B: I would like to express my thanks to my supervisor Dr. Andreé Grau for her useful comments on the draft of this paper and to my friends Steve and Eve for the polishing of the language.

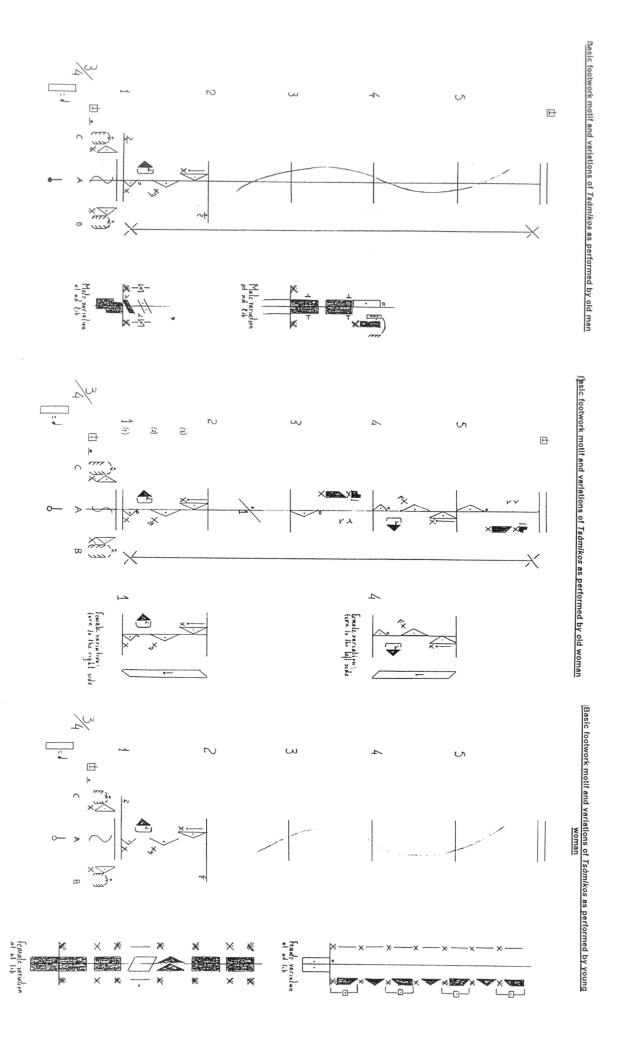

BIBLIOGRAPHY

Adshead, J.,   Dance Analysis:Theory and Practice, London: Dance Books, 1988.

Campell, J.K.,   Honour, Family and Patronage:A Study of Institutions and Moral
                        Values in a Greek Mountain Community, Oxford: Clarendon Press,
                        1964.

Cowan, J.,   Dance and the Body Politic in Northern Greece, Princeton:
                        Princeton University Press, 1990.

Danforth, M. L.,   Symbolic Aspects of Male/Female Relations in Greece, Journal of
                        Modern Greek Studies, vol.:1, no:1, May 1983, pp:157-160.

Dimas, E.,   Elliniki Paradosiaki Hori (Greek Traditional Dances), Athens, 1976.

Dimas, E.,   I Horeftiki Paradosi tis Ipirou (The Dance Tradition of Epirus),
                        Athens, 1993.

Dubisch, J.,   Gender and Power in Rural Greece, Princeton: Princeton
                        University Press, 1986.

du Boulay, J.,   The Meaning of Dowry:Changing Values in Rural Greece, Journal
                        of Modern Greek Studies, vol.:1, no:1, May 1983, pp:243-270.

Frazer, N. & Nicholson, L.,   Social Criticism Without Philosophy:An Encounter Between
                        Feminism and Postmodernism, Social Text, vol.:7, no:3, Winter 1989
                        pp:83-104.

Friedl, E.,   Men and Women:An Anthropologist's View, New York:Holt,
                        Rinehart and Winston, 1975.

Herzfeld, M.,   Within and Without:The Category of "Female" in the Ethnography of
                        Modern Greece, in Dubisch, J., Gender and Power in Rural Greece,
                        Princeton:Princeton University Press, 1986, pp:215-234.

Holden, R. & Vouras, M.,   Greek Folk Dances, Brussels:Folkraft Europe, 1976.

Koutsouba, M.,   Greek Dance Groups of Plaka:A Case of "Airport Art", unpublished
                        M.A. dissertation, University of Surrey, 1991.

Loizos, P. & Papataxiarchis, E.,   Contested Identities:Gender and Kinship in Modern
                        Greece, Princeton: Princeton University Press, 1991.

Loutzaki, R.,   O Horos sto Egeo (Dance at the Aegean Sea), Athens: Ministry of
                        Tourism and Aegean Ministry, 1987.

Mazaraki, D.,   To Laiko Klarino stin Ellada (The Popular Clarinet in Greece), Athens
                        Kedros, 1984, 2nd ed.

Meraklis, M.G.,   Laographika Zitimata (Folklore Issues), Athens: Bouras, 1989.

Raftis, A.,   O Kosmos tou Ellinikou Horou (The World of Greek Dance), Athens:
                        Polytropo, 1985.

Salamone, S. D. & Stanton, J.B., Introducing the *Nikokyra*:Identity and Reality in Social Process, in in Dubisch, J., <u>Gender and Power in Rural Greece</u>, Princeton:Princeton University Press, 1986, pp:97-120.

Schieffelin, L.E.,   <u>The Sorrow of the Lonely and the Burning of the Dancers</u>, New York: St. Martin's Press, 1976.

Skouteri-Didaskalou, N., <u>Anthropologika gia ti Gynekio Zitima</u> (Anthropological Concerns for the Female Issue), Athens: Politis, 1984.

Tirovola, V.,   <u>Elliniki Paradosiaki Horeftiki Rhythmi</u> (Greek Traditional Dance Rhythms), Athens: Gutenberg, 1992.

Zografou, M.,   <u>Laographiki-Anthropologiki Prosegisi tou Sera-Horou ton Pontion</u> (Folkloristic-Anthropological Approach of the Pontic Sera-Dance), Ph.D. dissertation, University of Ioannina, 1989.

Susan Kozel
Independent

The Virtual World: New Frontiers for Dance and Philosophy

> For the last twenty years neither matter nor
> space nor time has been what it was from time
> immemorial. We must expect great innovations
> to transform the entire technique of the arts,
> thereby affecting artistic invention itself
> and perhaps even bringing about an amazing
> change in our very notion of art.
> *Paul Valéry, (1930), Aesthetics, "The Conquest
> of Ubiquity"*

Technology in dance is regarded with a mixture of fascination and horror. The fascination stems from a sense of an extension of our abilities, a transformation of the shape of movement and choreography; yet there is also a fear for what may be lost. With the so-called *virtual* or immersive computer technologies, the potential for expansion and loss is greater than ever because it is the boundaries of the body which are expanded. And it is potentially the body itself which is lost. In literary and philosophical circles it is common to hear virtual reality praised for being a way to leave "the meat" (in other words the body) behind in order to voyage in the non-space of the mind. As a privileging of mind over body it seems like a vicious Cartesianism making a last gasp. This interpretation of the virtual world is, of course, a horror to a dancer because the result is an equation between technology and annihilation. So are dancers who embrace virtual technology nihilists of the most extreme kind? My answer to this question is no. I suggest that technology in dance is about the extension of the body and capabilities of a dancer through the manipulation of time, space, matter and movement. Virtual reality, when experienced through dance, can be seen as an amplification of materiality, rather than an immaterial space in which our bodies are represented only visually.

In an earlier paper I discussed mimesis in dance and philosophy, and left off by gesturing towards the combined participation of the dancing body and advancements in virtual technology as crucial ingredients in creating a new cultural symbolic.[1] In this paper, I take these themes further by examining the role for the dancing body in the new physical and philosophical space opened up by the virtual world. I present a glimpse of Gilles Deleuze's philosophy and sketch its relevance both to dancing bodies and virtual reality. In my final section, I introduce a few overtly aesthetic concerns based on creating work with the so-called 'new' technologies. By 'virtual technology' I mean a mixture of computer, video, audio and light in the context of live performance. Computer programmes such as *Lifeforms*, as well as dance on film and video, are undeniably examples of dance and technology, but they are beyond the scope of this discussion.

I   "Technologically Naive People"

In my efforts to derive a physical account of the virtual world which could be used in an aesthetic context, I turned for inspiration to three Americans who work at the design and construction of virtual worlds, and who also write about their projects. I thought their combination of theory and practice would be provocative. Myron Krueger is a pioneer of virtual reality research and has created interactive, full-body computer generated 'realities' since the 1960's. He reflects upon the reactions to one of his installations (*Videoplace*, 1983).

> It is impressive to observe how technologically naive people naturally accepted these projected experiences as reality... They regarded their electronic image as an extension of themselves. What happened to their image also happened to them; they felt what touched their image.[2]

How humbling to have to admit to being naive, let alone technologically naive. It seems like an indication of being backward, out of touch or fearful of change. When I agree to Myron Krueger's terms and adopt a position of technological naiveté, it is not out of a romantic sense of the power of child-like wonder. It is because I believe my electronic moving image *is* an extension of myself, and because I see this as a valid phenomenological experience of effective 'immersive' technology, whether this is achieved with sophisticated computer graphics or through use of other media frequently used in dance performance such as video, lighting and sound. Krueger identified the experiential space of dancing in a technological environment, but seemed to think it did not have philosophical validity.

After Krueger, I was lured to the writing of Brenda Laurel and Randall Walser by enticing quotes which appeared in other sources. They insist that advancements in virtual technology need to be informed, and possibly led, by the aesthetic concerns of art and theatre. Walser insists that knowledge of theatre, sports, dance and film are as important as programming; Laurel claims to use Aristotle's poetics to inform the creation of artificial realities in which the potential for action is cognitively, emotionally, and aesthetically enhanced. She states, in a highly dramatic way, that "Computers are Theatre." He is fond of saying that "cyberspace embodies."

Nevertheless, I found their writing jointly and severally disappointing. Their radicality seems to begin and end by acknowledging theatre to be a useful paradigm for understanding virtual interaction, and for designing interface software. Yet the understanding of 'theatre' they employ is highly limited. Walser's claim that cyberspace is fundamentally a theatrical medium is based on the simple fact that people invent and communicate realities by "acting them out."[3] Laurel in *Computers as Theatre* (1990) claims to present a "poetics of human-computer activity," but her highly conservative reading of Aristotle's poetics consists in using the principles of dramatic form and structure to design interesting and satisfying human-computer activities, which mainly take the shape of computer games.[4]

Their theoretical paradigms are not wrong, but they are limited; and as dancers or artists interested in using technology it is difficult to be satisfied with them. They do not challenge any theoretical boundaries, nor do they adequately account for movement or physicality. When Laurel and Walser gesture towards art as crucial to the future development of virtual theories and technologies, they must be taken seriously as *extending an invitation* to others to take up where they left off. They provide an opening, they do not do the work for us.

A strikingly underdeveloped, or uninspiringly developed, theme in their writing is mimesis. I suggest that one way to grasp the philosophical and practical radicality of virtual technology is to consider it in the context of performance, particularly dance. Central to this is a notion of embodied mimesis.

II   Distortion in Mimesis

> The body mutated to survive perpetual migration between interlaced realities...
> *Frank Lantz, Bioapparatus*

Mimesis is the theme which I use to link dance and virtual reality. It is the Greek word for artistic representation, and traditionally has been used in Western aesthetics to refer to the faithful pictorial representation of organic forms.[5] This narrow, or purely imitative, conception of representation is relevant to virtual technologies in as much as they frequently rely on sophisticated computer graphics to emulate and exceed the mimetic capability of photography. Yet, in stark opposition to this, I suggest that the understanding of mimesis underlying an aesthetics of virtual reality is not one of faithful imitation or mimicry. As such, it does not provide grounds for a distinction between artifice and reality, between the virtual and the real; it is embodied and based on the controversial idea of distortion.

Distortion, or indeed "mutation" as in the quote at the top of this section, implies a challenge to existing senses of order and normality by partially conforming to and partially transgressing the usual. It is a process of twisting free from existing structures of thought, language and movement. When, by computer or video manipulation, the image of an arm is bent backwards or a dancer is slowed, increased in size or rotated in mid-leap, it is not just a sense of anatomical structure which is breached. The laws of physics, our ingrained idea of what a body *ought* to do, and the aesthetic norms it must correspond to are also challenged. The challenge is particularly powerful when, as with dance, a physical basis is preserved, since the link with concrete reality is maintained and transformation is less likely to be cast aside as abstract or fictional. The quality of the image is less important than how it is integrated into performance. Grainy video images can have as powerful and destabilising an effect on our sense of 'normal' time and space as expensive computer graphics. Even simple projections on transparent screens can be used to create the transformed perspective of a virtual world.

Mimesis in dance is the conjunction of representation and kinaesthetics.[6] In our current cultural and intellectual climate, the practice of representation has strong symbolic, linguistic and visual relevance, but without a continued emphasis on the kinaesthetic moment there is a risk of losing physicality from the mimetic process. This is strongly evident in accounts of virtual reality which take it to refer only to the experience of wearing eyephones, earphones and a dataglove to access a computer generated space. When Simon Penny, a professor of art and robotics, examines the philosophical underpinnings of virtuality he sees an extreme form of the Cartesian preference of mind over body, he claims that virtual reality exhibits an "abhorrence of the body" rooted in Christian dogma. "In my assessment," he writes "VR blithely reifies a mind/body split that is essentially patriarchal and a paradigm of viewing that is phallic, colonializing, and panoptic."[7] He wonders if this technology would have a different attitude to the body if it were created by a non-Western culture, and then, strikingly, he mentions Indian dance as a possible alternative perspective. He romanticizes for a moment on how Indian dance could have provided an alternative path of development without realising that dance, Western dance, can be used to expand the conception of mimesis as it functions in virtual reality. Penny comes to his gloomy conclusion because of the parameters he sets for himself, both philosophical and physical. Once the definition of the nature of virtual reality is expanded beyond the goggles and glove scenario to include a truly kinaesthetic moment it invites the development of new philosophical paradigms, freeing the debate from the limited domain of Descartes and Saint Augustine.

III Deleuze: Lines of Flight

> Speed turns the point into a line...
> Line of chance, line of hips, line of flight.
> *Gilles Deleuze, (1980), A Thousand Plateaus, p.24-5.*

It is a line of flight, and a very rapid one, which I take through the vast intellectual project of Gilles Deleuze in order to show why he is heralded as the premier philosopher of virtual reality, and how his work provides a 'tool box' for constructing a philosophical account of the dancing body in the virtual world.[8]

In short, his work is useful for two reasons. Firstly, his project is motivated by the desire to undermine the basis of representation as it shapes our linguistic, intellectual, political and artistic structures. He objects to the static law of symmetry which governs the elements in all representative structures.[9] This basic challenge to the mechanics of representation can be translated into an objection to mimesis as simple imitation. Secondly, Deleuze generates a philosophy which is fundamentally dynamic, based on flows, desire and energy. When his emphasis on fluidity is combined with his critique of representation, it is possible to derive an understanding of mimesis based on distortion, where distortion is the transformation of thought and bodies through movement and image manipulation in an aesthetic context.

Deleuze's fluid dynamics of movement is a powerful, and often highly poetic, way to account for the body moving through space. In many ways, I believe dancers are more open to his philosophical descriptions because we have a physical experience which lends validity to his philosophical descriptions, making them at once theoretical and phenomenological. He claims that it is better to view our bodies not as matter, but as intensity;[10] and writes of,

> ...opening the body to connections that presuppose an entire assemblage, circuits, conjunctions, levels and thresholds, passages and distributions of intensity, and territories and deterritorialisations...[11]

His plan for developing a new sense of our bodies, called bodies without organs, sounds like the instructions for an improvisation exercise,

> Lodge yourself on a stratum, experiment with the opportunities it offers, find an advantageous place on it, find potential movements of deterritorialisation, possible lines of flight, causing conjugated flows to pass and escape and bring forth continuous intensities...[12]

One way of making technology seem less foreign to dancing bodies is to expand our conceptions of what technology and bodies are. If technology is regarded as abstract and logical and mechanical, and bodies are only seen to be organic matter then the two will seem mutually hostile. But if both technology and bodies are seen additionally in terms of flows of energy, or intensities then there is a ground for collaboration. Deleuze's vocabulary is remarkable for *combining* the machinic and organic.[13] He emphasises connections, conjunctions and disjunctions, rather than a simplistic understanding of postmodern fragmentation.

One of the greatest strengths of Deleuze's thought is that it provides a multi-dimensional context for virtual technology, so as to prevent it from being ghettoised in science or business. He affirms the interconnectedness of the conceptual and physical, molecular and metaphysical, political and artistic by exposing a common dynamic structure.

Deleuze is more than a provider of a tool box, as I said above, in a sense his work is like raw energy. His ideas need to be shaped and redirected by others who need to use them. Two feminist writers in particular stand out in my mind as providing paths for his thought. They are Rosi Braidotti and Donna Haraway, and unfortunately I only have time to briefly situate their work in the context of this discussion. Braidotti is valuable for her link between mimesis and materiality, as well as for the way she places both within a clear social and political context. She believes that a new form of materialism is the starting point for most feminist redefinitions of subjectivity,

> In a new form of 'corporeal materialism', the body is seen as an inter-face, a threshold, a field of intersection of material and symbolic forces;[14]

Donna Haraway effects an even more radical change to our conceptions of subjectivity and our bodies by introducing the idea that we are all cyborgs: hybrids of machine and organism which are a compound of the organic, technical, mythic, textual and political.[15]

Both Haraway and Braidotti have as their goal a change in the existing social and theoretical positions of women, and both see a strategy of mimesis as central to achieving this. For them, mimetic activity is physical and technological, and our bodies are a complex combination of the material and the immaterial. A dancer in a technological performance environment is, in many ways, the epitome of the embodied subject in their work.

IV   Multi-Mediocrity

> The work of art is valuable only in so far as it is vibrated by the reflexes of the future.
> **Andre Bréton, circa 1930, cited in Illuminations**

Once technological advancements are integrated into performance without the fear of leaving the body behind, another issue emerges. I call it The Aesthetics of Banality, or Multi-Mediocrity. Technological manipulations of the dancing body can produce five minutes worth of interesting viewing but then give way into tedium and predictability. We are such sophisticated consumers of technology that a complicated or clever effect will not sustain our attention for long. We demand more. Even as a performer, the novelty of dancing through video projections, or with sensors attached to your body becomes dull if it is nothing more than exercising your equipment. Marshall McLuhan's famous statement "the medium is the message" was culturally groundbreaking but not a recipe for good dance.

There is a creative risk associated with the 'expertise-gap' which faces many dancers who come to use complicated technology in a performance context. Most dancers have not spent years studying computer science, and there is considerable effort involved in understanding what the technology can and cannot contribute to choreography, followed by getting the equipment to carry out a choreographic vision. I recently took a crash multi-media interactive authoring course and found it frustrating at best, demoralising at worst. As I struggled with the Macintosh programmes *Director* and *Premier* to manipulate a video sequence with illustrative techniques, I found myself doing what I was technically able to do, rather than what I wanted to do from a choreographic standpoint. The gap between the two was enormous, and was only reinforced when the instructor looked over my shoulder and cried with dismay, "You've gone linear, that wasn't the point!" I realised then that I was light years away from being able to use the technology in a creative way.

In the light of the expertise gap, it is not surprising that one of the big artistic issues affecting live performance more strongly than ever is collaboration. In the dance world we often look to the legendary collaborations between Cunningham, Cage and Rauschenberg as being the organic ideal, but the reality is that collaborative multi-media performances are not effortless aesthetic endeavours. This is another way in which the reality of producing art does not correspond to many of the theoretical ideas on the nature of the artistic process, or of the functioning of mimesis. Mimesis cannot be seen as pure imitation of an object or idea if it is constantly affected by what is possible within given technological, financial, and space constraints. Distortion in the mimetic process, as discussed above, is not always an aesthetic or political strategy, it is also the result of coping with practical limitations; and, as any dancer knows, such limitations do not need to be seen as creative impediments, but can be used to shape the final product in an aesthetically constructive way.

It is ironically comforting that despite incredible technological advancements the same aesthetic question surfaces, "What makes a work a *work of art*?", "What makes a performance good?". Despite our many philosophical and technological advancements, this question is still nearly impossible to answer, with technology sometimes acting to obfuscate things even further.

V   Concluding and Continuing

This paper is another instalment in an on-going project to construct an aesthetics of virtual reality based on the dancing body.[16] Artistic practices, from visual to musical, from architectural to performance, are being profoundly affected by a radical expansion of physical and conceptual space stimulated by technology. With virtual technologies there is undeniably a danger of conceptual abstraction reinforcing a Cartesian split between body and mind, by privileging the mind. When dancing bodies are maintained as a reference point we not only prevent the tendency towards abstraction into pure cognition, but we give new significance to theory and practice. Dancers already experience a variation of the transformation of time, space and matter which technology is bringing about. So an aesthetics of virtual reality is not only a way for dance to expand into technological space, but it is a way for the experience of dancers to participate in the future development of experience altering technology, and to be central in the evaluation of the work of philosophers and theorists.

Notes:

1. Susan Kozel, "The Story is told as a History of the Body: Strategies of Mimesis in the work of Irigaray and Bausch." Forthcoming in *Meaning in Motion: New Cultural Studies in Dance*, ed. Jane C. Desmond, Duke University Press, 1995.

2. Myron Krueger, "Artificial Reality: Past and Future," *Virtual Reality: Theory, Practice and Promise*, ed. S.K. Helsel & J.P. Roth (London: Meckler 1991), p. 20.

3. Cited in Howard Rheingold's *Virtual Reality* (London: Mandarin, 1992), p.51.

4. Brenda Laurel, *Computers as Theatre* (Massachusets: Addison-Wesley Publishing Co, 1991), p.93.

5. The mimetic practices of art have famously been evaluated according to the ability to 'fool,' or deceive, the viewer with their life-like qualities. The story of a competition between two Greek painters is as follows:

> Parrhasius entered into a competition with Zeuxis. Zeuxis produced a picture of grapes so dexterously represented that birds began to fly down to eat from the painted vine. Where-upon Parrhasius designed so life-like a picture of a curtain that Zeuxis, proud of the verdict of the birds, requested that the curtain should now be drawn back and the picture displayed. When he realized his mistake, with a modesty that did him honor, he yielded up the palm, saying that whereas he had managed to deceive only the birds, Parrhasius had deceived an artist.

See Stephen Bann, *The True Vine: On Visual Representation and the Western Tradition* (1989), p.27.

6. Simon Penny, in "Virtual Reality as the Completion of the Enlightenment Project," *Culture on the Brink: Ideologies of Technology* (Seattle: Bay Press, 1994), p.244, calls VR an augmented case of representation where "the object is simultaneously a representation and (in a limited way - [sic]) a kinesthetically experiential phenomenon." He never makes a link with dance or performance.

7. Penny, p.236-8.

8. See Gilles Deleuze & Felix Guattari, *Anti-Oedipus* (London: The Athlone Press, 1984), and *A Thousand Plateaus: Capitalism and Schizophrenia* (London: The Athlone Press, 1988). Deleuze has been called the philosopher and Guattari the political militant (*Anti-Oedipus*, p.xix). For the sake of brevity I refer to the ideas as being Deleuze's, although they are obviously both Deleuze's and Guattari's.

9. In art the symmetry is between art object and its referent, in language between signified and signifier, in thought between thinking subject, concepts and the objects in the world, and finally in politics the symmetry is between actions and laws. See *A Thousand Plateaus*, p.xi.

10. *A Thousand Plateaus*, p. 153.

11. *A Thousand Plateaus*, p. 160.

12. *A Thousand Plateaus*, p. 161.

13. *A Thousand Plateaus*, p. 4.

14. Rosi Braidotti, *Patterns of Dissonance* (Cambridge: Polity Press, 1991), p. 219.

15. Donna Haraway, "A Cyborg Manifesto: Science, Technology and Socialist-feminism in the Late Twentieth Century," *Simians, Cyborgs and Women: the Reinvention of Nature* (New York: Routledge, 1991), p. 149-50.

16. For other relevant articles see Kozel, "The Story is told as a History of the Body: Strategies of Mimesis in the work of Irigaray and Bausch" (cited above in note 1); "Virtual Trajectories: Technology in Performance." Forthcoming in *Total Theatre*, Volume 7, Number 1, Spring 1995; "Spacemaking: Experiences of a Virtual Body." *Dance Theatre Journal*, Volume 11, No.3, Autumn 1994; "Choreographing Cyberspace: An assessment of the possiblity for dance in Virtual Reality". *Dance Theatre Journal*, Volume 11, No.2, Spring/Summer 1994.

Bibliography:

Bann, Stephen. *The True Vine: On Visual Representation and the Western Tradition* (New York: Cambridge University Press, 1989).

Benjamin, Walter. "The Work of Art in the Age of Mechanical Reproduction," *Illuminations* (London: Fontana, 1973).

Bioapparatus, Proceedings of a Seminar on Technology and Culture. (The Banff Centre for the Arts, Banff, Canada, 1991).

Braidotti, Rosi. *Patterns of Dissonance* (Cambridge: Polity Press, 1991).

_____. *Nomadic Subjects: Embodiment and Sexual Difference in Contemporary Feminist Theory* (New York: Columbia University Press, 1994).

Deleuze, Gilles & Guattari Felix. *Anti-Oedipus* (London: The Athlone Press, 1984).

_____. *A Thousand Plateaus: Capitalism and Schizophrenia*, trans. B Massumi (London: The Athlone Press, 1988).

Haraway, Donna. "A Cyborg Manifesto: Science, Technology and Socialist-feminism in the Late Twentieth Century," *Simians, Cyborgs and Women: the Reinvention of Nature* (New York: Routledge, 1991).

Kozel, Susan. "The Story is told as a History of the Body: Strategies of Mimesis in the work of Irigaray and Bausch." Forthcoming in *Meaning in Motion: New Cultural Studies in Dance*, ed. Jane C. Desmond, Duke University Press, 1995.

Krueger, Myron W. "Artificial Reality: Past and Future," *Virtual Reality: Theory, Practice and Promise*, ed. S.K. Helsel & J.P. Roth (London: Meckler 1991).

Laurel, Brenda. *Computers as Theatre* (Massachusets: Addison-Wesley Publishing Co, 1991).

McLuhan, Marshall. *Understanding Media: The Extensions of Man* (New York: McGraw-Hill, 1964).

Penny, Simon. "Virtual Reality as the Completion of the Enlightenment Project," *Culture on the Brink: Ideologies of Technology* (Seattle: Bay Press, 1994).

Rheingold, Howard. *Virtual Reality* (London: Mandarin, 1992).

Valéry, Paul. *The Collected Works of Paul Valéry*, ed. J. Mathews (London: Routledge & Kegan Paul, 1957).

Walser, Randal. "Elements of a Cyberspace Playhouse," *Virtual Reality: Theory, Practice and Promise*, ed. S.K. Helsel & J.P. Roth (London: Meckler 1991).

TENSION AND RELEASE ACROSS THE BORDERS OF DANCE AND MUSIC

Sophia Preston
University of Surrey

The focus of this paper is the identification and examination of what have been called the "inner workings" (La Fave cited in Hodgins 1992 p20) of dance and music compositions in order to be able to make a detailed study of dance/music relationships. The work taken as an example is Bridge the Distance made by Siobhan Davies in 1985 for London Contemporary Dance Theatre to Benjamin Britten's String Quartet No.3 (1975). A particular theory of meaning and expression in the arts is employed to construct points of comparison between the dance and the music in order to arrive at a greater understanding of the relationships between them and, ultimately, of the work as a whole. The theory, propounded by the philosopher and musicologist Stephen Davies (1994), draws on the way in which conceptions of tension and release in Western tonal music give rise to a perception of motion in music. This musical motion through aural space can be compared and contrasted with the movement observed in the dance and the paper demonstrates this process with the first phrase of the work. The phrase can be placed in a range of contexts, both structural and associative, leading to detailed and sophisticated interpretive possibilities.

In the existing literature on the role of music in Western theatre dance strong opinions are expressed on what should be the nature of dance/music relationships. Many writers agree that the dance should not fit the music too closely. Louis Horst (Martha Graham's musical advisor) asserts that

> it is not necessary for the music to fit the dance like a glove; in fact it should not fit too tightly. There are times when a unison is desirable for strength and dramatic effect...However this exact mirroring should be used sparingly or its effectiveness is destroyed.
>
> Horst 1963 p7

The composer Constant Lambert makes an impassioned plea against too close a fit between music and dance, writing,

> I am sure there must be innumerable musicians beside myself who experience the same feeling of exasperation when the choreographer turns the stage into a vast lecturer's blackboard and by associating certain dancers with certain themes, proceeds to underline obvious formal devices in the music which any one of average intelligence can appreciate with half an ear.
>
> Lambert cited in Steinberg 1980 p136

Writers disagree, however, in determining just what constitutes too close a fit. Horst describes the process of working on Frontier with Martha Graham, who, he says, "choreographed the entire routine to counts. After she showed me the dance I wrote the music to the counts she gave me" (1963 p6). Dello Joio (who also wrote music for Graham) describes an identical situation with horror:

> I could not compose according to a plan that had been pre-set, for I would have had to follow arbitrarily a scheme conceived by somebody else, a scheme conceived without musical values. It would have made me feel rather like a typewriter, just filling in empty spaces.
>
> 1963 p18

On the other hand Balanchine recounts,

> when I listen to a score by [Stravinsky] I am moved...to try to make visible not only the rhythm, melody and harmony, but even the timbres of the instruments.
>
> Balanchine 1980 p150

Austin questions the result of Balanchine's enthusiasm here, going so far as to suggest that

> there is indeed, a considerable monotony in Balanchine's work...It is a choreography invented rather than created, and its lack of true musicality as against musical exactitude, is what, in the last analysis, condemns it to sterility and a dead end.
>
> Austin 1975 p67

La Fave on the other hand contends that in Balanchine's choreography

> it isn't a matter of a certain kind of sound translating into a certain kind of step, but of a composition's inner workings being grasped by the choreographer and infused into the dance.
>
> La Fave cited in Hodgins 1992 p20

Paul Hodgins, who cites the La Fave quotation in his book devoted entirely to relationships between music and choreography in C20 dance, makes it clear that there is still the problem of "what elements of a composition could be considered to be its inner workings?" (Hodgins 1992 p20). Hodgins's own survey of the existing literature also finds that

> many writers critically or creatively associated with dance talk freely and disagree fundamentally about dance-music affinities without ever precisely defining the nature or parameters of those affinities.
>
> Hodgins 1992 p20

Hodgins, himself, develops an evocative metaphor of time as "the unavoidable x-axis, the structural spine upon which all musical and choreographic events are ordered" (1992 piii). He adds to this, however, the assertion that

> on a deeper level, though, a powerful and universally recognizable symbiosis resonates through the music-movement relationship.
>
> Hodgins 1992 pv

I am here attempting to clarify what might be this symbiosis, leaving aside any notion of its universality, which I doubt. In his book Hodgins considers questions of expression and meaning in dance and music as a point of contact beyond the merely temporal and structural, and I am sure he is right to do so. Because he investigates a number of large-scale works, however, he is never able to anlayse the dance in any depth and he frequently takes the meaning (often the narrative) of the dance for granted. My contention is that when we investigate the capacity for expression, meaning or significance in both dance and music, then we can make a detailed comparison and discover the relationship between them.

The philosopher Stephen Davies in his recent work <u>Musical meaning and expres-</u>

sion (1994) reviews the main historical and contemporary theories on how music, as a non-sentient being, can be considered to be expressive and he comes to the conclusion that "the expressiveness in music consists in its presenting emotion characteristics in its appearance" (1992 p228). That is, we feel that music is 'sad' (for example) in the same way that we see that a person looks sad without needing to know any object for this sadness, or even whether the person is sad or not. As Davies writes

> emotion characteristics in appearance are attributed without regard to the feelings or thoughts of that to which they are predicated.
> Davies 1992 p228

What is particularly interesting to the dance analyst is that Davies goes on to suggest that

> the expressiveness of music depends mainly on a resemblance we perceive between the dynamic character of music and human movement, gait, bearing or carriage.
> Motion is heard in music, and that motion presents emotion characteristics much as do the movements giving a person her bearing or gait.
> Davies 1992 p229

But how is motion heard in music? If we can establish what constitutes the motion and, therefore, (according to Davies) the capacity for emotional expressiveness, in music, might we also be able to compare this with the actual human bodily motion, gait or bearing that we see in dance? When Horst talks of "exact mirroring" and Lambert of "associating certain dancers with certain themes", what do they mean? How can we determine whether Balanchine's undoubted skill in following a musical score results in a slavish step-for-beat in his choreography or an "infusion of the composition's inner workings into his dance".

Hodgins has already given us the most obvious common parameter in dance and music, that of time. I would like to suggest that this goes deeper than simply the level of rhythm and form by employing the muiscologist D.B. Fry's characterisation of music as "a chinese box arrangement" which I developed in my Masters thesis (1989). This model works down from the architectonic level of the overall structure of a work built up of sections which are themselves made of phrases heard through time. These phrases are made up of rhythmic elements counted in, or against, pulses per minute and melodic and harmonic patterns made up of pitches, which are of course pulses per second. Even Balanchine's timbres are the effect of a selection of harmonics heard above the fundamental pitch also measurable in cycles per second. The volume of the music (what musicians, confusingly for dancers, call the 'dynamics'), the loudness and quietness, are also determined by speed, in this case the speed of the bow across the strings, or the speed of the column of air down the pipe. Even the stylistic characteristics of attack, the particular quality of a Beethovian *sforzando* rather than an Elgarian one is a matter of how long the player plays loud (fast), before reducing the bow (or air) speed to produce the rapidly following *piano*. It's all a question of duration.

This satisfyingly neat reduction of music to the single element, time, might seem redundant when we are considering perceived relationships between dance and music which we hear as a combination of pitch, timbre and rhythm. What it can do, however, is provide a common denominator for the comparison of dance and music. We are used in dance to considering dynamics as being dependent on speed, both on the large scale of speeds of whole sections of movement and also in terms of the quantity of attack and force in a movement. Laban defines his effort shapes in terms of the amount that they "indulge in" or "fight against" weight, space and time (1948). He draws attention to the importance of the duration of a movement when he writes that

> bodily actions of quickness cannot be prolonged without losing their char-
> acter. A punch, when slowed down, becomes a sustained pressure.
>
> 1948 p64

It becomes less confusing that musicians and dancers mean such different things by the term 'dynamics' when they are both seen to depend on the same factor, the same 'structural spine', of time.

If time can be thus established as a commonality between music and dance what about space, the other necessary factor for movement? Davies tells us that

> it is claimed that music unfolds within and through aural space. Aural
> space is not to be confused with real space; it has no location relative to
> the equator, for instance. Crucial to the experience of aural space is the
> recognition that notes at different, determinative pitches are high and
> low with respect to each other. Basic here is the fact that, at the interval
> of an octave, a note is identified as of a type that previously appeared in
> one "place" and now reappears higher or lower in the pitch continuum.
>
> 1992 p231

In this aural space, then, pitches can be situated and can be heard to move through time. As Davies notes, however, a large part of our understanding of this movement is influenced by the teleological aspect of so many (if not all) musics. There is what Davies calls a "gravitational pull" to the closure of a phrase or composition, whether the home, the point of repose, to which the music appears to be moving is the tonic (as in tonal music) or the final gong stroke of each cycle of a Javanese gamelan composition. The sonata form in Western tonal music is a familiar example of the employment of the different relationships notes of the scale are perceived to have towards the tonic. As Davies writes,

> in the major scale, melodically the leading note is the most strongly drawn
> towards the tonic. Chords are comparatively tense or relaxed (discordant
> or concordant) in relation to the tonic chord; discords strain for resolu-
> tion. As a result, the course of music, its motion, corresponds to an
> experience of increasing or diminishing tension, push and pull, pulse and
> decay, with closure achieved at the arrival of the final tonic.
>
> Davies 1994 p236

Tradition leads us to expect the first movement of a string quartet to be in sonata form and Hans Keller (the dedicatee of Britten's String Quartet No.3) states that "the first movement unfolds in fact an extremely subtle and innovative sonata scheme" (1994 p112). Other musicologists are not so sure. Arnold Whittall talks of the movement as having an "allusive sonata form and floating tonality" (1982 p282), and David Matthews talks of "a sonata movement, if a veiled one" (1984 p390). Donald Mitchell (1987 p91), on the other hand, suggests that Britten "regarded the Third Quartet as a signifi-cant achievement in his escape from the sonata aesthetic," and Evans suggests that

> a fluid succession of textural variants is to be more important for
> this work than an embracing argument, tensed by motivic concen-
> tration and schematic tonal opposition.
>
> 1979 p340

This debate can also be applied to a characterisation of the overall structure of the first section of the dance. There is, however, plenty of evidence to support an argument that the dance material for this section is structured under the sonata principle. The deciding factor, for me, was that after Davies has presented two distinct phrases and repeated them with subtle variations of direction and spacing on stage (very much in the manner of an exposition and its repeat) her subsequent phrases can be seen to be <u>developments</u> of the exposition material, rather than simply a new section. Thus she immediately moves away from an ABA ternary form to the exposition, development and recapitulation of the sonata form.

As well as comparing the music and the dance in terms of the overall structure of this first section, it is now possible to look at each phrase individually and to select these elusive internal characteristics for comparison. One direct comparison that can be made between the dance and the music on the level of individual phrases is in terms of shape. The first phrase of the dance has been identified as that occurring up to bar 10 of the music (see Fig. 1). An outline of this first phrase of the dance in terms of the height of the movements for both the men and the women is represented in the 'dance shape graph' (Fig. 2). The mid-line running through the centre of the diagram represents a standing position. The bottom line represents lying down on the floor, the top line represents one dancer being lifted to the full extension of another's arms (the highest position in the phrase). The time line of the bars of the music provides "the common x-axis".

The dance shape diagram can be overlaid with a similar representation of the shape of the music (Fig. 3). Each of the two instruments has been represented on the graph. Just as the bottom line of the dance shape graph is the lowest movement possible for the dancers so the bottom line of the music shape graph is the lowest note possible for the lower instrument (the C one octave below middle C). The top line of the music shape graph is the highest note of the phrase, the D one octave and a tone above middle C. The same time line in terms of bars of the music is used as in the dance graph allowing a direct comparison between the two.

A consistent difference observable between the two diagrams is in the shape of the outline of 'height'. Whilst the music lines are stepped, the movement ones follow a curved pathway. This is almost bound to be the case because of the nature of the two art forms. The only way the height of the pitches of the music could be outlined in a curve would be if the instrumentalists were at least running through fast scalic passages or frequent *glissandi*, if not performing all their phrases with constant *portamenti*. In dance, however, the change of height is almost bound to be continuous since the body must move through all the intervening space between one position and the next. Clearly a fast jump or rapid jerky movements will lead to a sharper angled line on a height graph, but the vertical steps equivalent to, say, a double octave interval in music can never occur. It is pertinent to note that this height graph of a Davies phrase has such a smooth, gently curved outline, reflecting the gradual changes in height, taking place over a length of time, which has led reviewers so often to describe her work as 'lyrical'. It is also interesting to note that the women in general diverge from the mid (standing) line much more than the men, who remain largely at this level in order to manipulate the women either into drops (forward or back) or lifts.

The first similarity to be observed between the two graphs is in the overall shape of the phrases although with some differences in detail. The women are lifted in bar 1 a beat <u>before</u> the two instruments move up a fourth from their opening pitches. This movement in the pitch of the music is, instead, reflected in the dance by a big <u>drop</u> back by the women over the men's bent legs. Similarly, as the violin moves up in pitch at the end of bar 4 the women kneel down and the men are slightly stooped over them. It is interesting to note, however, that in both these cases the relative heights of both

Preston

Fig. 1 Music score of the first phrase.

Fig. 2 'Height graph' of the movements of Phrase 1 of the dance

- - - - = men, ——— = women

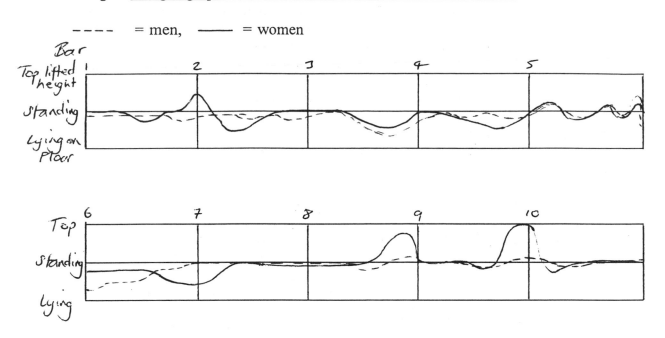

Fig. 3 'Height graph' of the pitches of Phrase A of the music

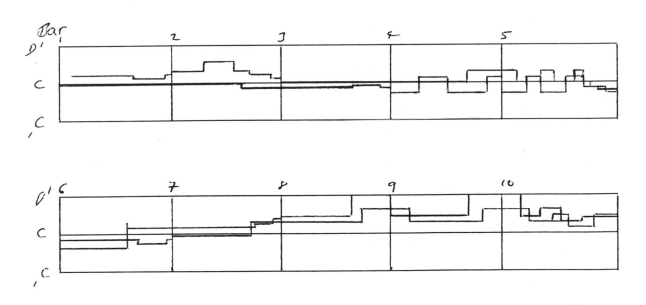

the dancers and the pitches of the two instruments have diverged from their previously closely connected lines. Evans (1979) has noted a gradual expansion of the intervals between the two instruments as the phrase progresses and this seems to be reflected in an expansion of the size of the movements of the dance. Of course an understanding of the 'size' of the dance movements depends not just on their height but also their volume. This is an instance in which Laban Movement Analysis has been particularly useful in its employment of notional kinespheres around each dancer both in terms of the size of each dancer's movements and also the distance between the kinespheres of the pairs of dancers and the extent to which they overlap. A graph of the changes in these 'sizes' is just one of many that can be compared with a whole range of music graphs.

The most obvious parallel between the two diagrams is at the ends of bars 8 and 9 when the two lifts of the women by the men are matched by the highest pitches of the music. The dips in the height line of the men just before each lift is caused by their preparations for the lifts. One of the differences revealed by the two graphs is that, whereas the music is an exact repeat in both bars, the first lift in the dance is lower than the second. The overall shape of both the dance and the music phrases is the same, however, with the highest point in both cases occurring just before the end of the phrase.

The two phrases end differently in that, whilst the dancers return to their opening position height, at the end of the music phrase the oscillating figure is repeated a minor sixth higher than at the opening. Thus this diagram does not reveal one of the similarities between the dance and music components of the phrase. To reveal that return to original material another particular aspect of the music needs to be represented, namely the size of intervals between notes. This could in turn be compared with a dance 'size' graph. These and many other graphs can be drawn giving an immediate graphic representation of relationships between the two components. For example comparisons can be made between the speed, dynamics and orchestration of the music and the speed, 'flow', stage-spacing and emphasis on different parts of the body in the dance.

Summary

The range of levels of structural analysis can thus be seen to extend from a micro level of the internal structure not only of individual phrases but even of particular movements, to a macro level of the structure of a whole section of the dance, or movement of the music. Both the dance and the music have evolved their own, independent, structural identities. They have achieved this, however, through a common concern with movement through space and time incorporating notions of tension and release.

I am fully aware of the reductionist problems inherent in extracting particular aspects of the work in this way (never mind the problems of observational and analytical method which is clearly never neutral). I contend, however, that these visual comparisons of a whole range of aspects of both components can substantiate and clarify claims to relationships between them. The comparisons here reveal an acute awareness of the music in the dance, a shifting in and out of parallels and contrasts throughout the phrase, which work on such a sophisticated level that the analysis needs to be as detailed as this in order to be able to articulate it.

The formulation and development of analytical procedures for the study of internal structural relationships between music and dance forms part of a larger study I am undertaking as my doctorial thesis on dance/music relationships in the work of Siobhan Davies. Just as music is able "in the world of extended tonality, to imply—by allusion and association" (Whittall 1982 p8), so dance references can be drawn from the reappearance of motifs, structures or even dynamics from work to work within a choreographer's oeuvre. Similarly, both dance and music bring with them a while range of contexts providing more resonances and allusions. The thesis explores the interplay between these structural relationships and external associations and references brought to the work by both the dance and the music.

Bibliography

Austin, R. Images of the dance London, Vision Press, 1975

Balanchine, G. 'The Dance Element in Stravinsky's Music' in Steinberg, C. (ed) The Dance Anthology New York: Plume, 1980 (pp149 - 152)

Britten, B. String quartet No. 3. London: Faber Music Ltd, 1977.

Davies, Stephen Musical meaning and expression Ithaca: Cornell University Press, 1994

Evans, P. The Music of Benjamin Britten 1979

Fry, D.B. Some effects of music London: Institute for Cultural Research, 1971

Hodgins, P. Relationships between score and choreography in twentieth century dance: music, movement and metaphor Lampeter: Edwin Mellen Press,1992

Horst, L. Composer/Choreographer: A Symposium Dance Perspectives No 16 New York 1963 pp6-8

dello Joio, N. Composer/Choreographer: A Symposium Dance Perspectives No 16 New York, 1963 pp

Keller, H. Essays on music (C. Wintle, editor) Cambridge: Cambridge University Press, 1994

Lambert, C. Music and action in Steinberg, C. (ed) The dance anthology Plume: New York, 1980 pp131-137

Martin, J. America Dancing New York: Dance Horizons, 1936, 1968

Matthews, D. The String Quartets and some other Chamber Works in Palmer, C. (ed) The Britten Companion London: Faber and Faber 1984 pp383-392

Mitchell, D. (ed) Benjamin Britten, Death in Venice Cambridge Opera Handbooks: Cambridge: Cambridge University Press, 1987 pp154 - 161

Preston, S. Dance to the music of time University of Surrey: unpublished M.A. dissertation, 1989

Whittall, A. The Music of Britten and Tippett: Studies in themes and techniques Cambridge: Cambridge University Press, 1982

JOE GOODE: BLURRING EDGES OF DIFFERENCE
IN PERFORMANCE AND SOCIETY

STACEY PRICKETT
INDEPENDENT SCHOLAR, OAKLAND, CALIFORNIA

Joe Goode's work presents a rich example for interdisciplinary analysis as it crosses over boundaries of dance and theatre. Dance is the constant thread pulling together diverse elements of performance, such as text, sets, costumes, music and props. In addition to integrating diverse performance media, the three male and three female members of the Joe Goode Performance Group challenge social boundaries of gender, sexual orientation, mainstream and subcultural identities. The group is based in San Francisco, and performs to critical and audience acclaim. Goode is also the recipient of numerous federal and private arts grants, such as a recent $25,000 National Endowment of the Arts award and $100,000 for artistic development from the National Dance Residency Program. Goode's work evokes a broad humanism through its focus on the extremes of everyday life, from loss to bliss, as subcultural identities are celebrated as components of a larger cultural pluralism. Goode's appeal remains mainstream, to the extent that modern dance is mainstream, rather than marginalising the subcultural identities evoked in his works.

Joe Goode calls his works "Human Dances" based on what he refers to as "little subjects" which open levels of accessibility through an integration of the familiar, the everyday, often revealed in an unusual light. His professed goal is to bridge the gap between interior and exterior lives. The full-length works are comprised of short modular dances created on one theme, such as the *Disaster Series* (on chaos), *Convenience Boy* (on consumerism in contemporary society), and *Remembering the Pool at the Best Western* (about loss). Goode blends site specific elements into his works, often expanding the performance space into the house or other part of the theatre, adding an installation atmosphere to each performance venue. While the dances are discussed in this context in terms of identity, for Goode the artistic process involves a giving up of self, believing that: "Passion in art is facilitated by a loss of self".[1]

A primary component of Joe Goode's identity is his homosexual orientation, highlighted in promotional articles and evident in the content of his work. Although the gay community is marginalised in broader American society, there is an increasing visibility and integration of the subculture into a mainstream social framework.[2] In particular, San Francisco is a bastion of gay activism, at the forefront of gay civil rights and a vibrant place for the expression of difference through artistic practice. On a legislative level, for example, discrimination in the workplace against the City's 6,000 transgendered individuals has been ruled a civil rights violation. San Francisco's liberalism towards its homosexual community is not matched even statewide, however, as an ongoing struggle continues for acceptance of "otherness". Goode's dances span from those that earned him the title of "bad boy", with sexually explicit language to the creations of today. In 1991 he explained, "I'm interested in creating a voice that's very clear and very human, that gets under people's skin. .... My goal has been to become a citizen of the world. I don't want to go back to purposefully marginalising myself."[3]

Peggy Phelan's book Unmarked examines representational visibility and political power, providing a starting point for my analysis of identity in Goode's works. Phelan questions conventional relationships between visibility and power developed in cultural studies wherein increased visibility is equated with political power. The essays in Unmarked explore various representational strategies, utilizing Lacanian psychoanalysis and feminism to examine negotiations between the real and the representational. Phelan explores the relationship between the self and the "other" as represented in art and political protests, focusing on the politics of the exchange of gaze.[4] For Phelan, the unmarked "other" is woman, whereas I viewed Goode's work as making visible a gay male "other". I draw from cultural and dance studies to examine the representations of both heterosexual and homosexual identity in some of Goode's works.

Rather than identifying the gay otherness by a single stylistic marker or set of markers, the defining parameters of homosexual subculture evoked in the dances are drawn from a larger foundation, as the mark of membership is fundamentally invisible. Dick Hebdige defined subcultural style as manifestations of "culture in the broader sense, as systems of communication, forms of expression and representation."[5] Out of the broader culture, for example, British punk rockers and Black reggae fans evolved the stylistic markers which set them apart as members of a subculture. The styles emerge as coded exchanges of reciprocal messages, "not as timeless objects, judged by the immutable criteria of traditional aesthetics, but as 'appropriations', 'thefts', subversive transformations, as movement."[6] Instead of using subversive transformations as stylistic markers, Joe Goode is a master manipulator of the hegemonic manifestations of American culture, toying with gender, consumerism and tradition aimed at universalizing experience.

Institutions of the family, shopping, the chain store sameness of American society, middle-class aspirations and expectations are elements of mainstream culture Goode freely subverts and appropriates. A critique takes place from within, to an extent, as Goode eases in and out of performative norms. The dancers flesh out conventional roles of middle class society so the critiques appear as self-parodies, occurring from within the mainstream, albeit momentarily. For example, Remembering the Pool at the Best Western opens with Goode sitting in his bathrobe contemplating a cup of coffee and the previous night's dreams. A window into the mundane soon evaporates with the appearance of a spirit guide of sorts, whose gestures shadow Goode's own. The set-up of normalcy usually occurs through text, establishing a narrative structure. John Fiske contends that cultural material "cannot be read off the primary texts themselves but only in their social uses and in their relationships with other texts."[7] Therefore, in Markers, it is not merely Goode's appearance as a country-western singer/narrator which stands out, rather inherent meanings in the popular image of the singer create subversive tension when juxtaposed against the modern dance performance. Like Hebdige's analysis of punk style, it is not the safety pins which shocked, it is where they were placed which turned heads.

Establishing narrative elements through the text opens areas of manipulation between the physical body and social body as manifest in Goode's treatment of gender conventions. Ted Pohlemus contends that dance embodies and identifies a division of cultural realities premised upon 'maleness' and 'femaleness', and *"for any given individual* the experience of gender identity is an absolute boundary which is existentially insurmountable."[8] In contrast, Goode's focus on gender and interpersonal relationships calls into question strict masculine/feminine and homosexual/heterosexual distinctions, at the level of their social construction. Such challenges to convention do not advocate a unisex or androgenous disappearance of boundary, however, as the interplay between dancers retains a level of sensuality, thus creating a more fluid boundary between oppositional categories of gender and sexual orientation.

The social construction of gender is taken to its extreme, with Goode occasionally manipulating his own gender identity by cross-dressing. His drag characters present a contrast to the cross-dressed or transgendered voguers seen in Jennie Livingston's 1991 film, <u>Paris Is Burning</u>. Phelan notes that "the balls reveal the performers' longing to be made unremarkable - to pass as "normative" (and thus be unnoticed) rather than to be seen as "other" (and constantly surveyed by the upholders of the normative)."[9] Goode's drag characterizations remain transparent, in contrast, his manipulation of gender identities appear incomplete by design, unlike those in Mark Morris' *Hard Nut* which it can be argued, are designed to pass as normative. In *Stareways*, a site-specific work integrating video transmissions of a dance created and performed in part on stairs in the backstage area of the theatre, Goode's visual gender transformation is limited to the application of make-up in front of the audience, with magnified images transmitted to onstage video screens. In *Convenience Boy*, the transformation extends to clothing in Goode's appearance in a sequined dress, high-heels and wig, the personification of a torch singer referenced in the previous vignette, the vision complete with Goode twirling a flaming baton.

In movement terms rather than through cross-dress, the dance *Twenty-nine Effeminate Gestures* begins by reinforcing stereotypes of an effeminate gay male, then proceeds to undermine them. The twenty-nine gestures include the exaggerated limp-wristed outstretched arm, hand on hip with head turned back over the shoulder, caressing of the face. The chosen gestures affirm a stereotype during their first appearance, although repetition of the gestures with changes in dynamic quality and rhythm, ultimately alters their effeminate air. The gestures become part of larger movements, the verbal text shifts from the lofty topic of the aesthetics of "too much" to sound effects of destruction and tonal incantations. The gestures increase in size, and in doing so, the stereotype vanishes, becoming unaffected movement. A broadcast version of the dance additionally challenges notions of masculinity through its location in a car repair shop and the mechanic's overalls Goode wears.

In contrast to the gender-bending examples, Goode comments upon contemporary society through vignettes which evoke a nostalgic reading of heterosexual romance. Often told through the female voice, the narratives of longing are developed with references to idealized norms, the ubiquitous "family values" which pervade the sound bites of conservative politicians in the U.S. There are subversive twists evident in these portraits, however, such as in "Doris in a Dust Bowl". In a wedding dress, Liz Burritt muses over expectations of the path her life would take. She proclaimed, "I thought Doris Day", naming titles of films and situations in which Doris Day would be found. The modern bride is joined by a debonair suitor à la Rock Hudson, evoking the perfect cinematic couple, in reality undermined by Hudson's sexual orientation kept hidden for so long, in addition to the reality of Burritt not being the girl next door. Setting up a scene, Doris yearns for a kiss, yet senses that the longing somehow misplaced, that "he might not be the marrying kind". In this instance, the narrative's subversive elements are drawn from the real life biographies of the actors, relying on the audience's knowledge to infer a myriad of underlying messages. In another monologue, Liz Burritt proclaims that she is not Doris Day, she is not a perennial virgin, doesn't get to chose between three eligible bachelors or fly off to Paris on a whim. Instead, she cannot even keep a boyfriend. Movement and text are interwoven, ironic on two levels -- in terms of the characters Doris Day played counterpointed against the reality of single life in the 1990s, and with reference to Rock Hudson's secret sexual orientation in tension with his Hollywood characters.

The question arises whether Goode is celebrating difference, the otherness of homosexual orientation, or contributing to an increased acceptance of difference within society with reference to issues of power in relation to visibility. Goode's work effectively shatters illusions regarding sexual orientation while integrating some commentary on race (through narratives which reveal the Hispanic/Latino roots of one of the dancers) and class (by embracing elements of material culture which are associated with middle-class America).

Universalised gender experience is prevalent at times, as in the "Convenience Lover" section of *Convenience Boy*. Marit Brook-Kothlow speaks of relationships, citing excuses to avoid commitment while couples interweave around her and she is drawn in to duets. Although the gender make-up of the couples shift seamlessly, the universality of the text strikes a resonant note with many, regardless of sexual preference. Revelations of similarity occur on two levels in this section, through the narrative and through the movement, as two women, two men, and mixed sex duets perform the same dance phrases.

Sections of *Convenience Boy* exemplify Goode's subversion of gender conventions through movement alone. Dancers switch partners and levels of sensuality remain between the partners regardless of gender. Female dancers match their male partners in terms of strength, evident through intrinsic analysis of gender balances in the partnering work. Stephanie Jordan's reading of Siobhan Davies' "Rushes" highlights the choreographic use of the male in a physically stronger role than the female dancer. Instead of lifting the male dancer off the ground, the woman would initiate movements through a light push or touch as a signal.[10] Goode's duets give the women dancers more agency, breaking through conventional male/female partnering relationships, with the women effortlessly lifting their partners. The nature of the lifts differ from conventional ballet partnering, due to the technical grounding of the movement in contact improvisation.

Partnering work in *Take/Place/This Is Where I Am Now* shifts between an egalitarian balance in the male/female partnering and one which stems from the narrative in which a heterosexual relationship is established. In the latter instances, the partnering reverts to the male with a more strength-dominant role than that of the female dancer. Thus, Goode can be seen to switch between an ideal of equality and a holdover of male dominance in heterosexual relationships, as in this section which refers back to a sarcastic monologue about a happy parental relationship, free of conflict.

In conclusion, Goode's work succeeds in transcending the personal sexual orientation of its viewers and creator, attracting a diverse audience which speaks beyond a gay male "otherness". Socially constructed gender issues are both celebrated and subverted through the manipulation of male and female identities and relationships.[11] Although the issue of gender representation and homosexual identity is raised in the dances, it is only one element among many. His most recent work, *Take/Place/This is Where I Am Now* makes little explicit reference to sexual orientation. The work is about location, identity with reference to finding or creating one's home and community. Nayland Blake, one of the curators of a recent exhibition on the gay/lesbian experience in American art entitled "In a Different Light", noted the absence of a specific culture passed on through the family among the homosexual minority: "All the words that serve as touchstones for cultural identification - 'family', 'home', 'people', 'neighborhood', 'heritage' - must be recognized as constructions."[12] An underlying emphasis on human agency recurs in Goode's works, resulting in an uplifting yet poignant reflection on contemporary life through dance.

ENDNOTES

1. Interview, promotional video excerpt provided by the Joe Goode Performance Group.

2. For example, in an NBC network television production, <u>Serving in Silence</u>, Glen Close portrayed the real life lesbian military officer, Col. Margareth Cammermeyer, in her struggle to maintain her career without revoking her sexual orientation. Arguments abound, however, that many portrayals of homosexual relationships within a mainstream media are devoid of realistic expressions of physical affection between partners.

3. Zimmer, Elizabeth, 1991, p. 38.

4. Phelan, Peggy, 1994, p. 8.

5. Hebdige, Dick, 1988, p. 129.

6. Ibid.

7. Fiske, John, 1989, p. 3.

8. Polhemus, Ted, 1995, p. 11.

9. Phelan, op. cit., p. 93.

10.   Jordan, Stephanie and Thomas, Helen, 1995, p. 4.

11.   The extent to which Goode's enhancement of visibility of the gay male other can be equated with political power raises disturbing questions, especially in light of an increasingly conservative political climate in the United States. While I was writing this paper, the state of Montana ruled that persons convicted of consensual homosexual sex, currently illegal, would be required to register with the police as a violent criminal offender, along with convicted rapists and murderers. The strength of the nationwide outcry prompted a swift turnaround, however, the homophobic sentiment still exists. In rereading Phelan's introduction to <u>Unmarked</u>, a new sentence grabbed my attention: "While there is a deeply ethical appeal in the desire for a more inclusive representational landscape and certainly underrepresented communities can be empowered by an enhanced visibility, the terms of this visibility often enervate the putative power of these identities." Phelan, op. cit., p. 7.

12.   Blake, Nayland, quoted in Due, Linnea, 1995, p. 14.

Bibliography

Videos

The Disaster Series.

29 Effeminate Gestures

Remembering the Pool at the Best Western, Theater Artaud; April 20, 1991.

Take/Place and *Convenience Boy*, Theater Artaud; May 29, 1994.

Take/Place/This is Where I Am Now; The Cowell Theater, February 17, 1995.

Other References

Due, Linnea. "A Shade of Difference, The Queering of Contemporary Art", Express. Berkeley, California, Vol. 17, No. 26, April 7, 1995, pp. 1-17.

During, Simon, ed. The Cultural Studies Reader. London: Routledge, 1993.

Fiske, John. Reading the Popular. Boston: Unwin Hyman, 1989.

Hebdige, Dick. Hiding in the Light. London: Routledge, 1988.

_____. Subculture: The Meaning of Style. London: Methuen & Co., 1979. Routledge, 1991 reprint.

Jordan, Stephanie and Thomas, Helen, "Dance and Gender: Formalism and Semiotics Reconsidered", Dance Research. Vol. XII, No. 2., Autumn, 1994, pp. 1-14.

Phelan, Peggy. Unmarked: The Politics of Performance. London and New York: Routledge, 1994.

Polhemus, Ted, "Dance, Gender and Culture, Dance, Gender, and Culture, Thomas, Helen, Ed. London: Macmillan Press, Ltd., 1993, pp. 3-15.

Wilson, Elizabeth. Adorned in Dreams: Fashion and Modernity. Berkeley: University of California Press, 1987.

Zimmerman, Elizabeth. "Joe Goode's Wild Ride", Inside Arts, June, 1991, Vol. 3, No. 2, p. 34.

BEYOND DRAMA, BEYOND MUSIC:
MUSIC AND GESTURE IN ANTONY TUDOR'S BALLETS

Rachel Richardson
Manchester Metropolitan University

In this paper I intend to look at some of the ways in which the movement vocabulary in Tudor's ballets is abstracted from realistic or dramatic gesture, to create apparently significant but often ambiguous or inscrutable images, and at some of the ways in which dance-music relationships allow for these visual images to resonate with further interpretative possibilities.

In considering the question whether dance-music relationships are conjunctive or disjunctive it might be argued that the simple answer is often simplistic rather than accurate or revealing. That is, to say that dance and music work together 'conjunctively', or have a 'close relationship' may only be true on one level. It is likely that the closeness of the relationship immediately discerned by the viewer in many cases occurs at a level of overall structure and/or dynamic shape. As other writers have illustrated (cf. Jordan, Topaz), examination of the *detail* of structural and rhythmic relationships between choreography and music may reveal complex and subtle variations which contribute significantly to the construction of possible 'meanings' in a way which simple 'conjunctiveness' may not. The extent to which either designation may disguise more complex strands of inter-relationship, and a shifting interplay between the two media, is explored in this paper with reference to specific choreographic examples. Further, the importance of music to Tudor suggests the possibility of considering some movement images in the light of musical conventions or compositional devices.

In looking at the use of realistic or dramatic gesture it is apparent that movement vocabulary is increasingly difficult to interpret in dramatic terms as it becomes more 'abstract' or more distant from movement which lends itself to being 'read' in significant gestural terms implying personality traits or psychological states.

In all of this discussion, as noted, the focus is directed towards detail and nuance, rather than over-arching characteristics or music-dance structural relationships, although these are clearly of fundamental importance.

Most of the examples come from a group of movements or distinctive gestures which, while not being immediately recognisable as relating to the movement and gesture of human beings in everyday life (Western conventions being taken in account), seem to have, nonetheless, something of the same function. They have been identified initially as 'gestures' because of their apparently similar function to other varieties of gesture, specifically 'realistic gesture', that is, revealing aspects of character, psychological experience, or mood. However, the expressive potential of these actions does not appear to be limited by specific notions of character or circumstance, and the extent to which either a dramatic or a musical perspective may illuminate certain moments in three ballets is explored in this set of examples.

The three ballets to be looked at are from the late 1930s and early 1940s.[1] Two, Tudor made in England—Jardin aux Lilas and Dark Elegies—and the other—Pillar of Fire—was his first major work after moving to America. All are set to music of the late nineteenth/early twentieth century: Chausson's Poème for violin and orchestra, Mahler's song-cycle Kindertotenlieder, and Schoenberg's Verklärte Nacht.

In all three ballets, important aspects of the music are the use of fluctuating tonality and chromaticism, and asymmetry in melodic phrasing, all of which features are characteristic of much music of the late nineteenth and early twentieth centuries. The choice of late-Romantic music is interesting and significant, in particular because

Tudor frequently complements the rich sweep of melodic line and chromaticism with a movement style which is austere by comparison.

Chromatic means, literally, 'coloured' and, in music, is a term applied to melodic lines or harmony which include notes which are 'foreign' to the key. A small proportion of chromatic notes will normally be heard as embellishment, but a more widespread use will often result in the de-stabilising of a sense of established tonality, resulting in a degree of tension or ambiguity. As Leonard Meyer has written:

> The affective aesthetic power of chromaticism [sometimes] arises because chromatic alterations delay or block the expected motion to the normal diatonic tones.
>
> 1956 p218

Several of the actions discussed here could also, perhaps, be likened to the use of chromaticism in music in that they serve a similar function, namely that of delaying the expected resolution of a particular phrase or passage.

All the examples may be seen as forming an integral part of the choreographic language but, while certain moments and images in a ballet may still suggest ideas relating to character or mood or situation, others do not do this in such a straightforward way, but may, instead, contribute to the depth of meaning possible; resonating, as it were, with unarticulated meaning which stimulates 'sympathetic vibrations' through the choreography, thus adding to the overall effect. Music does this more easily, because it is not so obviously linked to the human form and all the connotations attendant upon that.[2]

There are, then, images in Tudor's ballets which, while apparently contributing to possible interpretations of the ballets, are not necessarily tied to specific characters or circumstances, and have, therefore, no easily definable function. There is always some sense of atmosphere, tension or ambiguity arising, however, and the following examples either contribute to an intensification of the present mood (by drawing attention to it through their unexpectedness or ambiguity), or in some way alter it, without any specific change in dramatic development.

Certain moments or images may suggest a suspension in time because of their apparent significance at the same time as a lack of clear dramatic development in terms of action. The 'frozen tableau' (Jardin aux Lilas Example 1) is, of course, the most famous moment in Jardin. It is an example of the extreme contrast possible between dance and music; the music has reached its climax in the Poème, when the main theme (Example 1b) is heard *fortissimo*, in full orchestra, and the action on stage is frozen completely.

The music affirms its central theme in a particularly strong manner; it is not new material, but familiar material being returned to, offering the possibility of recalling earlier responses to it when heard in whole or in part, with different preceding and succeeding material, different orchestration, different context. Dramatically, it comes at the climax of the ballet. Caroline seems to swoon in the arms of her fiancé, with whom she is about to enter upon a marriage of convenience. Her Lover, and her fiancé's former mistress, look on.

The arrangement of dancers on stage, it is argued, is highly significant; Caroline central, with the focus of the Lover, the Episode and the Man directed towards her, while other guests either stand and look on or are absorbed in each other: a variety of responses to the situation, showing a variety of degrees of interest and perception on the part of the group of guests. This is the moment when the notion of 'psychological time' is most forcefully present, the music's surge being allowed to suggest a parallel surge of conflicting emotions in the mind of the character who draws our focus, that is,

Caroline herself, while the rest of the characters are differently affected. The Man appears not to be affected at all, there is nothing tense in his posture, bending over Caroline's hand as if to kiss it. The Episode and the Lover both stand straight, looking on, and indeed the moment is one of psychological importance for them, too. The guests, whether they look on or not, are less immediately affected, and this is shown through their physical distance from the central characters as well as through their individual postures (which offer the notion of a variety of degrees of involvement, as suggested). Again, the music and dance together combine to create or construct an image of potentially many layers of meaning in the context of the theme in general and the individual experiences of characters in particular.

The subtle interaction of dance and music in Tudor's ballets, however, often happens at a level of relatively small detail, although this detail may be equally significant in the overall context of the ballet.

In Pillar of Fire there are many images which relate in some clear way to character and/or circumstance. There are some, however, which resist interpretation in this way. The first occurs in Example 2 at bar 9, when one Lover-in-Innocence turns her head to look at her partner, not in a single, smooth movement, but in three quick, accented movements. This is surprising in the context; so far most movement has been sustained or controlled, except for some of Hagar's sudden movements and gestures as she turns away from the Maiden Ladies Out Walking, for example. The Lovers-in-Innocence enter with an easy, natural style of movement—walking hand in hand—so this sudden disjunction is notable and memorable and the music suggests no rhythmic imperative for this departure from the norm. Indeed, the rhythmic pattern of the movement introduces an irregular counterpoint with that in the music (see Example 2b).

The movement seems not to suggest anything about the character who performs it but, rather, to hint at something beyond, suggesting, again, as in Jardin, certain possible layers of meaning not tied to specific characters or circumstances, perhaps, but significant in the context of the theme as a whole. The dance, therefore, while drawing on drama and music, creates something beyond these in choreographic terms.

Example 3 shows another version performed by two Lovers-in-Innocence girls. This time the *staccato* movement is shown in arm gestures; firstly an arm drawing inwards with accented contractions, then the other arm extending outwards in the same way. In the music the dynamic is *pianissimo* and the strings muted so that the sound is very soft. The rhythmic patterns comprise quavers, dotted quavers and semiquavers, and quaver triplets all played at the same time, so the effect is very fluid, contrasting with the sharp, distinct movement seen. In neither of these appearances does the music seem in any way to dictate or even suggest the rhythm of the movement, so that complexity is increased.

The development of the theme is facilitated by means of this kind of movement manipulation and creation of links across the ballet, working in a way which is different from the dramatic characterisation of individuals and their circumstances, and is also different from the more formalist structuring devices of repetition, development and variation which dance may share with music. But it is linked to both these, and in some way draws upon both, drawing also upon something further in the creation of the whole.

Another example of the subtle interaction of dance and music happening at a level of relatively small detail occurs in the first song of Dark Elegies. This phrase (Example 4) involves both soloist and *ensemble*. The soloist begins to reach upwards with one arm, the other hand clasping the elbow in characteristic pose, while the *ensemble* slowly turn and kneel, then begin an arch back with extended arms, which completes the image. The picture is one of extreme tension, between the upward reach of the soloist and the long extension away in opposite directions by the *corps* at a much lower level. This tension is released by the sudden, small contraction of the soloist's upper body and arms immediately afterwards, and the rising of the *ensemble* to join with the soloist in a gentle circling phrase of movement. As with many of the images in this ballet, the relationship between dance and music is close, both in terms of larger-scale structure and in phrasing. Here, for example, the extent of the image is reached at the end of the long melodic phrase and orchestral cadence, the contraction coming in the final half-bar of this whole phrase. However, in dynamic and rhythmic aspects, there is some room for exploration of subtlety. For example, although the movement is controlled and sustained, there is also, as described, a strong element of tension within it. The music, however (Example 4b), is soft, lyrical, and with no 'angularity' of either melody or rhythm; the rhythmic pattern of the music is regular, and the apparent chromaticism is in fact in keeping with the overall D minor tonality, (apart from one F sharp in bar 70, which itself suggests the tonic major, so is not altogether 'foreign'). The first steps of the *ensemble* do coincide with the pulse of the music, as is often the case in Elegies, but thereafter there is no precise rhythmical relationship and, indeed, the soloist's contraction—the culmination of or postscript to the image—occurs on the second beat of the final bar of the phrase, not on the strong first beat, or slightly less strong third beat as might be expected, so there is some disjunction there.[3]

In the exit of the Episode, fanning (Jardin aux Lilas, Example 5), the rhythmic relationship of dance and music is very fluid; at this point in the musical score (Fig 2 bar 1) the immediately preceding ascending motif (Example 5b) arrives at the dominant seventh chord in E flat (built on B flat, but in its second inversion, that is, with F at the bottom, the root of the chord entering below that one beat later, *tremolo*). The unresolved dominant seventh chord itself is conducive to the sense of imminence, and the weak inversion adds a sense of instability. The Episode exits, leaves Caroline, and at the end of the bar, the Lover enters and surprises Caroline by touching her hands. Dramatically, therefore, it is also a moment of change, and the semaphore-like gestures of the Episode seem to add to the atmosphere of foreboding, by implying some significance while clearly not indicating anything specific.[4]

Despite the emphasis on clarity of line and shape throughout Dark Elegies, certain moments do stand out as being especially distinctive. Some of these are memorable because of the time given to them to allow them to register clearly, as noted in the example above (and comparable to the 'frozen tableau' in Jardin), and some are impressed upon the memory through repetition. In others it is the nature of the relationship of dance and music at a given moment which makes it appear extraordinary. There is some overlap between these; in all of them the music plays an important part in terms of creating mood and atmosphere.

The semaphoric gestures of *ensemble* and soloist early on in the first song (Example 6) coincide with a rising, undulating melodic phrase in the music (Example 6b). The gestures are angular and contained, and different, therefore, from the broad sweep of the Episode's 'semaphore-like' movement. There is no rising undulation to match that in the music, indeed, the movement for the *ensemble* tends downwards at the end, with an arrow-shaped gesture of hands, palms touching, pushing away from the body, focus down. The search for meaning here is problematic: while the ballet clearly concerns the experience of a smitten community with illumination of both communal and individual experience, images such as this one do not seem to offer any direct insight into either communal or individual experience. There is no sense of character being illuminated, nor of community life being demonstrated, except insofar as the choreography is so structured as to allow for an image of one individual within a community to be presented. These gestures do not apparently relate to matters of character and, while their ritualistic aspect may tend towards the notion of a community act (and the soloist's own gestures recall the rocking of a child in the arms), it is a rather eccentric-looking one.

The gestures are angular in shape, as has been noted, especially those of the *ensemble* and, while their changes match the pulse of the music, their shape contradicts the rising swell of the melody. This is significant in the whole ballet because it embodies a characteristic feature. Tudor frequently allows the structure of rhythm and phrasing in the music to give structure to the dance while, at the same time, providing a striking contrast with the colour and dynamic of the music. This contrast allows for the possibility of different layers of meaning, as noted in relation to Jardin, although not necessarily in exactly the same way. The common feature is the shifting interplay between the two media of dance and music.

These various examples may be read in terms of the development of aspects of character in relation to the theme of the ballet, but still the particular relation of dance to music allows for further subtlety of interpretation to be suggested, and the two approaches are not necessarily mutually exclusive, suggesting, rather, the notion of a continuum of possibilities.

This is applicable to the fourth song, Example 7, where the music's rhythmic shape is even and steady (Example 7b) and, while the overall phrasing of the movement idea matches this, the movement within the dance phrase creates a much faster rhythm of steps. The soloist moves with small, rapid sideways steps down stage, while brushing her hand down the opposite side of her body to the ankle. In the context of the whole ballet, where much of the movement is apparently supported by the inner metre of the music, these moments stand out because of their relative complexity in terms of dance-music relations, as well as because of their difference from the rest of the movement material.

The opening phrase of Dark Elegies and its later recurrence (Examples 8 and 9), is significant in relation to its function as the opening and closing movement motif of the ballet. Comparison of the Labanotation and music scores shows clearly how the first appearance of the movement phrase is closely linked to the rhythm of the sung melody in terms of weight changes. The brushing and sliding movements of the feet, together with the use of *plié*, provide a sense of weight which also corresponds with the downward trend of the melody itself (Example 8b). The main contrast comes through the angular shape of the arms and the direct sideways focus of the dancer in profile, and it is this which ultimately creates a 'dance image'[5] of potentially multi-layered meaning. When the movement phrase recurs at the end, the music provides no rhythmic support because the final chord has sounded and is gradually dying away into silence (Example 9b). As has been suggested elsewhere[6] this adds a further dimension to the meaning not only through the context (that is, the re-appearance of an identical phrase after the progression of the ballet through various moods and towards 'Resignation') but also because of this very lack of musical support, suggesting the possibility that the character dancing now has greater personal strength or inner resources and can move forward without that support. Although this suggests an image which may be thus interpreted in the context of the theme, there is clearly complexity beyond this.[7]

Conclusion

Music and gesture, then, are manipulated in Tudor's ballets to make visual and aural images which contribute significantly to the complexity of the dance 'text' and, therefore, to the range of possible meanings which may be constructed through the spectator's engagement with them. In some instances, the dance action itself is what attracts attention, and its particular relationship to its music is an additional and significant factor. On the other hand, there are also images which seem to become significant *because* of their relationship with their music, in which it is music and dance together which create the unique impression. In some, this is because of a startling disjunction between the two, suggesting the possibility of perhaps very different layers of meaning. In others, the notion of conjunction or disjunction is more problematic because, while the dance and music are clearly not stating the same thing exactly, there is a strong link between the two (often in rhythmic shaping or dynamic), so that the suggested layers of meaning are subtly, rather than strikingly, different.

Some images also clearly work with the music in a way which seems to give specificity to the general mood/atmosphere of the music (particularly in the 'story' ballets which have distinct characters). Other images seem to take their colour from the music. Dark Elegies, as so often, embraces all possibilities, it seems.

What is clear is the fact that there are images in Tudor's ballets which, while apparently contributing to the overall interpretation of the theme, are not tied to specific characters or circumstances, and have no easily definable function. There is always some sense of atmosphere or mood evoked, however, most importantly through the interaction of dance and music, and the images described above either contribute to an intensification of the present mood, or in some way alter it, without any specific change in dramatic development: beyond drama, beyond music.

Notes

1.   Jardin aux Lilas (1936) concerns a marriage of convenience. Caroline is engaged to the Man She Must Marry and, at her engagement party, seeks to snatch a few moments with her Lover. The Man is himself anxious to avoid the company of an Episode in His Past. The ballet shows aborted meetings between the various characters against the backdrop of a party in action.

In Dark Elegies (1937) a community mourns the loss of its children through some unspecified disaster. The two scenes are entitled *Lamentations of the Bereaved* and *Resignation*.

Pillar of Fire (1942) shows how the central character, Hagar, throws herself at the Young Man from the House Opposite in a fit of desperation, fearing the the Friend, whom she loves, prefers her younger sister. Despite her shame and inhibitions, all is resolved happily eventually.

2.   See Tudor's remarks to Gruen (1975) about 'abstract ballet' .

3.   Cf the exit of the two dancing guests in Jardin aux Lilas. The waltzing steps suggest the continuation of the party regardless of the personal dramas being enacted amongst individuals. This is underlined by the fact that the dancing guests do not link their waltz step to the pulse in the music, the implication being that they hear different music, that is, the 'party' music. The music that the audience hears, then, is associated instead with the inner experience of specific individuals. The case in Elegies might be seen as similar, suggesting, again, further possible layers of meaning, different aspects of experience being presented.

4.   De Mille describes this exit: 'It is not just an *arabesque* turn, it's an invitation to go and join her or to enquire what's happening or to say, watch out' (in Anon, 1974 p42).

5.   Fernau Hall used the phrase 'dance image' in the 1940s, for example here, in relation to the Mars and Neptune sections of The Planets (1934): 'Tudor showed for

the first time his gift for the invention of dance-images to express the most delicate and subtle shades of emotion' (1950 p109).

6.   Richardson, R (1985) *Future Light* (unpublished MA dissertation, University of Surrey).

7.   It is the structural placement of the image, rather than specific properties of the image itself, which tend towards the overall interpretation in the context of the theme; the dance image itself still eludes interpretation.

References

Anon (1974), Dance Magazine Awards, *Dance Magazine*, pp40-42, May 1974.

Chausson, E., *Poeme fur Violine und Orchestre* op25. Germany: Edition Breitkopf Nr2507.

Gruen, J. (1975), *The Private World of Ballet.* Middlesex: Penguin Books.

Hall, F. (1950), *Modern English Ballet*. London: Melrose.

Jordan, S., Ballet Imperial, *Dance Now* vol.2 no.4 pp28-37, Winter 1993-94.

Mahler, G., *Kindertotenlieder* (1901-1904). New York: International Music Company (1952).

Meyer, L. (1956), *Emotion and Meaning in Music*. Chicago, London: Chicago University Press.

Richardson, R. (1985), *Future Light*, unpublished MA dissertation, University of Surrey.

_____. (1994), *Beyond Drama, Beyond Music: The Choreography of Antony Tudor*. Unpublished PhD thesis, University of Surrey.

Schoenberg, A., *Verklärte Nacht* op4 (1899). Verlag Dreililien (Richard Birnbach).

Topaz, M.(1988), Specifics of Style in the Works of Balanchine and Tudor. *Choreography and Dance* vol.1.

Tudor, A., *Jardin aux Lilas* (1936). Notation by Topaz, M (1967), Hyninnen, A (1981). New York: Dance Notation Bureau.

_____, *Dark Elegies* (1937). Notation by Hyninnen, A (1980). New York: Dance Notation Bureau.

_____, *Pillar of Fire* (1942). Notation by Hyninnen, A (1982). New York: Dance Notation Bureau.

Dance Makers: Antony Tudor. BBCTV 1992.

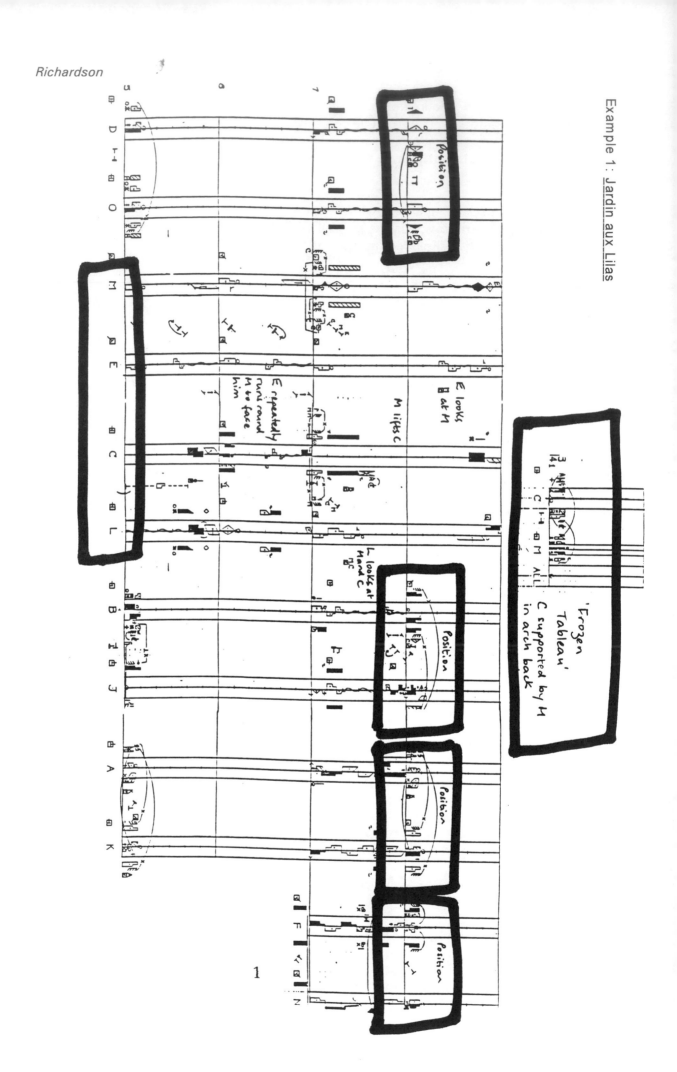

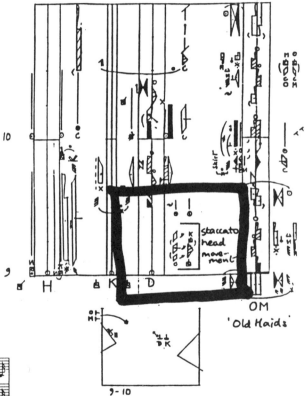

Example 1b *(above)*: <u>Jardin aux Lilas</u> (music)

Example 2 *(right)*: <u>Pillar of Fire</u>

Example 2b *(below)*: <u>Pillar of Fire</u> (music)

<u>Music rhythm</u>

<u>Dance rhythm</u>

255

Richardson

Example 3: <u>Pillar of Fire</u>

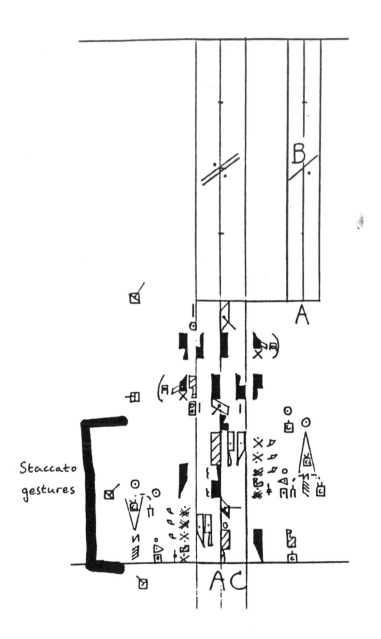

Staccato
gestures

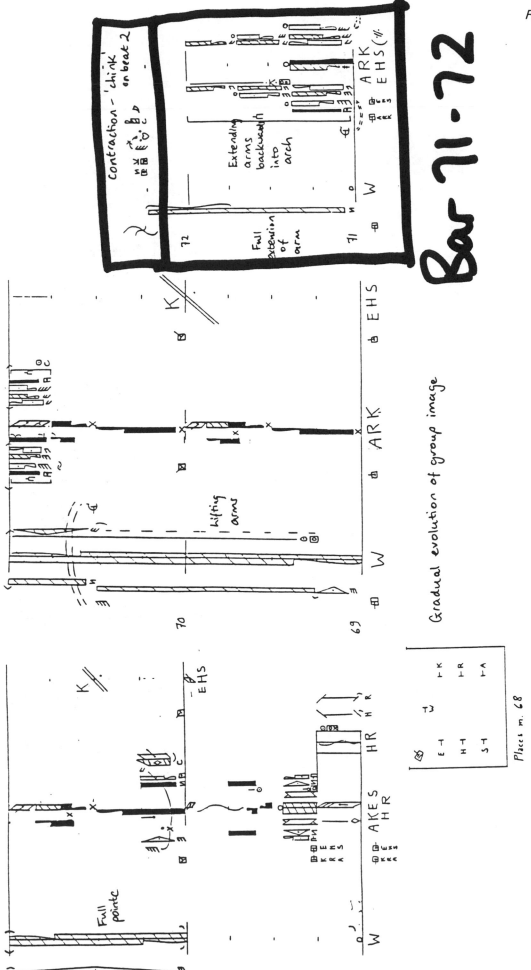

Richardson

Example 4: Dark Elegies

257

Example 4b: <u>Dark Elegies</u> (music)

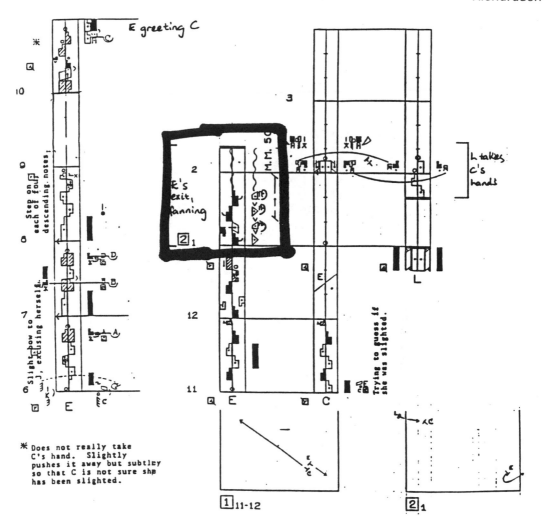

Example 5 *(above)*: <u>Jardin aux Lilas</u>

Example 5b *(below)*: <u>Jardin aux Lilas</u>

Example 6: <u>Dark Elegies</u>

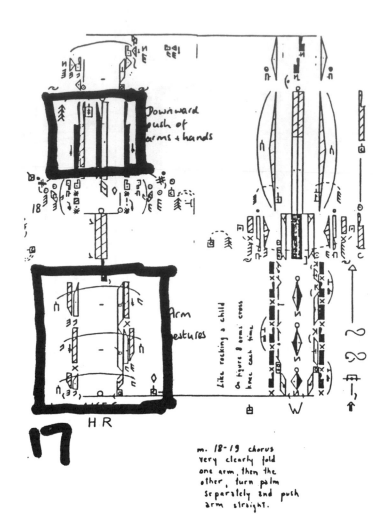

Example 6b: <u>Dark Elegies</u> (music)

Example 7: <u>Dark Elegies</u>

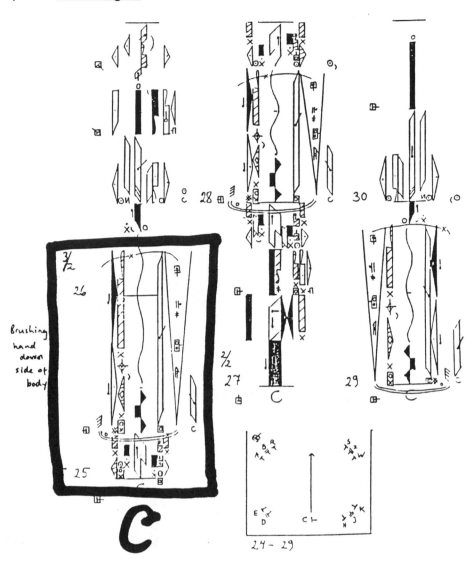

Example 7b: <u>Dark Elegies</u> (music)

Example 8 : Dark Elegies

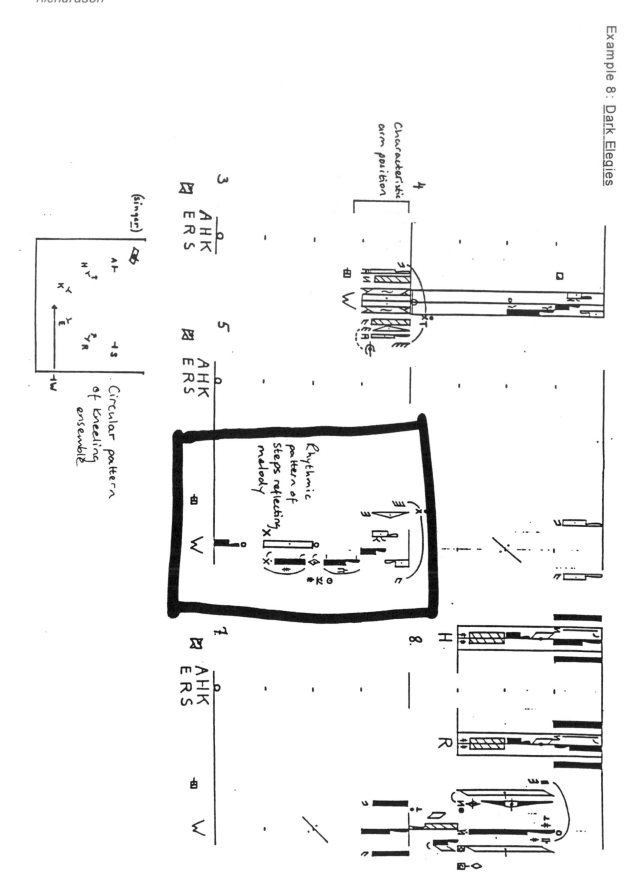

Example 8b: <u>Dark Elegies</u> (music)

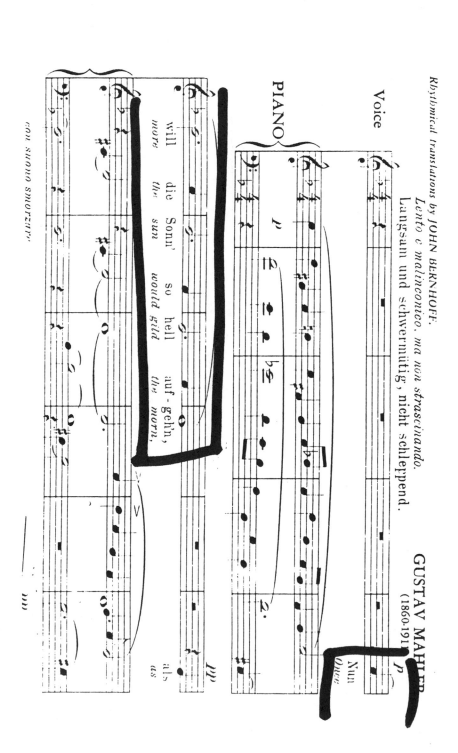

Example 9: <u>Dark Elegies</u>

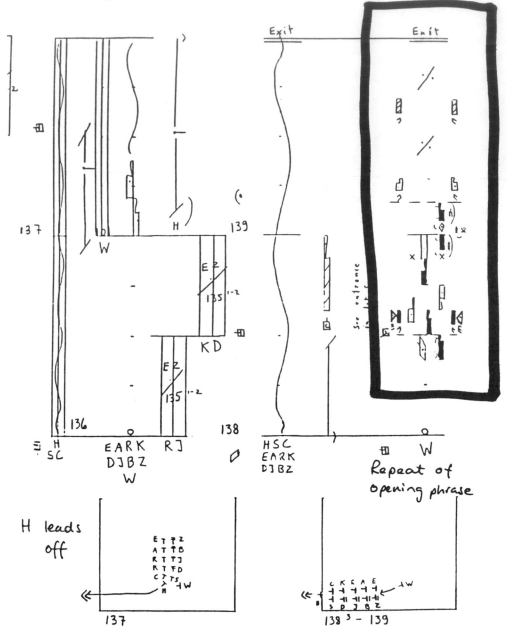

Example 9b: <u>Dark Elegies</u> (music)

GISELLE AND ROMANTICISM

VAL RIMMER: LABAN CENTRE FOR MOVEMENT AND DANCE

Despite the fact that all dance texts are semiological and rhetorical, structures of meaning in relation to dance works are frequently accountd for, historically, by a version of the historical which is given as an a priori, established fact. Consequently when discussing Giselle, an immediate question can be anticipated from dance historians - which Giselle? - as if there is an authentic original work in relation to which all other interpretations of Giselle must be considered. And as if there is a legitimating discourse, dance history, which in a hierarchy of discourses, is privileged over all others. This contrasts with drama, for example, where one can discuss Macbeth or The Importance of Being Earnest without necessarily being side tracked into extended discussions about which particular writing and performance one is talking.

A traditional dance history "paraphrases" the meaning of the dance text in terms of what is exterior or anterior to it and there appears in this position to be a turning away from the legacy of the structuralist and post structuralist perspectives which, instead of trying to tie meaning to a particular privileged version of events etc., have shown how a text achieves its particular meaning/s. The implication of this way of working (with a few notable exceptions such as the work of Mark Franko and Susan Foster) is that dance history follows a genetic pattern which narrativises all dance texts, treating them as being a significant moment in a chain which is on its way to a teleological end.

There are some works that have been canonically defined as embodying the generative principle of Romanticism and these works make up what is called in dance historical terms, the Romantic genre in ballet. Giselle is one such work and it is utilised retrospectively to justify a claim that the Romantic ballet is both the culmination and the beginning of an account of meaning that has its relevance in explanations of dance technique and dance technical developments. Discussing the latter part of the 18th century, Clarke and Crisp write that "innovators of the time - Noverre, Vigano, Blasis and Dauberval - were in a sense preparing the ground for a new form of dance" and that "the use of pointe work, the impression of ethereal lightness, are indicative of the change which not only altered the outward aspect of dancing but also the themes which it treated." (1) This perspective then reduces what is fundamentally Romantic about Romantic ballet to an explanation of what constitues classical ballet at this time (1830's-40's), or as Clarke and Crisp say what is outward. And dance history then is given as an account of events ordered in time (E.g., the evolution of ballet from Court ballet to the present day) or as an organic account of the development of technique, and dance texts are interpreted unproblematically as evidence of both.

To discuss Romantic ballet in terms of dance related developments raises another problematic issue which is the way such accounts of meaning ignore what would, in the other arts, be conventional accounts of Romanticism - that it demonstarates the passage from a mimetic to an expressive concept of art (Abrams), or that it is a movement from a Platonic towards a Hegelian model of the universe. Consequently dance history ignores the

border implicit in any discussions of Romantic ballet between Romanticism
and ballet. Or rather reduces the relationship between the two areas to a
simplistic account of themes. For example Cyril Beaumont talks about La
Sylphide and Giselle demonstrating "the four colours of the Romantic
palette" which he lists in relation to the first Act as being: the life of
ordinary folk, specific geographical location, the historical colour of
perhaps another age "perhaps the 17th century" and in Act 2 as new world of
supernatural visions. This oppositional relationship between classical
ballet and romanticism is then, one border tension which I will address in
this paper.

Cyril Beaumont in The ballet called Giselle talks about the differentiation
between Acts one and two of the ballet in terms of action. Gautier's
original idea for Giselle of making the first act a mimed version of Hugo's
poem was abandoned because, as it was conceived there would have been "a
complete absence of action...of an ordered drama, with its introduction,
plot, and climax" (2) Ultimately, engaging the help of Saint-Georges,
Gautier and Saint-Georges produced a work divided into two Acts the first
of which is described by Beaumont as "an undistinguished piece of stage
carpentry" and the second "as a genuinely poetic conception". I want to
consider the differentiation between the two Acts as a border tension. I
shall be looking at this differentiation not in terms of an examination of
narrative, or in terms of authenticity of choreography, or as an account of
technique, but in terms of the fundamentally defining characteristic of the
Romantic aesthetic which is contained in the opposition between symbol and
allegory (as formulated by Goethe, Schlegel and Schelling).

A third border to which I wish to draw your attention, is that of
male/female embodiment. Discussions of the Romantic symbol will lead me to
consider the way in which an organicist dance historical account of
Romantic ballet treats the ballerina as the idealised and central image and
the male dancer as an auxillary one, "not worthy of serious consideration"
(3). However if we consider the relationship between Romanticism and ballet
differently, it would appear that there is a reversal of the above
position, which can be found in the disguises under which Image and
Imagination exist.

The Romantics claim that the work of art is a particular type of expression
which is unique and which cannot be reduced to explanation because art
allows the artist to express aesthetic ideas which defy ordinary verbal
representation, and therefore to express what would normally be
inexpressible. The basis for this view of art is to be found for the
Romantics in nature. Not as the Neo Classical framework of aesthetics would
insist, on the subservience of the work of art to the principle of
imitation subjecting works of art to a consideration that is exterior to
them - in this case the way in which the work of art would imitate nature.
But in the way the Romantic work of art is conceived as being like nature
in that it has an identical internal structure to nature which it is the
task of the artist to represent. Beauty in the work is not achieved in
terms of representing what is already formed but, as representing the
impression of a higher beauty which resides in the totality of nature. A
beauty that is produced as having a value in itself and which results from
the harmonious relationship between the parts, and of the parts to the
whole. This enables the work of art to be treated, like nature, as having

an unconscious organic life and therefore as a closed and autonomous
totality whose beauty lies in its internal coherence. The appeal of
Classical aesthetics to external finality, that submits beauty to an end
or purpose placing it in the service of something else, is converted into
an internal finality in which beauty has a value and purpose in itself.

The principle of internal coherence allows for a distinction to be made
between language that is used in the service of intelligibility as
explanation and discursive reason, and the symbolic use of language which
has no end outside of itself, and which operates as a reincarnation of
beauty in which the internal organisation of the work is produced as its
organising principle. Although different writers of the time treat this
differentiation between the transitive and the intransitive use of language
differently, they all redefine the symbol/and the symbolic as fundamental
to the Romantic aesthetic, and differentiate the symbolic from the
allegorical use of language.

Allegorical use of language is transitive - there is an immediate movement
through the signifying face of the sign towards what is signified and
therefore allegory is utilitarian and functional in the sense that it is
without a value in itself. Its value is to be found in the service of
something else - the knowledge that is signified. It is here that I want to
turn to the different use of movement language between Act one and Act two
of Giselle. Firstly Act one is characterised by the amount of mime that is
used as a way of furthering the narrative action. Mime is treated in the
work as a mute gestural language through which there is a direct passage
between the mime and the information signified. An example would be when
Berthe, Giselle's mother warns her not to overexcite herself dancing
because if she is not careful she will suffer the fate of the Wilis. What
becomes clear from this example is that mime is a particular type of
vocabulary, with designated meanings which can be acquired and learnt, and
which are determined by convention. Mime is treated in Giselle
allegorically in that it is both arbitrary and conventional; it proceeds
like allegory from conventions that are arbitrarily imposed and which have
to be acquired and learnt before it can be understood. It therefore has a
rational character which operates as a form of explanation thus speaking to
deductive reason and intellection alone. This speaks of a particular view
of art which differentiates between art which has an end in itself, which
is expressed in the intrinsic beauty of form, and art which is subjected
to external demands - an opposition which is found in the Kantian
distinction between pure and applied art, and which is developed in the
writings of Novalis who speaks of art that is subjected by determined
communication and therefore adapts to an intention foreign to itself. This
is precisely the function of mime, to communicate a definitive message by
using a substitutive language.

The opposition between symbol and allegory resides in a distinction being
made between mechanical and organic form. Form is mechanical when it is
ordered externally, when certain conventions are imposed on the work making
the work obey a particular set of rules which are given without reference
to quality. Whereas organic form unfolds from within, appealing to a higher
order of existence which is produced out of the inner recesses of the
speaker's mind. As such it represents the concepts constructed by the
intellect in the process of creativity, which is in the service of

imagination. The Romantic work of art would therefore not be haphazard and determined by sterile convention, but would demonstrate a particular coherence which is demonstrated in the network of relations between its constitutent parts. The truth of the work is then to be found in the truth of the harmonious linking of all the particular instances in a living body of work.

The symbol is both concrete, in that it is visually apprehended, and it is at the same time fluid and suggestive. In it existence and essence coincide at all times. But in order for the Image to work metaphorically we have to forget all we know about language as a particular type of communication that is established by convention and which can be confirmed and recognised as such. Because as we have shown the Image is determined by the manner in which it originates as an expression of the essence or spirit of nature. What takes place within Romanticism is that there is a return, in respect of the various art forms, to a greater concreteness of expression. This can be found in the proliferation of the natural which restores to the language used a material substantiality whilst at the same time, language becomes increasingly metaphorical with the symbol coming to be the most prominent dimension of style.

The different use of movement between Acts one and two of <u>Giselle</u> demonstrates this process. Act one shows us a naturalised world – a peasant community – where the language used is naturalised. The use of mime as a particular type of communication, and dance steps such as glissades, chasses, pas de basques, poses, etc. combine to give an earthly nature to the steps, which have a special, light quality but which rarely lose contact with the ground. In fact in Lawson's work on classical ballet she talks of the preparatory or transitory steps of classical ballet as having been derived from folk dance and which are used to produce an affective quality and vitality of expression (4). In this work it is precisely the "affective" quality that dominates act one which leads to the symbolically enacted death of expressivity. Whereas in Act two the dance language and the dancer become synonymous, producing symbolically the Romantic Image. Mime has almost disappeared and the movements used are larger and the combinations produced more virtuosic – Arabesques, grand rond de jambes, developpe, grand jete, etc,. There is also a comparative use of the same movements such as the pas de bouree. In Act one it is used to indicate Giselle's special dancerly quality, whereas in Act two the quality of the movement is altered to suggest a floating, fluid effect, to give the impression of flight. If we return to the point made in relation to the relation between language and nature we remember that the resemblance between dance and nature is not a matter of external finality but is a matter of origination. The art work expresses the essence of nature and what this means is that art originates like nature and therefore the Romantic Image, or symbol, is determined by the manner in which it originates. So in the character of Giselle there is an appeal to the concrete, she loves to dance and this is what gives her a defining and differentiating identity within the work. And it is this identity that provides her condition of possibility as a Wili enabling her becoming to coincide with her mode of origination, her essence/being. As a Wili she is defined by their identity, as super – natural, as more than natural. She has in this world no beginning and no end, and she, like the Wilis, does not follow a model other than herself because her origin is determined by her own being. The discontinuity of death which causes her to relinquish her specificity as character determined in a series of actions, is left behind. And she is reincarnated as a natural (more than natural) entity which originates out of a being which does not differ from her in essence but which contains the totality of her individual manifestations within itself. She becomes a particular manifestation of an archetype and therefore a natural object, conceived in terms of origin, which as we have shown in the way in which the Romantics formulated the symbol, leads to the transcendental concept of the Idea. Giselle, like the Wilis, is material form – reincarnated out of the material body of a young girl. And therefore in Act two, she originates as a natural emanation of a transcendental principle. Albrecht, as the Romantic hero in his quest for the Idea therefore takes the natural object, Giselle, as his starting point and searches for the Image as the transcendental manifestation of a divine or super human principle in the world of the Wilis.

This awareness of the Image resulted in the french Romantics being drawn into an isolated position, feeling themselves to be irreconcilably different from their society – a society that was dominated, and in the eyes of the Romantics corrupted, by reasoned and rational knowledge. The Image, as representative of a transcendent order, provides a means to the ideas of a different order of truth and as a consequence isolation is the fate of those who were devoted to the dream of Imagination. However, not all men were recalled to the truth of Imagination. The presence of a transcendental principle was not available to all men because it could be hidden from man by his own volition. The manifestation of the divine appears always in the guise of a beginning. It has an outward appearance which operates essentially to conceal the truth and therefore initially there is a poetic seduction of beginnings – to be found in the ballet in the love story – which depends on a misrecognition of the transcendental nature of the source. This differentiation between misrecognition and disguise are fundamentally important in the ballet.

In the first act of the ballet, Albrecht, disguised as Loys , a simple peasant, demonstrates his estrangement both from his own community and the peasant community. The fantasised, or narrativised peasant world, is located between the true earthly and material world of nature – it refers in its description and expression to this world – and the false, humanised, aristocratic world of Albrecht, from which it is separated. The tension between these two extremes is contained in the disguise which is waiting to explode the fantasy. It is the action of disguise which eventually brings about Giselle's collapse into madness and her premature death. This provides the movement by which the poetic Imagination – characterised in Albrecht – is torn away from the terrestial, the material, the sterile and the decadent, and moves towards an other order. Albrecht, as himself, is led into the world of the imagination which is embodied and mythologised in the super natural world of the destructive but beautiful Wilis.

The world of the Wilis is constituted as an underworld that rises, literally in the work from beneath the ground, and the process that is being described in this movement is one of ascendance. This is clearly expressed in the contrast between the movement/mime of Giselle in Act one and her movements as a member of the Wilis. And, in the contrast between the ethereal movements of the Wilis, and the movements of Albrecht, which

are earthbound. Expressed in the contrasting movement quality is the desire
to escape earthbound matter and to be relieved of the weight of gravity
and a new relationship between nature and consciousness is uncovered in
which the transparency of air and the reverie of flight represent a
fluidity of a consciousness/being that is un-earthed. By going towards the
Image - symbolically embodied in the figure of Giselle - Albrecht
experiences a life-in-death. The death of one way of life, which is
represented by his inability to locate himself comfortably in either the
aristocratic world of his background which is shown in the work to be a
world of superficiality and governed by sterile conventions. Or, in
Giselle's world, where he is revealed as a fraud, by Hilarion.

There is an ontological priority which is located in the character of
Giselle. She is treated as an object that is intrinsically desirable - this
desire is placed in her capacity to dance which differentiates her from the
rest of her community - and it is through the experience of the material
presence of Giselle that the desire arises, in the gap between Act one and
Act two, for Albrecht to be reborn in the manner of natural creation.
Desire for Giselle is then embedded as a type of forgotten presence and
eventually it is re-presented as a desire for the origin of the object and
is converted into a desire to possess the image. The epiphany which was
initially misrecognised, is transposed into an entity that is still called
nature but is no longer equated with matter, and nostalgia for Giselle
enacted as Albrecht visits her grave, is converted into a nostalgia and a
desire for an entity which could never by its very nature be realised as a
particularised form of presence. The differentiation between the two Acts
expresses a typically Romantic position which is that of a consciousness
trapped between the real and the divine in its attempt to reach the
transcendental idea figured in the Image.

Giselle offers a contradiction in that it appears as a free and autonomous
Romantic expression but is in fact subjected to a classically ordered
regularity. The classical referred to here is that which has an allegiance
to the classical framework of Greek art which insists on the submission of
art to the principle of imitation which is governed by the invisible ideal
of beauty. Enlightenment thinking about art shows its beauty to be created
out of a symmetry that is produced in the way that the parts are organised
according to certain principles. This allows for the dance ideal to
designate a stable plenitude that is essentially definitive of an ideal
subjectivity that exists undisturbed by any conflict or tension. The ideal
then conforms to the Grecian ideal of human nature as a perfect unison
between all powers as the most perfect realisation of human subjectivity
and as its originating condition.

The classical technique drives towards the projection of a perfectly imaged
ideal. So what we call Romantic ballet is still performed according to
academic principles of line, placing, balance and symmetry, which operate
according to a set of technical rules and conventions. And the aim of this
classically ordered structure is to locate or effect a state that is proper
to beauty. The Romantic symbol, as expressive of a higher order of
existence, has its own set of structuring rules which are the rules of
aesthetics and not the rules of nature. And consequently the Image must
possess qualities of order, balance and harmony in order to prevent the
chaos of a meaning - less state. A dance example that I will use to develop

this is that of the pose. The use of the pose creates a stillness in an abstract flow of contour and surface. What the pose achieves is a demonstration of the ability to find and maintain, albeit momentarily, equilibrium. It therefore has the effect of demonstrating prowess. It offers a placing of the body/bodies in relation to the space in which they dance and, it displays the beauty of the relation bewteen the individual and the group. One can think of many moments in Act two of Giselle where the Wilis hold a pose, or the Queen or Giselle, hold an arabesque at some moment in a long enchainment giving the impression of a continuous, flowing line that is stilled momentarily to pause the spirit and give the audience access to Albrecht's vision. A vision in which the differentiated movements and forms melt into a continuous flowing image which expresses through the purity and simplicity of form a fantasised, self-sufficient and harmonious condition of humanity.

The Enlightenment ideal of self plenitude and harmony as an originating condition of humanity is one that the Romantics rejected as an impossible ideal. Ultimately the task of the Romantic work of art is to recognise internal discord in terms of an oppositional state that is the essential, natural human condition and to reconcile oppositional elements in such a way that they are blended insolubly together. This is achieved in the work of art through the property of internal coherence which offers a type of classicism which produces an expression which is always in the state of becoming, and allows individual and oppositional elements to cohere into an expressive whole. The fundamentally expressive feature of the Romantic aesthetic is the reliance of the work of art on the symbol. The symbol achieves a fusion of contraries in that it signifies and it is the thing itself at the same time, it is intransitive yet it expresses the inexpressible. It is a meaningful image which can bring to life what is infinite. Through its external surfaces it signifies its inner being and therefore "speaks" of itself. These are the terms in which Gautier speaks of Taglioni. "Taglioni is one of the greatest poets of our time...she is not just the dancer, but the dance itself" (5) When she dances the role of Giselle there is an effacement of the distance between signifier and signified in which the work of art is conceived as a closed totality whose resemblance is not a matter of the appearance of ideal forms found in nature, but is produced in the way in which the work of art is seen to possess an internal structure identical to nature. The way in which the parts of a work interrelate with each other and the whole is then not a matter of being converted to the imitation of harmonious, idealised form, but it is the condition of the work's status as a beautiful object that it has a clarity that is produced in this interrelationship. It is an autonomous totality that is expressive of itself, and which is not in the service of something else and therfore posseses an identical internal structure to nature. Beauty is therefore in the service of this internal organisation which can express only itself.

Interestingly 18th century discourse in relation to the Classical ideal perpetuated an exclusion of the feminine as the site of idealised subjectivity. The ideal female body in art had a conventionally straightforward function as a signifier of sensuous beauty in which the feminine ideal was remade in the image of abstract, perfect beauty which dissociated itself "from any recalcitrant flesh and bloods signs of its humanity".(6) In this placing it was uncomplicated by associations with ideas of freedom and heroism which were conventionally located in the male, Classical ideal. So, for example, the Wilis are treated as abstract ciphers drained of identity, feeling, materiality and consciousness. They are converted into outlines of ideal form and narratively constructed as occupying territory beyond the range of desire. Their concreteness and clarity is constructed from within the formal simplicity of the principles of dance classicism and it is this symbolically constructed world that offers a centredness to the instabilities and complexities of the modern R omantic soul. So we see the site of the feminine being used to supplement and purify this self as a visual expression of inner being. Constructed from within the principles of Classicism the Image is used as a gendered embodiment of the expression of male inner being. Within the classically ordered world of the Wilis there is implied a separation between the literal substance of the dance work - the material body - and its representation, its ideal reification, as an expression of imagination.

There is a differentiation made in the ballet between the image of life in death, that is embodied by the Wilis and evidenced in the reincarnation of Giselle as the most perfect product of the Romantic Imagination, and an image of death that is finite - the death of Giselle in Act one and the death of Hilarion in Act two. This contrast describes symbolically the moral argument of Romanticism that is expressed in relation to creativity. Neo Classical creativity, a creativity that insists on the submission of the work of art to the principle of imitation, was considered to be reproduced from the repetition of sterile convention and therefore could only lead to a compromise of life and art, and ultimately to the subsequent death of the soul. Whereas the act of the Imagination, which distinguishes the Romantic artist from other men - as Albrecht is differentiated from other men in the ballet - enables insight and sensibility to be the organs of moral knowledge. Sensibility is not however not just an organ of fine feelings but it is shown to be an organ of moral discrimination and perception because it demonstrates a belief in the higher degree of sensory organisation that distinguishes the artist from other men. This belief is not based on the artist merely feeling more deeply than others - and here the role of Hilarion is crucial in the ballet because it provides an essential contrast between the feelings of Hilarion and the feelings of Albrecht - but because there is a dangerous aspect to the gift of Imagination.

This danger is located in the mode of origination of the object. The object is present as a natural emanation of a transcendental principle and this necessitates that any quest for the Idea must take the natural object as its starting point. It is fundamental however that there is a separation between the material and the Idea which converts sensuous qualities into idealised form in such a way that sensuous desire is embedded as a forgotten presence. Because of the necessary presence of the sensuous in the ideal, the Romantic artist has to be cautious with his sensual appetites. The improper focus and expression of these can lead to, at the very least, misrecognition, but ultimately, could lead to destruction.

The combination in the ballet between the Classical, confined within the limits of pure form, and the Romantic as an expression of search for the ontological status of the aesthetic object, becomes focused around the issue of creativity which is expressed in the ballet through the metaphor of disguise. The creation of Loys, effected by a simple reclothing of the body, is a carefully qualified betrayal that results in death. The death of rationality as Giselle collapses into madness and ulimately her physical death. However if we take the character of Albrecht to be expressive of the spiritual journey of the Romantic artist, and follow the movement between the two Acts from action to contemplation, it is possible to perceive that the Classical ideal that is embodied in the world of the Wilis is used not to a Neo Classical end which is governed by external finality, but as an expression of life itself as the vision of actual experience in which spirit and matter combine under their purest and most perfect conditions. Mind and image are inseparable because the danced thought is identical with its sensuous form as it resists the Neo Classical separation between matter and form – dancer and dance are a totality.

Within the differentiation between the two Acts there is therefore a certain pragmatic and moral functionality which is concerned with the victory of the Image – as symbolic embodiment – over the larger organisation of words and their discursive truth. The fundamental quality of the symbol – that is active, living and infinite – enables Albrecht to temporarily access poetic transcendental form that is embodied in the totality of the world of the Wilis and which provides a moment of repose from loneliness and death. The differentiation between the two Acts that is particularly evidenced in the use of mime and dance, describes for the audience two different orders. One is a world ordered by the logic of causality which circulates around events, actions and truths which are constructed as being false, and which lead to a type of death in life. And the other is the transcendental dream world of the Imagination which drives towards possession of the Image, and which offers life at its most intense and significant. The products of the Imagination, which are presented as a dance vision, can only be accessed by Albrecht at the cost of continued self expenditure and immense effort, as he engages with the destructive force of the Wilis, whose motivation is to dance any male mortals that enter their world to their death. The archetypal heroine, Giselle, serves to provide the dramatic pattern for the narration of this quest.

The use of dance as a fundamentally defining quality that is a natural emanantion of an epiphany, is very interesting. Enlightenment society was dominated by the word as the privileged mode of expression and communication, with all that is linked to the body being carefully located through the abstract structure of form in order that the problems of materiality could be bypassed. Dance then, as the art that uses the body to become an ever more expressive instrument of choreographic thought, necessarily needs to be highly rationalised as a version of unified coherence and differentiated from the literal by the condition of figurality – figuring as idealised form. So although in the ballet it would appear that Giselle's ability to dance is evidence of her sensitivity, her spontaneity and her delicacy, it is also linked to a darker other nature., which is her essential instability.

I would argue that in this work there is put in place around the female image a negativity that sustains the view of the feminine as unstable, irrational and potentially dangerous to the dominant order (the rational, stable and the certain) unless brought under proper control. Proper control

romantically speaking would mean the dematerialisation of the feminine and
its re-placement as the embodiment of beautiful form as evidence of a
higher degree of sensory organisation. Through this movement the sensual,
the material and the potentially impure can be relocated to function as
pure, spiritual beauty that is ordered to be expressive symbolically, of a
transcendental principle. The symbol then functions, through the act of
Imagination, as life producing, and provides the condition of possibility
for the Romantic artist to pursue life defined by the Image and withdraw
from another type of life which can only ultimately lead to the death of
creativity.

What is demonstrated in this position is that although a conventional dance
history would tell us that the Romantic era is the era of the ballerina,
any serious consideration of the border between ballet and Romanticism
would lead us to the conclusion that the feminine is used to demonstrate
the special sensitivity of the male artist as an individual of special
moral discrimination and perception.There is therefore a placing of the
feminine as an embodied ideal which operates not as the dominant force to
which the male is subservient but as an objectified image as the image of,
and for, his contemplation. This would appear to be a reversal of
traditional dance historical accounts which locate the Romantic movement in
ballet as the era of the ballerina's dominance in which there occurred a
degradation of the danseur. The only point at which such an explanation
would hold would be if dance history was determined to account for dance
meaning in terms of an a priori - in this case technique - and relegate all
other interpretations as a disruption of this fetishistic fantasy.

FOOTNOTES

1. Clarke M. & Crisp C: <u>Ballet:An Illustrated History:</u> Adam & Charles Black:London: 1978: P64

2. Beaumont C: <u>The Ballet Called Giselle</u>: Dance Books Ltd: London: 1982: P20

3. Clarke M. & Crisp C: <u>Ballet: An Illustrated History</u>: Adam & Charles Black: London: 1978: P67

4. Lawson J: <u>Classical Ballet: Its Style and Technique</u>: Adam &Charles Black: London: 1960: P119

5. Guest I: <u>Gautier On Dance:</u> Dance Books Ltd: London: 1986: P2

6. Potts A: <u>Flesh and the Ideal: Wincklemann and the Origins of Art History:</u> Yale University Press: London: 1994: P164

BIBLIOGRAPHY

ABRAMS M: <u>The Mirror and the Lamp</u>: Oxford University Press: New York: 1953

BEAUMONT C: <u>The Ballet Called Giselle:</u> Dance Books Ltd: London: 1982

GUEST I: <u>The Romantic Ballet in Paris</u>: Issac Pitman & Sons: London: 1966

GUEST I: <u>Jules Perrot: Master of the Romantic Ballet</u>: Dance Books Ltd: London: 1984

GUEST I: <u>Gautier On Dance:</u> Dance Books Ltd: London: 1986

KERMODE F: <u>Romantic Image</u>: Routledge & Kegan Paul: London: 1986

LEVINSON A: Trans. S. Cook Summer: <u>Ballet Old and New</u>: Dance Horizons: New York: 1982

DE MAN P: <u>Rhetoric of Romanticism:</u> Columbia University Press: New York: 1983

POTTS A: <u>Flesh and the Ideal: Wincklemann and the Origins of Art History:</u> Yale University Press: London: 1994

RESOURCE-BASED TEACHING and INTERACTIVE VIDEO

Jacqueline Smith-Autard – De Montfort University Bedford
and Bedford Interactive
Jim Schofield – Bedford Interactive

Abstract: *First, it is proposed that the art of dance in education and training demands a resource-based teaching methodology as the central and most important approach. Next, it is established that through interactive video techniques professional dance exemplars can be flexibly and creatively employed to develop the students' own performance, composition and appreciation skills. Finally, a detailed expose of our creative ways of applying multimedia technology to dance education determines the relevance of it in resource-based dance teaching environments and provides an indication of the content and range of interactive facilities in our future resource pack publications.*

1) RESOURCE-BASED TEACHING:

The following text which derives largely from *The Art of Dance in Education* (1994) provides a short rationale for the resource-based teaching approach and explains briefly how professional dance resources might be employed in dance education at all levels.

Rationale:
A good professional example demonstrates artistic and aesthetic quality in its composition and its performance. It also has implicit cultural and historical significance. Resource-based teaching through interactive video permits repeated viewings of phrases, sections or the whole work and offers tasks at different levels attached to each part of the work to provide starting points for the students own learning about the dance work - style, form, expression, accompaniment, stage/costume/lighting design, and performance. The dance work can be studied to learn more about the choreographer and the traditions, trends or shifts away from conventions which are evident in the work.

Consequently, the students' artistic learning can be augmented through the appropriate use of dance works in resource-based teaching/learning activities. Moreover, if the experiences of engagement with an art work are feelingful in the sense that the individual's own feelings and emotions can enter the processes, they can be labelled aesthetic experiences. In our view, aesthetic interaction between students and art works is an important aim for resource-based teaching/learning and teachers/lecturers should ensure that their students' perceptions of sensory, expressive and formal qualities in art works are awakened and developed through the tasks they are given.

Resource-based teaching will work well if the resources selected are appropriate to the objectives of the lessons/lectures, rich in artistic, aesthetic and cultural features and used sparingly within the total programme. In most instances, dance works should not be studied in their every detail and analysed with infinite precision. This kind of scrutiny kills the artistic and aesthetic dimensions of the work and makes the study into a pseudo-scientific chore. It serves no purpose unless the intention is to reconstruct the work. If this is the case, the detailed analysis is a means to an end - a reconstructed section or whole dance **re-interpreted** in the students' own way. Hence, as in music, analysis of a professional performance of a work serves only as a qualitative example. It cannot and should not be **copied exactly**, rather it acts as a detailed reference text against which the students place their own interpretations. In other words, a dance ready-made is a **resource** to be employed in support of the students' own learning. It is not a **set formula** to be learned by rote and copied in exact form in reconstruction of the choreography. Neither is it a supply of content for the students' own choreography. This amounts to choreographic plagiarism! Rather, the movement vocabulary and choreographic techniques in a dance work resource should become part of a bank or repertoire of ideas and formuli for the students from which they select and develop in their own ways. Making the movements or choreographic principles **your own** is a very important principle to maintain in resource-based learning.

The above makes clear the rationale for resource-based teaching/learning approach in the art of dance in education model. However, in order to learn from complex and highly developed examples of dance works, students need to be guided through structured tasks which are sufficiently open for them to make their own responses to the art work, yet structured enough to aid progression and constructive learning. The following methods may help achieve these objectives.

Viewing tasks:
Watching dance is difficult. Movements are transient, illusive and complex. The view of dancers on video is two dimensional though, of course, the movement itself is three dimensional. The spatial canvas of dance is never visible- it has to be imagined by the viewer. A simple example of this non-visible and abstract nature of spatial patterning is a dancer travelling on a circular pathway - the circle is not there, it is constructed by the viewer while the dancer travels. For these and other reasons, the teacher/lecturer needs to help learners to **see** the dance as it passes through time.

In order to do this without telling the students what to see, however, it is necessary to provide frameworks or leading questions to guide perception. It would be quite wrong in an artistic/aesthetic context to determine exactly what they should notice by directive means. Hence, a student-centred approach is beneficial for most of the viewing tasks and interactive video is an ideal medium towards this end.

Methods might include use of teacher prepared questions on worksheets, which may be presented on screen or on paper to promote discussion, requiring students to observe, make comparisons, describe, interpret and make evaluative comment on what they see.

On almost every occasion of viewing a work, students should have opportunity to reflect on or talk about the feelings that the work evokes in them. These feelings could be positive or negative, but should be backed by reasons. Tasks to make known the viewers' feelings even if only for themselves is important if the art of dance is to contribute effectively to aesthetic education.

Viewing tasks are often necessary precursors of performing and composing tasks since the dance work resource is the starting point for such work in resource- based teaching/learning.

Performing tasks:
A most beneficial way of "getting inside" a dance work, especially for older students, is to dance the whole or parts of the work. In order to learn a section, for example, the teacher or, occasionally, a dance artist might employ a directed teaching approach so that the students replicate as accurately as possible the choreographed movements. Use of notation, graphics and slow motion video to demonstrate the qualitative aspects of the professional dancers' performance enhances the learning process. However, once the piece is learned this instructive approach should end because students need to colour the movements in their own ways to express the perceived choreographic intention.

This kind of experience is a very valuable way of coming to know a work. To be able to dance a piece of repertoire, it is necessary to learn how to perform the actions, rhythmic, dynamic, spatial and relationship patterning in order to understand how the choreographer expresses the idea. Without altering the style and content of the work, the students then have to make their performances their own so that they show understanding of the 'text' through their presentation. The resource, then, constitutes a professional and expert example against which the students can reference and check their own work.

Composing tasks:
There are many ways in which a dance ready-made can be employed as a basis for creative work. Students may learn part of a phrase and then end it in their own way building on and perhaps developing the material. Secondary students for

example, might view a section noting the kinds of leaning and counter balance actions the pairs of dancers are using and extract them to use in their own choreography. University students may study the style of movement or choreographic devices used and extract the essence of the style and/or the principles behind the choreographic devices to use in their own work.

Numerous examples could be given here, but the above are perhaps sufficient to indicate the advantages of resource-based teaching in developing the students' creative abilities in choreography. Learning from 'givens', - choreographically rich examples, and working on these bases towards something new, individual and of creative value **depends** on coming to know and understand the discipline/techniques of the art form through in depth study of its art works. Moreover, carefully formulated tasks which guide the students' perceptions of the way in which the dance work has been choreographed will teach them as much if not more about the processes than practical choreography experiences themselves. Thus artistic and aesthetic **appreciation** of the choreographer's skill and originality should be a primary objective in all resource-based teaching/learning creating tasks.

Historical/cultural context tasks:

This kind of study is important for older students in that in order to understand a dance work they need to put it into a context of time and place. As indicated above, a study of dance works as historical phenomena provides students with knowledge of the practices, trends, styles and genres evident at any one time and changes that occur in time. A study of dance works as cultural products provides students with knowledge of possible reasons for the characteristics contained in the works and the changes that can be seen in time. Looking inwards at the art work itself and looking outwards at the society from which it emerged, provides a problem-solving means of study whereby students interpret evidence in dance works against their findings about the choreographers and the cultures in which the works were created.

Multiple resources are needed in this context. Through reading about works, watching them and making critical comparisons and contrasts, the students gradually become aware of classifications of genre and style and the difficulties that some works pose in not fitting easily into such classifications. The students should be lead to support their study of a dance resource with research from books, programmes, choreographers' writings or interviews, critics' writings and television documentaries, photographs, and any published views of the dancers. A full range of such content could be available on a CD video disc - more on this below. However, opportunities to work with the choreographers or dancers themselves cannot be replaced by such a resource alone. Such a mixture of primary and secondary sources should offer multiple means of looking **into** the dance works.

At the same time, however, such study should be complemented with study of **external influences** -political, social, economic and cultural which affect and are reflected in the choreographers' works. Justifications and explanations of the characteristics in the works can then be supported by evidence.

Resource packs:
The above indicates a need for **a resource pack** containing a variety of materials in addition to a video performance of the dance work studied. Moreover, if resource-based teaching/learning is to be fully effective, activities should be student-centred so that individually or in groups students build up their knowledge of a dance by working through the pack systematically. For example, worksheets could direct them to read biographical excerpts, newspaper articles etc. and then answer questions which require them to reflect on the content or style of the dance work, for instance, in relation to the information gained about the choreographer's background.

A comprehensive pack would contain the following to aid the students' knowledge and understanding of a dance work:
- a video, CD ROM or video CD of the work (including detailed analysis of parts)
- a documentary programme or commentary on the work including voice-overs/interviews with the choreographer.
- a chronology of the choreographer's work and the dates and places of their premieres
- video snippets of other works by the choreographer if available
- written materials about the work, about the choreographer, about the dancers, the designer/s, the music and the composer if appropriate
- notated scores of the dance and music
- photographs showing costumes and designs
- press cuttings about the dance, the choreographer, the dancers and the company
- writings about the historical/cultural influences on the work and/or references to books or other sources from which information can be gathered.

In addition, and of great importance, the pack should contain worksheets with progressive viewing, performing, creating and historical/cultural study tasks for the students to undertake. Through these means, the students will develop their **appreciation** of the dance works studied.

INTERACTIVE VIDEO FOR RESOURCE-BASED TEACHING/LEARNING

CD video resource packs will contain all of the above content and much more.

Our proposed CD video on a Siobhan Davies work will provide different levels of viewing, composing and performing tasks to promote appreciation of Siobhan Davies' choreography.

The research problem has been to discern ways in which doors can be opened in helping students to see what is there in the work without directing them to perceive in a particular way or be influenced in interpretation of the piece. Meanings whether explicit or implicit should not be ascribed to the piece. Rather questions might be asked or discussion topics posed to promote the students' own interpretation of meanings.

To this end the following example shows how interactive video might be structured to provide a flexible and creative bank of resource materials. Open ended student-centred learning assignments will extend knowledge and understanding of the work itself and develop the students' own choreography and performance skills.

In the context of our pilot laser disc 1994-5, there are many options available for study of the one a quarter minute long quartet in Chorale 1 of *White Bird Featherless* choreographed by Siobhan Davies in 1992. These options have been designed to make accessible the distinctive features of the quartet. On first viewing one notices the unison movement and close proximity of the four dancers while they step, turn and travel across and close to the floor. The complexity of the choreography becomes more and more apparent in recurrent viewings by looking at the changing relationship of the dancers, the constant directional facing changes and the ongoing continuous flow of the piece through the actions of tipping, curving, leaning, tilting and initiation of momentum from different parts of the body.

It is proposed here that by taking the various routes through the quartet as described below, students led to perceive such richness in choreography might become better educated to appreciate the complexities for themselves on viewing the choreographer's works in the theatre.

EXAMPLE: The pilot laser disc on *White Bird Featherless* together with our multimedia investigations feature the following options of analysis of the quartet in Chorale 1 -

- text to show the relative position of this section in the whole dance work.

- text to describe the content, form and motivations behind the piece in Siobhan Davies' own words.

-voice-over descriptions of distinctive aspects in the choreography and options available to users in accessing them.

-lists of key words to describe
   a) distinctive features and
   b) dominant actions used.

- graphic representations and animations to show
   a) positioning of dancers in relation to each other,
   b) spatial pathways,
   c) directional facings,
   d) rhythmic and structural information.

- marks/highlights on the bodies of dancers to show the parts initiating momentum

- notation accompanying dancers with
   a) indications of beats and
   b) cues through a moving highlight on the notation or still frames of the movement content at key points.

- split screen showing two sections of the dance work successively and simultaneously to demonstrate repetition and development of material i.e. this quartet in relation to the solo in Chorale 4. The latter is a development of the movements in the quartet in that the movements are larger and additional actions of the head changes the rhythm.
The quartet in Chorale 1 is in itself a reduced version of a gross body action section to be seen later on in Chorale 2. The interrelationship of these parts within the whole work should be studied through worksheet tasks requiring students to discern how the choreographer uses such devices to achieve form.

- split screen showing simultaneous close-ups of body parts to identify detail.

- phrase analysis to show detailed content and relationship between key movements and transitions.

- a slow motion and frame by frame controlled progression forward and backwards through the material

- worksheets offering teachers/learners access to the richness and flexibility of the resource

(Information data on the music including relevant reference to the score, lighting, costumes, and a bibliography of critics writings, books, articles about this work and about Siobhan Davies - her choreography, company, background etc. would also be available on a future published disc. This could be accompanied by small movie pictures to illustrate points or stills).

We are continually inventing new and exciting ways of applying multimedia technology to the analysis and documentation of dance resources. The following text explains the current range of applications we intend to employ in our major project with Siobhan Davies. We are seeking sufficient funding for this project so that a very close working relationship with the choreographer results in co-publication of a CD video resource pack. In this context, the way in which the dance work is analysed will be strongly influenced by the choreographer herself.

2) INTERACTIVE VIDEO:

Interactive methodology:
This part of the paper describes how the authors have dealt with the problems defined in the earlier section by the development of original and appropriate use of interactive multimedia.

Several phrases from the earlier section define the flavour of the problems to be addressed.

>   *....movements are transient, illusive and complex*

>   *....(in video) the spatial canvas is never visible*

>   *....how to perform the actions rhythmic, dynamic,*
>   *spatial and relationship patterning*

>   *....(how to reveal) kinds of leaning, counter balance*
>   *actions (etc)...*

In addressing these, and many other problems, it is clear that solutions could not simply be a case of applying "multimedia techniques" to dance. Such a technology-led approach would not only be wrong and wholly inappropriate, but also predictably unsuccessful. Rather, it was necessary to start with the resource-based dance teaching approach, and, in addressing the problems that arise in its implementation, ADAPT, DEVELOP or, if necessary, INVENT appropriate means of handling the material using the possibilities inherent in interactive multimedia.

There are two fundamentals in the authors' approach. First, is the insistence on using only very high quality, full screen, moving video sequences, and on delivering immediate, flexible and full finger tip control of these images to the user. Secondly, there is the requirement to ADD VALUE to these images with graphic overlays, notation, animations and text, and in particular to use such means to address the problem of the contradiction between displaying the DYNAMIC and the CONTEXTUAL in movement.

The elements of dance video access:
The essence of the authors' approach is to base everything on very high quality full screen moving video sequences of the work to be studied and....

- to make any such images immediately available on screen at the touch of a button
- to allow full speed or slow motion running of the sequences
- to allow stills at any moment
- to enable a single shot, frame by frame mode of access
- to provide forward or backward movement, or loops around a particular phrase
- to allow switching to alternative views of the same sequence or..
- to allow close ups and a synchronised reference view to be on screen at the same time.

Adding value to video:
- **Early features:** The authors have engaged in a great deal of research into possible ways of adding value to such video images. In particular, they have developed the means to add synchronised animated graphic overlays to the underlying video sequence. Early examples of this in *Dance Disc 1* include:

- a map of the dance space with a moving dot for the position of the dancer in the floor pattern
- a "thermometer-like" time indicator, to show the current moment within the piece
- a display of synchronised dance notation on screen simultaneously with the moving image
- a synchronised bar count overlay
- immediately accessible phrase access lists.

- **Technological developments:** Since the completion of *Dance Disc I*, there has been a revolution in the technology of interactive video or multimedia, as it is now termed. The main development has been in the storing of video and sound in a digital, rather than analogue, format. This has resulted in a technology where the elements of a multimedia presentation are not only all stored on the same source medium, but are also all available for manipulation or processing by computer, both in the development of the product and "real time", that is, at its point of use - by the user.

Such processing allows a much more intrinsic involvement of the computer than the simple "overlaying" of computer graphics upon an unaltered, underlying video image. The images can be:
- scaled to any appropriate size
- brought together on screen in any arrangement or juxtaposition
- extracted to be used in tailor made animations
- processed to superimpose one image on another, either for comparison or as a means of analysis of a given sequence.

These developments have had a surprising effect on the area of multimedia productions. On the one hand, they have given it a very gimmicky, latest technology slant, which has emphasized such things as games and special effects, and at the same time, held back a mature application of the possibilities inherent in these technologies, until such time as it became clear which of the many competing systems would become the de facto standard and guarantee the big money returns.

Innovations: As far as the authors are concerned, these delays were unnecessary, as the important considerations had to be ones of methodology within the discipline of dance rather than technology, and these considerations are relatively independent of any particular implementation of technology.

We have concentrated, therefore, on the development of a series of techniques for presenting, studying and analysing dance movement in interactive multimedia. We believe that use of these new and powerful facilities is not only original, but makes a significant contribution to methodologies of teaching dance.

Recent Developments – CONTEXT versus DYNAMICS:
Significant recent developments have been made in tackling the major problems of the CONTEXT of a movement or its position within the phrase or section of the dance as a whole. The difficulty is that the moving image leaves no trace of what has happened before, nor does it in any way indicate how subsequent events will unfold. In our view, the use of notation to accompany the moving image does not really solve this problem, as there are many aspects that can only be found in the moving image itself.

The second problem is that any freezing of the moving image into a still, immediately loses all dynamic elements of the movement phrase and is mostly about instantaneous relative positions of the moving parts or dancers.

Historical or Context displays:
What is needed is a simultaneous display of the dynamic moving video, **and** some sort of "historical" information showing what has gone before, and, in addition, what is to come. To this end the authors have developed a series of techniques which attempt to deliver these facilities.

The first technique has been termed:

H.E.I.S.S. – Historical Equal Interval Still Sequences:
This method takes stills at equal intervals of time throughout the movement to be studied, and presents them on screen together as an array of still images or of derived diagrams. In addition to this array of stills, we show simultaneously, the moving video sequence, either immediately below or in the

middle of the still array. Also, it is possible to highlight whichever still portrays the current moment as the moving video runs, and, of course, all this is available with the full set of video controls as outlined above - that is forward, backward, stop, start, single shot, full speed, slow motion and so on.

These still sequences can simply be still video images extracted from the movie itself, but they can also be drawings specially drawn to highlight particular spatial positions, dancer orientations or directions of movement, for example.

A particularly powerful example of such drawings is termed "movement pathways". Here, a given position of a moving limb can be indicated by a dot then linked to a series of such dots as the movement unfolds. The resultant line of dots reveals the "pathway" of that movement through space and this HEISS drawing is not only shown alongside the moving image, but even more successfully, as a see-through overlay upon it. The information conveyed by such a HEISS pathway is not only in the line in space traced out by the movement, but in the indirect inferences that can be made from the spacing of the dots with regard to both velocity and acceleration.

The tracing out of the pathway as the moving video proceeds beneath it, is only one way of using this facility, while another is to manipulate the moving image, forward, backward, slow motion etc. beneath the complete HEISS pathway.

Further developments are being investigated with HEISS pathways, in particular the addition of rhythm and accent to the overlays.

The whole area of the context of a movement or phrase is not exhausted by the techniques of HEISS representations. Another development pioneered by the authors is termed:

K.E.S.S - Key Event Still Sequences:
The speciality of HEISS sequences is in detailed analysis of individual movements but another area where context needs to be displayed alongside the actual moving image is in the study of transitions between given positions.

A good example of this occurs in one of the quartet sections in *White Bird Featherless* where the four dancers move across the floor together but constantly change their relative positions within the group. To portray what is happening here it is essential not only to see the dynamic movement as it unfolds but also to indicate the differing arrangements as they occur **and** to show the whole sequence of relative positions as a context to the individual changes.

The essence of this technique, once more, is in an array of stills shown against the moving video. However, here the stills are not extracted at equal intervals of time but instead reflect "key positions" within the whole sequence of movements - hence, the description Key Event Still Sequences.

Again, these stills can be images extracted from the moving video, or, when appropriate, can be drawings.

The use of drawings has been particularly useful in the *White Bird Featherless* quartet mentioned above. Here, the KESS layout is an array of drawings showing the relative positions of the four dancers indicated by four differently coloured dots. A superimposition of these dots on the video itself would be confusing, so instead they are used in diagrams of the "plan" of the dancers (i.e. seen from above). As before, highlighting of the current position as the movie proceeds is helpful, and of course, the usual total control of the moving image allows quite detailed study of the transitions, but, in addition, a separate animated drawing version of the KESS positions is shown to "abstract" the changes of relative position from the movie. This animation is, of course, synchronised with the moving video and its "overhead view" reveals, at a glance, the transitions between adjacent Key Events.

A particularly fruitful use of KESSs, has been in looking at the key events in a sequence of two duos within *White Bird Featherless,* where the movements are connections between a series of positions of support, either mutually supporting, or by one dancer of the other.

As can be imagined, these support positions become the elements of our KESS array displayed with the moving image, but in this case, it was found useful to overlay drawn "support diagrams" on the momentarily paused video. Options for the array in this form could simply be either the images with overlay, the overlays alone as diagrams, or even some simple symbol representing the form of the support.

In another development, still images frozen from the moving video are used as a KESS facility and this is being developed into part of our P.A.T.(Phrase analysis Tool) mentioned later.

The authors have already begun to consider where both KESS and HEISS features could be made available for the same movement sequence either used as separate options, or together as an effective combination.

One other area where these ideas have been developed in a rather different direction, is in what is called:

Animated Lists:
Animated lists relate most closely to Key Event Still Sequences though here it is not video stills or drawings that we use but WORDS or PHRASES. Once again the approach is to

provide a context for the dynamically unfolding video, by the provision of an array to identify key events occurring within the particular sequence under scrutiny.

This array is a list of words or phrases that draw the users attention to some feature of the video. To link a particular phrase to the appropriate action in the video it is highlighted for a moment or two. The usual features of video control allow looping, slow motion, step by step movement etc. so the highlighted feature can be thoroughly explored in the context of the immediate transitions **and** as moments in the wider context.

Developments are now being considered to add optional audio value to these sequences where appropriate. These could be commentary, audible rhythm indicators, or dynamic audible prompts, such as a dance teacher might utter to focus the movement of his/her dancers.

An effective, if straightforward, facility which has been developed is what the authors term the:

"Living Page":
This involves use of text, stills, moving images and audio overlays. Here the form is of images surrounded by text as in a book, but with the significant difference that the image can be made to move with accompanying music and is controllable by the usual methods to give total access. In addition, optional voice overs could be brought in at the touch of a button.

An appropriate use of this facility has been in juxtaposing the choreographer's own explanations, descriptions or motivations concerning the piece alongside the moving image itself, and even his/her audible prompts and instructions to the dancers as the piece is performed.

Notation as contextual information:
Labanotation alongside the moving video image or, in the case of Benesh notation, underneath it, provides a short contextual analysis of the movement. More recent additions by the authors have included an overlayed graphic pulsating beat or moving bar line as the dancer performs the movements and cues of still or moving images at appropriate moments in the score. Multimedia processes also provide facilities to separate the notation from the moving image, enlarge it and display it elsewhere, including, of course, printed out on paper.

Montage and other layouts:
All these new facilities are based on the addition of extra information to high quality video, but just how these are brought together as an on-screen montage is not a trivial matter and requires great care and sensitivity to the needs of the user/dance teacher in relation to the purposes of the multimedia author. To simply crowd in as much as possible onto

the screen, with movement of different kinds taking place simultaneously, would generally be confusing. What is needed is a clear idea of which is the major element, how big it must be to perform the function adequately, and how the other elements are accessed as a movement proceeds. It could be that the moving video and dance notation elements are equally important during the learning of the movement, so that a 50/50 split screen is the best layout. Later on, when reference to the notation is there merely as a prompt or reminder, the optimum screen might have a much bigger video element and a see-through, so called head-up-display (HUD) for the notation.

Access to and manipulation of the resource is by on-screen menus that are controlled by a keyboard, mouse or joy-stick, so these are ever present. In addition, the more common elements are:
Video Windows
    Animation Windows
        HEISS Array Areas
            KESS Array Areas
                Notation Areas
                    Animated List Areas
                        Text Areas

These elements can be scaled to appropriate sizes, and can be OVERLAPPED, TILED or presented as transparent HUD displays.

It is even possible to have the same elements, doing the same things brought together in quite different layouts, depending on the stage the user is at, or the particular use the dance teacher is making of the materials.

A full discussion of all the layouts the authors have used in the current project alone would be too long to undertake in this paper, so we will at this stage simply list the most useful types that have been used. These are:

HEISS Array Layout (HAL)	- uses Video Window, Animation Window, Menus & HEISS Array
KESS Array Layout (KAL)	- uses Video Window, Animation Window, Menus & KESS Array
Still HEISS Array Layout (S-HAL)	- uses an Array of HEISS stills & Menus
Animated HEISS Array Layout (A-HAL)	- uses Animation Window, Array of HEISS stills & Menus
Detail and Reference Layout including Split Screen (DAR-LISS)	- uses two Video Windows, one giving a close up of detail the other a reference picture to give context, plus menus

Comparative Layout including Split Screen (C-LISS)	- uses two Video Windows, usually equal in size, of different parts of the dance, text area & menus
Animated List Layout (ALL)	- uses Video Window, Animated List Area and menus
Text Overlay Layout (TOL)	- uses Video Window, Text Area and menus - "Living Page" Layout
Notation Overlay Layout (NOL)	- uses Video Window, Notation Area & menus

SUMMARY AND CONCLUSION:

The above innovations have resulted in an extended library of facilities for application of multimedia to video material in dance and other movement fields. There is no doubt that this work constitutes the basis for further development and for very successful production of much needed materials for dance education and training.

Each of the processes described above has been written as an editor so that the discipline expert (in this instance in dance education) can access and manipulate the image and accompanying overlays/notation etc. to best effect for teaching/learning purposes. So far, we have six such editors - the

> **Synchro Editor** written for *Dance Disc 1*
> **Historical Equal Interval Still Sequence Editor HEISS**
> **Key Event Still Sequence Editor KESS**
> **Animated List Editor**
> **Notation Editor**
> **Text Editor**

Digital Video is of course a major break through and the obvious advantages of this technology will be fully utilised in our future work. To date, **digitised loops of movement phrases, canon effects, pathways of movements, and notation cues/graphic beat/bar indicators** are some of the processes we have employed in the pilot project. Many more applications will emerge as the research progresses towards our major project.

Two major problems of digital multimedia for dance/movement are a) the size of the files and b) the number of frames per second capability of the system. In the latter case, the minimum requirements for dance/movement is 25 frames per second. Although in some instances pictures could be quite small and a moving image at six frames per second could be used as reference for notation for example, in the majority of the resource pack full frame and full speed motion pictures are essential. To this end and to date therefore we are insistent upon production of materials in CDi or its equivalent technology for our future products. Also, CDi is exceptionally cheap and user friendly for dance teachers/students. This is an important consideration.

However, it is clear that we should be capable of delivering to the full range of the market including VHS video, CDROM and CDi. Future proposals will encompass all of these outlets.

References and relevant further reading:

Schofield J.   1988   Developing Expert Systems for Biological Keys on the IBM PC in *Research and Academic Users Guide to the IBM PC.* Vol. 2.

Schofield J.   1993   Multimedia in the Teaching of Dance Performance in *The Choreologist 44* Winter 1992/3.

Schofield J.   1992   The Use of Interactive Video and Superimposed Animated Parametered Figures in Dance Teaching and Choreography in *Compugraphics Proceedings* Dec. 1992. Calouste Gulbenkian Foundation, Lisbon.

Smith   J.M.   1991   Teaching Dance Performance in Secondary Education in *British Journal of Physical Education* Winter 1991

Smith-Autard J.1992   *Dance Composition: A Practical Guide for Teachers 2nd Edition* - reprinted 1994 A.& C. Black.

Smith-Autard J.1994   Expression and Form in the Art of Dance in Education in *6th Triennial daCi Conference Proceedings* Macquarie University.

Smith-Autard J.1994   *The Art of Dance in Education* A. &. C. Black.

Other publications by the above authors:
               1989   *Dance Disc 1-* Interactive laser disc Bedford College of Higher Education.

               1995   *Demonstration Reel** - VHS video Bedford Interactive.

* This free video is available to universities, dance training institutions, dance companies and choreographers who might be interested to work with us in developing multimedia resources for dance education and training. Apply to: Bedford Interactive, 35 Castle Road, Bedford MK40 3PL

COLLABORATIONS

Ian Spink
Second Stride

in discussion with

Richard Allen Cave
Royal Holloway, University of London

RAC: While the audience were assembling you chose to show extracts on video of *Escape at Sea*, which was staged in 1993. That was an unusual piece in that, while you were working with several people like Orlando Gough and Antony McDonald with whom you have collaborated before, you were actually sharing the choreography with Ashley Page. The original intention had been to share the work between three choreographers. Would you like to say something about this?

Ian Spink: Antony McDonald, who was to direct *Escape at Sea*, was interested in a number of ideas. There was the fairy story of *The Sleeping Beauty* which, with its many connections with ballet, he felt had considerable resonance. He was also interested in Chekhov's play, *The Seagull*, and he felt there was some kind of connection between these two pieces of theatre. He was also fascinated by a story that he had been shown which was written by a Russian oceanographer who, in the days when it was difficult to get out of Russia, went on a Pacific cruise and jumped overboard somewhere off the Philippines, thinking that he would be only two or three miles from the shore. He ended up spending about four days in the sea before finally coming to land; he is now living in America. His account of his journey is entitled *Escape in the Ocean*.

Antony was interested in the idea of someone escaping from their homeland and of going to a new place. There is an element in *The Seagull* that has to do with people becoming dispossessed. I think most of Chekhov's plays are about people moving into new times and coming to grips with social change. And Antony felt that the story of *The Sleeping Beauty* was similar to the story of Russia. Possibly during the period of the Tsars or during the final years of the Communist period, Russia had a sense of being asleep.

He decided he wanted to work with three choreographers who, moving through different styles, would each deal with one of these different starting points. The performers were all to be dancers. We set to work to try and make this happen. As Anthony was also designing the piece during rehearsals, he had quite a lot on his plate. We three choreographers also had a lot to do, as we realised quite swiftly that Antony was not going to be sitting out there as director giving instructions to us as to what to do. We were in the room with the dancers, and we had to make things happen and make sense of things.

We decided on a structure based on the story, *Escape in the Ocean*, beginning with the man talking about Russia and why he wanted to get away. In another section he was talking about being on the ship and what was going on around him there. He also spoke about the preparations for diving overboard. Another section had to do with his actual dive, which may have taken only a few seconds, but which lasted quite some time in his mind. Then there was the period when he was in the sea and after a day or two he started to hallucinate through, I suppose, sheer tiredness and to remember things in his past or imagine there were things in the sea with him. We had a section on this, dealing with dreams and memories. Then we added a final section which had to do with arriving in a new place. We decided he would reach America in the Thirties and so complete his journey.

There was an element in the way the piece developed which was rather organic. We spent a lot of time trying to work out a structure that we felt was straightforward and clear. In some ways we constructed the story independently of the material, and in some ways we were using the material itself to dictate how the structure and the narrative should work. Because there was a combined input from the composer, Orlando Gough, and from Antony, Ashley Page, the other choreographer, and myself (we lost a choreographer [Eval Rubin] somewhere along the way for various reasons), we all had a slightly different influence on how each of the sections worked and on what it comprised. The first section, for example, became a rather monolithic, unison movement for four couples wearing heavy greatcoats, whereas the second section was a series of dances for groups of people that were interspersed with sections of text from *The Seagull* spoken in Russian by the performers through hand-held microphones. Within this section, therefore, there were a couple of different elements at work, and there was too a distancing effect in the handling of some of the material. For a later section we created text for the dancers: it was a kind of collage, mixing text with taped, spoken and sung sounds which drew on a mass of material concerning memories that we got through interviews with people who had lived in Russia during the early part of this century. Much of this had to do with early experimental data relating to the oceans, sea currents and so on. We were trying through this to find a way of communicating the things that might have been going through the man's head as he drifted in the Pacific.

Antony was quite preoccupied with the idea of people speaking in languages that most of us would not understand. Hence the idea of using the original Russian text for the Chekhov was important to him. He was also keen to put in parts of the original fairy story of *The Sleeping Beauty*.[1] At the beginning of several major sections of the piece different stages of the story were related in French. The effect of this on the audience may have been to excite them to find connections: they would be aware of someone saying something to them, and they would have to discover clues as to what it was all about.[2]

RAC: This multi-layered quality is a distinctive characteristic of your work and the collaborations you have pursued with a number of people. Is this one inevitable outcome of so many people contributing to the art work, that it builds up these layers of ideas and possible meanings?

Ian Spink: I think it is. It is a very dangerous kind of situation because naturally we tend to try and protect the areas that we understand and know and can deal with—and try to keep the unknown at bay. With *Escape at Sea* I sense that we are doing two things at once: we are trying to introduce things that we know will de-stabilise the whole structure; yet at the same time we are trying to hang on to something that we know. Generally that's the way that Second Stride works: we tend to walk the razor edge between keeping control of the whole thing and losing it. That is quite an interesting dynamic.

RAC: Do you ever feel you have "lost it"?

Ian Spink: Yes. It is a traumatic period making this dynamic work, where you have possibly to compromise or adjust or change because of other elements that have suddenly become important—so much so that you lose sight of where you are going.

Maybe this is something that naturally happens in the creation of anything like this. It is certainly a principle that underlies all the work we set out to do: we set up a group of people and confront them with a series of ideas and then leave them to deal with each other.

RAC: You have become more and more daring over the years with each collaboration. You started working with designers and musicians in unusual ways. But all theatre dance involves collaboration to some degree with designers and musicians, so that initial experimenting on your part was in a sense working within known parameters. But then you began to introduce dramatists, writers of opera, creators of film into the equation, and in so doing you have pushed more and more against the borders separating art forms. Why have you felt impelled to do that? What has been the inspiration and the impulse?

Ian Spink: I'm really interested in making work that hasn't solved itself, that presents a series of questions or problems that might be solved, ideally, in any number of different ways. I want to make work where the viewer or the audience can connect parts together in an individual way. I know from experience that some audiences can find this rather irritating or incredibly obscure.[3] But I like to feel, if I am watching a performance like this, that every time I see it I will see something new in it, something different, that is not merely to do with the way it is being performed but to do with the way I perceive it, the way I taste it, that I hear it and understand it. In order to achieve responses like that, it is important to keep feeding ideas and people into the working situation, so that it is not just a single viewpoint or a single idea that emerges, but a *series* of responses and ideas that have moved together within the creative process.

I suppose it is true that formerly when I was getting grants from dance departments, I had to produce work that had the look of dance and had dancers in it and sometimes music and special costumes.[4] But then when I was working on a piece which was eventually entitled *Bosendorfer Waltzes*,[5] the designer [Antony McDonald] chose to set up an element within the piece that was nothing to do with design but was purely to do with characters, characterisation and using text. He required the six dancers involved to engage in an improvisation: they were to go away for two weeks and research a surrealist of their choice. Then they had to give a 20-minute lecture in the style of this artist, and they did this in various living rooms around London. For some of the performers it was quite a shock being asked to improvise in that fashion. They each had to research a subject very precisely and thoroughly, and then the rest of the group had to do an improvisation based on the surrealist who had been researched. Subsequently that material was fitted into the piece that we were creating and became one of the threads. Perhaps as the choreographer or director of that work, I could have decided that the improvisations were just part of the rehearsal process, which we could then throw away and pass on. But I felt quite strongly that we should include that process as part of the product. You will find that happening in a lot of the works that Second Stride stage. There are things that we do in the process that may be just improvisations or mad ideas that we ultimately decide to keep, because we think they are valuable to the final structure.

RAC: Improvisation happens often in rehearsal with actors but less often with dancers, I suppose?

Ian Spink: In my experience there is a phase that some actors go through where they have to do a lot of improvisation so that they know how to do something very simple like sitting down on a chair. You can say to a dancer: "Just walk over there and sit on that chair"; and they do not need to ask questions about how to do that, because it is not something that worries them. But some actors actually have problems doing that.

With actors there is another interesting stage that you go through in rehearsal. In *A Mouthful Of Birds*, for example, we spent four or five weeks improvising. Some fine material came out of those improvisations, yet the material never ended up in the final product because there was a further stage that that particular piece went through. The two playwrights [Caryl Churchill and David Lan] went away and wrote scenes that were devised out of their responses to the improvisations. That was another invention on top of the improvisations. It's a pity that in *A Mouthful Of Birds* we were not able to translate more of the improvisatory work directly into the final piece!

The way that I personally work when arranging movement is that I generally do not tell people what to do. I try and get them to do it; I like being fed information that is coming from the performers rather than me saying, "I want you to put your foot here." There are choreographers who show a step to the dancer and the dancer repeats. It is useful to work with people again, if the relationship is meaningful for both parties, because you develop a shorthand. You can communicate things and create material very rapidly without having to go through lots of explanation. I think it is important that the performers that I work with have a creative stake in the work, so that they are not doing something that is imposed on them. Every performer is different in what they will give and the risks they are prepared to take. Some people I have worked with are prepared to take the most incredible risks, and that is wonderful and very exciting. But one has to be careful when one has those people alongside people who have to know absolutely and precisely everything that they are doing and need to protect themselves. I am not interested in having a company that is completely one or the other. I quite like having those differences, having those individual responses.[6]

RAC: You have moved on to talk of Caryl Churchill in referring to *A Mouthful Of Birds*, so shall we discuss your work with her in more detail? It seems to me that it is in your collaborations with her that you have really been pushing most creatively against the borders dividing dance from drama. What has been the attraction in this for you? You've worked on four projects with her to date: *A Mouthful Of Birds*, *Fugue*, *Lives of the Great Poisoners*, and *The Skriker*.[7]

Ian Spink: A Mouthful of Birds[8] was the first time I worked with her. I was invited into this project that had been set up by the now defunct Joint Stock Theatre Company, which had probably started off with the two writers and it was decided to bring in a choreographer. Joint Stock had a creative method which involved a director taking a writer and a group of actors and doing a period of improvisations around a given theme. Then they would take a break during which the writer would go away and write a play based on those initial improvisations—which were designed to provide the dramatist with ideas and material. The whole group would then reconvene and rehearse the finished play. *A Mouthful Of Birds* was an extension of that method, in that they decided they wanted to involve a choreographer in the process and that they did not want to have a separate writing period. Improvisation, writing and rehearsal would be a continuous process with no standing-back period. We worked with a group of four actors and three dancers and were trying through improvisation to break down the barriers that have existed between these two different camps. To a certain extent, we were successful; particularly so for me in scenes where you were not quite sure what element, dance or drama, you were experiencing. There was one plot in the piece, for example, that had to do with a businessman, Paul, who falls in love with a pig. That was written by Caryl and the stage directions were quite simple sometimes: "PAUL dances with the PIG, tenderly."[9] We had to figure out how that could happen within the structure which had Paul stepping out from an acted episode with another actor into a scene that was danced, and the shift had to seem effortless.

During the process we were working out how far we could go with each other. There were sometimes situations where we felt restricted by somebody else's idea of what the structure should be or what the appropriate style should be. I certainly felt restricted at times by the way the writers were protective of their work and would not allow it to be moved around.

RAC: Did they give a reason why they wanted you to join them in the first place? Because obviously they had initiated the project and knew where they were going with it. Then you were invited in on it, when it was already in a *formed* state.

Ian Spink: I think there were probably two reasons. One was that Caryl was fascinated by working with dance and for a number of years she had been trying to get hold of me or Sue [Siobhan] Davies to collaborate on something. The other reason was a classic case of pigeon holing: one of the source materials for *A Mouthful Of Birds* was Euripides' tragedy, *Bacchae*, and as soon as anyone attempts to stage that play, they have call in a movement expert. They feel that a choreographer is the only person who can deal with the kinds of problems the play sets a cast and director: people being torn apart or going mad.

RAC: In subsequent collaborations you have done with Caryl Churchill have you been in on the act right from the start, or again as with *A Mouthful Of Birds* were you brought in after the work had in large measure been shaped?

Ian Spink: The next project we did together was *Fugue.*[10] I was offered a film-slot on one of the Dance on Four programmes, and I said I wanted both to direct and choreograph and to work with Caryl and create a piece that contained text and movement. We talked at length about a possible structure and, for some reason, we started looking at the Bach fugues which I had worked with in the past. Caryl became fascinated by the fugue form and the potential of writing dialogue that was fugal. She decided to write about death and memory because that would allow her to keep coming back to themes and phrases.

Possibly what we set out to do could have been done better in a theatre or a studio, because I soon realised that directing a film is difficult when you are also involved in creating, rehearsing and constructing parts of it. We also took on quite a task by working in a number of different locations (many outside, which at the time were freezing cold). Mainly what Caryl and I got out of the experience was a greater sense of how one use a musical structure for a play, though we both realised we had used a difficult example to test out our premise.

I next worked with Caryl on a project on which she and Orlando Gough had decided to collaborate with each other. It took a year of discussions before we finished up with the idea of a performance peopled with famous poisoners throughout history. Caryl wished to explore the idea of performers doubling parts and characters—virtually transforming into different characters in history, which was a device she had used before in plays like *Top Girls,*[11] where she takes people from different points in history and juxtaposes them together.

After a period of working closely together, Caryl and Orlando came up with *Lives of the Great Poisoners,*[12] in a form that was like an opera. There were to be five *a cappella* singers—that is, without accompaniment. We decided that the rest of the performers would have a character in each historical sequence, but that they would work in their own medium, not stepping out of it at all. There was a group of dancers who danced their characters throughout the piece; the singers sang their characters; the two actors acted their way through the piece. It proved quite a difficult process keeping people working strictly within their own original territory. Feedback I subsequently got from some of the dancers suggested that they felt unhappy about being restricted and not being able to use their voices either to sing or express their characters by using text. We experimented with pursuing our way within very strict guidelines and following these right to the end, which we succeeded in doing. Orlando, for example, had decided that he would not use any instruments in composing for the piece and he managed to do that.

RAC: How did you rehearse *Lives of the Great Poisoners*, given the multiple kinds of expertise that you were using in every scene?

Ian Spink: It was rather like rehearsing an opera, since the all-important musical element had to be rehearsed separately before we could get the rest off the ground. There was also a choreographed element which had to be worked out separately. So actually there were many separate threads to rehearse and then we had to edge them together and make necessary adjustments. Some of the scenes were highly complex. For example, towards the end in the section dealing with Mme de Brinvilliers there is a gambling party involving considerable intrigue between the various characters. This involved characters having to move across stage to make connections with an accomplice or confidant. These characters were all singing while moving into their different formations, and all the time a rather bizarre ballet for the dancers [representing a chorus of poisons] was taking place between them. Some kind of logic had to be followed, and I had to keep taking the dancers away to alter their material so that it would fit within the larger stage patterns of movement. The actors had to concentrate on whom they were watching as distinct from whom they were talking to and on where they were positioned within the stage space. Within all this complex action the card game continued to be played. Devising the scene felt like trying to put some amazing jigsaw puzzle together.

With *Lives of the Great Poisoners* Caryl decided we should have a director to handle the material involving spoken text [James MacDonald, who had directed several of her earlier plays]. So we had a director who worked mostly with the actors and singers on the scenes that seemed to require that kind of input, while I worked on and directed scenes that were much more choreographed or "moved". I did not really see myself as a choreographer on the piece; rather I felt I was a co-director within a rather special working structure of relationships.

RAC: So staging the play was a major collaboration in its own right?

Ian Spink: Yes: it was really quite a test in many ways. We also discovered that the actual material that the singers had to deal with (because in fact they are singing from beginning to end) was quite difficult, and so they needed constant help from a musical director. There were many unknown and unexpected things that we discovered during the rehearsals, and we had to be able to adjust quite rapidly to change.

RAC: Some time ago when you and I were discussing your work with Caryl Churchill, you observed that the notable thing about Caryl is that she is always very loyal. I misinterpreted that remark, thinking you meant she was a reliably supportive person. What you actually meant was that she was always very focused on the original conception of a given piece. Did you find this difficult, seeing that you have said you like to enter rehearsals with a sense of an open end, of creative possibilities, of being prepared to let things go anywhere?

Ian Spink: I do, yes. I think that is something that I found difficult at times with Caryl. She says we are going to do it this way, and she clings on to that idea. I like making rules, but I like to make them knowing that I might well be changing them.

RAC: Are you suggesting that when Caryl writes she has a very clear sense in her own imagination of what she wants to see on the stage?

Ian Spink: No, she does not have a picture of what the work will look like. That's what I like about her so much. She has a strong feeling about what the piece is to be about, and that is a very good starting point for directing or choreographing the material. She gives you a starting point which is potentially very rich and has a number of possibilities. She is very generous; she will continue to follow you, as you search out the way of visualising or realising what the material could yield and become. I would be quite interested in seeing Caryl directing. She has worked closely with directors, and I would like to see her step into that position.

RAC: Does she ever exercise a right of veto and say, "No, I just don't like that; go and change it"?

Ian Spink: No, I don't think she does. There was another writer on *A Mouthful Of Birds* [David Lan] who was very clear about what he wanted. He had seen very precisely how his scenes would be set up and staged. I found that a problem sometimes. I was written into those scenes and had to create movement material for them. I felt occasionally I was coming up against a brick wall. I seem to recall hearing the line once or twice: "This is not what I want."

RAC: May we move on to your most recent collaboration with Caryl, which was *The Skriker* at the National Theatre, a very demanding piece.[13] Was that a collaboration from the start or did she conceive the play and bring you in on its production? How did *The Skriker* evolve?

Ian Spink: It was a play that Caryl had been writing for about nine years or so. She has certainly been writing it ever since I have known her, and she has kept talking about it, tantalisingly. Certainly her experience with some of our earlier pieces together, which used movement and deployed dancers and actors together, influenced the way that she came to see *The Skriker*: the ways that things might happen on stage, the ways characters would develop and scenes be shaped. She has created a play that is immensely rich. She has made a piece that is like two pieces occurring simultaneously in the same space. Caryl was eager that I be involved in the movement aspect of the whole piece. To be frank I was desperate to get my hands on directing the piece, but that was not to be. At least, not yet! So we had a director and a choreographer, a group of people who were not necessarily dancers but who did not have any spoken parts, and a small group of actors. We worked separately, in separate rooms.

RAC: Was there a reason for that?

Ian Spink: Possibly not a good reason. It was a tactical reason. The opening speech for the Skriker lasts for some five pages of the printed text and that speech had to be cracked very early in the rehearsal process. The way that Caryl writes scenes is sometimes quite difficult for people to get hold of. There needs to be quite a lot of rehearsal on how the characters work and the scenes work. Possibly because there was a director and a movement director that tended to channel things into separate ways of working. We would work for days and days without actually seeing what each other was doing.

RAC: So staging *Skriker* was not the collaborative venture you had experienced with *Poisoners*?

Ian Spink: I think it's so difficult with a play that's written completely. Obviously there was territory that the actors had to go through to get hold of their characters, but I think we should have set up situations where we worked together as an ensemble a lot more.

RAC: Again you had very little help in approaching the choreography other than bald stage directions, and yet you were required to create strange, other-worldly figures.[14] You mentioned your earnest wish to direct the play. How would you have directed it in ways that were different from the National Theatre production?

Ian Spink: I don't know whether the bulk of the problem I was having with the piece was because I was working with a director who seemed from a different world and a designer who seemed from a different world, or whether it was because I was working within the National Theatre, which has its own structure and way of working. It is rather difficult sometimes to get things done or to do things how you would wish. Certainly it might be possible for a production of the play to be created more organically, for it to shift and adjust, based on what you come up with in rehearsal. I feel that Caryl's work can be treated more like a list of possibilities rather than treated strictly according to the letter, so that one can interpret her stage directions, for example, in a number of ways.

RAC: Where are you likely to move after this in terms of future collaborations? Clearly the fact that you have gone on collaborating with a number of people several times over means that these projects do work very well, or else you would not come together to experiment in yet more adventurous ways. What might you do next?

Ian Spink: In August I am staging with the National Youth Dance Company and Peter Brooks, whom I have never worked with before, a play by Peter Handke which is called *The hour we knew nothing of each other*. It was at last year's Edinburgh Festival[15] and is a play entirely without words, with only stage directions, in which four hundred characters walk on stage, do something, and then leave. As you can see, the piece is a huge problem in terms of directing, but an exciting one.

I am also working with Second Stride on a new piece called *Badenheim*, based on a novel by a Jewish writer who was about nine years old when the Holocaust was happening.[16] He has written a story about a holiday resort in Austria in 1939, describing the things that go on in this town—like a music festival and the various characters there. Then at the end of the story everyone goes to the railway station and gets on a cattle train. We are making a theatre piece for a company of 14 musicians, dancers and actors, which is quite large for Second Stride. We plan to pick up an extra 10 performers in every place we go to and incorporate them into the production via a week-long period of workshopping. It could be a nightmare!

We have also involved the author of the book [Aron Appelfeld], and he is partly, I suppose, a collaborator in the venture. He was there as a child and he is writing about his parents. The way we plan to deconstruct and reconstruct his story should lead to interesting dialogues. We have researched the project for about a year through material that is grim, bleak and disturbing. *Badenheim* is about a group of people who in a very human sort of way deny that they are in any sort of danger; yet the danger is deadly. They deceive themselves, and they spend a lot of time trying to have a good time— enjoying the sun and walks in the hills—within the context of a terrifying period of European history.

RAC: When you say you have been researching, do you mean you have already got your cast and that you are involving them in the work?

Ian Spink: We have been interviewing and auditioning, and we should have decided within the next couple of weeks. We are hoping to be writing text for the actors and deciding on characters once we know precisely who the cast are.

RAC: Are you using the author to write your text, or are you bringing someone in as playwright?

Ian Spink: No, we are communicating with the author and occasionally having meetings with him, letting him know where we are and taking his comments. It feels like a rather dangerous situation to me.

RAC: Well, you said just now you like danger, which brings us nicely full circle.

Ian Spink: Actually as you were speaking, I was thinking that I do not consider myself a dangerous person. I think I'm a bit timid and careful, and perhaps what I am doing in these situations is facilitating a meeting point of different views with the intention of attempting to accommodate them all somehow. It is important that people within the collaborative situation can engage with each other, engage with different viewpoints. Structure is a very important part of the process—talking about structure and making structure (even if it eventually gets thrown away). There is always a point when people have to take control of their particular territory. There has to be a situation of trust and that can only be developed through people fighting everything out right to the bitter end, through knowing and being clear about what they want, and through being very honest about what they want and why. Sometimes the situation does feel very dangerous.

Notes

1.   *La Belle au bois dormant* was originally published by Charles Perrault in his *Contes de ma mere l'Oye* in 1697.

2.   Characteristically the reviewer for *The Times* (Nadine Meisner) was not impressed by this complexity of reference. Under a headline reading "Erudite but Empty", she concluded: "It must do wonders for the company's cultural education, but a reckless amalgam of literary parallels does not a show make" (*The Times*, 9 November 1993, p.33). *Escape At Sea* was a sell-out, however, at the box-office.

3.   David Dougill's review of *Escape At Sea* for *The Sunday Times* (14 November 1993) concludes by posing a whole series of questions about what certain moments of action or images in the work *mean* and adds that *"Escape At Sea* falls victim to a long-

proven pitfall of the mixed-media format: that it's impossible for an audience to con-centrate equally on dance and a spoken or sung text, if they are going on simultane-ously."

4.   Second Stride lost its Arts Council funding on the grounds that the company had forsaken dance. *Escape At Sea* was made possible by a Digital Dance Award.

In answer to a question from the audience at the end of the discussion as to whether he nowadays saw himself as a choreographer, Spink replied: "Certainly I would use the term 'choreographer' if I was working in a situation where there was a strict definition of that type of role, as in opera, or if I was working in a strict theatrical way, like when I worked once or twice with the RSC as the movement adviser. The work that I enjoy the most is being the kind of general, overall manipulator of people, and I consider that more to be a sort of director. I may go into the territory of just working with movement, or I may go into the territory of assembling a text, or I may get other people to make the movement. 'Choreographer' for me is an old connotation back in my past or back in *the* past."

5.   This collaboration between Spink, Orlando Gough and Antony McDonald was staged at the Place Theatre in March 1986. In addition to exploring a vein of ideas relating to the Surrealist movement, *Bosendorfer Waltzes* also deconstructed Fokine's *The Firebird*.

6.   In response to a question posed later from the floor, Spink elaborated on this point: "There was a time when I was possibly working more in situations where a lot of material was taken from the performer. Possibly not in a positive way, possibly expos-ing them. Maybe too much of the performer was being used as the material of the piece. I think I moved away from that a few years ago. I do not actually know how Pina Bausch works, but my impressions of seeing her work and talking with some of the people who have worked with her is that she gets quite a lot of material from people, from inside of people. I admire her work a lot, but there can sometimes be problems created by the performers themselves not having the technique to deal with the fact that they are actually exposed in a rather dangerous sort of way. I don't know whether her performers have worked out a way of dealing with that, but I was getting the impression a while ago that in fact some of them were not and they were ending up in rather distressing situations. They did not know how to deal with other people on stage in a performance, because they were not quite sure what the other performers were going to do."

7.   A question from a member of the audience asked how Spink felt about only the *text* of these collaborative performance-works being published, when one of the big issues in live performance today is how we document it. Spink replied that the first such piece that Second Stride had published was *Lives Of The Great Poisoners* and that he thought "publishing was a good thing— not so much because the text was pub-lished or that it was a piece that Second Stride had produced but the idea of a piece appearing in that form is a good one. The idea needs to go further. Unfortunately, it would be prohibitively expensive to pay a choreologist to write down what was hap-pening on stage." The text of *Poisoners* does, however, include the music and essays by each of the four collaborators: Churchill, Gough, Spink and MacDonald. The ques-tion was then posed whether Ian Spink minded being "written out of the published text." He answered: "I guess that's life, really. It did feel very strange with *A Mouthful Of Birds* that it was accepted that the writers would go away and write—that they could publish their plays and earn money and royalties—when in fact a lot of the

material that went into the piece came from the actors and a lot of ideas about the structure of the piece came from me. Those names do not appear on the title page (they do appear elsewhere). The idea of the author in the traditional sense obviously does not work very well in these kinds of pieces."

8.   *A Mouthful Of Birds* opened at the Birmingham Repertory Theatre in September 1986 and toured nationally before opening for a season at the Royal Court Theatre in London on 26 November. The published text credits both Ian Spink and Les Waters with directing the production, which was designed by Annie Smart.

9.   Caryl Churchill and David Lan: *A Mouthful Of Birds* (London: Methuen, 1986) p.44.

10.   This was broadcast as part of the Dance on Four season for 1988 on 26 June.

11.   First staged at the Royal Court Theatre, London on 28 August 1982.

12.   The production was first performed at the Arnolfini, Bristol on 13 February 1991, and went on a short national tour before a series of performances at the Riverside Studios, London. The poisoners in question were Medea; Dr. Crippen; Mme de Brinvilliers; and Thomas Midgeley, the inventor of leaded petrol and CFCs, "who inadvertently became the *greatest* poisoner of all time."

13.   *The Skriker* was first performed at the Cottesloe Theatre on 20 January 1994. The director was Les Waters and the designer Annie Smart, the team that had worked with Caryl Churchill on *A Mouthful Of Birds*. The music was composed by Judith Weir. The demanding role of the Skriker was played by Kathryn Hunter, and the cast also included Philippe Giraudeau and Stephen Goff, dancers associated with Second Stride, who had previously played in *A Mouthful Of Birds*.

14.   The *danced* or *moved* characters are all drawn from English folk lore: Yallery Brown, the Black Dog, a Kelpie, a Green Lady, a Bogle, Rawheadandbloodybones, Nellie Longarms, the Spriggan, and Black Annis.

15.   This production was directed by Luc Bondy.

16.   Aron Appelfeld: *Badeheim, 1939*. trans. Dalya Bilu. (London: Dent, 1984).

New Formations in Dance Studies: A Critical Appraisal

Helen Thomas, Department of Sociology, Goldsmiths College,University of London

This paper[1] focuses on a consideration of certain aspects of developments in dance research that have taken place over the past several years that bear witness to a shift of interests towards the social, cultural sciences and humanities. The aim is to assess the value and/or the problems that arise from the growing predilection in what might be called 'new' dance studies [2] to graft discourses stemming from literary and/or cultural studies, particularly those informed by poststructuralism and postmodernism, onto the analysis of dance. In the course of this, I shall also consider what it is about these discourses that makes them so appealing to dance writers. This will entail some lengthy diversions away from dance towards a discussion of certain points of reference that seem to underpin the discourses. I shall focus on writing that addresses western theatrical dance, although the aforementioned discourses have also had an impact on dance analyses that are not centred on performance (see, for example, Cowan 1990, Novack 1990, Sklar 1991)[3].

However, I am not going to discuss the shift towards a theorization of 'culture' in dance scholarship in an objectivist manner. Rather, the intention is not only to locate these changes with reference to particular aspects of the work of writers like Foster (1986), Adair (1992), Dempster (1988) (Daly 1991a,b), Cooper Albright 1990), but also through the lenses of the evolution of my writing on dance over this time span. This relates to a commitment to the practice of self-reflexivity, to situate the discourses that ground my voice in relation to those of others with and of whom I speak. The individual is situated in and articulated through a complex web of social relations, discourses and practices. There is a constant interchange between the writing self(ves) (in this case the particular-woman-academic) and other(s) (texts, authors, discourses) and that interrelationship is worthy of exploration. So it is from this point that I wish to begin: from a space that is already enmeshed in a range of discourses and practices to the engagement with the others (texts, authors, discourses) I encounter(ed) through the journey into the dance research maze.

When I began to direct serious attention towards formulating a sociological framework for analysing dance in the early 1980s, there were very few places in dance scholarship or sociology where a budding sociologist of dance could go to directly to draw inspiration for theorizing the relations between dance and culture[4]. My attention was directed to just about everywhere apart from current dance research in order to set out the basis for a methodology that would attend to the specificity of dance as a reflexive practice on the one hand and the social facticity of dance on the other, except perhaps dance anthropology and certain aspects of the phenomenology of dance. Ultimately I found my direction through two main avenues: first, the idea of the text, image etc. being more than the some of the parts that comprise it, that was gaining credibility in the sociology of art and culture through the increasingly pervasive influence of structuralism and semiotics in Anglo-American academic circles; second, the contention that the body is a symbol of society that stemmed from the Durkheimian tradition of thought (see Polhemus 1975, Thomas 1995) which situated the body firmly in the domain of culture and as a site for sociological inquiry.

When I began to rework this material in 1992, it was clear that certain changes had taken place in dance scholarship both here and in the US since the late 1980s which have centred around a concern to explicate the relations between dance and culture and to analyze dance as a mode of representation. In many respects these shifts echoed changes that had reverberated through the social sciences and the humanities during the 1980s which were characterised by:

> ...a series of crises of representation, in which older modes of defining, appropriating and recomposing the objects of artistic, philosophical, literary and social scientific languages are no longer credible and in which one common aspect is the dissolution of the very boundary between language and its object, this in turn being related to the acceptance of the inevitability of a plurality of perspectives and the dissolution of various older polarities (popular/elite forms, subject/object) and boundaries (for instance between disciplines such as philosophy, sociology, history and psychoanalysis). (Boyne & Rattansi 1990: 12)

The 'crises in representation' in the various discourses, in part, can be characterized by the challenges to the dominant cultural hegemony of modernity posed by postmodernist, poststructuralist and feminist analyses. It would have been almost impossible for anyone engaged in the sociology of culture in the 1980s not to have been affected by the way in which the influential 'linguistic turn' of semiotics was itself being turned upon by deconstructionism. Similarly, the concepts of postmodernism/modernism and postmodernity/modernity and the related issues they engendered became highly contested areas (Featherstone 1988). What Stuart Hall once referred to as the 'steamroller' of structuralism' moving over cultural studies and the social sciences in the late 1970s could be used equally to point to the impact of postmodernism and poststructuralism in the 1980s.

In the early 1980s, 'culture' was seen as a rather marginal (and somewhat unworthy) area of sociological analyses, in comparison to the more established areas of class, power and social structure that emanated from the classical tradition. Sociologists of culture, for the most part, did not draw on other 'aesthetically' oriented frameworks like art history, literary criticism and philosophical aesthetics, but were more concerned with the extrinsic factors of social class, biography, taste and so on. As I have pointed out elsewhere, (Thomas 1995b), 'the relaxing of traditional disciplinary boundaries in sociology has been accompanied by a shift towards the theorisation of culture'. Cultural issues have been pushed to the centre of sociological discourse, so much so that it sometimes appears that we are in danger of losing sight of the fact that issues of class/race etc. are embedded in the discourses of taste and style of consumer capitalism (Bourdieu 1984). Although this shift was given impetus through other discourses such as marxism, semiotics and feminism, poststructuralism and postmodernism have accelerated the drift. The theorization of culture constitutes a common strand that runs across the chain of meanings that shelter under the umbrella of postmodernism and poststructuralism (Featherstone 1988). My approach to the sociology of dance began to develop and shift its grounds through the processes of my intellectual and institutional engagement with the changing discourses of the sociology of culture and cultural studies in the early 1980s. The subsequent confrontations with postmodernism and poststructuralism, in the late 1980s had implications for the re-writing of the work which was completed in the first half of the 1980s and for re-positioning or re-writing myself in relation to it. This entailed a re-working of and through the text and to a certain extent, the undoing of it, particularly in relation to issues such as modernism in the arts and dance, and the body in society and dance. Modernism, for example, can now only be seen by me and I suspect by others also, through the lenses of the modernism/postmodernism debate.

In the Introduction to the second edition of Terpsichore in Sneakers in 1987 Sally Banes indicated with some relief that, at that point, dance scholarship had not fallen prey to these intellectual fads which Boyne and Rattanisi (1990) considered contributed to the above named 'crises in representation'. These fads which were founded on the 'linguistic turn', for Banes, perhaps echoing what Lyotard's (1984) notion of the 'postmodern condition', constituted a response to a crisis for meaning in the arts and contemporary culture,

> The recent intellectual infatuation with structuralism and poststructuralism, symptomatic of our present rage for meaning and order, is in turn perhaps a symptom of our national, indeed global, sense of insecurity and doom. Scholars in every field turn to linguistic analysis and the jargon of new literary criticism and French psychoanalysis in attempts to make tidy sense of the messiness of experience....
> While the critical community in dance has not rushed to embrace semiotics and post-structuralism with the fervor found in other fields, choreographers (though not necessarily motivated by deeply theoretical concerns) have been exploring the implications of this perspective. (Banes 1987: xxiii-xxiv)

Banes, however, almost spoke too soon. The recent burgeoning interest in the interrelation between dance and culture within dance scholarship also carries the marks of the influence of semiotics, postmodernism, poststructuralism and feminism, encased in a cultural studies type framework. The work of Susan Foster (1986), Marianne Goldberg (1988), Ann Cooper Alright (1990), Susan Manning (1993), Ann Daly (1991a), Cynthia Novack (1990) and Roger Copeland (1993), despite his cries to the contrary, in the US, and Christy Adair (1992), Ana Sanchez-Colberg 1993, Valerie Rimmer (1993), and Jordan and Thomas (1994) to some extent in the UK to name but a few, bears witness to this. Although cultural studies started out in Britain in the late 1960s it was taken up in the USA in the 1980s and much of what now counts as 'critical' cultural studies emerges from the USA. Cultural studies, embraced postmodernism and poststructuralism like a new lover. The eclecticism in theory and method which lie at the very roots of the formation of cultural studies, lent itself well to the adaption and incorporation of the issues which these discourses brought to the fore.

Despite differences between the proponents of postmodernism, there are a number of commonalities. There is general agreement that the postmodern represents a cultural break or shift in sensibilities, practices and discourses that has taken place in western cultural formations since the end of the Second World War. Postmodernism stresses the collapsing of the boundaries between high art and popular culture, between art and life and a celebration of eclecticism through a mixing and matching of styles and genres. As the prefix suggests, Postmodernism (as with poststructuralism) is a relative term. In order to understand the otherness of postmodernism, 'the move beyond/away' from modernism and its 'links' with modernism (Kaplan 1989), we have to reconstruct the image that it has of modernism itself. And that image, according to Andreas Huyssen (1986), has changed and developed over the years.

While the emergence of postmodernism, as Huyssen (1986) argues, has to be seen against the backdrop of American culture in the 1960s, the rise of poststructuralism needs to be seen as a response to the failure of the political Left in Europe after 1968 (Eagleton 1983). Although there are differences in approaches and perspectives between those thinkers who have been labelled poststructuralist, there are here too, certain commonalities to be found. Central to these is the critique of the Cogito, the concept of the individual as a formally free, rational thinking, acting, unified self, which has been the cornerstone of the western humanist rationalist tradition of thought since the Enlightenment. Poststructuralism rejects the idea of a fixed subjectivity 'in favour of a dislocated, fragmented subjectivity which is not fixed but is constituted through language on each and every occasion on which we speak. The subject, in poststructuralist theory, contrary to the western humanist tradition is constructed in and through language' (Thomas 1985:15), as I shall go on to elaborate in relation to Lacanian psychoanalysis.

The challenges to modernity that are inscribed in the anti-humanist stance of poststructuralism are also visible in the modernism/postmodernism debate, as are other key ideas such as 'intertextuality, difference, plurality and reflexivity' (Thomas 1995:16). It is hardly surprising, then, that postmodernism is often used as an extended term to include the impact of the work of poststructuralists like Jacques Derrida in literary theory, Jacques Lacan in psychoanalysis, Michel Foucault in history and Richard Rorty in philosophy. A number of writers have warned of the dangers of collapsing poststructuralism into postmodernism because, not only are there variations within each but also across their divide (see Huyssen 1986: 179-221, Kaplan 1989:1-9, Boyne & Rattansi 1990: 1-43, 116-156, McNay 1992: 116-156). Nevertheless, given that the extension has to a great extent taken place, as Roy Boyne and Ali Rattansi (1990:11) argue, 'it is legitimate to use the term [postmodernism] broadly to include discussions of, especially, poststructuralism in literary theory, philosophy and historical and social analysis as the kind inspired by Foucault and Derrida'. However, they go on to stress that this should be done with the problems that might stem from this enterprise. But what makes this extension even more credible is that postmodernism and poststructuralism are also characterized by the aforementioned 'crisis in representation' (ibid: 12).

I want to turn back to dance now and consider the kinds of theories and issues that have drawn the interest of writers who are concerned to examine the relation between dance and feminism, largely because I consider that there is some very interesting work in this area. My concern, however, is toaddress the theories that seem to underpin these interests.

The 'new wave' of dance scholars, for the most part, have not turned to the more 'traditional' divergent approaches of 'liberal', 'radical' or 'socialist feminism' (Jagger 1983) for inspiration. Rather they have drawn on feminist analyses of representational systems that have been passed on through the route of critical cultural studies[5] and which point to the influences of psychoanalysis, semiotics, poststructuralism and postmodernism. Laura Mulvey's (1989) concept of the 'male gaze', for example, which has had a considerable impact on feminist film theory and on feminist cultural analyses of representations of women since it was first published in 1975, has also been used by the new generation of dance writers like Marianne Goldberg (1987), Ann Daly (1991a), Elizabeth Dempster (1988) and Ann Cooper Albright (1990), to criticise the notion of the 'to-be-looked-at-ness' of the appearing female body in performance, sometimes, as I hope to demonstrate, rather uncritically[6]. And it is for that reason that I think it is important to at least contextualize the frameworks that are cited or invoked. There are a number of occasions, for example, where writers are cited one after the other to support or advance a discussion, without acknowledging the fact that the citations are drawn from competing or contrary theoretical positions. I am thinking here of the all to easy running together of quotes from poststructuralist French feminists such as Luce Irigaray, Hélène Cixous and Julia Kristeva,

without pointing to their tense relationship with Lacanian
theory or to each other (Cooper Albright 1990, Daly 1990,
Copeland 1993, Adair 1992). It may be argued that this
does not matter because, in the endless play of signifiers
within postmodernism, it is quite legitimate to mix and
match and quotes from different perspectives. However, and
perhaps I betray my 'creeping rationalism' here, I think it
is important to be clear about the ways in which other
writers are invoked so as not to do violence to their
ideas, or the manner in which they are being interpreted,
despite the fact that those ideas may be read/written in a
variety of ways, and this goes for my reading also. Hence,
my frequent sorties into the realm of theory that dance
writers draw from before I discuss the dance texts
themselves.

The incorporation of psychoanalytic semiotics in film
theory and cultural analyses owes much to the formidable
influence of Jacques Lacan (1977) and his re-reading of
Freud. Before discussing Mulvey's analysis of the male
gaze and then going on to consider how it has been used by
dance writers, I want to give a brief if somewhat 'ideal
typical' description of the Lacanian problematic which
seems to inform much of the work and debates in feminist
film theory.

Lacanian psychoanalysis attempts to draw together the
Freudian problematic of the structuring of gender
subjectivity with the Saussurian paradigm of structural
linguistics, in order to provide a corrective for absences
and problems in both theories (Fraser 1992: 181-182). Freud
was concerned to reveal the construction of gender identity
through a complex process of psycho-sexual development. To
a certain extent his theory of the psycho-sexual
development of the subject challenges theories of innate
biological determined sexual identity because it insists
that the structures of psycho-sexual development form the
basis of social organisation. However, by claiming
universal status for the theory, psychoanalysis can be
criticised for reducing gender to the outcome of a set of
pre-ordered psycho-sexual processes and thus for shutting
off the issue of gender differences from historical
processes.

In his 'return' to Freud, Lacan stresses the link
between sexuality and the unconscious (Rose 1982). In
formulating his account of sexual desire, he returns to
Freud's central controversial concept of the castration
complex ie. to quote Mitchell,'the presence or absence of
the phallus and <u>nothing else</u> that marked the distinction
between the sexes' (Mitchell 1982: 7), which had split the
psychoanalytic community in the 1920s. The subject, for
Lacan however, is constituted through language, and the
unconscious is structured like a language. The loss of the
<u>imaginary</u> and the entry of the subject into the <u>symbolic</u>
has a correspondence with the child's entry into language:

> The mirror stage represents the moment when the
> subject is located in an order outside itself to which
> it will henceforth refer. The subject is the subject
> <u>of</u> speech (Lacan's parle-être), and subject <u>to</u> that
> order. (Rose 1982:31).

Lacan draws on Saussure's theory of language but rejects the 'correspondence between words and things' (Lacan 1977:151) that is implied in Saussure's concept of the arbitrary relation between the signifier and the signified, in favour of the poststructuralist idea of language as a chain of signifiers whose meanings are fixed temporarily in relation to their differences from one another. However, the process of signification, for Lacan, unlike Derrida's deconstructionist model for example, is not that of an <u>endless free play of signifiers</u> whose meanings are constantly in the process of being deferred. Lacan inverts Saussure's model of the linguistic sign and gives primacy to the determinacy of the signifier over the signified to produce certain meanings in relation to the production of the subject within the symbolic system.

In Lacan's model, as Nancy Fraser (Fraser 1992) notes, the speaking subject, which is absent in the Saussurian paradigm, appears to be given a voice through the introduction of the Freudian problematic and in so doing, seems to opens up a space for raising the vexing questions of identity, speech and social practice which Saussurian linguistics cannot address. At the same time, the notion that gender subjectivity is socially produced through the child's entry into the symbolic order which is structured and sanctioned by the rules of language, appears to offer the possibility of remedying the charges of biological reductionism directed at Freud.

Meaning and the symbolic order, for Lacan (Weedon 1987:53-54), is fixed in relation to the primary signifier of sexual difference, the phallus. And it is the phallus that guarantees the patriarchal structure of the social order. The phallus, as the privileged signifier, signifies power and control through authority over the satisfaction of desire. Women's relation to language in this framework is always negative. Woman, in Lacanian theory, signifies a lack or an absence. Men occupy a central position in relation to power in the symbolic order - they have access to it, by virtue of the fact that they possess a penis. Women, however, cannot aspire to power and control by virtue of the fact that they lack a penis - their difference, their identity, is defined in terms of what they are not. They constitute the 'Other' to language, power and control. In Lacan's framework:

> Sexual difference is [then] assigned according to whether individual subjects do or do not possess the phallus, which means not that anatomical difference <u>is</u> sexual difference...but that anatomical difference comes to <u>figure</u> sexual difference, that is, it becomes the sole representative of what difference is allowed to be. (Rose ibid:42)

Thus, Lacan claims to describe the mechanisms through which the people achieve subjectivity through their entry as young children into an already phallocentric symbolic order. The structure of the symbolic order which is patriarchal determines the attributes of individual subjectivity. At the same time, however, the framework affirms that the symbolic order has to be phallocentric because the achievement of subjectivity can only be reached through the submission to the 'rule of the father'. This circularity in the theory leads to an iron-cage from which there can be no escape. As Fraser (1992:182) argues, Lacan's various stages of development are coated in a theoretical frame of necessity and inevitability. There seems to be no way out of the patriarchal symbolic order, at least through social practice, which has been the driving force of feminism.

Like Fraser (ibid), I have always been somewhat sceptical of this framework which has come to have a such a powerful influence on feminist cultural analyses in recent years. Despite some persuasive arguments put forward in its defense (see Mitchell & Rose 1982, Kaplan 1983: 23-35, Phelan 1993), I appear unable to get over the fact that Lacanian theory, despite its claims to point to the 'fictive' character of the power of the phallus in the symbolic order (Rose 1982:38-41), is already implicated in sustaining its privileged position as the universal signifier. There seems to be no space for women, whenever or wherever they appear, they are always in masquerade. And it is precisely this spacelessness that has sent poststructuralist psychoanalytic feminists like Irigaray, Cixous and Kristeva scurrying in different but related directions to find a possible space from which the voice(s) of the feminine can be raised (Rose 1982). That space, they argue, albeit from different positions in the poststructuralist continuum, is locatable in the body: the female libido in Irigaray's case; the feminine of the pre-Oedipal phase for Cixous; the semiotic (imaginary) but non-sex specific phase for Kristeva, and thus, their concern with 'writing the body' (Weedon 1987:63-73).

Despite my reservations about Lacanian psychoanalytic semiotics, I think Toril Moi (1985) is correct when she says that the importance of psychoanalysis lies in its challenge to discourses that assume a unified self, a rational, free thinking subject which can be <u>entirely known</u>. In contestimg the very idea of the 'self' which is the central tenet of the humanist tradition, it demands that any analysis of the 'real' world must take account of these other determinants of which conscious thought is but one part. Thus, it points to the fact that any analysis can only be partial.

In her psychoanalytic semiotic approach to <u>Visual Pleasure and Narrative Cinema</u>, Laura Mulvey (1989:14-26) argues that the pleasure in looking in narrative Hollywood cinema comes from and replicates the structure of male looking. The woman in the film is the object of the 'male gaze' and the viewer is invited to see the film through the male look. Hence the female becomes objectified and this in turn replicates the unequal structure of power between the sexes. Feminist cinema, according to Mulvey, must disrupt the pleasure of the gaze. Mulvey's idea of the gaze is grounded in psychoanalytic theory and as such, it is difficult to move out of the way in which the individual (sexed) psyche is structured in an undifferentiated universal manner. In Mulvey's framework, as with Lacan, woman stands for what she is not, the phallus. The presence of women as an obsessive image is linked to male castration anxiety and its resolution. The body of the woman 'the other' is frightening for men. She signals the loss of 'active' phallic power. In order to deal with castration anxiety, men turn women into fetishized objects and thus 'women in representation can signify castration and activate the voyeuristic or fetishistic mechanisms to circumvent threat'. (Mulvey 1989:21) Mulvey's analysis of the 'male gaze' was important to feminist analysis because it offered a theoretical framework for understanding the association of the objectification of women through their bodies and their lack of cultural power within the discourse of patriarchy which had been implicit in earlier 'second wave' analysis (Gamman & Makinen 1994). However, it also incurred certain criticisms; the analysis proposes that 'all' gaze is male, and heterosexual, and that men, unlike women, are not objectified through the look (see Marshment and Gamman (1988). It does not take account of difference (except along the lines of the Lacanian binary divide) or change over time and thus its approach can be criticised for being monolithic and static.

In a later paper she attempts to address the issue of the 'male only gaze' in Visual Pleasure..., (Mulvey 1989:29-38). She maintains that the 'actual' sex of the spectator was not an issue for her at the time of writing. Rather, her 'interest lay in the relationship between the image of woman on the screen and the "masculinization" of the spectator position'(Mulvey 1989:29). In the later discussion, Mulvey extends her analysis of spectatorship to take account of some of the deficiencies in the earlier piece. She sees that the identification of the woman in the audience with the 'active' male gaze could speak to the rediscovery of the lost aspect of her sexual identity; ie the loss of the 'active' or phallic phase and thus the female spectator 'oscillates' between the active/male and passive/female subject positions. The consequence of this, however, is that the possibility of bringing women to the position of an active knowing subject depends not on <u>her</u> identity and difference, but, rather, on what she is not or what she lacks. She is constantly deferred or is deferring to the power of the privileged signifier, the phallus, the marker and measure of her difference. Mulvey does argue, however, that when the female protagonist occupies center stage in the narrative structure (revealing that 'she is unable to achieve a stable sexual identity' (Mulvey 1989:30), a discursive shift is produced and she no longer <u>represents</u> sexuality, but, rather the narrative becomes <u>about</u> sexuality.

Despite Mulvey's attempts to correct some of the problems inherent in the first piece, the fact remains that her model of the gaze is underpinned by psychoanalysis and thus, neglects considerations of historical change. This is because it ultimately locates explanations of representations and looking in the presumed trans-historical (dare I say essential) occurrence of male castration anxiety. This model, as Gamman and Makinen (1994:182) argue, cannot adequately address postmodernist aesthetic ideas such as 'kitsch, camp, pastiche and parody' which have come to pervade many of the representations we see on the billboards, the visual media (or in some dance performances). Nor can it address why different 'others' get pleasure from looking without resorting to what Mulvey calls 'psychic transvestism', ie oscillating between the active and the passive gaze (Gamman and Makinen ibid:182).

Given these various dilemmas I want to look at the ways in which some dance scholars have invoked the 'male gaze' (usually without elucidating its psychoanalytic grounding) and ask why they considered it (and its various revisions and developments) a useful concept to apply to dance in the first instance. The discussion will follow the routes taken by Christy Adair (1992), Ann Daly (1991a), Ann Cooper Albright (1990).

In her book, Women in Dance: Sylph and Sirens (1992), Christy Adair devotes a chapter to the ways in which women have been viewed in dance. In the preceding chapter Adair warns the reader to beware of the trap of essentialism vis à vis certain theories on sexual difference (she is discussing Irigaray and Cixous at this point), and wishes to stress the social construction of the (female) body in dance and culture. Drawing on Mulvey's concept of representation of women, dragging in the psychoanalytic constructs of voyeurism and desire, Adair sees that the importance of the bodily 'look' of the (female) dancer in the western theatrical dance tradition emphasises the 'to be looked-at-ness'.

> The audience is in the role of the voyeur in relationship to the dancer. The voyeur has power over the looked at, so that the dancer is traditionally displayed to gratify the audience's desire. (Adair ibid:72)

Adair suggests that some' dance work resists mainstream dance practices' implying a disordering of the gaze (as Mulvey too suggests that the task of feminist film making is to disrupt the gaze), by emphasizing the 'processes and performers' experiences and subjectivities' (ibid:74). Like Susan Foster (1986) and Cooper Albright (1990), Adair sees that these 'advanced' subject positions are taken up by particular contemporary (postmodern?) choreographers. The hierarchy that Phillip Auslander (1998) argues is inherent in Foster's work in particular is also visible in Adair's discussion, that is, the idea of a 'postmodernism of resistance' as a yardstick by which to measure other dance practices.

Adair cites Pina Bausch's Rite of Spring (1975) as an exemplar of dance work that resists mainstream practices that are ensnared in patriarchal discourse. Quoting from one of her own collaborative papers, Adair sees that in Bausch's work, 'women's experiences of the world is expressed in... [the] many grounded focussed, womb-like movements: there's not the extension and exposure of the body that we are used to seeing in many other dance works. The woman is subject' (ibid:74). Thus, although Adair argues against essentialist views of women, she too becomes caught up in them. There is more than a suggestion, here, that women experience themselves through their wombs (biology is destiny?) and that 'womb-like movements' express the 'real' of woman as subject as opposed to 'extension and exposure of the body', which, presumably, Adair views in terms of the fetishization of woman as object enmeshed in the male gaze.

Part of the problem is to be found, I think, in the sociologizing of psychoanalytically grounded constructs of spectatorship, without theorizing the oppositions between the social subject as agent, actor etc. and the subject of psychoanalysis as defined above. As Mary Anne Doane (1987:8) points out, traditionally, the problematic of spectatorship in film theory, stems from a 'psychoanalytically informed linguistics, not from a sociologically based analysis'. Feminist theory has set itself on course to show that this spectator 'has been constantly posited and delineated as masculine'. In so doing, argues Doane, feminist theory is forced to introduce the problematic of the social subject, 'but unfortunately, it frequently and overhastily collapses the opposition between social subjects and psychic subjects, closing the gap prematurely' (ibid).

Although this is a problem in Adair's work, it is not in Foster's (1986) text where, following Barthes, she purposely outlines her approach to 'the subject' through the poststructuralist notion that it comes into being through participation in a range of discursive practices. Although Foster recognises the influence of Lacan and Freud on Barthes' treatment of the subject and the body, she opts for the semiotic/structural side of the Barthes formula in which the body is seen as a 'locus of mindful articulations', rather than 'a sign for the structure of the unconscious' (Foster 1986:237).

Adair (1992) also discusses key psychoanalytic concepts such as 'desire' and 'pleasure' in looking and it is here that she topicalizes psychoanalysis as a useful resource for feminism because 'it has', she says,' attempted to extricate meanings from its cultural surroundings' (ibid:79). However, Adair does not elaborate on what this might mean and the notions of desire and pleasure that she discusses, once more, tend to collapse the psychoanalytic into the sociological frame. A further problem might also lie in the all too easy transfer from film spectatorship to that of performance. According to Adair:

> Dance provides an ideal opportunity for the voyeur. Sitting in the dark of the auditorium the spectator is offered the body endlessly displayed to gratify the desire of the looker. The woman is not as remote as she might appear to be in the screen. She is there in the flesh, constantly exposed (ibid)

Thus, for Adair, performance and film spectatorship have much in common, but there is something of an excess in performance. The presence of the real, live body, Adair seems to suggest, makes the (female) body more available and vulnerable to the gaze. But is there in fact such an unproblematic 'goodness of fit' between film and performance and need the possibility of the excess be viewed as more repressive? According to Peggy Phelan (1993) (drawing on psychoanalysis and feminist theories of representation), the import of performance in the ontological sense of the word, in contrast to film for example, lies in its non-reproducibility - 'Performance, Phelan states, 'implicates the real through the presence of living bodies' (ibid:148). Spectatorship involves consumption of performance as it appears and disappears into the memory. Phelan argues that unlike other arts involved in the system of mechanical reproduction, performance does not become enmeshed in the circulation of capital, rather, she ssays 'it resists balanced circulations of finance. It saves nothing; it only spends'(ibid). This excessive pouring out, she maintains, makes it susceptible to 'charges of valuelessness and emptiness'(ibid). In turn, however, this gives rise to the possibility of performance 'revaluing that emptiness, which 'gives performance art its distinctive oppositional edge'(ibid).

Ann Daly, (1991a) in her discussion on dance and feminist analysis, points out that contemporary feminist analysis focuses on the 'the entire process of representation' rather than a consideration of the image in itself and that this includes 'the spectator and his/her process of interpretation' (Daly ibid:2). Although Daly sees Mulvey's term for spectatorship as 'tiresome' (although she does not elaborate on this), she states, nevertheless, that the 'male gaze' remains 'a fundamental concept' which reveals the gendered positions inherent in the unequal structure of looking (active/male) and being looked at (passive/female) in contemporary western culture in which the male and/or female spectator is the consumer of the image. In the preceding paragraph, where she discusses the idea of woman as 'other' in western culture, Daly implicitly invokes psychoanalytic theory when she adds that this otherness has been defined according to 'the fantasies [my emphasis] and power structures of men'(ibid). However, as with Adair's (1992) discussion, the psychic subject which resides in the realm of the symbolic crosses over into the realm of the social subject, despite the fact that she indicates once more that the actual sex of the spectator is not an issue: 'The spectator is in the position of power: a traditionally male position. Thus, the term, "male gaze"'(Daly 1991a: 2).

Like Adair (1992), Daly sees that the theory of the male gaze has much to offer dance and vice versa: 'How can women represent themselves on stage without being co-opted by the conventions of the male gaze? Is it possible for women to reconstruct their own standards of beauty that need not depend on becoming the object of the male desire?' (Daly 1991a:3) Once again, the overriding message is that all gaze is male and heterosexual.

In a slightly later paper, however, Daly (1992b) does call into question the 'monolithic' male gaze and problematizes the all too easy transfer of concepts from film theory to that of dance. She proposes that' a new theory is required: one that inludes within its very structure the capacity for change'(Daly 1992b: 244). The theory that Daly finds illuminating, however, is that of the French psychoanalytic feminist, Julia Kristeva. Daly stresses what Fraser (1992:185)) terms the 'pragmatic dimension' of Kristeva's framework which is, 'the analysis of language as a social practice in a social context'. Nevertheless, as Fraser argues, despite Kristeva's attempts to transcend the limits of Lacanian theory, she ends up by operating in a similar dualistic model that privileges the symbolic order, thus, once more, locking us into the law of the father[7].

One of the most interesting dialogues with psychoanalytic film theory that I have encountered is in Yvonne Rainer's film <u>The Man who Envied Women</u>, as, indeed, the title's inversion of the Freudian problematic suggests. Rainer takes Mulvey's theory of the male gaze and pushes it to its logical conclusion and asks what happens when the object of the male gaze, the female protagonist, is not represented through her bodily image.

Trisha, Rainer's protagonist, is sight unseen throughout the film. She is 'off screen', like the viewer, with whom at times she seems to share a space as a spectator in her own story. Trisha's marks her presence in the film by a voice, not her body - the mark of what she is not in Lacanian theory - and thus, Rainer, as Phelan (1993:72) argues, 'implicitly challenges the nature of filmic presence'.

Rainer's erasure of the body of the female protagonist in the film is the starting point for Ann Cooper Albright's (1990) interesting discussion which centres on 'spectacle, moving subjects and feminist theory'. Cooper Albright (ibid:32) asks, rightly I think, if Rainer's strategy of erasure is the 'ultimate route for feminists to take'. This seems especially pertinent in relation to the tradition of western theatre dance where the body is the primary instrument of expression, with the female body as the dominant representational choreographed site (sight). How is it possible to create a space to represent the unrepresentable (female psychic subject) and the underepresented (female social subject) and thereby challenge the dominant (male centred) gendered discourses? Following, Teresa de Lauretis's (1987:26) concept of 'space off' or a view from 'elsewhere' ('the space not visible in the frame but inferable from what the frame makes visible'), Cooper Albright (1990:33) sees that by 'using Trisha's disembodied voice to fracture the conventions of the filmic gaze, Rainer envelopes her audience in this elsewhere'. De Lauretis's analysis of spectatorship attempts to go beyond Mulvey's view of the female spectator as 'oscillating' between male/active passive/female positions by positing the idea that there is a simultaneous movement between two kind of spaces, the 'represented space' and the 'space off, the elsewhere', which she maintains, 'coexist concurrently and in opposition' (de Lauretis 1987:26). For de Lauretis (ibid), 'the subject of feminism is en-gendered' in the elsewhere. Thus, in the final analysis, for de Lauretis, Rainer's film is also en-gendered.

Cooper Albright (1990:33) suggests that contemporary dancing can find ways to fracture the conventional reifications of body images and jolt the gaze of the spectator by shifting the discourse to another space or 'elsewhere'.

> Slipping in and out of their culturally determined frames, the bullient bodies in these [specific contemporary] dances elude a traditional gaze and defy the powerful pleasure of spectacle - that of looking at some-thing to-be-looked-at, the audience, in turn, can be pushed out of its conventional consumption of these bodies. (ibid)

This opens up the possibility for a different kind of spectatorship, one which looks at the 'physical experience of the dancer - her moving, her motion - her subjectivity'(ibid).

Although Cooper Albright recognises that dance performances are not 'the imaging machines in quite the same way that cameras are,' nevertheless, she argues, they do reveal 'a certain politics of imagery' that raises questions about ' "woman": woman as a spectacle, as an object to be admired, as a vision of beauty, and as a site of pleasure' (ibid:34). Dancers in ballet or the musical stage are often seen as embodying 'some kind of eternal or essential woman' (ibid). However, the image of ideal-typical dancer, according to Cooper Albright does not speak of or to the subjectivity of the dancer in question ,but, rather, '[of] her role in the lives and the fantasies of <u>male</u> directors, choreographers and audience members' (ibid:33). Once again, the psychic subject and the social subject are collapsed. Despite the fact that Cooper Albright places the term 'male gaze' in inverted commas, that gaze is still a monolithic one. The result of this is that, like de Lauretis and Mulvey, the male spectator is theorized as pure while the female spectator at some level is achieved through recourse to bisexuality - 'transvestism' in Mulvey's case and 'double identification' in de Lauretis's work (Doane 1987:9).

Cooper Albright's analysis, somewhat like Foster's (1986), implies a dance hierarchy: forms that reflexively disrupt the dominant canons of representation are politically more advanced and these are most likely to be found within postmodern or new dance. Like Foster, Cooper Albright sees that whilst some contemporary dances might have the appearance of being more politically advanced than others, they are not because they still operate within the dominant conventions of representation. Whilst, for example Molissa Fenley, Cooper Albright explains, makes 'fast dances that require that she and her dancers train rigorously for stamina and strength', her dances, nevertheless, 'fail to challenge a traditionally static "male gaze" because they continue to accept the classic split between the audience and the performer' (Cooper Albright 1990:34). Fenley seems to be more interested in displaying the body as opposed to the pleasure of moving. Cooper Albright considers that Fenley cannot jolt the perception of the audience into 'an awareness of the physical experience of those moving bodies' (ibid), because she remains within the bounds of conventional representation.

The problem with this view, however, is that it is

somewhat at odds with the postmodernist/poststructuralist rhetoric that the paper seems to celebrate, in that it assumes that it is through the relation of the creator/performer to the spectacle that the single reading that the audience is allowed/enabled to see is fixed. Postmodernism and poststructuralism, however, emphasise the 'death of the author' (the traditional privileged speaking subject), the unfixing of the text (that had been fixed by the arbitrary relation of the signifier and the signified in semiotics), and the shift towards the readers/ viewers as writing/choreographing the text/dance and combining the ingredients in any way they choose. This intertextuality calls into question traditional (logocentric) notions of 'true' 'real' 'fixed' meanings, and that goes for the audiences/spectators as well as texts/performances and authors/choreographers. In this view, there are potentially a multiplicity of voices/eyes at work in any discursive practice, the task for analysis is to hear/see and deconstruct them. Cooper Albright seems to get caught up unwittingly in a paradigm she wants to rupture, the monolithic pure male 'look'. She considers that audiences 'could be trained to see' the dancers experiencing themselves as subjects, thus implying that they cannot possibly see it now unless they are forced or instructed to 'look elsewhere' (ibid:39).

And certain dancers do create works that shift the focus to the 'space off', according to Cooper Albright, such as Pooh Kaye, Ann Carlson, Marie Chouinard and Jennifer Monson and in so doing, she states, 'often expose the problematic dynamic of a conventional performer / audience relationship'(ibid:40). These dancers/dances although different from each other, are exemplars of the top rung in the hierarchy of dance from a feminist perspective, she says 'it is in this space - this new frontier -that women dancers can begin to claim their subjectivity' (ibid) and presumably teach others (the audience) to 'see' difference. Thus, Cooper Albright ends up by privileging author over audience, 'art' over 'life', and by implication, art over popular culture, which, ironically, is the very antithesis of cultural postmodernism.

Despite the queries I have raised with regard to the use of the male gaze, and the unproblematic collapsing of the psychic subject into the social subject in the writing under discussion here, the theoretical intention behind the work is important; that is, to show that the ways in which we look at dance, are not quite as neutral or as individual as we might think but are inscribed in a chain of cultural codes and practices in and through which our bodies, our subjectivities, are situated and implicated.

This paper began by asking what it is about the discourses of postmodernism and poststructuralism that makes them so appealing to dance writers. In postmodernism and poststructuralism, the central issues of 'language and meaning and subjectivity' (Weedon 1987) are articulated in terms of a discourse of the body, and these are themes that are constantly being addressed in recent dance scholarship. In the light of the preceding discussion, I think that the key to understanding the sway of these discourses is to be found in the manner in which they have precipitated the elevation of culture into the academic arena and their re-positioning of the body to the centre of the discourse, which, in turn, offers dance (particularly western theatrical dance) the possibility of a new found (academic) legitimacy, an authorial voice that it had not achieved hitherto.

Endnotes

1   This discussion is a much shorter version of a paper that will appear in Gay Morris' collection <u>Rethinking Dance</u> (forthcoming 1996, Routledge). This is mostly a US collection.

2   Ann Daly (1991b), in an article entitled <u>"What Revolution?: the New Dance Scholarship in America</u>, gives a brief overview of what she sees as new dance scholarship in the United States. Here she points out the weaknesses (and some of the strengths) of 'old' dance scholarship and the emergence of 'new' dance analysis in which culture is a central concern. Daly explains that was once called' dance history' has expanded in terms of its 'approach, subjects and methodology' into what might be more appropriately termed 'dance studies'. The use of this term is significant because it follows the pattern of other multi-disciplinary based programmes of study like, cultural studies, literary studies, film studies. Although graduate courses at the Laban Centre in London were given the name Dance Studies at the beginning of the 1980s to indicate that dance analyses involved a range of disciplines, the particular disciplines that were taught, apart from the sociology of dance, did not particularly engage or draw on the other related areas, as perhaps they now do.

3   This is not to imply a hierarchy of forms of dance or the types of analyses involved. I think that one of the merits of postmodernism, although I must admit that I am not a convert, is that it points out that such divisions are spurious and that their retention speaks more about the 'hyperinstitutionalization' of the 'high' arts in western culture than anything else (Willis et al. 1990).

4   This is not to imply that dance history did not a provide valuable resource in terms of data, nor dance aesthetics/criticism in terms of focusing of the activity of dancing and moving, because they did (for example. (Banes 1987, Cohen 1982, Siegel 1979) and still do so. This discussion, however, is primarily concerned with the articulation of the relations between dance and culture.

5   I am using critical cultural studies, here, in a somewhat broader sense to include texts such as Laura Mulvey's (1989) <u>Visual Pleasure and Narrative Cinema</u> that might more correctly come under the heading of 'film theory'. As recently established areas of study like cultural studies and film studies, which are in themselves interdisciplinary, interact with each

other, the boundaries between them become increasingly blurred. See, for example, de Lauretis eds. (1987)

6   To a certain extent I have to include myself in this category because I have used a quotation from Mulvey's work, albeit with a proviso, to discuss an association between the active and the appearing body in the talk of the some young women dancers' I had been studying. See Thomas (1993:83).

7   The paper in Morris' book (see endnote 1) offers a more detailed discussion of this.

Bibliography

Adair, C. (1992) <u>Women and Dance: Sylphs and Sirens</u>, London: Macmillan.

Auslander, P. (1998, Winter) Embodiment: The Politics of Postmodern Dance (Review of Susan Leigh Foster's Reading Dancing), <u>The Drama Review</u> 32,4: 7-23.

Banes, S. (1989, Spring) Terpsichore in Combat Boots, <u>The Drama Review</u> 33,1: 13-16.

--- (1987) <u>Terpsichore in Sneakers: Post-Modern Dance</u>, Mifflin: Houghton.

Bourdieu, P. (1984) <u>Distinction: A Social Critique of the Judgement of Taste</u>, translated by R. Nice ed. London: Routledge & Kegan Paul.

Boyne, R. & Rattansi, A. (eds.) (1990) <u>Postmodernism and Society</u>, London: Macmillan.

Cohen, S.J. (1982) <u>Next Week, Swan Lake: Reflections On Dance and Dancers</u>, Middletown: Wesleyan University Press.

Cooper Albright, A. (1990, Spring/Summer) Mining the Dance Field: Spectacle, Moving Subjects, and Feminist Theory, <u>Contact Quarterly</u> 15,2: 32-41.

Copeland, R. (1993) Dance, Feminism and the Critique of the Visual, in H. Thomas (ed.) <u>Dance, Gender and Culture</u>, Basingstoke: Macmillan.

--- (1992) The Black Swan and the Dervishes, <u>Dance Theatre Journal</u> 9,4 Summer: 10-13, 41-43.

Cowan, J. (1990) <u>Dance and the Body Politic in Northern Greece</u>, Princeton: Princeton University Press.

Coward, R. & Ellis, J. (1977) <u>Language and Materialism: Developments in Semiology and the Theory of the Subject</u>, London: Routledge & Kegan Paul.

Daly, A.ed (1992a, Spring) What has Become of Postmodern Dance?, <u>The Drama Review</u> 36,1: 48-69.

--- (1992b) Dance History and Feminist Theory: Reconsidering Isadora Duncan and the Male Gaze, in L. Senelick (eds.), <u>Gender in Performance</u>, Hanover and London: Tufts University Press.

--- (1991a Spring) Unlimited Partnership: Dance and Feminist Analysis, <u>Dance Research Journal</u> 23, 1 (Spring),: 2-3.

--- (1991b, January) "What Revolution?": The New Dance Scholarship in America, <u>Ballet International</u> 14,1: 48-53.

--- (1987, Spring) The Balanchine Woman: Of Hummingbirds and Channel Swimmers, <u>The Drama Review</u> 31,1: 8-21.

Dempster, E. (1988) Women Writing the Body: Let's Watch a Little how she Dances, in S. Sheridan (ed.) <u>Grafts: Feminist Cultural Criticism</u>, London: Verso.

Doane, M.A. (1987) <u>The Desire to Desire: The Woman's Film of the 1940s</u>, London: Macmillan Press.

Eagleton, T. (1983) <u>Literary Theory: An Introduction</u>, Oxford: Basil Blackwell.

Featherstone, M. (1988) In Pursuit of the Postmodern: an Introduction, <u>Theory, Culture and Society</u> 5, 2-3,: 195-216.

Foster, S.L. (1986) <u>Reading Dancing: Bodies and Subjects in Contemporary American Dance</u>, Berkeley: University of California Press.

Fraser, N. (1992) The Uses and Abuses of French Discourse Theories of Feminist Politics, in N. Fraser & S.L. Bartky (eds.) <u>Revaluing French Feminism: Critical Essays on</u>

<u>Difference, Agency, & Culture</u>, Bloomington: Indiana University Press.

Gamman, L. & Makinen, M. (1994) <u>Female Fetishism: A New Look</u>, London: Lawrence & Wishart.

Gamman, L. & Marshment, M. (eds.) (1988) <u>The Female Gaze: Women As Viewers of Popular Culture</u>, London: The Women's Press.

Garfinkel, H. (1984) <u>Studies in Ethnomethodology</u>, Cambridge: Polity Press.

Goldberg, M. (1987/88) Ballerinas and Ball Passing, <u>Women & Performance</u> 3,2: 7-31.

Grau, A. (1993) John Blacking and the Development of Dance Anthropology in the UK, <u>Dance Research Journal</u> 25,2 Fall,: 21-32.

Hoare, Q. & Smith, G.N. (eds.) (1971) <u>Selections from the Prison Notebooks of Antonio Gramsci</u>, London: Lawrence & Wishart.

Huyssen, A. (1986) <u>After the Great Divide: Modernism, Mass Culture, Modernism</u>, London: Macmillan.

Jaggar, A. (1983) <u>Feminist Politics and Human Nature</u>, Sussex: Harvester Press.

Jenkins, R. (1992) <u>Pierre Bourdieu</u>, London: Routledge.

Jordan, S. & Thomas, S. (1994, Autumn) Dance and Gender: Formalism and Semiotics Reconsidered, <u>Dance Research</u> 12,2: 3-14.

Kaeppler, A. (1991) American Approaches to the Study of Dance, <u>Yearbook of Traditional Music</u> 23,: 11-21.

Kaplan, A.E. (ed.) (1989) <u>Postmodernism and Its Discontents</u>, London: Verso.

Kendall, E. (1979) <u>Where She Danced</u>, New York: Arnold A. Knopf.

Lacan, J. (1977) <u>Écrits: A Selection</u>, Translated from the French by Ann Sheridan ed. London: Tavistock.

de Lauretis, T. (1988) <u>Feminist Studies/Critical Studies</u>, Basingstoke: Macmillan Press Ltd.

de Lauretis, T. (1987) <u>Technologies of Gender</u>, Bloomington: Indiana University Press.

Lyotard, J.F. (1984) <u>The Postmodern Condition</u>, Manchester: Manchester University Press.

Manning, S.A. (1993) <u>Ecstasy and the Demon: Feminism and Nationalism in the Dances of Mary Wigman</u>, Berkeley: University of California Press.

--- (1989, Spring) Terpsichore in Combat Boots, <u>The Drama Review</u> 33,1: 17-18.

--- (1988, Winter) Modernist Dogma and Post-modern Rhetoric, <u>The Drama Review</u> 32,4: 32-39.

Wright Mills, C. (1970) <u>The Sociological Imagination</u>, Harmondsworth: Penguin Books.

Mitchell, J. (1982) Introduction 1, in J. Mitchell & J. Rose (eds.) <u>Feminine Sexuality: Jacques Lacan & the École Freudienne</u>, London: Macmillan Press.

Mitchell, J. & Rose, J. (eds.) (1982) <u>Feminism Sexuality: Jacques Lacan & the École Freudienne</u>, London: Macmillan Press.

Moi, T. (1985) <u>Sexual/Textual Politics</u>, London: Methuen.

Mulvey, L. (1989) <u>Visual and Other Pleasures</u>, Basingstoke: Macmillan.

Novack, C. (1990) <u>Sharing the Dance: Contact Improvisation</u>

and American Culture, Madison: University of Wisconsin Press.

Parker, R. & Pollock, G. (eds.) (1987) Framing Feminism, London: Pandora.

Phelan, P. (1993) Unmarked: The Politics of Performance, London: Routledge.

Polhemus, T. (1975) Social Bodies, in J. Benthall & T. Polhemus (eds.) The Body as a Medium of Expression, London: Allen Lane.

Rimmer, V. (1993) The Anxiety of Dance Performance, in H. Thomas (ed.) Dance, Gender and Culture, Basingstoke: Macmillan.

Rose, J. (1982) Introduction 2, in J. Mitchell & J. Rose (eds.) Feminine Sexuality: Jacques Lacan & the École Freudienne, London: Macmillan Press.

Sanchez-Colberg, A. (1993) 'You put your left foot in, then you shake it all about... ': Excursions and Incursions into Feminism and Bausch's Tanztheater, in H. Thomas (ed.) Dance, Gender and Culture, Basingstoke: Macmillan Press.

Shelton, S. (1981) Ruth St. Denis: A Biography of a Divine Dancer, Austin: University of Texas Press.

Siegel, M.B. (1979) The Shapes of Change, Boston: Houghton Mifflin.

Sklar, D. (1991) On Dance Ethnography, Dance Research Journal 23,1,: 6-10.

Sorell, W. (1981) Dance in Its Time: The Emergence of an Art Form, Garden City: Anchor Press/Doubleday.

Thomas, H. (1995) Dance, Modernity and Culture: Explorations in the Sociology of Dance, London: Routledge.

Weedon, C. (1987) Feminist Practice & Poststructuralist Theory, Oxford: Polity Press.

Williams, D. (1977) The Nature of Dance: An Anthropological Perspective, Dance Research Journal 9,1: 42-44.

Willis, P., with Jones, S., Canaan, J., & Hurd, G. (1990) Common Culture, Milton Keynes: Open University Press.

Youngerman, S. (1974) Curt Sachs and his Heritage: a Critical Review of World History of Dance with a Survey of Recent Studies that Perpetuate his Ideas, Cord News 6,2: 6-17.

GENDERING ENGLISH TRADITIONAL DANCE IN THE UNITED STATES

Linda J. Tomko
University of California, Riverside

My topic today is the transmission of English traditional dance to the United States, giving special attention to gender as a dimension of that transmission. I'll be focussing on traditional dance as it was produced or "revived" in the first two decades of the twentieth century, particularly the period when Cecil Sharp voyaged to the U.S., collected Appalachian materials, but taught English folk dance as well. I must confess, speaking here in England about England's traditional dance, I feel rather like I'm carrying coals to Newcastle. At the same time, there is compelling historical reason to speak from and about the Yankee perspective on English matters. In the nineteenth and early twentieth centuries, a strong and vibrant "transatlantic connection" operated between the two countries. They shared certain kinds of values: substantial literary transfer occurred, from Henry James to the program of Ruskin and Morris; the British model fueled the culminating phase of American suffrage agitation; and Americans in certain circles took up English traditional dance.

Today I propose consideration of, and indeed agitate for, gender as a focus for analysis in studying revived English traditional dance from the turn of the twentieth century. Those were years when an active folksong revival operated in Britain, in which waters Cecil Sharp swam after his return from Australia. Sharp constituted himself an expert, first in folksong, and then in folk dance, the latter including morris, sword, and English country dance. The literature on early twentieth-century revival movements is deep and thorough in regard to folksong, and analysis is mounting for the folk dance revival. My survey of the music and dance revival literature finds several kinds of analysis at work--but not yet application of sustained gender analysis. John Forrest's work, some ten years ago, took a positivist stance. Examining Sharp's ceremonial dance collecting practice, and his manuscript notes, Forrest then compared them with Sharp's published works. Claiming that Sharp regularized in print what in practice was anything but tidy, and demonstrating the selectivity of Sharp's collecting patterns, Forrest took the path of recovering the facts, righting the record, and damning along the way the functionality of dance manuals. Keith Chandler forcefully supplied a contextual approach, which shared much with what is called a social history perspective in the States. Chandler searched out records that documented morris dancers' lived experience of the morris resurgence in the late nineteenth century. Here the doers and their behavior, and in Chandler's terms, their humanity, were privileged rather than the collectors and their ideologies. Dave Harker's numerous articles and his book *Fakesong* worked skillfully to expose the hegemonic function of the folksong movement, arguing that collectors and authors strengthened and secured their class status by imposing an ideological view of the "folk" which he found "fake." Richard Sykes, in an article on the Englishness of English folksong, moved to the different ideological ground of nationalism, considering how national identity was forged through the folk music revival and its intersection with primitivist and antiquarian thought.1

Studies of English folk dance have gone much further than folk music writings in acknowledging the participation and contribution made by women. Theresa Buckland, writing about historical morris in Northwest England, pointed out the rising numbers of female, child, morris dancers, and she theorized this gendered shift in connection with changing conceptions of childhood, civic ceremony, and the shaping force of dancing masters. Studies of the folk dance revival have addressed women by writing Mary Neal back into the record. Thus, Roy Dommett, A.D. Townsend, and in great detail, Roy Judge have elaborated Neal's use of morris dance for social reform purposes, and Neal's early involvement with England's suffragette movement (via the Women's Social and Political Union). They detail the early harmony between Neal and Sharp, and the subsequent, caustic, and finally public break between the two over methods and authority in the national movement. But acknowledgement of Neal's activity, and explanations for the break, stop short of theorizing questions of gender. This lacuna signifies for the turn-of-the-century revival, and also for the transmission of revival dances by women teachers to the second revival dating from the 1930s and later.2

Thus the discourse on English traditional dance in its first revival presently begs considerations of gender, and one purpose of this paper is to press the discourse on this point. My own work on American uses of English traditional dance shows gender contest and recasting to be central. I turn to the transmission of revived traditional dance in the U.S., to push on the discourse of English traditional dance; to press and extend its borders to compass American practices, the pertinence of a transatlantic connection, and the salience of gender. I'll raise questions as I go about possible parallels and issues in the British movement.

Cecil Sharp first visited the U.S. in late 1914, to stage the dances for Harley Granville-Barker's New York production of *A Midsummer Night's Dream*. Sharp had been preceded in the U.S. by Mary Neal, with Florrie Warren in 1910-11, and by A. Claud Wright in 1913 and 1914. These parties positioned themselves as independent operators. Wright enlisted in the war, and Neal lost ground in the British revival--so Sharp arrived as the key man from the English Folk Dance Society (the EFDS), the formal society founded in 1911. Completing his obligation to Granville-Barker, Sharp travelled, lectured, and taught for several months. In that short time, he catalyzed formation of a federated American arm of the EFDS, with active

subsidiary branches or centers in New York, Boston,
Chicago, St. Louis, and Pittsburgh. The national
organization sponsored a three-week summer session in
Eliot, Maine, which Sharp directed. Sharp returned to
England at intervals but sojourned extensively in the
U.S. for the next four years. It is the urban centers
for English folk dance and the summer camp project that I
focus on from 1915 until about 1918. The centers and
camps (two more followed in 1916 and 1917 at Amherst,
Massachusetts) supplied the organizational nodes that
offered work to Sharp. It is very clear that Sharp
journeyed to America to make money--his collecting of
Appalachian materials was an unexpected boon. When he
returned permanently to Britain in 1918, it was to
negotiate, successfully, a secure paying position as
official inspector of folk dancing at training schools.3

The American centers were quite active 1915 to 1920
and their conduct constituted a gendered transmission of
folk dance in the U.S. The centers scheduled regular
dance instruction for their regional communities; engaged
Sharp and his amanuensis Maud Karpeles to teach
periodically; and sent members to the summer camps. Four
of the five centers were organized and driven in
important part by women's founding and organizational
energies.4

In Boston, Mrs. James J. Storrow backed the local
Center's founding, and she funded Sharp's Appalachian
collecting in part. Storrow was deeply entrenched in
reform causes. She sponsored a Boston working girls'
club for Jewish and Italian immigrant laborers, and she
founded the Paul Revere pottery, offering handicraft
employment at a living wage. She took active part in the
Playground Association of America (PAA), a voluntary
organization that linked urban reformers with the
burgeoning physical education profession. Storrow headed
the PAA committee on folk dancing in 1910, and later
involved Boston Girl Guides with English dancing.
Storrow also stood as guarantor for Lily Roberts, an EFDS
teacher Sharp secured to work in Boston while his
collecting proceded apace in the South. Storrow's reach
also extended to New York City, where she contributed
financially to the Girls' Branch of the Public Schools
Athletic League.5

In New York, the Girls' Branch provided after-school
instruction and club work in folk-dancing for school
girls hailing predominantly from the city's Lower East
Side. As an all-female voluntary group, the Girls'
Branch employed Elizabeth Burchenal to administer a
curriculum of traditional dances from foreign lands--
these "folk-dances" Burchenal collected on trips abroad
and by study with immigrants. Burchenal contacted Sharp
in 1908 for steerage in England toward village morris
dancers, with whom she made contact on several trips
abroad. She incorporated morris dances among the
materials that Girls' Branch school girls danced in
annual May fetes held in Central Park and other borough
parks.6

It was the Girls' Branch that sponsored Sharp's New York lecture and demonstration in February 1915, and it booked another appearance for its Brooklyn meeting in March. The Girls' Branch promoted as well a six-lesson course in English country dancing in March 1915--participants were then prepared to be examined by Sharp for an Elementary certificate. The Girls' Branch role in transmitting English folk dance was thus two-fold: it validated English traditional dance as part of a city-wide practice for school girls and it launched Sharp in America as an expert in pedagogy. Finally, several Girls' Branch instructors served loyally in the New York Center's activities, and Burchenal worked as the national organization's first treasurer, actively shaping policy along with Helen Storrow, the secretary, and George Pierce Baker, president.7

Already, I hope, the connection is clear between women's social reform work and transmission of English traditional dance in Progressive-era America. In Chicago, Mary Wood Hinman remained the organizational stalwart as secretary of the Chicago Center. Hinman has gained recognition as the early mentor of modern dance choreographer Doris Humphrey. Hinman had also taught folk dancing, court, and social dancing at Hull-House, one of America's premier social settlements, from 1897 to about 1908. In this context, she worked with immigrant children, offspring of the city's industrial labor force, bringing to bear dance materials she'd collected abroad, learned from immigrant people, or learned at the EFDS Stratford-on-Avon summer school. Hinman taught, too, at the University of Chicago Elementary School, a laboratory school for John Dewey's progressive education theory. And from 1904 she ran the Hinman Normal School, a training school for dance teachers. In similar vein to Burchenal and the Girls' Branch, Hinman's personal pedagogy and her organizational labor with the Chicago Center transmitted and promoted the study of English traditional dance to various class groups.8

In Pittsburgh Mrs. Dawson Callery's philanthropy and interest in traditional dance buoyed up the Pittsburgh Center in a manner similar to Helen Storrow's. St. Louis was the exception to the pattern of female-impelled networks. The banner of English traditional dance in St. Louis was carried by Percival Chubb, leader of the city's Ethical Culture Society. This was consistent with his earlier work in New York City's Ethical Culture School as director of school festivals, and with his position within the Ethical movement as one inclined toward ceremonial.9

With Chubb noted as the exception, four of the five American centers for English folk dance were founded and persisted through the agency of female networks, networks developed through women's philanthropy and social reform activity. Here the parallels to Neal's situation in England are quite strong--to her working girls group, the Esperance Club, she introduced traditional dance as a solvent for urban industrial conditions. (The American situation was compounded by the pressure from massive

flows of foreign immigration.) American middle class and
elite women rode the waves of demographic and industrial
crises to contest the structures of a nineteenth-century
separate spheres ideology, one which consigned women to
the home and domesticity. In temperance, poor relief,
recreation, Americanization, and settlement movements,
American women claimed public sphere presence and
instrumentality for political reasons: to recuperate the
effects of industrialization; to mediate (though not
finally change) class antagonism; and to bridge cultural
difference between immigrants and resident people. They
stepped into municipal and national voids by supplying
social welfare needs, unmet in American until formation
of the welfare state in the 1930s. It is germane to ask:
did, or how did, Neal's collecting and promotion of
morris dancing for working girls construe or trouble
gender ideology in England?10

Extant records from American certificate awards and
summer dance camps illuminate another dimension of the
gendered transmission of English dance. For three
summers, Sha rp directed the three-week sessions where
country, morris, and sword dance were taught, with the
help of Maud Karpeles, Lily Roberts, and Nora Jervis, the
latter an English-trained teacher employed at Goucher
College. Attendance lists at the 1915 camp show that
women outnumbered men by about three to one. Further,
each camp and Center-sponsored course concluded with
certificate exams in traditional dance subjects, at
Elementary, Intermediate, and Advanced levels. Records
of certificate winners show that in 1915, 1916 and 1917,
successful women outnumbered men in every category of
examination. The disproportion was greatest among
country dance certificate-holders, who were tested in
country dance and singing games. In 1915, 55 women
compared to five men earned the certificate. Even in
1917, when overall numbers were low, nine women compared
to one man earned the award. Certificate winners were
more closely balanced for the Elementary certificate,
which tested competence in country dance, morris dance,
and sword dance. In 1915 and 1917, seven women versus
four men earned the certificate. In 1916, however, 17
women compared to three men won the Elementary
certificate.11

Of course, the class basis of American course and
camp attendance may be argued--only middle and upper
class people could afford tuition and/or time away from
work. Gender and occupation figured in as well, for
teachers would be the most likely to pursue either a
short-term, high intensity branch course, or the camps'
three-week training. Hinman enrolled in camp, as did
several Girls' Branch instructors; Burchenal earned a
certificate at a branch course. Census data show that in
the early twentieth century, 75 to 85% of elementary and
secondary school teachers were female. The case was
different for teachers of dancing, however, and I
summarize the situation here. National census returns
did not recognize teachers of dancing as an occupational
category until 1910. At that time, the new category

comprised "teachers of athletics, dancing etc." In 1910,
men constituted 70% and women almost 30% of these
gainfully employed workers. In 1920 women climbed to
41%, and men fell to 59%, of these workers. Women's
dance teaching clearly did not comprise a simple
continuity with their contemporary predominance in
general school teaching. Rather, dance teaching in the
1900s and 1910s was taking shape as a new profession, one
not yet occupationally feminized, but with a trend
developing in that direction. Burchenal and Hinman made
careers for themselves as folk dance teachers at
precisely this time. The admittedly limited data from
the 1915 camp and the certificate awards exceed the
national pattern and lend support to my argument that
English traditional dance was transmitted as a gendered
practice.12

Finally, I want to sketch briefly a third way in
which English traditional dance was gendered female--and
performed cultural work in early twentieth-century
America. I return specifically to New York, which
boasted the country's largest consolidated city school
system. There Girls' Branch after-school work staked out
folk-dancing (including English traditional dance) as an
athletic activity specifically suited to girls. After-
school athletics for boys focussed on track, drill, and
team sports; boys' work featured competition between
schools across the system. Using a questionnaire
methodology promoted by the child study movement, the
Girls' Branch determined that folk-dancing elicited the
greatest "interest" among girls compared to gymnastics
and team games. In Progressive education theory,
"interest" was taken to signal appropriate curricular
materials. The Girls' Branch dropped gymnastics, and
dancing took pride of place in folk-dancing clubs girls
formed at each school. A morris dance like *Laudanum
Bunches* was thus performed by all-girl sides of six; the
country dance *Sellengers Round* united girls and only
girls. Girls' work was further distinguished from that
of boys by limiting competition to clubs within a school-
-no *inter*mural competition was permitted. In 1910,
school meet judges awarded points to clubs for the
memory, spirit, and form that girls showed in executing
dances. By 1914, the criterion of form was dropped,
thereby privileging girls' cooperative, interactive
qualities. While these interpersonal skills were
traditionally thought feminine in separate spheres
ideology, Girls' Branch annual park fetes recast them as
politically instrumental. Park fetes always closed with
a maypole dance, maypoles dotting the field, the girls
from each school clustering around their poles. Plaiting
the ribbons, they etched crystalline circles on grassy
lawns, their geometry captured by long-shot newspaper
photographs. Still other photos, closer-up, caught
girls' swaying limb-reach and throat-bared heads. Park
fete choreographies framed the girls' group-oriented,
relational qualities in tension with the pleasure and
passion suffusing individual dancing bodies. This
unstable equilibrium embodied and worried conflicting

Progressive-era claims re the individual and the group,
matters of political moment in a society wrestling with
the effects of laissez-faire economic and social
practices. The gendered construction of girls' folk-
dancing functioned politically, mobilizing the body as
site for ideological contest.13

For the English movement, we might well ask: what
cultural work was performed by the Esperance girls giving
public demonstrations or dancing in connection with a
major suffrage exhibition? What work was done by Neal's
adding boys to the all-girl group?14 Or by Sharp's
privileging of his all-male morris demonstration team?
And whence Sharp's penetrating, enduring sense of loss
when half of them were killed during the war? These
questions proceed from concern with ways in which dancing
performs cultural work. I submit that English
traditional dance, in America, and surely England, too,
troubled, challenged, and even confirmed contemporary
constructions of gender. To this the traditional dance
discourse could profitably turn consideration. If we
look at traditional dance as performing cultural work, we
can articulate it with other acts and activities that
constitute social order and experience, thereby breaching
boundaries of another kind.

NOTES

1. See Maud Karpeles, *Cecil Sharp: His Life and Work*
(London: Routledge & Kegan Paul, 1967) for an account of
Sharp's life and work. See also articles and books
listed in this paper's bibliography, which elaborate and
qualify aspects of that account. For historians of the
dance revival named in the text, see John Forrest, "Here
We Come A-Fossiling," *Dance Research Journal* 17/1
(Spring/Summer 1985): 27-34; Keith Chandler, *"Ribbons,
Bells and Squeaking Fiddles"; the Social History of
Morris Dancing in the English South Midlands, 1660-1900*,
Publications of the Folklore Society: Tradition, 1
(Hisarlik Press, 1993); Dave Harker, *Fakesong; the
Manufacture of British 'Folksong' 1700 to the Present*
(Milton Keynes, England: Open University Press: 1985);
and Richard Sykes, "The Evolution of Englishness in the
English Folksong Revival, 1890-1914," *Folk Music Journal*
6, no. 4 (1993): 446-490.

2. See Theresa Buckland, "Institutions and Ideology in
the Dissemination of Morris Dances in the Northwest of
England," *Yearbook for Traditional Music* 23 (1991):53-
67; Roy Dommett, "How Did you Think it Was? The Political
Background to the Folk revival, 1903-1912," *Country
Dance and Song* 11/12 (1981): 47-52; A.D. Townsend, "Cecil
James Sharp as Collector and Editor of Traditional

Dance," *Traditional Dance* 5/6 (1988): 53-75; Roy Judge, "Mary Neal and the Esperance Morris," *Folk Music Journal* 5, no. 5 (1989): 545-591. For women's transmission of revival dances to later practitioners see for example Roy Dommett, "The Cotswold Morris in the Twentieth Century," *Traditional Dance* 1 (1981): 59-92.

3. On Neal, Warren and Wright in America see "English Experts Here to Teach the Famous Morris Dance," *New York Times*, 22 January 1911, part 5, p. 11; James. C. Brickwedde, "A. Claud Wright: Cecil Sharp's Forgotten Dancer," *Folk Music Journal* 6, no. 1 (1990): 5-36; and Rhett Krause, "Morris Dance and America Prior to 1913," *Country Dance and Song* 21 (March 1991): 1-18.

4. My understanding of the national American organization (the English Folk Dance Society--American Branch) and its urban centers is based primarily upon scrapbook materials housed in the Archives of the Country Dance and Song Society, the present-day successor to the national organization. Two scrapbooks are germane: "Federated American Branches of the English Folk Dance Society 1915-1927, Part I"; and "New York Branch of the English Folk Dance Society from the Organization on April 20, 1915 to, the end of the Season of 1930." The CDSS Archives were located in Darnestown, Maryland when I first used them; they were re-located to the University of New Hampshire.

5. On Mrs. Storrow see Leonard Ware, "Helen Osborne Storrow 1864-1944; A Memoir" (Northampton, Massachusetts: 1970), and "Program of the Rochester Play Congress," *The Playground* (May 1910):92. On the Paul Revere Pottery see Eileen Boris, *Art and Labor: Ruskin, Morris and the Craftsman Ideal in America* (Philadelphia: Temple University Press, 1986), 114. On Storrow's support for Lily Roberts see Cecil Sharp to Mrs. Roberts, 26 August 1915, in "My dear Lily, the Letters of Lily (nee Roberts) Conant from Cecil J. Sharp. Transcribed, with notes by Betty Conant Burchell," p. 15, part of "Lily Roberts in America," CDSS Archives.

6. Materials on the Girls' Branch and Burchenal's work are developed in Linda J. Tomko, "Women, Artistic Dance Practices, and Social Change in the United States, 1890-1920," Ph.D dissertation, University of California, Los Angeles, 1991, chapter 4. For Burchenal's contact with Sharp, see her letter 1 September 1908, Sharp Correspondence, Box 1, Vaughan Williams Memorial Library, London.

7. On Sharp at Girls' Branch meetings, see Elizabeth Burchenal, ed., *Official Handbook of the Girls' Branch of the Public Schools Athletic League of the City of New York 1915-1916* (New York: American Sports Publishing, 1915): 36. See also the printed course announcement in "Federation American Branches" scrapbook, and the

typescript "Report of the English Folk Dance Society
U.S.A. Branch for the Year 1915-1916" in "New York
Branch" scrapbook, both CDSS Archives.

8.   On Hinman see Tomko, "Women, Artistic Dance
Practices, and Social Change," chapter 3.

9.   See Chubb's *Festivals and Plays in Schools and
Elsewhere* (New York: Harper & Brothers, 1912). I develop
Chubb's connection with innovative New York dance
practices in my manuscript in progress *Dancing Class*.

10.   Barbara Welter identified this separate spheres
ideology in America in the seminal article "The Cult of
True Womanhood, 1820-1860," *American Quarterly* 18
(Summer 1966): 131-175. Subsequent scholarship has
traced and weighed the ideology's reach and effects.

11.   For camp attendance and certificate awards, see
items in the "Federation American Branches" scrapbook,
CDSS Archives: loose pages treating the 1915 Eliot camp;
"The English Folk Dance Society Report" (February 1917);
and "The English Folk Dance Society United States Branch,
Notes on the Season of 1917-1918." On the camp staff see
also "Lily Roberts in America; from her notes, somewhat
reorganized by Elizabeth Conant Burchell," p. 3, part of
"Lily Roberts in America," CDSS Archives.

12.   These census figures are developed and analyzed in
Tomko, *Dancing Class*, in progress. They draw from data
published in the Twelfth, Thirteenth, and Fourteenth
Census of the United States (Washington, D.C.: United
States Census Office (1900) and Government Printing
Office (1910, 1920) and from Joseph A. Hill, *Women in
Gainful Occupations 1870 to 1920*, Census Monographs IX,
(Washi ngton, D.C.: Government Printing Office, 1929).

13.   On the gendering of Girls' Branch folk-dancing, see
Tomko, "Women, Artistic Dance Practices, and Social
Change," chapter 4; and Tomko, "Fete Accompli: Gender,
`Folk-Dance,'and Progressive-era Political Ideals in New
York City," in *Corporealities*, ed. Susan Foster
(Routledge, forthcoming). For news photographs of the
dancing field see for example "When 7,000 School Girls
Danced Around Eighty-Two May Poles in Central Park," *New
York Times*, 25 May 1913, Picture sec., part 1, pp. 4-5
and "5,000 Schoolgirls Dance on the Green," *Brooklyn
Daily Eagle*, 19 May 1915, Picture and Sporting sec., p.
5.

14.   For Esperance girls' dancing on public and suffrage-
related occasions see Judge, "Mary Neal," p. 562 and
Dommett, "How Did You Think It Was?" p. 51.

BIBLIOGRAPHY

Barrand, Anthony G., Roy Leonard Dommett, Ivor Allsop. "Comments on John Forrest's `Here We Come A-Fossiling'." *Dance Research Journal* 17/1 (Spring/Summer 1985): 34-42.

Boris, Eileen. *Art & Labor*: *Ruskin, Morris and the Craftsman Ideal in America.* Philadelphia: Temple University Press, 1986.

Boyes, Georgina. *The Imagined Village; Culture, Ideology and the English Folk Revival.* Manchester and New York: Manchester University Press, 1993.

Brickwedde, James. C. "A. Claud Wright: Cecil Sharp's Forgotten Dancer." *Folk Music Journal* 6, no. 1 (1990): 5-36.

Buckland, Theresa. "English Folk Dance Scholarship: A Review." *Traditional Dance* 1 (1981): 3-18.

Buckland, Theresa. "Institutions and Ideology in the Dissemination of Morris Dances in the Northwest of England." *Yearbook for Traditional Music* 23 (1991):53-67.

Burchenal, Elizabeth. *Folk-Dances and Singing Games.* New York: G. Schirmer, 1909.

Burchenal, Elizabeth, ed. *Official Handbook of the Girls' Branch of the Public Schools Athletic League of the City of New York, 1915-16.* New York: American Sports Publishing Co., 1915. Burchenal-edited *Handbooks* for the 1914-15 through the 1917-18 years were issued by the same publisher.

Chandler, Keith. *"Ribbons, Bells and Squeaking Fiddles"; the Social History of Morris Dancing in the English South Midlands, 1660-1900.* Publications of the Folklore Society: Tradition, 1. Hisarlik Press, 1993.

Chubb, Percival. *Festivals and Plays in Schools and Elsewhere* (New York: Harper & Bros., 1912).

Dommett, Roy. "The Cotswold Morris in the Twentieth Century." *Traditional Dance* 1 (1981): 59-92.

Dommett, Roy. "How Did you Think it Was? The Political Background to the Folk revival, 1903-1912." *Country Dance and Song* 11/12 (1981): 47-52.

Forrest, John. "Here We Come A-Fossiling," and "Response." *Dance Research Journal* 17/1 (Spring/Summer 1985): 27-34 and 42.

Fourteenth Census of the United States taken in the Year 1920. Vol 4, "Population", 1920, Occupations. Washington: Government Printing Office, 1923.

Gulick, Luther H. *The Healthful Art of Dancing.* New York: Doubleday, Page & Co., 1910.

Gulick, Luther Halsey. "Teaching American Children to Play: Significance of the Revival of Folk Dances, Games and Festivals by the Playground Association." *The Craftsman* 15 (November 1908): 192-199.

Harker, Dave. *Fakesong; the Manufacture of British 'Folksong' 1700 to the present*. Milton Keynes, England: Open University Press: 1985.

Harker, Dave. "May Cecil Sharp be Praised?" *History Workshop Journal* 14 (Autumn 1982): 44-62.

Hill, Joseph A. *Women in Gainful Occupations 1870 to 1920*. Census Monographs 9. Washington, D.C.: Government Printing Office, 1929.

Hobsbawm, Eric and Terence Ranger, eds. *The Invention of Tradition*. Cambridge: Cambridge University Press, 1983.

Judge, Roy. "Mary Neal and the Esperance Morris." *Folk Music Journal* 5, no. 5 (1989): 545-591.

Judge, Roy. "May Day and Merrie England." *Folklore* 102, no. 2 (1991): 131-148.

Judge, Roy. "Merrie England and the Morris 1881-1910." *Folklore* 104, no. 1-2 (Spring-Autumn 1993): 124-143.

Karpeles, Maud. *Cecil Sharp: His Life and Work*. London: Routledge & Kegan Paul, 1967.

Krause, Rhett. "Morris Dance and America Prior to 1913." *Country Dance and Song* 21 (March 1991): 1-18.

Krause, Rhett. "Morris Dance and America Prior to 1913, Part II." *Country Dance and Song* 22 (June 1992): 20-35.

"Program of the Rochester Play Congress," *The Playground* (May 1910):77-102.

Schofield, Derek. "'Revival of the Folk Dance: An Artistic Movement': The Background to the Founding of The English Folk Dance Society in 1911." *Folk Music Journal* 5, no. 2 (1986): 215-219.

Scrapbooks of the Federation American Branches (1915-27) and the New York Branch (1915-30) of the English Folk Dance Society. Country Dance and Song Society Archives, University of New Hampshire.

Sharp, Cecil J. *Folk Dancing in Schools*. 3d ed. London: The English Folk Dance Society, 1920.

Sykes, Richard. "The Evolution of Englishness in the English Folksong Revival, 1890-1914." *Folk Music Journal* 6, no. 4 (1993): 446-490.

Thirteenth Census of the United States taken in the Year 1910. Volume 4, "Population", 1910, Occupation Statistics. Washington, D.C.: Government Printing Office, 1914.

Thompson, Allison, ed. "The Amherst Dance Camp: Reminiscences of Ted Viehman." *Country Dance and Song* 23 (April 1993): 11-18.

Tomko, Linda J. "Women, Artistic Dance Practices, and Social Change in the United States, 1890-1920." Ph.D dissertation, University of California, Los Angeles, 1991.

Townsend, A.D. "Cecil James Sharp as Collector and Editor of Traditional Dance." *Traditional Dance* 5/6 (1988): 53-75

Twelfth Census of the United States, Taken in the Year 1900. "Population," Part 2. Washington, D.C.: United States Census Office, 1902.

Ware, Leonard. "Helen Osborne Storrow 1864-1944; A Memoir." Northampton, Massachusetts: 1970.

Welter, Barbara. "The Cult of True Womanhood, 1820-1860." *American Quarterly* 18 (Summer 1966): 131-175.

"English Experts Here to Teach the Famous Morris Dance." *New York Times*, 22 January 1911, part 5, p. 11.

"When 7,000 School Girls Danced Around Eighty-Two May Poles in Central Park." *New York Times*, 25 May 1913, Picture sec., part 1, pp. 4-5.

"5,000 Schoolgirls Dance on the Green." *Brooklyn Daily Eagle*, 19 May 1915, Picture and Sporting sec., p. 5.

Control of the Passes, de - scribing the fictions of Bali.

by Jane Turner, Crewe & Alsager Faculty
Manchester Metropolitan University

The Secret Agent by W.H. Auden

Control of the passes was, he saw, the key
To this new district, but who would get it?
He, the trained spy, had walked into the trap
For a bogus guide, seduced by the old tricks.

Bali has been defined by its performance activities.[1] Temples are equated with theatres and performances are held to activate the temples. The passes between religion, ritual and everyday life have become so interwoven that it has proved difficult to control them but since the time of the Dutch colonisers Bali has been described, inscribed and prescribed by the west.. The flickering shadows of the Balinese performers, like the shadows in Plato's cave, have come to be a simulacrum of the ancient, exotic, mysticism of the east and it is these fictions that have controlled the passes into and out of Bali for the last three hundred years. Edward Said writes in **Orientalism**, that what the west writes as truth about the east is only representation.

  The Dutch went to Bali having heard tales that on this tiny island the ancient court of the Javanese could be rediscovered, preserved, as it were, in amber since the aristocracy fled Java with the Islamic invasion during the fourteenth century establishing their new kingdom in Bali. The early Dutch administrators wrote excitedly that indeed Bali did have an elite , refined culture that undoubtedly dated back to the Javanese **Majapahit.**

  Sadly, the colonising of the island was a bloody affair and a great embarrassment to the Dutch[2] . The Balinese had spent most of their history in a state of war and were found to be a violent, hostile people; a view that did not suit the Dutch at all. Through government policy the Dutch were able to impose peace and replace bloody battles with reports of an idyllic island paradise where everyone was happy, and peace and artistry were national characteristics. And as the Balinese did not see history as of especial importance, the Dutch had free rein to invent a narrative confirming the early tales and their present policy which showed the Balinese to be a traditional but mystical people, who sought non - progressive change and whose beliefs in Animism mixed with Hinduism were articulated day and night through their graceful dancing.

  Such stories of an island and its extraordinarily well balanced, dancing people arrived in Europe as the Modernist movement was seeking some sort of confirmation that human spirit could find harmony. The source of their lack was thought to be located in the exotic 'other', the primitive peoples of the east.

Western artists and anthropologists arrived in Bali in the late 1920's and were not disappointed by what they found and took it upon themselves to perpetuate the myths, but maybe in a more accessible form. The artist Walter Spies created two of the most popular tourist performances from sacred forms not easily seen by visitors[3] . The first, *Kecak* or monkey dance was initially constructed for a German film crew who wanted to include trance dance in their film *Island of the Demons* but had been denied permission to film in the temple. The resulting dance is derived from an ancient exorcism rite called *Sanghyang,* a pre - Hindu dance performed to prevent evil spirits from causing sickness and death in a community. The dance is performed by pre - pubescent girls, who go into a state of trance - possession. Spies adapted the dance by developing the male chorus chant and inserting an excerpt from the Indian epic *The Ramayana*, thus structuring the dancing around what the west would recognise as narrative.Having nullified the religious and ritual significance of the dance, it could be performed outside the temple but was seen as retaining a sense of mysticism and the exotic. It has remained a firm favourite with tourists, who often mis - identify it as being an authentic, ancient dance.

Spies was also instrumental in creating the *Barong and Kris dance*, another tourist performance originating from another exorcism performance depicting the encounter between two of the most potent forces on the island: *Rangda* and *Barong. Rangda* the widow witch has immense magical powers and can only be incarnated by very strong performers able to withstand her spirit. *Barong,* her adversary, is a playful beast whose 'good' magic is in opposition to *Rangda.* In the playing out of their conflict the drama is always curtailed before one or the other is destroyed[4]. The drama is one of two powers that need to be maintained in balance and does not follow a western narrative form. The extraction of the dance from the ritual *Calong Arang* again proved popular with tourists fascinated by the dangers of *Rangda's* magic and eager to see an example of trance dancing.

The fictions of the island were being re-written and modified, most notably by Spies but also by others. Hickman Powell in his book *The Last Paradise,* written in 1930, commented that Bali should be made into, 'an international theme park with special laws to maintain it as such', including a ban on 'all goods not essential to the natives' and a halt on democracy which, 'in Bali was preposterous'. Like Disney Land, Bali was being made into a place where a culture could be synthesised and packaged, to be consumed in a twenty - four hour stop over. The narrative created by the Dutch had been accepted and confirmed by the west and continued to thrive until it was picked up by the Indonesian government, who also recognised the economic potential of tourism and adapted the island's narrative once more.

Bali is seen as a culture that has remained distinctive despite the disparate influences imposed upon it. It has sustained its own narrative by modifying ideas from outside forces to fit in with its own cultural beliefs. Anthropologists consider Bali a bi - furcation,[5] a culture able to operate two separate systems simultaneously. Whether it be the Balinese acknowledging the Javanese rule, the Dutch rule or the Indonesian rule, quietly but persistently they are said to continue opperating at a separate level, whereby *Desa* and *Adat* (religious affairs and a matter of custom) have priority over *Banjar* and *Dinas* (state business and government law), maybe best illustrated by the persistence of cock - fighting, outlawed by the Indonesian government but still practised religiously by Balinese men.

In an attempt to regulate and differentiate between religious activity and tourist performances, the government, in the early 1980's, created different performance categories distinguishing sacred from secular performance. The decree argued that the use of non - consecrated costume and props freed a performance from any religious significance thus allowing for more tourist performances. These divisions, in terms of performance intention, have been argued to be a further indication of Bali being commodified as a tourist island. The construction of Bali as an island paradise was and is, a purely economic strategy, nurtured by the implementation of polices that have led to what has been called 'cultural tourism'[6]. The profanation that accompanies such exploitative commerciality has frequently been addressed by the ruling powers who have been able to authorise activities and adjustments to the culture without seeming to be hostage to a tourist economy simply by re - locating the boundaries. Terms like bi - furcation and boundary maintenance[7] explain, perhaps conveniently how the Balinese negotiate the absence of their voice in matters of *Dinas*. Dancers say that all performance has religious significance, despite the governments categories. For the performers, it is important for a dance to be well performed and spiritually efficacious, for this the performer must have *taksu*,[8] a spiritual energy given by the gods. Performance is a functional occupation that services both the community and the gods. Its primary function is not as spectacle for tourists but as a ritual enactment, an offering to the gods; either way the performer needs the spiritual energy to perform so whether a performance has been decreed *Wali* (sacred) or *Bali - Balihan* [9] (secular) the performer requires *taksu* and would therefore consider all performance as having a religious significance.

Traditionally performers learn to dance in the villages. This creates a kaleidoscope of interpretation and also ensures a diversity of forms, as each village may maintain a different repertoire. The range of dance - dramas on the island is extraordinary[10] and, contrary to the views that the island's culture is in a state of stasis, new forms are constantly evolving. This picture has been distorted by the opening of a government training academy, A.S.T.I., in 1967. The training here mitigates against the traditional practise of learning from older dancers in the villages. Here standards and styles are heavily influenced by economic viability, although its agenda incorporates a commitment to researching forms that have fallen out of favour and 'restoring behaviour'[11] , that will then be preserved in a 'seed bank'. However, the teaching dictates that students learn a standard repertoire in a standard form. Particular dances, deemed of specific interest to the tourist market are central to the curriculum. Students at the academy are seen to be privileged, initially because to go there costs a great deal of money so only the rich have access, and secondly because students who go there have easier access to the more lucrative work of dancing in the large tourist hotels and at overseas festivals. I Made Bandam, a major influence on the recent developments in Balinese performance, is not only the Principal of the Academy but also a member of the government. He, like many of the teachers at the Academy, went to America to gain a Masters degree and returned not only with the degree but also, inevitably, an American view of what education should privilege. Perhaps as a consequence of this I Made Bandam has recently been involved with a new television station, set up in Java, introducing a series of programmes on the 'history' and 'origins' of Balinese dance.[12] Responses to the programmes were that it was, of course, a fiction but that it would be accepted as a truth by younger generations, who saw television as projecting realism and therefore truth. As Baudrillard would have it, the fiction is 'realised' and the real becomes 'fictitious'.

In a similar way to how the Dutch, in the nineteenth century, created and wrote a history for the island, the Indonesian government and the west are continuing to shape, formalise and prescribe what Bali is by exerting influence through the mediated representations of performance.

The myth of Bali has been perpetuated and misrepresented by the west from **The Island of the Demons,** to the classics **Road to Bali** and **South Pacific,** and even **King Kong** makes some allusion to the beast being found in Bali. And contemporary fictions still abound, Odin's production of **The Million** clearly references both the **Baris** dance and **Rangda** in the figure of **Anabasis**. The political implications of appropriation are far more of an issue in performance now , although strangely at odds with post - modern thought which confidently declares that cultural boundaries are down and that notions such as truth are outmoded and certainly have no higher status to fictions. The figural now has priority over the discursive and stylistic diversity is essential.

The work of practitioners such as Robert Wilson, Robert Lepage and Arianne Mnouchkine illustrate many of these postmodern practises but there seems to be an integrity to their work. These practitioners have all referenced Balinese cultural performance in their work. The references, often visual, to non - western cultures create a resonance or tension in the text being performed. For example, in Lepage's production of **A Midsummer Night's Dream**, performed at the Royal National Theatre in1992, the fairies were presented as having blue painted faces, referencing a Congolese rites of passage ritual where the colour denotes the ghost of childhood, this and the swamp - like set, a reference to Bachofen's theory of swamp culture[13] and sexuality, gave a clear reading of the play as the lover's rite of passage from adolescence to adulthood, These rituals have been lost from our own culture and we can only reference existing rituals to point the importance of these liminal phases in our life.The success of the visual reference was off - set by the use of the **Kecak** chant by the lovers at the transition point of their return to the court. The decision to have a mere chorus of four (as opposed to the Balinese chorus of one hundred) chanting for a few minutes seemed to belie the complexity of the form and obscure a clear reading for its inclusion.

This and the decontextualised simulation of Balinese **Baris** in Odin's **The Million,** are no more critiqued than Dorethy Lamour's mock **Legong** in **Road to Bali** so is there a validity to this form of intercultural performance? **The Million** reflects Odin's own cultural encounters and misunderstandings. In an attempt to explore the bodies potential for creative expression Odin performers went and studied codified performance techniques in India, Japan and Bali. They then taught other members of the company and created **The Million,** a piece that shows what happens when a technique is not understood, or as their director, Eugenio Barba, went on to explore, the importance of the performer being able to work through their inculturated behaviour to incorporate an acculturated behaviour.[14] Inculturated behaviour is that which we have absorbed from the culture of our up - bringing, whereas acculturated behaviour is an imposition of an un - natural behaviour. Since **The Million** , where we see a poor reproduction of **Baris,** an example of performers having learnt a technique but understood it with their eye and not their body, the company have absorbed performance ideas and created their own body technique, what Kirsten Hastrup calls a creolisation.[15]

Cultural creativity is an evolutionary process. Part of the process of attaining a technique comes from a physical and mental understanding, what Barba calls an underscore, a way of focussing and controlling the energy in a performance. For the Balinese this comes from the gods in the form of **taksu** for Odin and other western performers we must create narratives that we can believe in.

The dichotomy created by a global culture, conceived by the west, that on the one hand wants to retain what are perceived as 'primitive' cultures in an 'authentic', 'primitive' state but, on the other hand, sees all art as a commodity with an economic value and therefore subject to market forces, has created in Bali, an 'international theme park'. This is only one narrative and underscoring it is a seemingly unlimited potential for human creativity. The boundaries may be down but the imagination has control of the passes.

1 See Geertz, Clifford (1980) *Negara: The Theatre State in Nineteenth Century Bali,* Princeton: Princeton University Press

2 For a more detailed appraisal of Bali at this time see Schulte Nordholt, H (1986) *Bali: Colonial Conceptions and Political Change 1700 - 1940 From Shifting Hierarchies to 'Fixed Order',* CASP 15

3 See Vickers, Adrian (1989) *Bali - a paradise created* Periplus Editions

4 See Eiseman, Fred B. (1989) *Bali: Sekala and Niskala Volume1 Essays on Religion, Ritual and Art* Periplus Editions.
See also Covarrubias, Miguel (1937) *Island of Bali* O.U.P.

5 See Picard, M (1990) *"Cultural Tourism" in Bali: Cultural Performances as Tourist Attraction* Indonesia No.49 (April)

6 Ibid.

7 Ibid., p.38

8 Suriyani,Luh Ketut and Jenson, Gordon D.(1993)*Trance and Possession in Bali* O.U.P. in Asia
Bandam, I Made and DeBoer, Fredrik E. (1995) *Balinese dance in Transition* O.U.P. in Asia

9 Ibid. Picard, Michel p.66

10 Still the most comprehensive guide to Balinese performance is De Zoete,Beryl and Spies, Walter (1938) *Dance and Drama in Bali* Faber and Faber.

11 See Schechner, Richard (1985) *Between Theatre and Anthropology* University of Pennsylvania Press

12 There is an on - going project based at SOAS surveying the output from the station, led by Mark Hobart and Felicia Hughes - Freeland.

13 See Bachofen, J.J. (1973) *Myth, Religion and Mother Right: selected writings* Princeton University Press.

14 See Barba, Eugenio and Savarese, Nicole (1991)*The Dictionary of Theatre Anthropology* C.P.R. and Routledge.

15 Unpublished article *Teatrum Mundi.*

Bibliography

Bachofen, J.J. (1973), *Myth, Religion and Mother Right: selected writings,* Princeton University Press.

Bandam, I Made and DeBoer, Fredrik E. (1995), *Balinese Dance in Transition,* Asia: Oxford University Press.

Barba, E. and Savarese, N. (1991) *The Dictionary of Theatre Anthropology,* Centre for Performance Research and Routledge.

Covarrubias, M. (1937), *Island of Bali,* Singapore: Oxford University Press.

De Zoete, B. and Spies, W. (1938), *Dance and Drama in Bali,* Faber and Faber.

Eiseman, Fred B. (1989), *Bali: Sekala and Niskala Volume 1, Essays on Religion and Art,* Periplus Editions.

Geertz, C. (1980), *Negara: The Theatre State in Nineteenth Century Bali,* Princeton: Princeton University Press.

Hastrup, K. unpublished paper *'Teatrum Mundi, Cultural creativity and the theatricality of the world'.*

Picard, M. (1990), ' *"Cultural Tourism" in Bali: Cultural Performances as Tourist Attraction',* Indonesia, No. 49 (April).

Powell, H. (1930), *The Last Paradise,* London: Jonathan Cape.

Schechner, R. (1985), *Between Theatre and Anthropology,* University of Pennsylvania Press.

Schulte Nordholt, H. (1986), *'Bali: Colonial Conceptions and Political Change 1700 - 1940 From Shifting Hierarchies to "Fixed Order"'.*CASP 15.

Suriyani, L. K. and Jenson G. D.,(1993), *Trance and Possession in Bali,* Kuala Lumpur: Oxford University Press.

Vickers, A. (1989), *Bali - A Paradise Created,* Periplus Editions.

An Exercise in Contradiction: Reading The Aerobics Video

Trish Winter

University of Newcastle upon Tyne

The aerobics video sits in a place where the female body confronts an ideal-feminine image on the screen. It spans representation and bodily practice, both constructing images of the body and offering itself as a self-help tool for women to produce femininity through work on the body. It explicitly and implicitly offers itself as a means of gaining health, fitness, beauty, transformation and empowerment through the vehicle of bodily activity matched in mirror-image to the body of a star on the screen. It is positioned not only at the interface of image and lived experience, but also spans and falls between categories such as work/leisure and sport/dance, and extends into the film, music, video, fitness, fashion, beauty, diet and advertising industries as well as the fields of sport, medicine and health. Sitting, then, at the point of intersection of a number of discourses which compound, contradict and compete with each other within the text, its main subject and object, the female body, can be viewed as its battleground.

The body represented in and addressed by the aerobics video is also situated at the intersection of a number of theoretical debates within feminism, media and cultural studies, some addressing themselves primarily to questions of representation and others focusing on the body itself. The status of the aerobics video as a text which both represents and speaks to the female body allows for the convergence of separately existing theoretical areas, and its study raises a number of issues in relation to them. I will be considering *CherFitness: A New Attitude* and *Body Confidence* in relation to some of these fields of study, focusing on the body as a site of tension, contradiction and ambiguity.

Consider first the body of the star Cher. As actress, singer and professional 'body', Cher occupies a market position which cuts across the film, music and entertainment industries. The meanings of the star-image 'Cher' circulate both within her filmic and other performances, and outside of them, via representations in the media, interviews, and so on. The *CherFitness* videos not only carry her star-image but have helped to define it. It is, perhaps, not surprising that this star vehicle for the aerobics video should be one whose image is founded on tropes of transformation, transgression and contradiction, and in whose image the body is of central importance.

The undoubted fascination of Cher's appearance seems to be related to its contradictions; hers is an image full of tensions. As Richard Dyer points out, the star-image can hold together contradictory elements. In the case of Cher, this seems to be echoed in her body itself. Her unusual and chimera-like appearance is intriguing partly because it is deceptively and 'un-naturally' youthful. This ambiguity is illustrated in an article in *Film Comment*, 1988:

> 'Ironically, while she has had everything known to woman done to her - nose bobbed, teeth capped, back tattooed, Mac the Knife knows what else - the thing you notice up close, or even in performance from the back row, is how ... absolutely *real* she seems.' (Jacobson, H., 1988: p.42)

She *seems* real or natural, even though we know she has reconstructed her body through means such as plastic surgery, and the natural/un-natural tension is as compelling in her image as it is in the sci-fi image of the cyborg.

The element of the un-natural in Cher's image resonates in these texts, opening up a space for the notion that gender might be a matter of performance rather than a natural result of the sexed body one is born with. The idea that the body can be understood as a cultural rather than a natural entity has contributed to feminist and other critiques of essentialism, and provides a tool for demystifying bodily matters which are conventionally consigned to the realm of the natural, and therefore the immutable.

This kind of theoretical position has led Judith Butler, for example, to a discussion of the radical possibilities of practices such as drag. She suggests that if gender is not an expression of inner truth but 'a fantasy instituted and inscribed on the surface of bodies' then the practice of drag has a potential to reveal 'one of the key fabricating mechanisms through which the social construction of gender takes place'. (Butler, 1990: p. 137) If, as Butler suggests, practices such as drag can be deployed or read subversively, can the performance of femininity within the aerobics text be read in this light? Although not an example of drag in the specific sense referred to by Butler, how far can the aerobics text and its practices be considered to have the potential to reveal the performativity of gender or to unsettle gender norms?

In the aerobics text, femininity is seen to be produced not only through the performance of a series of stylised acts, through clothing, hair and makeup and so on, but also through the transformation of bodily form, implying that bodily signs of femininity can be a matter of construction too. As Cher puts it, 'you don't get a body ... any kind of body ... by wishing for it. You get it by work.'

The female body has often been conceived of as transformable, but the work of transformation has generally been done through externally applied means, like corsetry, make-up and clothing, keeping intact the notion of a 'natural body' existing prior to these interventions. The notion that the actual shape of the female body itself can be transformed in a chosen image is a potentially more transgressive one. That the female bodily form is seen to be transformable, and the desirable feminine body to be, increasingly, self-produced not only through exercise and diet but also by and in association with other means such as plastic surgery, is a development which coexists uneasily with discourses of health, beauty and the 'natural body' which are more commonly associated with beauty and fitness practices. This leads to textual contradictions such as Cher's statement: 'You'll be able to make the curves you used to have naturally', presenting the ideal body as both natural and self-made.

Similarly, the feminine body constructed within the texts is produced through increased muscularity and, as Richard Dyer notes, muscles are both natural and constructed. They are also conventional signs of masculine strength and power. Creating further ambiguity, these ideal feminine bodies draw significantly on images of masculinity in their form, clothing and activity. The ideal body is a lean one in which some bodily signs of femininity, particularly breasts, tend to disappear. Similarly, these representations draw on the masculine iconography of body-building, albeit in a modified and eroticised form. For example, the 'resistance bands' included free with *Body Confidence*, are reminiscent of that icon of masculine physical culture, the bullworker.

In *A New Attitude*;. The 'ideal image' of the muscular female body reaches almost perfect expression in the figure of Kelly, the instructor. Her body is more bulky and muscular than Cher's. Her muscles are well defined and she is flat chested. Her outfit is like a wrestler's and, in common with the other participants, she wears substantial black ankle boots. Her physique is reminiscent of the sculptural image of the androgynous and athletic Classical Greek youth. Whilst Kelly's body approaches an androgynous appearance through muscularity, Cher's is more like that of a female impersonator. Her tight-waisted costume, for example, seems designed to create feminine curves on a lean body. Hers is an intriguing and compound image combining signs of masculinity, such as tattoos and flexed biceps, with an excessive performance of femininity in costume, hair and makeup.

Despite being, in some respects, ambiguously gendered, the muscular bodies of CherFitness clearly do not disrupt notions of femininity to the extent that, for example, the body of the female bodybuilder does. These bodies are all within a range which is considered acceptable, normal or desirable for women today. They do indicate, however, how far that 'normal' range has shifted; indeed the aerobics phenomenon is itself closely identified with this shift towards a more muscular 'ideal' and notion of 'normal'. This shift is an ambiguous phenomenon, which involves processes of transgression of the boundaries of what is considered 'feminine' as well as a making safe of potentially dangerous or transgressive images of womanhood through, for example, reference to the iconography of S&M. This makes available images of female strength and power which connote 'transgression', but at the same time are eroticised and within the bounds of the feminine.

Just as tensions and ambiguities are carried in the body and image of the star, they are written also into the content of the activities within the texts. The aerobics video contains a powerful metaphor for a contested female body; one in which struggles, conflicts and tensions are carried in the image of the woman in competition with herself.

One way in which this ambiguous image is compellingly created is through the trope of 'resistance'. As Margaret Morse points out in her analysis of *Jane Fonda's Workout*, (1988) muscular resistance is an important part of the way aerobics is performed. Exercises are done with resistance in the body: muscle strength is pitted against itself so that the body uses more energy than is simply required to execute the movement. The notion of resistance is further emphasised in *CherFitness* through the use of rubber 'resistance bands'. Whilst the texts present an image of active women, then, they are not seen to be active in the world, but appear as women whose activity is visibly turned in against themselves.

The image of activity presented is, in many respects, a contradictory one; a kind of active passivity. It is an image of vigorous physical work which spatially goes nowhere. It is not a complete movement experience; it is repetitive, has a limited spatial profile and exhibits very little dynamic range, for example. The women in the text are seen to be controlling their own bodies, but in submission to the directions of another. The appearance of the exercises is reminiscent both of soldiers and of follow-my-leader children's games. The participants are represented as both active and powerless, with responsibility and decision making taken away from the individual participant except in strictly controlled ways; choosing the height of the step from a menu of three possibilities, for example. This is work which aims to produce the participant's own body in a chosen image. It is an activity which, if it is to succeed, requires a substantial investment of time and energy: time and energy which could have been spent acting in the world.

The participants are represented in the act of writing signs of activity on the body, both by taking part in a display of activity and by enacting the transformation of the body into one which is lean and muscular - the body of an active person.   The text conflates and confuses the image of activity with agency, promising the latter and offering the former. Similarly, the image of the woman working with resistance is one of a curiously static activity, seeming to advance by frame-by-frame stasis. It is an image of women empowered beyond their immediate needs, more clearly an image of empowerment than its condition.

Another effect of working with resistance is that in the process of exercising the musculature is visibly displayed. The act of participating is also, therefore, one not only of producing but also of displaying signs of strength, both muscular and gestural. Whilst the activity of aerobics works to write muscular signs of strength on the body, as Morse points out this does not necessarily equate with functional strengthening. In fact, the isolations and fragmentations proposed by the exercises can be argued to compromise the strength of the body at the same time as they display the signs of strength on its surface.

The text presents and acts primarily to produce the body as 'seen', emphasising the appearance of the body rather than sensation. This is explicit, in that it declares itself to be a tool for transforming the shape or appearance of the body. Even though it claims to be concerned with well-being - 'Any woman who wants to give herself that fit feeling'. Feeling good follows primarily from looking good: 'Feeling your best' is offered more as a result of the promised transformation into a desirable shape than by a sense of power or agency rooted in the body.

The emphasis on the 'seen' body is also implicit, written into the content of the exercises. They are organised around a real or virtual mirror, carrying a sense of 'front' , a presentational emphasis, and the notion of being viewed, emphasising the body as something to be seen rather than felt or experienced. Related to this, there are ways in which the texts appear more like a performance than a participatory class. In CherFitness this is emphasised through the presentation of a visually unified style and of a routine which is declared to have been choreographed by the choreographer of Cher's stage show. High camera angles often position the viewer as if in the circle of a proscenium theatre. The locale refers not only to the culture of body building, itself a culture of display, but also to the proscenium arch. Cher's frequent but unseen costume changes emphasise the notion of performance, and also the continuity between Cher's performance of herself in her stage shows and in the aerobics videos, blurring the act of presentation with that of participation, and performance with 'real life'.

These texts address themselves to the body as a surface for inscription. Dealing in flat, two-dimensional images they reinforce an image of the body as surface, without depth and substance. There are few references to sensation or felt bodily experience; not even, as in *Jane Fonda's Workout,* references to pain. The *CherFitness* workout is offered as a means to an end 'which you might as well try and enjoy' (Cher), rather than something which is pleasurable or empowering in its own right. The *CherFitness* philosophy is to 'get in, do the work and get out', offering work on the body as something of a necessary evil, separate from the rest of one's life. rather than a part of everyday embodied experience.

What are the implications of this textual emphasis on the 'seen' body? If, as in Laura Mulvey's formulation, the 'looked at' position is a narratively passive one, the female protagonists of these texts can be seen to be in a position of tension. their vigorous physical work which signifies 'activity', and which is offered as a key to empowerment and agency, is overwhelmingly orientated towards producing themselves as spectacle. In the world of the aerobics text the female participant is offered an experience of her body as not only in a highly contradictory position, but also as to-be-looked-at.

The final point of tension to be considered is that which is situated over the body of the spectator. To an extent, as she positions herself in mirror-image to the image of the star's body, in the performance of aerobics, those textual contradictions already considered can be seen to be inscribed also on her own body. In considering the spectator, however, it is not enough simply to read her body. As Elizabeth Grosz argues, feminist accounts of the body require not only accounts of the ways in which bodies are culturally produced, controlled, manipulated, and so on, but also 'experiential or phenomenological concepts of the body' (Grosz, 1987: p.13). If this is the case, our account of the female spectator must approach her as both acculturated and embodied. What does it mean, then, for the embodied female subject to view these texts, undertake these activities, and attempt to produce the aerobics body?

Kagan and Morse (1988) argue that the mirror-relationship proposed by the activity of video aerobics can serve to disembody the viewer as feedback from her felt bodily sensation is subjugated to visual feedback from the mirror or screen. On the other hand, the act of 'embodying' the metaphorical spectator/star mirror-relationship could, rather than disembodying the spectator, serve instead to distance the reader from the text as it brings the somatic reality of the lived body right up against the screen image. Furthermore, it is likely that in the uncontrolled domestic context the attempted conjunction of reader and image is more likely to foreground the fact of the spectator's embodied existence. The sheer awkwardness and potential humour of the reality of trying to participate, of 'working out' in the home, stepping up and down on a plastic box in front of the TV set may, in many cases, be a more powerful deconstructive tool than textual analysis.

Of course, the act of approaching the body as a surface for the inscription of signs of strength and activity, even though these may not in themselves equate with the condition of strength or with agency, may for some women be a potentially empowering activity. The muscular body will be read culturally and this will affect the behaviour of others towards the female subject, which will in turn affect the way she experiences herself. At the same time, however, given the time consuming nature and difficulty of actually achieving a bodily transformation, the cultural imperative to do so is as likely to create anxiety and unhappiness as a sense of agency.

The analysis so far assumes that the spectator actually takes up the participating positions offered to her. To presume this is in danger of conceiving of her as passive, seduced by her pleasures, controlled by the stimulation of desire, duped into disciplining herself in line with patriarchal notions of femininity. In this respect, it is helpful to bear in mind the work of feminist writers who, going beyond Mulvey's notion of the male gaze, have considered the role of the female spectator in producing meaning and in taking up subject positions other than those constructed within the text. Radway (1984), for example, makes a useful analytical distinction between the meaning of the text as read, and the meaning of the 'act of reading'. She emphasises the importance of this act in the potentially oppositional pleasures taken by the female romance readers in her study.

The aerobics video explicitly offers itself as something to 'do'; the 'act of taking part' is offered as one of making a claim for agency. At the same time, the video aerobics project could be seen as a strategy of containment which channels women's desire for an active physicality into a form which will control it. Indeed, the 'making space' for physical activity could also be seen as removing that activity from the reader's life and setting it apart, so that the potentially empowering pleasures of bodily activity are seen as something specialised requiring instruction from experts. Any such notion of containment will always be unstable, however. The potential pleasures inherent in bodily activity threaten to exceed the discipline or control of the text, particularly in an uncontrolled domestic viewing situation.

Many readers will not use aerobics videos for the purpose for which they present themselves; as a fitness programme for regular home use. As well as those already mentioned, there are many other features which mitigate against easily being able to take part and follow these texts; it is often quite difficult to follow the exercises, for example. Although these texts explicitly present themselves as interactive, they do seem at times to offer themselves more for watching than taking part, and are quite likely not to be consumed as an interactive project. Some of the variety of fitness tapes on the market, such as Carolan Brown's Step Workout are clearly designed for participation. Others, like Marky Mark's Fitness Video, are designed more for watching, are virtually impossible to attempt without risk of injury and verge on the pornographic. The *CherFitness* texts occupy a middle, and often unstable, position somewhere between the two. The act of attempting to use them for the purpose for which they declare themselves is therefore likely to be something of a struggle.

The position occupied by the aerobics text between viewing and doing, work and leisure, practice and representation, is an ambiguous one, as full of tension as the bodies on the screen and the position occupied by the female body in our culture. As interactive texts, situated in a place where the body confronts the media, they foreground questions of readership. They have both cultural and corporeal significance, provoking a consideration of the relationship between representation and women's lived experience, and can not be considered fully without reflecting on the position of women as textual, social and embodied subjects.

References

BUTLER, J., *Gender Trouble,* Routledge, 1990

GROSZ, E., 'Notes Towards a Corporeal Feminism', *Australian Feminist Studies,* Vol. 5, 1987, pp. 1-5

JACOBSON, H., 'Cher: Chez la femme', *Film comment,* January/February 1988

Bibliography

BORDO, S., 'Reading the Slender Body' in KELLER, J.M. and SHUTTLEWORTH, S., ed., *Body/Politics*, Routledge, 1990

BUTLER, J., *Gender Trouble*, Routledge, 1990

DYER, R., *Stars*, BFI, 1979

GLEDHILL, C., *Stardom, Industry of Desire*, Routledge, 1991

GROSZ, E., 'Notes Towards a Corporeal Feminism', *Australian Feminist Studies,* Vol. 5, 1987, pp. 105

JACOBSON, H., 'Cher: Chez la femme', *Film Comment,* January/February 1988

KAGAN, E and MORSE, M., 'The Body Electronic', *The Drama Review*, vol. 32, no. 4, Winter 1988

KUHN, A., 'The Body and Cinema: Some Problems for Feminism' in SHERIDAN, S., ed., *Grafts,* Verso, 1988

MCNAY, L, *Foucault and Feminism,* Polity Press, 1986

MORSE, M., 'Artemis Aging: Exercise and the Female Body on Video'. *Discourse,* Winter 1987, pp. 20-53

RADWAY, J.A., *Reading the Romance*, Verso, 1984

SCHWARTZ, H., *Never Satisfied: A Cultural History of Diets, Fantasies and Fat,* The Free Press, 1986

TASKER, Y., *Spectacular Bodies*, Routledge, 1993

WILLIS, S., *A Primer for Daily Life,* Routledge, 1991

Other Presentations

THE OBSCENE/OFF-SCREEN BODY: *LOVERS FRAGMENTS*

Johannes Birringer
Northwestern University

[Film/video production for this new performance-work started in December 1994; stage rehearsals began in March, and Act I was premiered at the Cleveland Perform- ance Art Festival in mid-April 1995. The completed work is to be shown in Chicago during May 5-15. Yet we are somewhere still at the beginning, asking questions about the stories and fantasies we are telling each other. So we meet in a dance/photo studio and tell stories while we dance and shoot film.]

Lovers Fragments is a work in progress that began in December 1994 after an intensive weekend spent in the snow-landscape surrounding a friend's pottery farm in Wisconsin. Our personal relations, passions and fantasies helped us to get started on a project that intends to raise questions about collaboration, sexuality, queer conscious- ness, political analysis and desire.

We are particularly interested in the relations between sexual pleasure, the erotic, and performance, and in the role of images that move (us). We began shooting film and video back in January, and some earlier footage or dreams were created in Cuba. After shooting film scenes based on personal fantasies and memories, we began the dance rehearsals, trying to figure out where our stories were moving, where they had begun, and how our differences became intertwined and our fantasies complementary.

We meet in the dance studio or the photo studio and show/tell each other our stories. In our rehearsals we try to remember what it was that developed, and how we can un-develop the images. Or how we might interpret the filmic images of ourselves, at a later stage, on stage, off stage, as figures of our love lives and the strange logic of the rituals we create to explain emotions to us or others. There is an even stranger logic in the way we repeat ourselves, not knowing why we feel love, why we feel loss, and why sexual intimacy or the erotic appear dangerous once we lose control over the projections we make of ourselves.

Is the film the recording or does the dance and the music record something else? What is the whole story, and can there ever be one story when we stumble, blind- folded, over so many different desires and sexual possibilities?

"It was a game at first. I can't remember now how it began. Perhaps I shed my dress. Perhaps she tore it as we fought. Perhaps we were naked over dinner. Like all games, it was a licence of sorts—a licence to touch. A licence to hurt. A licence to struggle, to resist, to restrain. To keep holding. To cry out. To feel fear. Did you see it happen? The circling, the clinch, the rocking and slaps of flesh. It was real enough at the time. Time after time. Because it never had to stop. No one ever won. No one ever came. No one ever got married, or paid the mortgage. The children never left home, or died in car wrecks. Like in a story, or in memory...."

Margaret's monologue comes half-way through the first Act; she has been seen standing on the edge between the abstract, asymmetric steel sculpture (which repre- sents perhaps the real forest we discovered in Wisconsin, or another kind of labyrinth of dreams or entangled threads of stories) and the white screen that closes one side of the upstage area. She carries a coat in her arms, a piece of clothing that is shared by other dancers in the performance, worn by others, used by others to cover their naked-ness or their uneasy memory. When she speaks of "licence" in games and in fiction/memory, she's of course also commenting on the freedom we took to invent or recre-ate the various individual choreographies of the body's memory. We also saw them as geographies of memory, each particular one connected to an experience of a lover and place in time—reconstituted through the gestures of longing and loss, of irony and reflection, of disavowal and impassioned insistence.

"Cada dia regreso a esta playa donde por primera vez me besaste debajo de la luna llena y con el sonido de las olas golpeando contra las rocas y acariciando la arena blanca. Te espero..."

Catherine, Venezuelan-born actress, reads from the letter she is writing at her little table where she patiently plays a poker game against herself, enacting perhaps what Roland Barthes, in *A Lover's Discourse,* has described as the extreme solitude of the one who loves and waits, engulfed in fantasies fending off the absence of the other. "Absence can exist only as a consequence of the other: it is the other who leaves, it is I who remain" (Barthes).

Our performance moves into another direction, deeply into that absence which is not caused (only) by the other but by our own fortunate narcissism, our stubbornness which clings and drives us into the many stories we invent and act out, the scenarios of sexual pleasure that turn us on and cannot be written but are sensed, in the contact of skin and breath, hands sliding over sweat-drenched body muscles nerve-ends nipples, curves of flesh.

Sex for its own sake. Movement born out of passion or a desire too frightening or unexplored or tender to express in words, still grappling, with absence and waiting for emotion to be recognizable. How do we know our emotions? Is it a certain rhythm or the lightness or heaviness of touch, weight upon weight, or gravity floating in an invis-ible color, tasting like the juices of wet tongue savoring tropical fruit? Margaret returns to the stage with a large pineapple, her "vegetable love", luscious secret seated inside the mouth, *peso del sabor* (weight of taste), yet also carried as a concrete metaphor of displacement, the deviation of her desire, centerpiece of the table at the dinner she later stages for her male and female lovers.

Dance for the sake of loving or translating the body into incestuousness: the body cannot be alone. And it blurs all the lines of sexual and gender identities others worry about in their theory or soulless hatred of what they call obscene, dirty, perverse, shameless, imperfect, abject.

Dance for the sake of loving and embracing culturally degraded projections of forbidden love: sweet licence to delve into our own images, nothing to hide except our own awkward force, a strength that allows us to set our own rules, when we dance the tango or invent a triple *pas de deux* or wrestle with ghost images of our film personae. Our films have become strange mirrors, we are inside and outside at the same time. No duplication or refraction but breaks and silences, in the simultaneity of all our stories crossing and departing and never identical. Our kinematics move like the spurts of the saxophone, a frozen still-image, a sudden turn, a backward glance, hands touching eyes, a fluttering of fingers, a sequence of quick kisses on the ear, the rubbing of necks against each other. Sharing the stage with three other women, Shannon stands alone and sings an old blues song, "I'm gonna love you like no one", and at this point I'm not sure anymore how to explain the visibility of touch, since her voice reaches inside us in a way I had never felt before. On our bodies: traces left by voice, the film goes black.

"If I can't forget, is that because it never happened?"

© 1995 by Johannes Birringer

THE MECHANICS OF FLUIDS

Carol Brown

This solo performance is composed of three sections—*The Anatomy of Reason, The Mechanics of Fluids,* and *Acts of Becoming*—collectively titled, *The Mechanics of Fluids. The Anatomy of Reason* was devised in November/December 1994 and had its first performance at the Lilian Baylis Theatre, 9 December 1994. *The Mechanics of Fluids* was first performed at the Lilian Baylis Theatre, 6 October 1994 and has been extensively reworked since then. *Acts of Becoming* received its premiere performance on 15 March 1995 at the University of Surrey. Together with the thesis *Inscribing the Body: Feminist Choreographic Practices* (1994), *The Mechanics of Fluids* represents the culmination of Carol Brown's PhD research. Although the three works that comprise the programme are differentiated in style and subject matter, they are intended to be seen collectively as a trilogy of representations exploring issues of the female body in performance.

In *The Anatomy of Reason,* the polarities of passion and reason, form and matter are negotiated through the combinatory possibilities of selected texts, movements, objects and costumes. The "body" of reason and its feminine subtext is here signified through devices of parody and mimicry. Ideas about the female body and femininity are explicitly referenced in the performance texts (these are reproduced below) as well as through the use of costume, "posture" and gesture. The "baggage" referred to in the work is clearly not solely "critical" but also material. The sexual specificity of the body is gesturally registered as nipples are tweaked and the contents of underpants becomes a site of anxiety (the search for the lost object?). By these means the notion that Woman connotes a lack or absence is playfully interrogated. The significance of the doll is crucial in this context. "She" is set apart from my own body but as an actual object which can be manipulated, shaped and controlled, draws attention to the object-like status of the female body in performance.

However the physicality of the work displaces the freezing of my own image into any singular category: pedestrian movement, walking, crouching and standing, is combined with more stylised sections of movement, mermaid-like humping across the floor; sharp cuts of limbs through space and music-box like posturings. How the female body is "divided by language" and "inscribed by ideas" (Foucault, 1984, p 88) is in this work playfully interrogated through pointed texts and movements which attempt to instal, in order to subvert, images of her/my body as a bound and contained object, idealised and fetishised but also oddly resistant to territorialisation. Though she appears with the accoutrements of feminine passivity, she is not reducible to this image, there is a fierceness in the striking of limbs across the floor and an ironical glint in the eye as the text is spoken.

The presentational mode of this performance involved my direct engagement with the audience through eye contact and speech as well as through the spatial organisation of the dance. In questioning the audience, and in positioning myself as an audience member who steps into the performance space, the traditional boundary between invisible audience and over-exposed performer is transgressed. This is in direct contrast to the following section, *The Mechanics of Fluids,* which apart from its initial "set-up" within the performance—"How to Become an Object..."—turns the focus inward, on the "mechanics" of bodily composition as organism and object. This section is organised into four distinct parts, its fractured form is denoted through dramatic shifts in lighting environments, subdivided by blackouts, as well as contrasting music. In the first section, "the body" is positioned on the plinth for display. Awkward and resistant "it" is an object gone hard. This section evolved out of explorations into the tradition of the female nude in art history and the problematic representation of the female figure — prone and naked — in performance. In particular the issue of how to de-eroticise and de-naturalise the image of a silent and still female body was explored. Through distortions and tensile stillness, "her" body can be seen as both derelict and resistant. The wig, as a device of feminine disguise, serves to heighten this effect, making Her more vulnerable in one sense, as "living doll," and in another sense, further distancing Herself from my-self, opening a gap between the representation of my body as object and myself as cultural agent.

The section on the plinth is followed by three different kinds of journeys. The first travels across the back of the stage in short bursts of fretting, halting and tip-toeing, moving "into the light" and extinguishing it. A second journey begins with a precarious balancing game through which I re-dress my own body and, reiterate some of the still poses from the plinth. In the slow traversing of a diagonally lit strip of the stage, moving precariously from upstage left to downstage right, shifts in weight from one leg to another are-negotiated as if "through a minefield". In the final passage the doll becomes the focus for a transformation of focus and energy. Through these passages I envisage myself as a journeywoman, mapping differing trajectories of space-time and energy and beginning, again and again, without resolution nor ending. The edgy quality of the plinth section is maintained until the final section when the gestural motility shifts to an-other space and is externalised as a contradictory array of gestures — imploring, supplicating and teasing — towards the doll.

Acts of Becoming represents an attempt to draw and reflect upon aspects of my own experience in the processes of becoming a dancer through the animation of boundaries between dancer and choreographer, performer and spectator. In utilising recognisably stylised dance language, it shifts gear from the other two sections of the work into a space where the genealogy of my own dancing body becomes the subject of the work itself. The dance within a dance operates reflexively in the context of the performance drawing attention to the discursive spaces of dance practices. The form of the choreography interposes dance and spoken texts, segmenting and dividing roles as speaker/mover so as to heighten the effect of differing modes of perception inside and outside the dance. The initial phrase of the "dance" is repeated four times with minor variations in detail. Each section of spinning which follows this initial phrase is differentiated by name, the "schlinger," the "schöpf kreis," the "arm kreis," and the "impuls," names given to specific movements common to the Bodenwieser technique and here incorporated into the action of spinning. In this way my own specific inheritance as a dancer is signified within the work. Whilst the repeated enactment of the dance reiterates its form, the momentum increases across these repetitions and builds until the final section of spinning which, with its continuity, its shifts of axis and percussive thrusts breaks with the controlled formalism of what has gone before. The alternation between forms of activity — spinning and "directing" — is a deliberate device intended to break the flow and lyricism of the dance with the poetics of words positioned outside of, but in reference to, the dance. This follows feminists' claims of the need to break with acquired patterns of movement which risk naturalising assumptions about the body as well as the ongoing need to acknowledge female genealogies. At the same time this work attempts to move into a more poetic space through its privileging of rhythm, pulse and spinning.

In this context the choreography can be seen as a metaphor for the becoming spaces of the feminine imaginary as articulated in the writings of Luce Irigaray. The spoken texts refer to both an inheritance of codes and correctives received as a dancer, and feminist writings which attempt to retrieve the body for women (these are repro-duced below). The co-presence of other voices—"I" as other, "I" as another—attests to the differences within and between women as they negotiate their real and imaginary inheritances. In this sense an attempt is made to override and collapse subject and object positions within the dance. This situation is not resolved but shifts to an-other space as the dancer, "I" relocates her/my "baggages" and addressing her audience begins—dancing beyond the ending.

The open-ended structure of this performance suggests passage, on-goingness and non-bounded space wherein the fluid interventions of the feminist subject are enabled.

References

Foucault, Michel. Nietzsche, genealogy, history. In Rabinow, P. (ed.), *The Foucault Reader.* London: Penguin, 1984, pp 76-100.

Irigaray, Luce. When our lips speak together. In Humm, M. (ed.), *Feminisms: A Reader.* London and New York: Harvester Wheatsheaf, 1992, pp 204-206.

du Plessis, Rachel Blau. *The pink guitar: writing as feminist practice.* New York and London: Routledge, 1990.

Biographies

Carol Brown is originally from New Zealand. Her early training was in the Central Euro-pean dance theatre techniques of Gertrude Bodenwieser (1890-1958) which she stud-ied with Shona Dunlop-MacTavish in New Zealand, and subsequently with Bettina Vernon, Evelyn Ippen and Hilda Holger in England. She has performed and choreographed exten-sively throughout New Zealand with Dunedin Dance Theatre, Carousel, Dance = Arts and Bronwen Judge. In 1987-88 Carol completed an MA in Dance Studies at the Uni-versity of Surrey. Returning to New Zealand in 1989 she worked as a freelance chore-ographer, performer and teacher. In 1992, she returned to England to begin a PhD at the Department of Dance Studies, University of Surrey. She completed her PhD in Feminist Choreography in March 1995. While working on her doctorate, she presented *Dancing Through the Wild Zone*, in 1992, and *Bloodsongs*, which had a South East regional tour in 1993-4.

Original music for the piece is by New Zealand composer **Russell Scoones**. Scored for voice, guitars, percussion and found sounds, his compositions are characterised by their varied textures, haunting qualities and driving rhythms.

Brown

The Mechanics of Fluids: Programme Details

Friday 21 April, 1995 at 8:00 p.m.
Main Hall, University of Surrey

Choreographed and performed by Carol Brown
With original music by Russell Scoones
Additional music by Iva Bittova, *Ne-Neh* and Arvo Part, *Frates*
Lighting design by Phillippa Wickham
Premiered March 15 1995, under the aegis of the University's Choreographic Laboratory

Performance Texts

The Anatomy of Reason

This is my Brainchild. Well haven't you ever wondered what it would be like to be pregnant with an idea? Imagine the indigestion from all those words, and what old man philosophers we'd give birth to, Plato for instance.

I'm miming philosophy, partaking in the phallocentric phantasmagoria of post-Freudian anal-ysis.

Psychobabble.

I'm miming philosophy, partaking in the phallocentric phantasmagoria of post-Freudian anal-ysis.

The hegemony of languages, dizzying spells of glossolalia. In speaking, repeating, past narrations of he-she fantasies.

Is reason sexed?

[Whisper to doll] Look, if you're going to go into the forest you're going to have to take a clean handkerchief, carry some spare change with you, and whatever you do, don't talk to strangers.

I have all these bits and pieces, a left side and a right side, an upper body, a middle body and a lower body, a front side and a back side, a top and a bottom, an inside and an outside, and when I was very young, I imagined that all of these bits, and pieces, could fold in on themselves, and that I could make myself into a work of origami. And then I'd imagine that I had a join through the middle, running from the top of my head to the base of my pubic bone and that I could fold in half. like a suitcase.

Are you following me?

[Whisper] Mother. Sacred. Machine. Soiled.

I have all this critical baggage, I hope you don't mind if I share some of it with you.

How to become an Object. Number one, remove all clothing. Number two, position the body for display, a raised surface will do. Number three, pose.
[To the doll] Don't move, I'll be right back.

Acts of Becoming

I'm speaking to you.
Ready the space, make it possible, make it real.

Mark/sign/imprint/trace/seal.

Step together, stop, wind, unwind, step, turn, thrust, schlinger and breathe.

And speak to me in this silence.

....

The 'I' stretches through the tendons and spilling, spinning, tripping, moves to an-other place.

Never to close the circle, keep it open, keep it whole.

The schöpf kreis.

....

Listen, I want the feeling of listening, of listening and leaping, of leaping into listening.

Put rhythm, pulse and humming space into movement [adapted from du Plessis 1990].

Oh, and don't forget to breathe.

The arm kreis.

....

And why stop. You must keep going.

Your body is not the same today as it was yesterday.

Be what you are becoming, not what you might have been [adapted from Irigaray in Humm 1992, p210].

The impuls.

BODY AS SITE

Rosemary Butcher

Body as Site had its première in February 1993 at the Centre for Contemporary Arts, Glasgow, and was performed again in January 1995 at Guildford Cathedral in a slightly reworked version that took account of the different surroundings.

In making the work, I looked at the body almost as a place, as a site, and I wanted to place this body in an environment—so that the body as site was itself put in a site. The work is made up of four pieces, and in each I collaborated with a different artist or architect. Each artist was asked to create a physical environment to allow for the development of choreographic events. The restriction on the choreography, therefore, was the environment, which also gave the key to the movement material.

The idea behind the work was to change the audience's perception of performance—in that the dances, as well as the environments, were to be seen as installations, rather than as theatrical performances. The dance, in consequence, evokes a feeling of indeterminate time, just as installations exist in indeterminate time, without beginning or end.

I have an overriding interest in form and structure; the content *is* the form. The four pieces that constitute *Body as Site* are no exception.

Image as Event

The set of designer Paul Elliman consists of large photographs of the dancers and a grid of cat's eyes on the floor. The photographs have a grid superimposed on them, and this subdivision is reflected in the grid on the floor. The placing of photographs of the performers in the performance space plays with the idea of live image against recorded image. In the movement, I worked with distortion of images and the placing of original movement ideas against the distorted versions.

Wasp

In sculptor Ron Haselden's installation, a large oval mirror is hung near the back of the space. Onto it is projected a changing skyscape of sun and clouds. The mirror reflects these onto the floor, creating an oval of light in which the dancer moves. The vibration of the soundtrack—a buzz of a wasp—makes the mirror hover.

A theme in the piece is how things are seen. As the clouds come over the skyscape, the lighted area on the floor goes dark and the dancer is hardly visible. When the clouds pass and the sun returns, the pool on the floor becomes light and the dancer is seen more clearly. She can also be viewed in the suspended mirror, so that her movements can be seen from above as well as at audience level.

The movement is an expression of functionalism; it eliminates the decorative. Confining it to a small illuminated area centres the eye on every aspect of its breakdown. The movement material is shown forwards, backwards, and upside down—as well as reflected and in and out of darkness.

Tension and Compression

The architect John Lyall provided four long, thin wooden boards with two ropes running from one end to the other. Pulling the ropes tighter causes the boards to buckle, making a semi-circular shape. During the work, the dancers change the positions of the boards in the space, stacking them, or laying them on edge at various places around the performance area.

The boards define and divide the space, and inform the movement content. The dance takes on the physicality of the boards' shape and adopts similar positions in space. Their curved form might recall sails, and the dancers, too, sometimes look like ships or sailing objects. The physical displacement of the boards is picked up by the dancers, who push and pull each other.

Recover

Visual artist Anya Gallaccio contributed a carpet of white nylon threads. Her metaphor was of recycling—these nylon threads would be made into things. I used the idea of recycling in thinking of recovery, of going over something.

The movement material had to be limited because the thread was difficult to walk on and caught around the dancers' feet. I concentrated on people slowly walking, falling, and being caught. Everything a dancer does is with the support of another person; she or he is linked with somebody else.

The overall effect of the piece is one of sustainment. Time seems to be absorbed as events are recycled, seen again in different points of the space, continuing indefinitely.

....

Programme Details: *Body as Site*

Choreographer: Rosemary Butcher
Lighting Designer: Gian Carlo Rossi

Image as Event

Artist: Paul Elliman
Composer: Simon Fisher Turner
Dancers: Deborah Jones
              Michael Popper
              Fin Walker

Wasp

Artist: Ron Haselden
Composer: Peter Cusack
Dancers: Gill Clarke

Tension and Compression

Artist: John Lyall
Composer: Simon Fisher Turner
Dancers: Dennis Greenwood
              Deborah Jones
              Michael Popper
              Fin Walker

Recover

Artist: Anya Gallaccio
Composer: Simon Fisher Turner
Dancers: Gill Clarke
              Dennis Greenwood
              Deborah Jones
              Michael Popper
              Fin Walker

Biographies

In collaboration with visual artists and contemporary composers, **Rosemary Butcher** makes live art pieces with a strong conceptual and structural base. She has made 35 dance works over the past 15 years. Her collaboration with composer, Michael Nyman, in 1985, produced *Flying Lines,* a piece which marked a move towards larger works, notably, *After the Crying and the Shouting* and *d1, d2, 3D*, where contemporary music, architecture and movement combined on an ambitious scale. Since then, a new collaboration with Nicola Baldwin and Jim Fulkerson, *Of Shadows and Walls*, has given Rosemary's work fresh impetus, providing the catalyst for a new direction of movement which she has called Athletic Realism. It signals the beginning of a new phase in her work, while continuing to preserve the integrity of the pure artistic abstraction which has always distinguished her art.

After an early training in classical ballet, **Gill Clarke** became interested in contemporary dance whilst studying for a degree in English at York University. Her dance career began with Ross McKim and Dancework. In 1978 she began working with Janet Smith and Dancers, performing, teaching and choreographing until 1988 when she joined Siobhan Davies and Dancers. In addition to working on projects such as *Spatial Decay* with Laurie Booth, she teaches regularly for dance companies and courses throughout Britain and abroad. She has recently choreographed for Uppercut Dance Theatre, Copenhagen and Ricochet Company, London. Her work with Rosemary Butcher started in 1990 with *d1, d2, 3D*.

Paul Elliman has established an international reputation as a designer, working in Japan, North America and Europe. London-based clients include the Royal Shakespeare Company, the British Film Institute, the Tate Gallery and the publishers Routledge and Verso Books. In the late 1980s he won awards for his design of *Wire*, the jazz and new music magazine, and in the 1991 D&AD awards he received a silver and a gold medal for the self-published magazine *Box Space*. He is Associate Lecturer in the Visual Communication Department at the University of East London, and Visiting Lecturer in Design at Ravensbourne and St Martins in London, Syracuse University in New York and the State University of Stuttgart, Germany. *Body as Site* is Paul's first collaboration with Rosemary Butcher.

Anya Gallaccio's sculpture and installation pieces have been exhibited widely over the past four years. In London she has shown at the ICA, the Serpentine, Karsten Schubert and Surrey Docks, while abroad she has exhibited in Brussels, Italy, New York, Los Angeles and Spain. Her work has been widely published and reviewed in journals. "I see my works as being a performance and a collaboration. It adds something to the work that isn't obvious. It is like the hidden domestic activities of how many times you cook diners and how many times you clean the bath, but I don't want it to become a chore. The magic and the pleasure have to be the most important thing."

Dennis Greenwood has performed with American choreographer, Mary Fulkerson and many of the earliest British experimental choreographers, including Rosemary Butcher and Miranda Tufnell. He was a founder member of Strider, directed by Richard Alston, and has worked with visual artists Tim Head, Bruce McLean and David Ward. During the 20 or so years that he has worked with Rosemary Butcher, he has not only performed but played an important role in the development of her work.

For more than 10 years, **Ron Haselden** has been conjuring with light, movement and sound. He trained as a sculptor but soon defined that term for himself to encompass the ephemeral and transient. His installations always evolve out of direct confrontation and his immediate surroundings, resulting in works specifically made for the public arena of street, park, and building as well as the gallery. Ron has been involved in a number of collaborations with architects and performers.

Deborah Jones trained in ballet and performed with the Royal Ballet between 1984 and 1992, taking part in the award-winning 1992 production of William Forsythe's *In the middle somewhat elevated*. She has been a member of the Jonathan Burrows Group since 1989, collaborating on three projects: *Dull Morning* (1980), *Stoics* (1991) and *Very* (1992).

John Lyall is an architect based in London. He achieved international success in 1971 when, as students, he and a group of colleagues were second in the Centre Pompidou competition in Paris. Buildings of note in the UK include "The Splash" swimming pool in Sheringham, Norfolk, the new Cloth Hall in Leeds, and the floating fire station on the Thames at Lambeth. Current work includes a large urban renewal project in Leeds, a strategic planning scheme in Halifax, and underground stations at North Greenwich and Tottenham Hale. He has designed travelling stage systems and opera sets for Opera 80 and is an active member of the art-and-architecture movement. His collaborative work with Rosemary Butcher started in 1989 when they worked on a tour of UK art galleries and then developed specific performances for Christ's Church, Spitalfields and the Tramway Theatre, Glasgow.

Michael Popper has appeared as a dancer, actor and singer with Ballet Rambert, Direct Current, Second Stride, Women's Comedy Workshop, Compagnie Renaud Barrault and Insomniac. He has choreographed and directed work for Direct Current, the Royal Shakespeare Company, the Royal National Theatre, Buxton Festival Opera, the Turkish Ballet in Ankara, Vocem and the legendary Gateway to Freedom. He is building an international reputation as choreographer, teacher and artist. He has worked on three pieces with Rosemary Butcher since 1990.

Gian Carlo Rossi is currently a lecturer at the Holborn Centre for the Performing Arts.

Simon Fisher Turner has worked in the film industry, as an actor (*Caravaggio* and *The Party*), director, casting director, runner and extra. For the past eight years, however, he has concentrated on music for the big screen, producing the soundtrack for six of Derek Jarman's films (including *The Garden* and *Edward II*). Most recently, he has scored Isfi's *Elenya*, the centrepiece of the 1992 London Film Festival. He has made numerous recordings and his audio-visual concerts with Derek Jarman have toured the world. *Body as Site* is his first collaboration with Rosemary Butcher.

Fin Walker graduated from Leicester Polytechnic with a BA in Performing Arts and has worked since then with choreographers Gary Rowe and Greg Nash and with Extemporary Dance, where she won an apprentice place. She has danced with Sue MacLennan, Duncan MacFarland in America, Laurie Booth and Loredo Dance Theatre and has recently been on tour to Japan with the Frank Chickens. In 1995, she received a training bursary from the Arts Council and was the recipient of an award from the Creative Developments in Dance Project Fund 1992/93. She has been working with Rosemary Butcher for four years.

[*Note:* A video of *Body as Site*, as performed in Guildford Cathedral, is available from: National Resource Centre for Dance, University of Surrey, Guildford, Surrey GU2 5LG.]

HI JINX and *THE FETCHING BRIDE*

Divas

Based in Brighton, Divas is co-directed by Liz Aggiss and Billy Cowie, who have been hailed in Britain and Europe for their extraordinary and entertaining dance/drama and music performance pieces. Aggiss and Cowie present their work as a visual, choreographic, alternative movement aesthetic that puts the dancer, and particularly the female dancer, in the forefront of the work. They engage in the surreal and recognise the bizarre and political nature of performance. The choreographic and dance performance style that has emerged through their work has evolved from their formative years working in alternative spaces—spaces that at the time reflected in Brighton, London and Europe a developing alternative theatre culture and a growing trend towards denying theatrical exclusivity.

Divas researches the "lost" European dance tradition of Central Europe pre- and post-war, for example in the work of Impekoven, Gert, Sent M'Ahesa. In new pieces Liz Aggiss uses "historical sampling" to stimulate and develop choreography. Her vocabulary draws upon postmodern and expressionist dance and is influenced by her training with Nikolais, Holm, and Holger.

The University of Surrey's Choreographic Laboratory awarded its 1994/5 commission to Divas, allowing Aggiss and Cowie to create two new works: *Hi Jinx* and *The Fetching Bride*. These were shown first at the Wilde Theatre, South Hill Park, Bracknell, before their performance at the University of Surrey during the *Border Tensions: Dance and Discourse* conference. They were also performed at the 1995 Brighton Festival.

Hi Jinx, a Dadaist lecture-demonstration about the work of a 1930s German expressionist dance/choreographer, is a solo piece that includes film footage, live action, and spoken word. Research and development funding from the Arts Council of England's dance panel (obtained by the University's Choreographic Laboratory) assisted the company in the development of *Hi Jinx*. Research led to choreographic archives in Berlin and the Museum of Erotic Art in Hamburg, and to collaboration with Lea Anderson of the Cholmondeleys and Hilde Holger, a German expressionist choreographer who worked in the 1930s.

The Fetching Bride is a duet featuring an opera singer and dancer in an erotic black satire on a journey from innocence to corruption and death. The piece is accompanied by live music composed by Billy Cowie.

Divas

Programme Details

Saturday 22 April 1995 at 8:00 p.m.
Main Hall, University of Surrey

Commissioned by the University of Surrey's Choreographic Laboratory

Hi Jinx

Choreography	Liz Aggiss and Billy Cowie
Text	Billy Cowie
Performer	Liz Aggiss
Music	Billy Cowie
Singers	Sarah Jane Dale, Rowan Godel, Liz Aggiss
Joints performed by	Kirsty Jennings
Lighting Design	Jeff Baynes
Costumes	Kate Strachan
Film Director/Lighting Camera	Jeff Baynes
Film Performers	Lea Anderson and Akiko Kajihara
Camera Assistant	Martin Millband
Film Technician	Andy Cheng
Editors	Liz Aggiss, Billy Cowie, Jeff Baynes
Film Costumes	Tig Evans
Translations by	Mine Kaylan, Dominique Rivoal, Pia Roca

The Fetching Bride

Groom	Chloe Wright
Bride	Liz Aggiss
Piano	Billy Cowie
Cello	Sian Bell
Violin	Ann Stephenson
Choreography	Liz Aggiss and Billy Cowie
Music	Billy Cowie
Wedding Dress	e-Garbs Leather & Rubber Tailoring, Brighton
Costumes & Props	Kate Strachan
Text	Billy Cowie
Lighting Design	Jeff Baynes
Translations by	Pia Roca

Biographies

Liz Aggiss studied dance in New York with Murray Louis and Alwin Nikolais, in Colorado with Hanya Holm, and in London with Hilde Holger. In 1986, with composer **Billy Cowie**, she formed the company Divas. They have performed widely in Britain and in Europe—and in major festivals in Vienna, Amsterdam, Budapest, Freiburg, Hanover, and Mainz. Divas represented Britain at Bagnolet in Paris in 1990. Numerous awards for their work include Brighton Festival Awards for Dance and Contemporary Music, the Alliance and Leicester Award, and the Time Out/Dance Umbrella Award. In 1993, they received the BBC2/Arts Council Dance for Camera Award, which resulted in the film *Beethoven in Love*. Liz and Billy have also worked extensively with other companies, including Extemporary Dance Theatre, Mantis, Transitions and the performance group Carousel, for whom they choreographed the award-winning *Banda Banda* and *La Soupe*. Both lecture at the University of Brighton on the BA (Hons) Performance with Visual Practice degree courses.

Lea Anderson trained at St Martins School of Art and at the Laban Centre. In 1984 she was a founder member of the Cholmondeleys, an all-female company. Her choreographic style is defined both in the work of the Cholmondeleys and in that of the all-male company the Featherstonehaughs, which she established in 1988. The two companies were brought together in 1992 for *Birthday*, which won a Time Out Dance Award, and again in 1993 for *Precious. Metalcholica* (1994) is her most recent production for the Cholmondeleys, and in spring 1995 she choreographed *Featherstonehaughs Go Las Vegas*. Lea has created many works specifically for television, and wrote and presented the series 'Tights, Camera, Action' in 1992 and 1994. She has also choreographed for the National Theatre, Transitions, Opera North and the Women's Playhouse Trust.

Jeff Baynes first worked with Divas as Lighting Cameraman on their film *Beethoven in Love*, directed by Bob Bentley. His extensive range of drama and dance works as Director of Photography includes DV8 Physical Theatre and Freefall, both directed by Bob Bentley for Songbird/Channel 4; CanDoCo, directed by Margaret Williams for Arts Council/BBC2; and Stephen Frears's *The Bullshitters*, a Comic Strip Production for Channel 4. Jeff has also directed many music videos with artists such as the Beautiful South and Carter USM. His documentary work has been with directors such as Deborah May, Pratibha Palmar and Annieszka Piotrawska.

Akiko Kajihara was born in Tokyo and trained initially with Kayoko Takasawa. She has a degree in physical education, majoring in dance, from the Tsukuba University. While studying for her degree, Akiko danced for the Miki Wakamatsu Free Dance Company. She co-choreographed the winning entry for the NHK prize in the 1991 All Japan Dance Festival held in Kobe. After graduating in 1993 Akiko took the Professional Diploma in Dance Studies at the Laban Centre. She performed for Vital Theatre at the 1993 Edinburgh Fringe Festival. Following her year in Transitions, Akiko intends to take the knowledge and experience gained in England back to Japan and continue to work there.

Chloe Wright is currently training at the Guildhall School of Music and Drama, graduating in July 1995. Her experience is already extensive and includes Britten's *War Requiem* and Ravel's *L'enfant et les sortileges* at the Guildhall. She has also sung the soprano solo in Purcell's *Fairy Queen* with Morley Opera and in Verdi's *La Traviata* with Bath and Wessex Opera. Her many oratorio solos include Mozart's *Coronation Mass,* Vivaldi's *Gloria,* and Faure's *Requiem*. In 1994, Chloe was awarded the Freda Parry Memorial Prize.

DIFFICULT JOYS

Jools Gilson-Ellis
Dartington College of Arts

Let me write this to you.

I can't sleep anymore. This is difficult, and my joys run before me. Write to me here. Say it again simply. Write it down so I won't forget it. What is it? Happy Birthday Julie. You will understand again and again, but not in the water. It rains. It's. It's. I choke and sneeze in the water, and I can see little. Sometimes there are faces at the glass. Writing. It's peaceful down there. Quiet. And I cannot see myself being looked at. And I cannot write. What you can see, has everything to do with what you can say.

Let me describe this to you.

The performer is situated in a glass tank 4 ft long, 2 ft wide, and 2 ft 6' high, filled with water. The tank is placed at the end of two lengths of black dance floor which draws members of the audience to the performance site. Downstage of the tank, are three sets of frozen sculptural objects, placed at intervals before the tank. The first is a birthday card frozen within a block of ice, written in a scrawled hand. The second is a suspended oblong block of ice, which contains several dozen small bendy clowns, placed in various physical (dancerly) positions. This block melted onto a page of type-written text, which was placed on the ground beneath it. The last ice block was a page of frozen handwritten text. Ice melted as the performance progressed. The performance lasted one hour, and audience members were encouraged to stay for as long, or as little as they wished, or to make several visits. The performer worked repeatedly underwater, and came up for air when she needed it. Her breathing was amplified. The performance consisted of a combination of task-based movement and choreographed sequences in the water. The various tasks were involved with writing under water, both on the performer's own body, and on submerged paper. Choreographic sequences combined gestural signing sequences with movement derived from the manipulation of the task work. Audience members were encouraged to view the piece from close as well as distant perspectives.

Proper Analysis

Difficult Joys is a dance/installation, which is part of an on-going series of performance work, in relation to my research work into *Women Performance Writers*. This research work is part of a written and performed doctoral thesis in the areas of *Performance* and *Gender Studies*. I am using the term *Women Performance Writers* to refer to women who produce written texts as an integral part of their performance practice, and I am including myself amongst these women. The work attempts to locate writing as a bodily practise within an intellectual practise, and to explore how the physical dynamics of writing/the written text, permeate in the visual body, in performance space as well as in academic space. At this conference I performed *Difficult Joys* on the first evening of the conference, and gave a conference paper the following day. My interest in writing in performance, blurs here in these distinctions. I do not see the giving of a paper and the performance of *Difficult Joys* as different practices. The last page of my conference paper was part of the installation *Difficult Joys*; was placed on the ground beneath the iced clowns. The two women I focus on in the conference paper, I gave at *Border Tensions*, and included here in these proceedings; Rose English and Laurie Anderson, both verbalise their written texts. In *Difficult Joys*, there is no speaking of the texts placed in the space. Indeed all that is heard is the sound of breathing, and spluttering in the water. There is a play between the framing of this female body and the framing of the page in the space. The rectangular shape of the tank and of the texts, refer to each other, confuse and repeat each other. The water in the tank is reconvened as ice around texts and objects. I want to suggest in this work that acts of looking and reading/writing text are intimately connected.

Secrets

7a) The birthday card used in this piece was written by my grandmother who died a week after it was written.

b) moving swiftly and joyfully on.

....

Difficult Joys: Programme Details

Friday 21 April, 1995, at 5:30 p.m.
PATS Music Studio, University of Surrey

Created and performed by Jools Gilson-Ellis
Technical Director: Neil Smith
Tank made by: Aqua Stands, Whitchurch

Biography

Jools Gilson-Ellis won the 1988 Graduate Scholarship to the University of Colorado at Boulder, where she studied theatre and dance with Mel Wong, Bob Een, and Jawole Willa Jo Zollar. A lecturer, researcher, and performer, Gilson-Ellis is currently researching women writing *in relation to* performance. Special Lecturer in Drama at the University of Hull from 1990 to 1992, she is currently Lecturer in Theatre at Dartington College of Arts.

Appendices

A. Conference Programme

B. Speakers' Biographies

Thursday 20 April 1995

18:30 - 19:45	*Opening reception*
20:00 - 21:30	**Rosemary Butcher:** *Body as Site* (film of a performance, with discussion by the choreographer)

Friday 21 April 1995

9:30 - 10:15	**Professor Patrick Dowling,** Vice-Chancellor of the University of Surrey: Opening Remarks **Professor Janet Adshead-Lansdale:** Discourse in Dance: Its Changing Character		
10:15 - 10:45	*Coffee break • NRCD Laban Exhibit (Library Foyer)*		
10:45 - 11:45	**Dr Sally Bowden:** Reading Ballets of Early Modernism: Diaghilev and Medievalism **Iris Garland:** Modernist Values and Historical Neglect: Tortola Valencia Chair: **Joan White,** University of Surrey	**Dr Theresa Buckland:** Dance, Gender and Music Video **Trish Winter:** Reading the Aerobics Video Chair: **Sophia Preston,** University of Surrey	
12:00 - 13:00	**Dr Alexandra Carter:** Narratives, Meta-narratives and Women in the Music Hall Ballet, 1884-1915 **Dr Ann Daly:** Isadora Duncan and the Distinction of Dance Chair: **Ann Nugent,** University of Surrey	**Dr Anna Aalten:** Constructing the Body of the Ballerina **Dr Andrée Grau:** On the Notion of Bodily Intelligence Chair: **Dr Helen Thomas,** Goldsmiths College	**Johannes Birringer:** The Obscene/Off-Screen Body [multimedia presentation] Chair: **Sophie Lycouris,** University of Surrey
13:00 - 14:00	*Lunch break • Conference Bookshop • NRCD Laban Exhibit (Library Foyer)*		
14:00 - 15:30	**Mo Dodson:** Taxonomies of Dance and Powers of Exclusion: Jazz Dance **Caroline Kershaw:** Clog Dancing in the Victorian Music Hall **Dr Linda Tomko:** Gendering English Traditional Dance in the U.S. Chair: **Dr Georgiana Gore,** Université de Clermont-Ferrand, France	**Sherril Dodds:** Lea Anderson and the Television Text **Dr Susan Kozel:** The Virtual World: New Frontiers for Dance and Philosophy Chair: **Professor Roger Copeland,** Oberlin College, USA	**Ian Spink:** Practical workshop
15:30 - 16:00	*Tea break • Conference Bookshop • NRCD Exhibit (Library Foyer)*		
16:00 - 17:00	**Dr Helen Thomas:** New Formations in Dance Studies: A Critical Appraisal Chair: **Dr Theresa Buckland,** University of Surrey	**Ian Spink and Professor Richard Cave:** Collaborations: A Discussion	
17:00 - 18:00	*Wine reception hosted by Routledge •* <u>*Difficult Joys*</u>*, an installation by* **Jools Gilson-Ellis**		
17:15 - 19:45	*Break for evening meal • Conference Bookshop • Demonstrations in the Performing Arts Multi-Media Research Room*		
20:00 - 21:00	*Performance in the Main Hall* **Carol Brown:** <u>The Mechanics of Fluids</u>		

Saturday 22 April 1995

9:30 - 10:15	**Professor Roger Copeland:** Abstraction and Hysteria: The Place of the Body in American Non-Literary Theatre Chair: **Dr Alexandra Carter,** Middlesex University
10:15 - 10:45	*Coffee break • NRCD Laban Exhibit (Library Foyer)*

10:45 - 11:45	**Sherrie Barr and Dr Philip Lewin:** Straddling Borders: Proto-Narrative Unit **Dr Ramsay Burt:** 'Purity' vs 'Theatricality': A Re-reading of the Position of Minimalist Theatre Dance Chair: **Valerie Briginshaw,** Chichester Institute of Higher Education	**M.A. Greenstein:** Border Art, Border Town: Los Angeles Dances on the Edge **Dr Stacey Prickett:** Joe Goode: Blurring the Edges of Difference in Performance and Society Chair: **Dr Ann Daly,** University of Texas at Austin, USA	**Ian Spink:** Practical workshop
12:00 - 13:00	**Raphael Akopian-Schupp:** The Way Questions Become Dance: 'Und Die Pina [Bausch] Hat Gefragt' Chair: **Sophia Preston,** University of Surrey	**Jools Gilson-Ellis:** Text and the Dancing Body in the Work of Rose English and Laurie Anderson **Dr Valerie Rimmer:** Giselle and Romanticism Chair: **Professor Susan Foster,** University of California, Riverside	
13:00 - 14:00	*Lunch break • Conference Bookshop • NRCD Laban Exhibit (Library Foyer)*		
14:00 - 15:30	**Linda Jasper:** Tensions in the Definition of Community Dance **Maria Koutsouba:** Restoration or Collapse of the (Dance) Tradition? The Dance *Tsámikos* on the Island of Lefkada, Greece **Dr Georgiana Gore:** Rhythm, Representation, and Ritual: The Rave and the Religious Cult Chair: **Joan W. White,** University of Surrey	**Rachel Richardson:** Music and Gesture in Antony Tudor's Ballets **Sophia Preston:** Tension and Release Across the Borders of Dance and Music **Professor Stephanie Jordan:** Narratives for Eye and Ear: Integrating the Musical Contribution Chair: **Dr Alexandra Carter,** Middlesex University	**Ian Spink:** Practical workshop
15:30 - 16:00	*Tea break • Conference Bookshop • NRCD Exhibit (Library Foyer)*		
16:00 - 17:00	**Shobana Jeyasingh:** Imaginary Homelands: Creating a New Dance Language [paper with demonstration] Chair: **Ann Nugent,** University of Surrey		
17:15 - 19:45	*Break for evening meal • Conference Bookshop • Demonstrations in the Performing Arts Multi-Media Research Room*		
20:00 - 22:00	*Performance in the Main Hall* **Divas (Liz Aggiss and Billy Cowie):** <u>Hi Jinx</u> and <u>The Fetching Bride</u>		
22:00	*Reception hosted by Campusdance to mark the presentation of these two new works, commissioned by the University of Surrey's Choreographic Laboratory*		

Sunday 23 April 1995

9:30 - 10:15	**Valerie Briginshaw**: Metaphors of Travel and Mapping in Postmodern Dance and Discourse Chair: **Dr Theresa Buckland,** University of Surrey
10:15 - 10:45	*Coffee break*

10:45 - 11:45	**Simon Dove**: The New Authenticity: South Asian Dance in the 1990s **Dr Jane Turner**: Control of the Passes Chair: **Linda Jasper**, University of Surrey	**Dr Michael Huxley, Jayne Stevens, and Martin Leach:** An Interdisciplinary Perspective on the Ideas of F.M. Alexander and the Theory and Practice of Dance [paper with demonstration]	**Jackie Smith-Autard and Jim Schofield:** Resource-based Teaching in Dance and Interactive Video [paper with demonstration]

12:00 - 13:00	**Professor Susan Foster**: Harder, Faster, Longer, Higher—A Postmortem Inquiry into the Ballerina's Making Chair: **Professor Janet Adshead-Lansdale,** University of Surrey
13:00 - 14:00	*Lunch break*

SPEAKERS' BIOGRAPHIES

Dr. Anna Aalten teaches feminist anthropology at the Department of Anthropology, University of Amsterdam, The Netherlands. In 1979-80, she did fieldwork on women's labour in agriculture in Spain. In 1985, she conducted an anthropological study of female entrepreneurship in The Netherlands and published the book *Businesswomen: Crossing the Boundaries of Femininity in The Netherlands since 1945*. Her current research project on the relationship between dance, culture and cultural constructions of the body crosses the border between anthropology, women's studies and cultural studies.

Professor Janet Adshead-Lansdale is Head of the Department of Dance Studies, University of Surrey. She heads the research endeavour at the University and teaches on the MA Dance Studies. Her research is in the field of dance analysis, critical theory in interpretation and theoretical issues in the structure of the discipline of dance studies. Publications include *Dance Analysis: Theory and Practice* (ed 1988); *Choreography: Principles and Practice* (ed 1987), which arose from a previous conference at the University of Surrey; and, jointly edited with June Layson, *Dance History: An Introduction* (1994).

Sherrie Barr, MFA, is Assistant Professor of Dance at the University of Oregon, USA. In 1987, she became certified as a Laban Movement Analyst. Her presentations have focused on the learning and teaching strategies which occur in dance technique and theory classes. She is also artistic co-director of TwoDance, a Eugene-based duet contemporary troupe. The paper presented at this conference marks her second collaboration with Dr. Philip Lewin. Their first paper, "Learning Movement: Integrating Kinaesthetic Sense with Cognitive Skills," appeared in the Spring 1994 issue of *Journal of Aesthetic Education*.

Johannes Birringer is a performance/video artist and choreographer currently in residence at the Performance Studies programme of Northwestern University (Evanston, Illinois, USA). His last dance-theatre work, *AlienNation*, has toured the U.S., Europe, and Cuba. He is a contributing editor of *Performing Arts Journal*, and his most recent books include *Theatre, Theory, Postmodernism* (1991) and *Border-Work* (forthcoming).

Dr. Sally Bowden is a theatre historian working as teacher and choreographer in drama and dance theatre in London. Her research centres on the early twentieth century avant-garde. In her PhD thesis, she explored the diverse strands of modernist and pre-Revolutionary Russian theatre history as they illuminate understanding of the 1911 performances of *Petrouchka*.

Valerie A. Briginshaw is a Principal Lecturer and Head of Dance at Chichester Institute of Higher Education, where she teaches on undergraduate courses in Dance, Related Arts, Media Studies, and Women's Studies (in 1996). She also leads courses in Dance and Postmodernism on the MA Related Arts. Her recent publications include a chapter on postmodern dance and politics for a book entitled *Analysing Performance*, forthcoming from Manchester University Press.

Dr. Theresa Buckland is currently Senior Lecturer and MA Course Director in Dance Studies at the University of Surrey, where she teaches dance anthropology and dance as popular culture. She has published in *Dance Research Journal, The Yearbook for*

Traditional Music, Dance Research, and *Folk Music Journal* and contributed chapters to *Dance History: An Introduction* (eds Adshead-Lansdale and Layson, 1994) and *Parallel Lines: Media Representations of Dance* (eds Jordan and Allen, 1993).

Dr. Ramsay Burt recently completed a doctoral thesis on representations of masculinity in British new dance, and a book, *The Male Dancer,* which was published by Routledge this spring. He is married with three children and is currently teaching part-time at De Montfort University: Leicester.

Dr. Alexandra Carter is Principal Lecturer in the School of Dance at Middlesex University. Her teaching and research interests in feminist theory, history and dance analysis were combined in her thesis on representation, hegemony and ballet in the British music hall for which she was awarded a PhD from the University of Surrey in 1993.

Professor Richard Cave is Head of Drama and Theatre Arts at Royal Holloway, University of London. He has published extensively on aspects of Renaissance theatre, Anglo-Irish theatre, contemporary theatre in performance, and dance drama. Currently, chairperson of the National Consortium of Drama and Media in Higher Education, he is co-Artistic Director of Border Crossings Theatre Company.

Professor Roger Copeland is a Professor of Theater and Dance at Oberlin College (Oberlin, Ohio, USA). He is co-editor of the anthology *What is Dance?* and author of the forthcoming *Cunningham's Legacy: The Nature of Post-Modern Dance.* He has published frequently in the dance, theatre, and film pages of *The New York Times*, and his essays have also appeared in *The Village Voice, Partisan Review, The New Republic* and most of the major dance publications.

Dr. Ann Daly is Assistant Professor of Dance History/Criticism at the University of Texas at Austin (USA). She has written on dance, gender, and culture for publications including *TDR, Ballett International, Dance Research Journal, High Performance, Women and Performance, Theatre Journal, Performing Arts Journal, American Studies,* and *DanceView*. She is contributing editor and co-book review editor for *TDR*. A past president of the Dance Critics Association, she serves on the editorial boards of several journals. Her book *"Done into Dance": Isadora Duncan in America* will be published by Indiana University Press later this year.

Sherril Dodds completed a MA in Dance Studies at the University of Surrey in 1993. She then took up a position as Lecturer in Dance at the City of Liverpool Community College. In 1994, she returned to Surrey to commence a PhD. Her area of research is the relationship between dance and film.

Mo Dodson started in art history, worked with Robert North and others in the early 1970s, trained in film-making, and finally joined what is now London Guildhall University. His main influences have been Buber, Laing, Quirey, and Blacking. He is now researching a thesis under John Baily and Andrée Grau at Goldsmiths College.

Professor Susan Leigh Foster, choreographer, dancer, writer, is Professor and Chair of the Department of Dance at the University of California at Riverside (USA). She is the author of *Reading Dancing: Bodies and Subjects in Contemporary American Dance* (University of California Press, 1986) and *Storying Bodies: The Choreography of Narrative and Gender in the French Action Ballet* (Indiana University Press, 1996). She is the editor of two new anthologies: *Choreographing History* (Indiana University Press) and

Corporealities (Routledge), both forthcoming in spring 1995.

Iris Garland is Professor of Dance in the School for the Contemporary Arts at Simon Fraser University (Burnaby, British Columbia, Canada). She is founder of the Dance Program at Simon Fraser and is active as an independent choreographer. She teaches dance history, is a Certified Laban Movement Analyst, and is the recipient of three Canada Council project grants.

Jools Gilson-Ellis won the 1988 Graduate Scholarship to the University of Colorado at Boulder, where she studied theatre and dance with Mel Wong, Bob Een, and Jawole Willa Jo Zollar. A lecturer, researcher, and performer, Gilson-Ellis is currently researching women writing *in relation to* performance. Special Lecturer in Drama at the University of Hull from 1990 to 1992, she is currently Lecturer in Theatre at Dartington College of Arts.

Dr. Georgiana Gore is based in France as a free-lance lecturer and writer in dance and anthropology. She has recently initiated courses in intercultural studies at Blaise-Pascal University, Clermont-Ferrand (France). Previously, she was Lecturer in Dance Anthropology at the University of Surrey and spent the 1980s in Nigeria establishing a dance section in the Department of Theatre Arts, University of Benin.

Dr. Andrée Grau is a Benesh choreologist and anthropologist. She has carried out field-work among the Venda (South Africa); among the Tiwi (Northern Australia); and in London, where she looked at "intercultural" performance within a Western setting. She is currently a Senior Research Fellow in Dance at Roehampton Institute and also teaches Anthropology at Richmond College, the American International University in London.

M.A. Greenstein is Lecturer in Critical Theory at Art Center College of Design (Pasadena, California, USA) and in World Performance at Scripps College (Claremont, California, USA). She is also a contributing editor to the American journal *Artweek*. At present, she is co-curating regional and international exhibitions for the 1995 season in Los Angeles.

Michael Huxley researches in and teaches dance and performance history at De Montfort University: Leicester, where he is Chair of the School of Arts and Humanities Research Committee. He has taught and researched there for fifteen years and has been Head of Dance and Acting Head of the Department of Performing Arts. He contributed to *La Danse au Défi* (1987), *Dance Analysis: Theory and Practice* (1988), *Dance History: An Introduction* (1994) and to a number of journals. He is co-editing/co-authoring *Twentieth Century Performance* with Noel Witts for publication by Routledge in January 1996.

Linda Jasper, Chair of the Community Dance and Mime Foundation since 1993, is responsible for undergraduate professional studies courses in the Department of Dance Studies at the University of Surrey. She was formerly Dance Development Officer for Berkshire, based at South Hill Park Arts Centre, Bracknell. Prior to this, she was a member of the Footloose Dance in Education and Community Company, Powys, and taught at Bedford and Worcester Colleges of Higher Education.

Shobana Jeyasingh has directed the Shobana Jeyasingh Dance Company since 1988. Her choreography for the Company includes *Romance ... with footnotes* (1993), *Making of Maps* (1992), *New Cities Ancient Lands* (1991), *Correspondences* (1990), *Defilé* (1989), and *Configurations* (1988). She has created a number of works for television, including *Duets with Automobiles*, which was shortlisted for the 1993 IMZ Dance

Screen Award. In 1993, her company was the overall winner of the Prudential Award for the Arts, one of the UK's most prestigious awards. She was awarded the MBE in this year's New Year's Honours.

Professor Stephanie Jordan is Professor of Dance Studies at Roehampton Institute, leading the postgraduate and research programmes. She trained in both dance and music, and has taught both practical and theoretical aspects of dance in Europe and North America. Her books include *Striding Out: Aspects of Contemporary and New Dance in Britain* and *Parallel Lines: Media Representations of Dance* (edited with Dave Allen). An established dance critic, she has contributed many scholarly articles and conference papers. She has received a research grant from the Radcliffe Trust to write a book on music and dance.

Caroline Kershaw is a doctoral candidate in theatre and cultural studies at Royal Holloway and Bedford New College, University of London, writing a thesis on the Victorian performer Dan Leno, under the supervision of J.S. Bratton. Originally trained as a musician, she concurrently works as an oboist in period instrument orchestras and ensembles.

Maria Koutsouba has been a dancer and a dance teacher for almost ten years. She graduated from the Department of Physical Education and Sports, University of Athens in 1989, specialising in Greek folk dances. She gained her MA in Dance Studies from the University of Surrey in 1991, writing a dissertation on urban dance folklore. She is currently a PhD candidate at Goldsmiths College, University of London. She has regularly presented papers in seminars and conferences.

Dr. Susan Kozel is a free-lance dancer and writer. She wrote a PhD on the phenomenology of dance for the Philosophy Department of the University of Essex. Recent publications include: "Virtual Reality: Choreographing Cyberspace" (*Dance Theatre Journal*, Summer 1994) and "Spacemaking: Experiences of a Virtual Body" (*DTJ*, Autumn 1994). She performed in a virtual reality installation in Amsterdam in 1994 and is currently working with a composer and a video artist to further explore dance and interactive technology.

Martin Leach read English and Drama at Hull University before studying theatre directing in Poland. He went on to study the Alexander Technique and qualified as a teacher with the Professional Association of Alexander Teachers in 1989. He now teaches a series of modules in the Alexander Technique for Performers at De Montfort University: Leicester, as well as teaching in private practice.

Dr. Philip Lewin is Associate Professor of Humanities at Clarkson University, New York. He earned his doctorate in Interdisciplinary Studies from Emory University, Atlanta, Georgia. His most recent articles have appeared in *Metaphor and Symbolic Activity, Tradition and Discovery, Issues in Integrative Studies,* and *Soundings*.

Terry Monaghan, BSc (Econ), PGCE, Dip. Ed. Tech, co-founded the Jiving Lindy Hoppers in 1984, partly as a result of his academic interest in U.S. history in WW2, and his personal interests in jazz dance and music. He has researched and produced an Arts Council "Taped" funded video *Jazz Dance*, has won a Lisa Ullman Travel Scholarship and in June 1995 was awarded a Wingate Scholarship which has enabled him to take early retirement from London Guildhall University in order to pursue his research interests on a full-time basis.

Sophia Preston is a Lecturer at the University of Surrey. Her first degree was in music from York University, and she was a professional double-bass player for ten years, giving solo concerts and playing in a contemporary music ensemble. She also played for London Contemporary Dance Theatre and the Rambert Dance Company. Ms. Preston gained an M.A. (Dist.) in Dance Studies from the University of Surrey in 1989 and went on to undertake research for a PhD there on dance/music relationships in the work of Siobhan Davies.

Dr. Stacey Prickett wrote her MA and PhD dissertations on the American revolutionary dance movement at the Laban Centre for Movement and Dance, London. She recently lectured at the University of California, Berkeley, and is published in journals such as *Studies in Dance History, Dance Research, Dance Theatre Journal,* and *DanceView.*

Dr. Rachel Richardson is Subject Leader in Dance at the Crewe + Alsager Faculty of Manchester Metropolitan University. She trained in ballet and Graham technique at the Hammond School of Dancing in Chester. She later took a first-class Honours degree in Dance and Music at Crewe + Alsager and an MA in Dance Studies at the University of Surrey. She submitted her PhD thesis on the choreographies of Antony Tudor to the University of Surrey in December 1994.

Dr. Valerie Rimmer lectures in dance politics at the Laban Centre for Movement and Dance, London. Her publications include essays on psychoanalytic and deconstructionist approaches to dance, and her current work on Dada and the body is soon to be published.

Jim Schofield, BSc (Hons), is a partner in Bedford Interactive. A teacher and lecturer, he recently retired as Director of Information Technology at Goldsmiths College, University of London. A computer control specialist, he is also an interdisciplinary researcher, scientist, sculptor, and author.

Jacqueline Smith-Autard, MA, is a partner in Bedford Interactive at De Montfort University: Bedford, and Principal Lecturer and Leader of Dance and Drama in the BA (Hons) degree there. She has 30 years' lecturing experience and is a leading exponent of resource-based teaching methodology in arts education. She is an author and researcher into multi-media applications in dance for further and higher education.

Ian Spink has choreographed and directed many works for Second Stride since its formation in 1982, originally working with Richard Alston and Siobhan Davies, and becoming sole Artistic Director in 1986. He has worked extensively with the UK's major opera companies, choreographing *The Trojans* (Scottish Opera/Opera North/Royal Opera House) and *Death in Venice* (Glyndebourne Festival Opera), among others. His work in the theatre includes the movement for Caryl Churchill's *The Skriker* (Royal National Theatre) and *Antony and Cleopatra* (Royal Shakespeare Company). He also choreographed Churchill's *Fugue* for television.

Jayne Stevens is Head of Dance at De Montfort University: Leicester. Until 1994, she was co-Artistic Director, with Jo Breslin, of Glasshouses Dance Company. She will be publishing a retrospective catalogue of her choreographic research undertaken by the company later this year. She qualified as a teacher of the Alexander Technique in 1987 and is a member of the Professional Association of Alexander Teachers.

Dr. Helen Thomas is Senior Lecturer in Sociology at Goldsmiths College, University of

London. She has published a number of articles on dance and is editor of and contributor to *Dance, Gender and Culture* (Macmillan, 1993). She is author of large-scale survey on *Equal Opportunities in the Mechanical Media* (1992). Her book, *Dance, Modernity, and Culture* (Routledge, 1995) will be published in September. She is the Project Director of *Unequal Pay for Equal Parts*, funded by the Leverhulme Trust.

Dr. Linda J. Tomko is a historian, dancer, and reconstructor of period choreographies. She earned a PhD in History at UCLA and focuses her research in two areas: dance and gender in the early 20th-century United States, and reconstruction of early 18th-century court and theatre dance. She is a faculty member of the Dance Department of the University of California, Riverside, and co-directs with Wendy Hilton the annual summer Stanford University Baroque Dance Workshop. She directs Les Menus Plaisirs, a baroque dance troupe.

Dr. Jane Turner is a Lecturer in Drama at Crewe + Alsager Faculty, Manchester Metropolitan University. She has been involved in performance work, documentation of the performance process and investigating and interrogating the relationship between Eastern performance (specifically Bali) and the West.

Trish Winter is Demonstrator in Dance at Newcastle University, having been an independent dancer/choreographer for nearly ten years. She continues to make performance and is about to embark on PhD research on the aerobics video. She has an MA in Cultural and Textual Studies (with Distinction) from the University of Sunderland.